October 9, 1988

To John,

With gratitude for your
many contributions to this
book, which are only inade-
quately noted on p IX.

Michael

The Fate of Nations

Also by Michael Mandelbaum

*The Nuclear Question: The United States and Nuclear
Weapons, 1946–1976*
*The Nuclear Revolution: International Politics
Before and After Hiroshima*
The Nuclear Future
(With Strobe Talbott) *Reagan and Gorbachev*
(With Seweryn Bialer) *The Global Rivals*

The Fate of Nations

The Search for National Security in the Nineteenth and Twentieth Centuries

MICHAEL MANDELBAUM

The Council on Foreign Relations

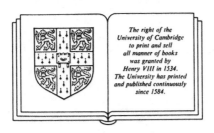

The right of the
University of Cambridge
to print and sell
all manner of books
was granted by
Henry VIII in 1534.
The University has printed
and published continuously
since 1584.

Cambridge University Press

Cambridge
New York   New Rochelle   Melbourne   Sydney

Published by the Press Syndicate of the University of Cambridge
The Pitt Building, Trumpington Street, Cambridge CB2 1RP
32 East 57th Street, New York, NY 10022, USA
10 Stamford Road, Oakleigh, Melbourne 3166, Australia

First published 1988

Printed in the United States of America

Library of Congress Cataloging-in-Publication Data
Mandelbaum, Michael.
The fate of nations: the search for national security in the
nineteenth and twentieth centuries / Michael Mandelbaum.
p.   cm.
Includes bibliographical references.
ISBN 0 521 35527 3.   ISBN 0 521 35790 X (pbk.)
1. World politics – 19th century.   2. World politics – 20th century.
3. National security.   I. Title.
D363.M29   1988
327.1′1 – dc19   87–33838
                                                                CIP

British Library Cataloguing in Publication Data
Mandelbaum, Michael
The fate of nations: the search for
national security in the nineteenth and
twentieth centuries.
1. National security. Policies, 1800–1985
of governments
I. Title
327′.09′03

ISBN 0 521 35527 3 hard covers
ISBN 0 521 35790 X paperback

To Seweryn Bialer, Stanley Hoffmann,
and David Riesman
and to the memory of Harry J. Benda:
teachers, colleagues, friends

Contents

vii

Acknowledgments

I am happy to record my thanks to several institutions that sponsored this book. I began writing *The Fate of Nations* at Harvard University with a grant from the Institute for the Study of World Politics. I completed it as Senior Fellow and Director of the Project on East–West Relations at the Council on Foreign Relations in New York. I wrote most of it during the time that I was Research and Editorial Director of the Lehrman Institute of New York, which provided a congenial and stimulating environment in which to write and think.

My greatest debt is to Nicholas X. Rizopoulos, formerly the Vice-President and Executive Director of the Lehrman Institute, without whose support, encouragement, and advice this book would not have been written. I am also grateful to Robert W. Tucker, the Institute's President during my time there, for his good counsel, and to Linda Wrigley, its Associate Director, and Marel Harayda and Annabel Allafriz of the Institute for their assistance and many kindnesses.

The Lehrman Institute organized seminars to discuss earlier versions of each of the chapters of this book. I owe a considerable debt to Donald Kagan, who chaired the meetings, and to those who participated in them, for giving me the benefit of their expertise and critical judgment. Among the participants I should like to single out for special thanks John Lukacs, whose detailed comments on Chapters 2 and 3 saved me from many errors of fact and interpretation.

I am grateful also to Harry Harding for his comments on Chapter 4 and to Strobe Talbott and Stanley Hoffmann, who read an earlier version of the entire book. My wife, Anne Mandelbaum, edited the manuscript with extraordinary sensitivity and insight. Carol Rath and Cynthia Paddock typed it with efficiency, dispatch, and good cheer.

A Note on Sources
and Citations

Each chapter of *The Fate of Nations* is an interpretive essay on a historical episode. None is, strictly speaking, a work of history itself. None draws directly on original source material – the government documents and personal papers from which historical monographs are written. Each relies on secondary works, books and articles, in this case almost all of them in English, that are based on primary materials. Over the past forty years a large and varied body of historical studies of the international history of the nineteenth and twentieth centuries has been created. This book is both a commentary on and, indirectly, a tribute to the efforts of those who have created it, for without this literature more strictly interpretive works like this one would not be possible.

The footnotes have three purposes: to expand ideas mentioned in the body of the book, to give sources of quotations and statistics, and to provide references for points that are controversial or obscure. The works cited in the footnotes in each chapter constitute many, but not all, of the secondary sources that were consulted in the writing of this book. Not all of the historical studies in English of any of the six subjects, moreover, were consulted. Chapter 1, for example, covers a century of European history. Hundreds of books have been written on the many events in this period, but only a small fraction contributed to this chapter. Like the others, it is intended to offer an interpretation rather than an authoritative reconstruction of an important episode in recent history.

Introduction

The subject of this book is the impact of the international system on the sovereign states that comprise it. It is the fate of every independent nation to have to protect itself against the possibility of external attack, because there is no supreme international authority to protect all states as government protects individuals within states. But the fate of every state is not the same; the problem of national security, and thus the policies that address it, take several basic forms. One of this book's two main purposes is to identify and illustrate the basic varieties of security policy. They are created by variations of the international system itself. The six chapters that make up the book illustrate one or another of these basic varieties. The book's second purpose is to reinterpret a number of well-documented and extensively analyzed historical episodes in order to show that they were responses by particular states to the demands and constraints of the international system. The aim is to demonstrate the ways in which security policies were shaped by the character of the international system and by the positions of particular states within it.

The international system varies in two fundamental ways. One involves its organizing principle, which is anarchy in the literal sense of the term, meaning the absence of formal organs of government, rather than chaos. It is anarchy that creates the insecurity that is the fate of every country. Although they have never wholly abolished anarchy, on a few occasions states have tried to cooperate to make the international order less anarchic and more like –

although never exactly like – the state itself. On these occasions
the members of the international system have practiced security
policies that are here called collective because they involved the
participation of all states, or at least all of the important ones.

The other way that the international system varies is in the
distribution of power within it. The security policies of very strong
states are different from those of very weak ones, and both differ
from those of states that are neither very strong nor very weak.
Like its organizing principle, the distribution of power within the
international system is a property of the system itself, not of its
individual units. It is true that it is the member states of the system
that possess the military might and economic power on which
strength depends. Population, resources, and geography are characteristics of particular countries. But no state is strong simply in
the abstract. The strength of one state has meaning only in relation
to the strength of others. In 1980, for example, Britain was a much
stronger military power in absolute terms than it had been in 1880,
but it was a weaker member of the international system than it had
been a century earlier because other countries were comparatively
stronger in the twentieth century than they had been in the
nineteenth.[1]

It is a fundamental assumption of *The Fate of Nations* that a
state's security policy is determined in the first instance by the
features of the international system, not of the state itself. Thus
two states that are similarly situated in the system but have different
domestic orders will tend to pursue similar security policies. In
contrast, states that are alike in domestic terms but different in
their relationship to the international system will carry out different
security policies.

Two chapters of this book are devoted to periods during which
collective security policies were undertaken. Chapter 1 reviews
relations among the great powers of Europe from the end of the
Napoleonic Wars to the aftermath of World War I, a time when
they intermittently engaged in deliberate although limited cooperative efforts to keep the peace. While the chapter scrutinizes

---

[1] On this point, see Kenneth N. Waltz, *Theory of International Politics* (Reading,
Mass.: Addison-Wesley, 1979), p. 98; the conceptual framework of the present
volume owes a great deal to this book.

Europe as a whole, special attention is given to the perspective of Great Britain, which had a singular role in the establishment, operation, and decline of the collective European order between 1815 and 1919.

The other case study, Chapter 6, stretches the definition of collective security to include the realm of economics. It concerns the international economic order that was established after 1945, an open one in the sense that goods and capital could move relatively freely across national borders. Like the efforts of the great powers after 1815 to promote political tranquility in Europe, the open economic order was the work of more than one sovereign state. Both involved cooperative efforts not to abolish but to mitigate the anarchy of the international system. The country that is singled out for special attention in Chapter 6 is Japan. Like Britain and the international political arrangements in nineteenth-century Europe, Japan received extensive benefits from the international economic order after 1945 although making modest contributions to its maintenance.

Most sovereign states have not been able to depend on others to help ensure their security. Most have had to cope with the universal problem of insecurity on their own. They have practiced "self-help" rather than collective security policies. It is these self-help policies that vary according to the strength of a state. The representative strong state examined in this book is the United States during the years from 1945 to 1980 (Chapter 3); the weak state is the People's Republic of China between 1949 and 1976 (Chapter 4).

Most states have been neither very strong nor exceptionally weak. The case studies in this large in-between category are France from 1919 to 1940 (Chapter 2) and Israel from 1948 to 1979 (Chapter 5). France was roughly equal in strength to Germany in 1940 in the sense that neither country was so overwhelmingly weaker than the other as to have no chance to defend itself successfully. The same was true of Israel and its Arab adversaries from 1948 to 1979. Neither pair was precisely matched, of course, and the differences proved decisive in the Franco-German war of 1940 and in the various Arab–Israeli conflicts. But those crucial discrepancies were not self-evident in advance; they did not become apparent until the wars themselves were fought.

Chapter 2, on France in the interwar period, illustrates the range of strategies available to a state that pursues a self-help approach to national security. The choices that such a state makes invariably involve a particular kind of uncertainty, which is here, as elsewhere in the literature of international politics, called the security dilemma. That dilemma was especially important for Israel's policies from the 1967 war to the peace treaty with Egypt in 1979; it is the subject of Chapter 5.

The six chapters that follow can thus be seen as three pairs. Each of them – Britain and Japan, France and Israel, the United States and China – illustrates the same type or complementary types of security policy. The first pair involves collective policies. The second emphasizes issues relevant to countries that are roughly equal in strength. The third concerns policies that are at the extremes of the spectrum of strength along which all states vary.

The chapters are presented in chronological order: nineteenth-century Europe and Great Britain, France, the United States, China, Israel, and finally the postwar international economic order and Japan.

Each chapter has a comparative aspect, to demonstrate that similar security policies recur throughout history and across the international system in states that, whatever their differences, occupy similar positions in the system. The comparisons are not uniform, however, and the differences among them reflect differences among the main varieties of security policy.

Collective approaches to security are not national policies at all. No state can carry them out alone; a number of states must adopt them. Such approaches have been prominent after wars involving all the great powers of the international system. There have been three in the modern era: the Wars of the French Revolution from 1792 to 1815, World War I, and World War II. The collective policies that are subject of Chapter 1 followed the Wars of the French Revolution. They are compared with the collective efforts made in the aftermath of the two world wars of the twentieth century. Chapter 6 compares Britain's relations with the other great powers in the nineteenth century and Japan's place in the open international economic order after 1945. Chapter 1 also includes a comparison between the collective policies of the nineteenth century, called the managed balance of power system, and a cartel, the cooperative arrangements among firms in the same industry. This is an analytical rather than a historical comparison, highlighting the logic of the formation and disintegration of the collective efforts of the great powers of Europe to achieve security.

In the chapters on self-help security policies the comparisons are more explicit for the very strong – the United States – and the very weak – China – than for the two countries in between – France and Israel. The reason is that the influence of the international system differs among states in different positions in that system.

Weak and strong states exhibit more regular patterns of international conduct than do sovereign states that are neither. Their behavior is determined to a greater extent by their position in the international system than is that of states in the "middle" category. For states such as France in the interwar period and Israel from 1948 to 1979, the anarchic international system imposes the need for self-protection and provides several broad approaches to achieving it. But neither the character of the international system, nor the position of such states within it, determines the combination of policies that these states will employ or whether their policies will succeed or fail. So numerous are the states in this intermediate category, and so modest are the effects of the system on them, that France and Israel are compared with general patterns of international conduct, rather than with other states.

In addition to including a comparison of some kind, each of the six chapters is written from a particular point of view. Each begins with the impact of the international system on its member states, thereby interpreting the particular historical period "from the outside in." Each takes as its starting point the restraints and limits that the character of the international system and the state's place in it impose on national security policies. Being subject to these restraints and limits is the fate of every sovereign state.

Such a view stands in contrast to interpretations of foreign policy as an outward expression of the internal features of states. "Inside-out" interpretations are often apt. In the twentieth century, domestic politics has intruded ever more extensively into security policy. In carrying out security policies, governments everywhere have become less independent of the societies they govern.

Inside-out accounts do in fact appear in the chapters in this book. Domestic divisions affected Britain in the eve of World War I and

France in the face of the German threat between the two wars. Driven by conflicting views of the appropriate way to respond to worsening international conditions, both countries were on occasion unable to take decisive action to safeguard their interests. Similarly, the United States and the People's Republic of China have been motivated by ideology – anticommunism in the American case, the Maoist version of Marxism–Leninism in the Chinese – in their relations with the rest of the world. A feature of domestic society that is akin to ideology, national character – specifically stubbornness and anxiety rooted in historical experience – helps to explain Israel's policies toward the Arab states.

Domestic divisions have particular influence on foreign policy when they are acute, when a government is unstable, and when the legitimacy of a regime itself is in dispute. These conditions have been widespread in the second half of the twentieth century. Chapter 5, on Israel's security policy, in fact refers primarily to domestic politics in explaining the conduct of the Arab states. Moreover, domestic influences are most pronounced when the power of the international system is least decisive, in the cases of states that are neither strong nor weak. Domestic influence on security policy has thus been considerable in the twentieth century.

The subject of this book, however, is the limits that membership in the international system imposes on states whatever their internal arrangements, limits that are as old as the anarchy of the system itself, limits that have shaped the history of international politics in the twentieth as in other centuries.

An approach that stresses these limits runs two related risks. One is the risk of suggesting that security policy is determined wholly by forces external to, and beyond the control of, sovereign states. It is the risk of implying that a nation's fate in one sense of the word – its basic condition, its lot in life – is determined by fate in another sense – a predetermined and unalterable plan. The approach thereby also risks excusing from responsibility those who carried out the policies in question.

No state is entirely free of external constraints, but neither is any wholly restricted by forces beyond its control, its policy determined totally by its position in the system. Even where the pull of the system is strongest, a margin of choice remains, and so therefore does the burden of individual responsibility.

Still, the outside-in approach does impart a particular bias to each chapter. That bias is sympathetic to the particular countries and to those responsible for conducting their security policies. Each chapter emphasizes the fate with which they had to contend. Each portrays them as responding, usually sensibly, if not always successfully, to the circumstances that the international system imposed on them. Whether and where this interpretation is appropriate is a matter of judgment, a subject for the endless argument that is the process of writing history. It does, however, represent the author's belief that, in the twentieth century, a bloody, contentious, and in many ways terrible era in world history, national security policies, especially in the democracies – and five of the six countries that are the subjects of this book are democracies – have been more sensible and prudent, even when unsuccessful, than they have often been retrospectively judged.

1

Collective Approaches to Security

The Nineteenth-Century Managed Balance of Power System and Great Britain

I

In the eighteenth century there was a balance of power in Europe. Although the leading states were not precisely equal in strength, none so far outstripped the others as to be able to subdue them and dominate the Continent. Each state pursued its own interests, which meant that each strove to expand its power and influence, chiefly by increasing the territory and population under its control. None was so successful that it gained mastery over the others.

One or another of the European powers had from time to time threatened to achieve dominance: first the Spanish, then the German Hapsburgs, then Louis XIV of France. On each occasion the lesser states came together to thwart the power seeking hegemony. The threat of domination produced an opposing coalition, which, after defeating the state making the bid for mastery, dissolved into uncoordinated rivalries for territory and influence.

The European powers did not design their foreign policies so as to contrive equilibrium among themselves. The coalitions that formed to thwart efforts to dominate the Continent arose not from a grand Europe-wide scheme but rather from the uncoordinated pursuit by each power of its own interest, which was defined, even above self-aggrandizement, as independence. The balance of power was the unintended outcome of these individual strivings. Rousseau described it as a kind of mechanical marvel: "The actual system of Europe has precisely the degree of solidity which maintains it in a constant state of motion without upsetting it. The balance existing between the power of these diverse members of the European society is more the work of nature than of art. It maintains itself without effort, in such a manner that if it sinks on one side it reestablishes itself very soon on the other."[1]

The balance can be compared with the workings of the market in the classical version of economics. There individual selfishness – the search for personal gain – produces overall harmony, as resources are put to their most productive uses through the operation of the laws of supply and demand. In the eighteenth-century balance of power system, the self-assertion of sovereign states led to an outcome that, like the equilibrium of the market, was willed by none but was more or less acceptable to all.

The eighteenth-century system reflected similarities and differences between the international system and the state of nature that Hobbes describes. States, like men, are in competition with one another because of the absence of a governing authority. Structure determines behavior. But the result of the operation of the balance of power was precisely the opposite of the outcome to which Hobbes says men in the state of nature are inevitably driven. Individuals, according to Hobbes, give up their independence and form a commonwealth, a "Leviathan," that is, a state. The states of the eighteenth century retained their sovereign independence. Individuals form the state because they find life without it, in the state of nature, unbearable. Because states are tougher, more resilient, less vulnerable to one another than are individuals, their common condition, anarchy, was not intolerable. To the contrary, it was desirable. To perpetuate it was the chief purpose of the policies of the individual states, or rather the consequence of the workings of the balance of power. Independence, with all its hazards, was deemed preferable to peace through subservience. The balance of power preserved precisely what Hobbes says men in the state of nature must escape. The European states were prepared to fight to preserve it, to avoid what Hobbes portrays as the salvation of individuals. For eighteenth-century Europe, anarchy itself provided a kind of order.

[1] Quoted in Inis L. Claude, *Power and International Relations* (New York: Random House, 1962), pp. 43–4.

Then came the Wars of the French Revolution. The conflict between France and a shifting combination of the other powers that began shortly after the overthrow of the French king and continued to the final defeat of Napoleon in 1815 resembled the great wars of the European past. The strongest power sought to dominate the Continent. The others resisted and finally prevailed. This conflict differed from the campaigns against the Bourbons and the Hapsburgs, however, in its scale, its intensity, and most importantly in its political implications.

It ranged over more of Europe and the rest of the world and was bloodier and more destructive than its predecessors. The armies that France was able to put into the field were much larger than any that had existed previously because there were many more Frenchmen than there had been in centuries past and because the French Revolution rallied them to arms. France had a vast citizen army instead of the much smaller bands of mercenaries that had fought the preceding wars of the century.[2] The size of the "Grand Armée" made new tactics possible. Instead of cautious maneuvering while avoiding engagement with the enemy, which was the customary practice of eighteenth-century armies, the French generals moved their forces swiftly, concentrated them for battle, and attacked. Their conquests were more extensive than any since Roman times.

France was beaten, but only after a long struggle and at enormous cost. The balance of power system had worked, but its natural, spontaneous working had become much more expensive than ever before. For a different, although related reason, the eighteenth-century procedures also seemed dangerous to those who finally defeated France. The French carried with them the new ideas of nationalism and liberalism. Their victories advanced the causes these ideas inspired even when they were achieved under the leadership of Napoleon, who abolished many of the revolutionary liberties and proclaimed himself emperor.

The new dogmas posed a mortal threat to the three eastern great powers of Europe: Prussia, Russia, and Austria. None was either

---

[2] In 1789 there were 160,000 regular French troops. By 1794 France had 750,000 men under arms. Derek McKay and H. M. Scott, *The Rise of the Great Powers, 1648–1815* (New York: Longman, 1983), p. 287.

liberal or a nation-state. All were multinational autocracies ruled by hereditary monarchs. In a world of political units organized according to nationality and governed by popular sovereignty, the houses of Hohenzollern, Romanov, and Habsburg would have no place. The French Revolution had unseated the king, and although Napoleon took his place and put his relatives on other European thrones, the fate of the Bourbons was an abiding nightmare and a great cautionary lesson for the other monarchs. So was the way that the successor regimes harnessed popular enthusiasm for revolutionary causes, including war. The combination of French military power and revolutionary ideas made the dynastic regimes seem suddenly fragile.

In the eighteenth-century balance of power system each great power opposed the designs of all the others in pursuing its own, but none challenged the others' legitimacy. The kings and emperors might lose territory in the ongoing competition for power and place, but none would lose his throne. The French Revolution introduced precisely that threat. Regimes were shown to be perishable. They were therefore much more vulnerable, much more like men in Hobbes's state of nature, than before. War, as the byproduct of anarchy, had been a normal part of the life of states; after the French Revolution and Napoleon, it seemed unacceptably dangerous.

War was dangerous, of course, if it ended in defeat. But it was dangerous even if it were won, because victory would require an active alliance between the people and the rulers that could subvert the monarchical system. In the wake of the war against France, therefore, for the first time, the great powers adopted policies designed to modify the anarchy of European politics.

They did not embrace the Hobbesian solution of an all-powerful Leviathan. They were frightened by the Revolution, but not so frightened as to forsake the charms of sovereignty. The European powers valued independence as highly as ever. They merely wanted to avoid having to fight great wars to ensure it. They established procedures and unwritten, informal rules designed to avoid conflicts of the scope of the one just concluded and so avert the revolutionary upheavals that such wars threatened. These procedures and rules did not put an end to the competition among the great powers; they did, for a time, regulate it. At their center

was the idea of equilibrium, defined not in terms of some arith-
metical formula but simply as the absence of any preponderant
power. Whereas in the eighteenth century equilibrium came about
spontaneously through the uncoordinated actions of each of the
major states, in the nineteenth century the powers tried to contrive
it deliberately, through cooperation. The eighteenth-century balance of power was like a law of physics, a pattern that existed
independent of any deliberate design. The nineteenth-century balance more closely resembled a social rule, which governed the
conscious conduct of the states involved.

The main business of the Congress of Vienna in 1815, where the
victorious powers assembled after the defeat of Napoleon, was to
divide France's conquests among themselves in a way that was
consistent with a stable balance of power. For four decades thereafter they generally – although not always and certainly not everywhere – observed two rules whose purpose was to sustain the
equilibrium and thus the tranquility of Europe. First, each power
restrained its appetite for more territory in Europe – not entirely,
to be sure, but at least to the point of avoiding a major war. Second,
when internal turmoil on the Continent or rival claims there threatened war, the great powers moved to resolve the issue at hand
jointly and peacefully, usually at meetings of their representatives.

Equilibrium, restraint, and cooperation were the hallmarks of
European politics for forty years after the defeat of France. The
great powers aimed to preserve peacefully, by a loose kind of joint
management, what the eighteenth century had achieved by uncoordinated individual policies that included war: a balance of
power. These nineteenth-century procedures and norms can therefore be called a "managed balance of power system."

The managed balance of power system was a departure from the
normal international practice in which states seek security individually, through "self-help" policies. It represented a collective approach to the security problem. It was collective because it involved
all of the European powers, or at least all of the important ones.
The participation of each depended, in the end, on the participation
of all the others. As with individuals in Hobbes's state of nature,
each would have found itself worse off by practicing restraint unless
all the others did the same. The pattern of cooperation among the
great powers can thus be said to have been a property of the

international system as a whole. The pattern was contrived, not the unintended sum of individually determined policies. The great powers were well aware of their duties as "managers" of the balance of power system. They were conscious that there was a European interest distinct from the interests of Europe's individual states.

The nineteenth-century balance of power system was collective as well because it modified the basic anarchy of the international system. The powers accepted restraints on the pursuit of their own interests beyond those imposed by the countervailing military might of others; or to put it differently, they redefined their interests to include cooperation to avoid war as well as competition to acquire more territory. They also accepted the obligation to consult with one another on matters that threatened the peace. The practice of resolving Continental problems jointly came to be known as the Concert of Europe.

Collective security policies are those that attempt to modify the anarchic structure of the international system. The nineteenth-century balance of power system represents the most extensive, successful collective approach to security in modern times. It is therefore a significant development in the history of international relations.

The achievement of the Concert of Europe should not be overstated. It is not a towering landmark in international history on the scale of the French Revolution or World War I. Although it modified the international system, it certainly did not transform relations among sovereign states. If it was the zenith of the collective approach to security, if it marks the farthest the world has moved from uncoordinated self-help policies toward cooperative measures to provide common security, it also shows how resilient the anarchic structure of international policies is and how unyielding traditional self-help international policies therefore are; for the nineteenth-century managed balance of power system did not, in the end, move very far from the norm of unfettered anarchy.

Although the practices of the Concert were well understood, they were not embedded in formal international organizations. The familiar striving for advantage among the powers continued. Ambition and rivalry remained at the center of European affairs. Russia sought to advance to the south and west, France to regain privileges in Italy and Spain that Napoleon had enjoyed. The Austrian prime minister, Metternich, and the British foreign secretary for much of the period, Lord Palmerston, were rivals for the leadership of the Concert. For a time there was a persistent split between Britain and France on one side and the three eastern monarchies on the other.

Still, the nineteenth century was recognizably different from the eighteenth. It was more peaceful, and this was not simply by chance. It was partly attributable to the rules and procedures that the great powers acknowledged and followed. Collective practices became part of European politics. The idea of the interest of Europe as a whole – that is, of the claims of the system – influenced individual policies.

The Concert of Europe, defined as a set of regular procedures, did not last much beyond midcentury. Vestiges of the managed balance of power system did crop up in Europe for the next half-century after its demise, however. Something of its spirit, at least, could be discerned until the outbreak of World War I, which swept away all that remained of the old order on the continent. The ideas and practices that were born in 1815 became steadily less important for the policies of the great powers the farther in time they moved from the great war against France, with one notable exception. The spirit and the letter of the managed balance of power system continued to exercise an important influence on the foreign policies of Great Britain.

Britain had a special place in European affairs; it was both part of the politics of the Continent and detached from them. The English Channel afforded the British Isles a layer of protection from Europe; but the Channel was narrow enough, and the mainland close enough, for the British to count what happened there as having a direct bearing on their own security. Geography and economics combined to give Britain a definition of security that had two principal features.

The first was the need for maritime supremacy. To keep their island and their empire secure from foreign challenges the British needed control of the seas. Throughout the eighteenth and nineteenth centuries the Royal Navy provided it. The world's oceans were the highways connecting Great Britain with its overseas possessions. British prosperity depended heavily on trade. In the nineteenth century the British economy increasingly emphasized manufacturing rather than agriculture. The country needed markets abroad to sell what it made at home. Mastery of the seas was crucial, as well, for the defense of the home islands. Britain could be invaded only across water, and an invading force would first have to defeat the Royal Navy.

The second pillar of British security was a balance of power in Europe; that is, the absence of a single power dominating the Continent. A European hegemon could seal off the Continent from British trade. It could use Europe as the base for a navy of its own, which could interfere with imperial communications. It could blockade, harass, and even invade the British Isles.[3]

The British requirements for security differed from those of the continental powers. Each of the European states wished to hold as much territory as it could get in Europe while keeping each of the others from achieving dominion there. The British shared only the second goal. Britain's holdings expanded in spectacular fashion in the nineteenth century, but in Africa and Asia rather than on the other side of the English Channel. The British had no territorial ambitions in Europe. So while the Europeans worried about their neighbors, their frontiers, their armies and those of the states on their borders, the British were concerned with the balance of forces in Europe as a whole. Both the Continental powers and the British sought to advance their own interests; but the British conceived of their interests as a particular configuration on the Continent. Each European state sought to be as powerful as possible in Eu-

---

[3] The often cited memorandum of January 1, 1907, by Eyre Crowe of the British Foreign Office summarized this second requirement of the nation's security and the method by which the British acted on occasion to achieve it: "The only check on the abuse of political predominance derived from such a position [of hegemony in Europe] has always consisted in the opposition of an equally formidable rival, or of a combination of several countries forming leagues of defense. The equilibrium established by such a grouping of forces is technically known as the balance of power, and it has become almost an historical truism to identify England's secular policy with the maintenance of this balance by throwing her weight now in this scale and now in that, but ever on the side opposed to the political dictatorship of the strongest single State or group at a given time." "Memorandum by Mr. Eyre Crowe on the Present State of British Relations with France and Germany," Foreign Office, January 1, 1907. Reprinted in G. P. Gooch and Harold Temperley, eds., *British Documents on the Origins of the War, 1898–1904*, Vol. 2: *The Testing of the Entente 1904–06* (London: His Majesty's Stationery Office, 1928), p. 403.

rope. Britain was not, on the whole, concerned with which state was powerful as long as none became too powerful.

The concept of the balance of power was more firmly established and more explicitly a part of foreign policy in Britain than on the Continent. Britain was accustomed to thinking about Europe as a whole and the distribution of power within it. When Palmerston said, "We have no eternal allies and we have no perpetual enemies. Our interests are eternal and perpetual and those interests it is our duty to follow," one of the interests to which he was referring was equilibrium in Europe.[4]

In the wake of the Wars of the French Revolution the Continental powers came to define their security more along British lines than they had before. They, too, came to favor equilibrium. They, too, made this an explicit goal of their relations with other states. Like Britain, they conducted deliberate balance of power policies.

Their motives were different from those of Great Britain, however. They feared the revolutionary upheavals that were the likely consequences of wars for hegemony. The British were much less worried about revolution at home. They wanted, as always, to avoid the burden of coping with a hegemonic power. Equilibrium in Europe, not ideological probity there, was Britain's priority. Consequently, at the Congress of Vienna and for a decade thereafter the Europeans favored more extensive great-power collaboration than Britain was willing to countenance. Their goal was more ambitious than the establishment of a managed balance of power system. Metternich, especially, sought to maintain the victorious coalition in order to suppress revolutionary movements across Europe. What he wanted was something like a global police force to monitor and control developments within the European states. Britain was concerned simply with the balance of external strength among them. Britain's preferences set the limits on great-power collaboration after the Wars of the French Revolution.

Over the course of the next hundred years the European gov-

---

[4] Quoted in Alan Palmer, *The Chancelleries of Europe* (London, Allen & Unwin, 1983), p.83. Britain was particularly concerned with several specific areas on the Continent – the Channel ports. These were the parts of Europe most directly connected with the safety of the British Isles. The British did not wish to control the ports themselves, however, simply to ensure that no power hostile to Great Britain got control of them.

ernments' sense of what their security required changed. Their fear of revolution abated, or at least the tactics they adopted to resist it shifted. The perils of war seemed less daunting, the goal of equilibrium less important, and the claims of Europe as a whole less pressing. The British definition of security, by contrast, remained the same. Britain's relationship to the Continental powers on the matter of collective approaches to security therefore underwent a reversal. At the outset of the hundred years between the defeat of Napoleon and the outbreak of World War I Britain was, in a sense, the least enthusiastic supporter of international collaboration – or, rather, enthusiastic about the least extensive form of collaboration. By the end of this period, the British were more committed than any of the other great powers to a collective approach, and they remained more committed after World War I.

II

The idea of a collective approach to European security was broached by British Prime Minister William Pitt in a letter to the czar of Russia in 1805. The two had discussed joining forces to oppose Napoleon. Pitt listed the objectives of such a partnership: to deliver Europe from French subjugation, to apportion the territories recovered from France, and "to form, at the Restoration of Peace, a general agreement and Guarantee for the mutual protection and Security of different Powers, and for re-establishing a general System of Public Law in Europe." He stressed the need to give "Solidity and Permanence to the System which shall thus have been established." He called for "a Treaty to which all the principal Powers of Europe should be Parties, by which their respective Rights and Possessions, as they shall then have been established, shall be fixed and recognized, and they should all bind themselves mutually to protect and support each other, against any attempt to infringe them." The signatories would oppose "projects of Aggrandizement and Ambition" like the one on which France was embarked.[5] This letter was the ancestor of the managed balance

---

[5] "Extract from Pitt's official communication made to the Russian Ambassador at London . . . explanatory of the views which His Majesty and the Emperor of Russia formed for the deliverance and security of Europe," January 19,

of power system. It emphasized three themes: equilibrium, collective action, and permanent procedures. These became the cardinal features of the Concert of Europe.

The proposal was in keeping with the consistent and explicit British concern with equilibrium. That concern had come to the forefront of British policy because France had upset the European balance. Napoleon posed the greatest direct threat to British security in two centuries. He proposed to do, and in part did do, exactly what it was the aim of British security policy to prevent. He overran much of the Continent. He tried to stop all British trade with Europe through his "Continental system." He went farther. Having seized the Channel ports, he twice assembled forces there for the purpose of crossing the Channel and invading the British Isles.

As a result, Britain was France's most persistent opponent through the long period of turmoil following the Revolution. At one point the British promised assistance to any power that would wage war against the French.

Not until ten years after Pitt made his proposal, however, was a coalition formed that was able to defeat Napoleon. Its formation required that all the Continental powers put the aim of frustrating France's bid for hegemony above the powerful impulse for their own aggrandizement. Before 1813, one or another of the other great powers sided with Napoleon in his campaigns, or at least did not resist him. Napoleon cultivated this tendency. He tried never to go to war without an ally.

The French invasion of Russia in 1812 proved to be a turning point. It demonstrated that Napoleon's ambitions were boundless. At the same time it weakened the French forces enough to make his defeat seem feasible. The Fourth Coalition against France succeeded where the others failed.[6]

<hr>

1805. Reprinted in Kenneth Bourne, *The Foreign Policy of Victorian England, 1830–1902* (Oxford: Clarendon Press, 1970), pp. 197–8.

[6] Paul Schroeder argues that a successful coalition against Napoleon could not be formed until each power was persuaded that the defeat of France would not come at its own expense as well. Each had to be confident that it would not be a loser in the peace settlement. This meant that there had to be a common commitment to equilibrium *before* the Congress of Vienna. "The European International System, 1789–1848: Is There a Problem? An Answer?" Woodrow

The defeat of Napoleon required, as well, a greater commitment by the British than they had initially been willing to make. Britain had traditionally thrown its weight on the scales of European politics not by armed intervention but through financial assistance to Continental states. The British had contributed to the First Coalition by hiring German mercenaries to fight France. They had hoped to defeat France overseas and with naval power, as in the Seven Years' War earlier in the century, rather than through decisive victories in large-scale engagements in Europe. To bring Napoleon down they had to go farther. They dispatched their own forces to the Continent. Wellington led troops on the Iberian Peninsula and later commanded the army, made up of non-British soldiers as well, that won the Battle of Waterloo. Just as important for the establishment of permanent methods for sustaining equilibrium, Britain took the lead in organizing the final coalition and, in an unusual step, sent its foreign secretary, Lord Castlereagh, to Europe in late 1813 to help weld it together.[7]

In his enthusiasm for collective action on the Continent, Castlereagh was the disciple of Pitt. He made it his business to persuade the Europeans of the value of collaboration in peacetime as well as in wartime and to obtain their commitment to it. In the Project of Alliance that he sent to the various European capitals in September 1815, he included a provision for a perpetual defensive alliance after the conclusion of hostilities. The Treaty of Chaumont of 1814, which gave the Fourth Coalition against France a formal basis, included a provision for a grand alliance to last twenty years beyond the defeat of Napoleon. Finally, the Treaty of Quadruple Alliance, which was concluded on November 20, 1815, after the Hundred Days, Waterloo, and the division of the territory that France had conquered, contained an article that announced:

> The High Contracting Parties have agreed to renew their meetings at fixed periods, either under the immediate auspices of the Sovereigns themselves or by their respective Ministers, for the purpose of consulting upon their common interests, and for the

Wilson International Center for Scholars Colloquium Paper (Washington, D.C., March 19, 1984), pp. 31–9.
[7] It was the first visit to the Continent of the person holding this office since 1743. Palmer, *Chancelleries*, p. 1.

consideration of the measures which at each of these periods shall be considered the most salutary for the repose and prosperity of nations and for the maintenance of the peace of Europe.[8]

This was the charter for several peacetime conferences and for the general practice of deciding issues affecting the peace of Europe collectively, which was at the heart of the managed balance of power system.

According to the terms of the First Peace of Paris of May 1814, France was to return to its borders of 1792, which meant that the map of Europe had to be redrawn and French territorial gains reallocated. The representatives of the coalition powers met to settle the details at Vienna in 1814. Castlereagh was joined there by Metternich and ministers of the king of Prussia and the czar of Russia.

The collaboration that had made possible the final coalition served as a precedent for the Congress of Vienna, which in effect continued the process by which the coalition was assembled. The Congress, in turn, was itself a precedent for subsequent gatherings at which the great powers jointly addressed potentially disruptive political questions. The Congress of Vienna was the founding meeting of the nineteenth-century managed balance of power system. At the same time it was the high point of that system, because great-power collaboration was more extensive and intimate at Vienna and the issues decided there were weightier than on later occasions.

The guiding concept of the Congress's deliberations was equilibrium. The parties said so themselves. The idea recurs in official documents and unofficial accounts of the proceedings.[9] The principle of equilibrium was the basis on which the main business of

---

[8] Quoted in Carsten Holdbraad, *The Concert of Europe: A Study of German and British International Theory, 1815–1914* (New York, Barnes & Noble, 1970), p. 1.

[9] Douglas Dakin, "The Congress of Vienna, 1814–15, and its Antecedents," in Alan Sked, ed., *Europe's Balance of Power, 1815–1848* (London: Macmillan, 1979), p.21; E. V. Gulick, "The Final Coalition and the Congress of Vienna, 1813–15," in C. W. Crawley, ed., *War and Peace in an Age of Upheaval 1793–1830*, The New Cambridge Modern History, Vol. 9 (Cambridge University Press, 1965), p. 665; McKay and Scott, *Great Powers*, p. 339; Harold Nicolson, *The Congress of Vienna: A Study in Allied Unity: 1812–1822* (New York, Viking, 1961; first published, 1946), p. 39.

the Congress, the distribution of territory, was conducted. Each of the European powers wanted as much of what France was being forced to give up as it could get; but in their deliberations there was a sense that none should get so much as to threaten the others.

The most difficult issues at Vienna involved the disposition of Poland and Saxony. Britain and especially Austria, whose holdings bordered these territories, were concerned that if Russia incorporated all of Poland it would become too powerful. The czar did get most of what he wanted there, but to keep Prussia from annexing Saxony and so upsetting the balance of power in Central Europe, again at Austria's expense, Castlereagh and Metternich were prepared to make common cause with France. They signed a secret agreement with the French representative, Talleyrand, to this effect. It was never invoked; a compromise was reached over Saxony. The fact that the British and the Austrians were prepared to make it, however, shows that they considered the cause of equilibrium more important than the solidarity of the wartime coalition.

Castlereagh took upon himself the task of promoting great-power collaboration and a stable balance. He carried considerable weight. Britain had made an important contribution to the Fourth Coalition's victory, particularly the final defeat of Napoleon at Waterloo. The British sought no territory in Europe for themselves. Their only European goal, as in the past, was a balance of power. They were therefore well placed to urge others to modify their own ambitions for the sake of equilibrium.[10]

There followed, over the next seven years, three additional full-fledged congresses, each attended by the foreign ministers of the great powers. The Congress of Aix-la-Chapelle in 1818, the first such European gathering to be held in peacetime, ratified the withdrawal of occupation troops from France and officially readmitted the French to the councils of Europe as a great power. The

---

[10] "Napoleon professed to be unable to understand British policy as directed by Castlereagh at Vienna. 'The peace he has made is the sort of peace he would have made if he had been beaten.' Clausewitz wrote more perceptively: 'Historically the English will play the better role in this catastrophe, because they do not seem to have come here with a passion for revenge . . . but rather like a master who wishes to discipline with proved coldness and immaculate purity.'" Christopher Bartlett, "Britain and the European Balance," in Sked, *Balance of Power*, p. 148.

Congress of Troppau and Laibach in 1820 was convened in response to a revolutionary upheaval in Naples and the threat of Austrian intervention there. The issue that dominated the Congress of Verona in 1822–3 was what appeared to be the start of a revolutionary uprising in Spain.

These three meetings, especially the last two, were not as successful as the Congress of Vienna. They were not nearly as harmonious. There was discord between Britain, on the one hand, and the Continental monarchies, especially Austria, on the other, over the proper scope of great-power collaboration. The discord had begun at Vienna. The Russian czar Alexander had offered a vague, mystical idea for a "Holy Alliance" of the powers to promote Christian virtue. Metternich turned the idea into a proposal for collective intervention to suppress revolutionary outbreaks in Europe. As the most cosmopolitan of the eastern empires, without a natural geographic or national basis, consisting as it did of German, Hungarian, Italian, and Slavic provinces, Austria was particularly vulnerable to revolutionary forces. Metternich was seeking an arrangement to protect the dynasty that he served.

Castlereagh rejected the idea. He refused to sign the Treaty of the Holy Alliance. It would have required a deeper involvement in the politics of the Continent than Britain's security warranted. It would have made Britain part of a European police force. On similar grounds the British opposed intervention in Italy and Spain. In a state paper written in early May 1820, Castlereagh said that the arrangement he had conceived at Vienna "never was . . . intended as a Union for the Government of the World or for the superintendence of the internal affairs of other States"[11] and that while "we shall be found in our place when actual danger menaces the System of Europe . . . this Country cannot, and will not, act upon abstract and speculative Principles of Precaution."[12]

Castlereagh died in 1822 and was succeeded by George Canning, who lacked his predecessor's commitment to the collective management of European affairs and was indeed scornful of Continental entanglements. The change of ministers did not really make for a change of policy, however. Canning did not turn his back on Eu-

[11] Quoted in Alan Sked, "Introduction," in ibid., p. 6.
[12] Quoted in Palmer, *Chancelleries*, pp. 31–2.

rope. He deprecated great-power conferences, but his representatives and successors attended them when Britain's interests were
involved. Castlereagh, for all his allegiance to the idea of the European Concert, was not prepared to join Metternich in forming
a Holy Alliance. Palmerston, their great successor, was an ardent
champion of the European balance but not of intervention in the
internal affairs of the Continent.

The three post-Vienna congresses are often portrayed as mark-
ing the failure and the disintegration of the Concert of Europe.[13]
It is more accurate to say that they set the limits of the managed
balance of power system. They established the practice of conven-
ing frequent if irregular peacetime international meetings and of
approaching certain kinds of disturbances in Europe in collective
fashion. The methods employed at Vienna were subsequently applied elsewhere. The later congresses also established the kinds of
issues to which these methods would be applied. Europe as a whole
would act not to preserve dynastic thrones but to sustain equilibrium. The powers would not jointly dictate how the states of Europe
were to be governed but would rather address themselves to
external considerations – the borders and the balance of power
between and among them. This they did, periodically and successfully, over the next three decades.

The European powers collaborated on the question of Greek
independence from Turkey. There was no full-scale congress to
take up the issue, but the Concert of Europe was nonetheless at
work. By the Treaty of London of 1827, Britain, France, and Russia
recognized Greek autonomy, called for an armistice between
Greece and Turkey, and approved the dispatch of a multinational
fleet to the Mediterranean to enforce the peace. A protocol signed
in London in 1829 and another the following year fixed the boundaries of the newly independent Greece, and the final details were
settled in 1832.

The issue of Belgian independence from Holland evoked a similarly collective response. The powers convened in London at the
end of 1830 and, in the first month of 1831, produced a protocol
recognizing the Belgian state and guaranteeing its perpetual neu-

---

[13] Henry Kissinger, *A World Restored* (New York, Grosset & Dunlap, 1964; first
published, 1957), and Nicolson, *Congress of Vienna*, take this line of argument.

trality. A treaty to that effect was enacted later in the year, although final agreement was not reached until 1839.

The perennial threat to European harmony throughout the nineteenth century – what came to be called the "Eastern Question" – was the slow, steady disintegration of the Ottoman Empire, which finally collapsed in defeat in World War I. Its European possessions, most of which were predominantly Christian, grew restless under Turkish control and clamored for independence. Greece was the first of them to do so. The great powers feared a total collapse of Ottoman rule, which, they anticipated, would touch off a dangerous scramble for the various pieces of the empire. Austria and Britain in particular worried that Russia would seize most of them and thereby upset the Continental balance. Hence the Concert of Europe was recurrently preoccupied with the Eastern Question.

But is was not only the European parts of the Ottoman Empire that struggled to break away. Turkey's Near Eastern possessions revolted as well. There was a rebellion in Egypt in 1839. The European powers sent a note to the Turks asserting their right to have a say in the matter. The following year in London a treaty was signed by all of them save France stipulating the terms of settlement between the Turks and the Egyptian rebel, Mehmet Ali. In the next year the great powers concluded the Straits Convention, reaffirming the principle of keeping the Dardanelles and the Bosphorus closed to warships.

Greece, Belgium, and Turkey were situated at the edges of Europe. It was relatively easy for the powers to collaborate in order to resolve such peripheral issues, especially when they were settled at the expense of Turkey or the Netherlands rather than one of the members of the Concert of Europe. Britain took a particular interest in these matters. The status of the Turkish Near East affected the security of India, the most important British imperial possession. Belgium had within its borders the strategically vital Channel ports. Britain's voice carried weight because at the extremities of the Continent British naval power could be brought to bear.

The Concert also operated, however, where issues closer to the geographic center of the Continent were involved. A London conference of 1852 worked out a solution to disputes surrounding the tangled question of who should control the duchies of Schleswig and Holstein, which lay between Germany and Denmark.

Neither Greece, Belgium, Egypt, nor Schleswig-Holstein was the subject of a full-scale congress, with the foreign ministers of the great powers present, like the Congress of Vienna and the three that followed it. The meetings devoted to each of these European problems were attended by lower-level representatives, often ambassadors. Sometimes one or another of the powers was not represented.[14] There were fundamental similarities and continuities, however, between the reorganization of Europe at Vienna and the resolution of potentially contentious issues during the next four decades. Collective procedures were employed; the issues to which they were applied were considered proper subjects for Europe as a whole. Equilibrium was the principal guideline for resolving those issues. In their deliberations the powers were concerned to make sure that none was imperiled by the gains of another.

The establishment of the Concert marked the beginning of the great age of European diplomacy. A diplomatic corps came into existence, which took ever greater responsibility for conducting the international relations of the Continent. The diplomats of the different powers had much in common. Their backgrounds were generally aristocratic. They were often related by marriage. They had a common political outlook. They even spoke the same language: French was the more or less official medium of diplomatic communication. These common characteristics lubricated the machinery of diplomacy. The basis of diplomatic cooperation, however, was a common purpose, the common commitment to tranquility and therefore to equilibrium that the managed balance of power system expressed.

After 1815, as at the Vienna meeting, Britain was a strong proponent of collective measures to maintain the European balance. The British took part in the deliberations of the Concert of Europe and occasionally served as a mediator among other, more directly engaged powers.[15] Palmerston was a great partisan of the balance

---

[14] F. H. Hinsley, *Power and the Pursuit of Peace: Theory and Practice in the History of Relations Between States* (Cambridge University Press, 1967), p. 214, provides a useful list of the great-power gatherings of the nineteenth century.

[15] This was the case with Belgian independence. See Bourne, *Foreign Policy*, p. 21.

of power. He identified Britain's interest with the effective working
of the Concert. But he insisted that it avoid internal issues. His
views on the proper governance of the European states were generally liberal. But he was prepared to sacrifice liberal and national
principles when they conflicted with the requirements of Continental equilibrium. He was unsympathetic to the Hungarian revolt
against Austria in 1848, for example, because it threatened the
Hapsburg monarchy and thus the balance of power at the center
of Europe.

If the Concert of Europe can be said to have begun at the
Congress of Vienna, the Crimean War of 1854–6 marked its end,
at least as a set of quasi-formal procedures that the great powers
felt some ongoing obligation to follow. The Crimean War was a
conflict over Turkey between Britain and France on one side and
Russia on the other. It was followed by three more wars within
fifteen years that pitted European great powers against one another. France and Austria fought in Italy in 1859. The French
victory obtained Lombardy for the Italian king, Victor Emmanuel,
setting in motion a series of events that led to the unification of
the entire peninsula under Italian rule. Prussia defeated Austria
in 1866 and annexed the previously independent North German
states. Five years later Prussia defeated France and incorporated
the rest of the German states into a new, Prussian-dominated German empire.

Each of these wars violated the spirit of the managed balance of
power system, the unwritten rules that the great powers had followed since 1815. Each was a war between great powers, something
the Concert of Europe had been formed to avoid. The last three
changed the map of Europe, and thus the distribution of power on
the Continent, not by collective but by unilateral measures and
not by agreement but by the use of force. The unification of Italy
and Germany changed the territorial dispensation of 1815 by methods wholly inconsistent with the managed balance of power system.
Still, the wars did not have the dire consequences that the great
powers had feared in 1815 and afterward and had established the
Concert of Europe to avert. They did not lead to conflict on the
scale of the Wars of the French Revolution. No potential hegemonic
power strong enough to threaten the independence of the others
emerged from them. They did not touch off revolutionary up-

heavals. The year of greatest internal turmoil on the Continent was 1848, well before the Crimean War, not to mention the Prussian conquests. And the spirit of collaboration reappeared from time to time in the sixty years between the outbreak of the Crimean conflict and the beginning of World War I.

The Crimean War was itself fought by Britain to vindicate the principles of the balance of power. At issue was whether these principles would extend to the Turkish holdings outside Europe. The British and French victory ensured that they would. The Eastern Question was kept under control for fifty years more.

The European wars that followed the Crimean conflict were brief. None lasted more than seven months. They were "cabinet wars" fought for specific political purposes, not vast sprawling wars of conquest like the French campaigns of fifty years earlier. And although the habit of frequent collaboration among the great powers was not fully resumed after the Franco-Prussian War of 1871, neither was there another war among the great powers until 1914.

Nor did the results of the wars of midcentury upset the balance of the Continent. The unification of Italy and Germany came chiefly at Austria's expense. But the Hapsburg monarchy did not disappear. It remained a great power, although reduced in size and prestige. Prussia emerged a much greater power than before but was not an immediate threat to the European equilibrium. The Prussian victories seemed, in fact, to reinforce the balance by establishing the newly unified Germany as a bulwark against the two ambitious flanking powers, France and Russia, which were widely regarded as the likeliest to bid for mastery of the Continent. This, at any rate, was the British view. Britain was not tempted to try to stop the Prussian conquests because these were thought to serve the British interest by counterbalancing France and Russia.[16]

In the wake of Prussia's victories, Otto von Bismarck, the German chancellor, became the most important figure in European affairs. For his own reasons and in his own way he conducted policies consistent at least with the spirit of the managed balance

---

[16] There was anti-French feeling in Britain in 1871 because Bismarck had disclosed documents suggesting French designs on the Channel ports. The British were in any case not in a position to intervene effectively. Although it had been won, the Crimean War had gone badly enough to create a public and official bias against fighting on the Continent that still lingered.

of power system. After rearranging the map of Europe in favor of Prussia, he became the staunch champion of the status quo. His methods were not precisely those of the Concert of Europe. Rather than relying on meetings of all the great powers to address troublesome issues, he constructed a series of overlapping alliances to keep potential enemies from combining against Germany. The intent, however, was similar: to keep peace on the Continent. Bismarck even had occasional recourse to the diplomatic procedures of the first half of the century. He convened the Congress of Berlin in 1878 to deal, successfully, with another flare-up of the Eastern Question. Once again the Turkish Empire, weak and ramshackle though it had become, was preserved.

III

The collective arrangements of the nineteenth century were a response to the destructiveness of the Wars of the French Revolution. Those wars constituted one of three great conflicts in modern history. World Wars I and II were also long and bloody. They, too, scrambled the map of Europe. They, too, introduced a revolutionary mode of warfare – mechanized war in the first case, atomic weapons in the second – which made the war itself far more destructive than had been anticipated and promised to make the next round, if there should be one, catastrophic.[17] World Wars I and II, like the Wars of the French Revolution, gave rise to a widely shared impulse to avoid another, similar one. That impulse, in turn, led to efforts to contrive collective arrangements for security. Those efforts, and the relations among the great powers in the wake of the two great wars of the twentieth century, may be compared with the Concert of Europe. The great powers failed to establish successful collective arrangements after World War I. The peace settlement of 1919 came apart within two decades.[18] The aftermath of World War II has more closely resembled the decades following

---

[17] On the three modern "military revolutions," see Michael Mandelbaum, *The Nuclear Revolution: International Politics Before and After Hiroshima* (Cambridge University Press, 1981), pp. 14–21.

[18] The failure to reconstitute a managed balance of power system or something like it after World War I is the subject of Section V. See also Chapter 3, Section II.

the defeat of Napoleon than the politics and diplomacy of the post–
World War I period. Nuclear weapons have provided a powerful
incentive to avoid a major war. For forty years and more no such
war has been fought. After 1945 there came to be a stable balance
of power between the two strongest states, the United States and
the Soviet Union, at least at the heart of the international system
– in Europe.

If the achievement of the Concert of Europe was repeated in
some measure after 1945, however, the forms, the diplomatic procedures of the first half of the nineteenth century, were not. No
periodic meetings took place between the United States and the
Soviet Union for the purpose of resolving contentious political questions by negotiation, mutual adjustment, and concessions. A number of issues on which the two great powers had competing interests
did arise after 1945, both in Europe – in Hungary, Czechoslovakia,
and Poland – and elsewhere – in Korea, Southeast Asia, and Afghanistan, for instance. These were settled by force.

There has been no equivalent of the Concert of Europe since
1945 because the attitude of each great power toward the other
has differed in one fundamental respect from the norm of the
nineteenth century. In 1815 and afterward each great power considered the status of the others legitimate. Each conceded the right
of the others to the prerogatives of great power. Each acknowledged, specifically, the right of all the others to have a say in
resolving European questions. Neither the United States nor the
Soviet Union, by contrast, has accepted the legitimacy of the other's
role as a great power. The United States is not willing to endorse
Soviet control over Eastern Europe. The Soviet Union will not
explicitly concede to the United States a rightful part in the military
and political affairs of Europe. Indeed, neither the United States
nor the Soviet Union considers the other's government a wholly
legitimate regime.

Each has had to accept the other's form of government and its
sphere of influence as unwelcome, unpleasant, but established
facts. But neither will acknowledge these as part of the natural,
proper order of international affairs. Such an acknowledgment,
however, has proved unnecessary. Nuclear weapons are such powerful disincentives for war that the United States and the Soviet
Union have been able to avoid one without a twentieth-century

version of what Castlereagh called the "great machine of European safety." In the absence of explicit cooperation they have practiced tacit parallel restraint.

The United States and the Soviet Union have also been able to do without formal procedures similar to those of the nineteenth-century balance of power system because there are only two of them. Each can readily monitor the conduct of the other.[19]

Meetings like those of the Concert of Europe to resolve political disputes were not convened after 1945. But by then they were less important for the maintenance of peace than they had been in the nineteenth century, because military power, and thus European and global equilibrium, had come to depend less on the control of territory and more on armaments made within a state's own borders. Balancing the other great power became largely an internal affair for each, a matter of building more weapons. The disposition of territory outside their borders was not as easy for the United States and the Soviet Union to arrange to their mutual satisfaction as it had been for the conquerors of Napoleon; but this was also a less crucial matter for the great powers after World War II.

The two have negotiated, at great length, about the stockpiles of nuclear weapons they have built. One of the purposes of these negotiations has been to secure a military equilibrium. Arms control talks can therefore be considered the closest approximation, after 1945, of the workings of the Concert of Europe.

There was a peace conference of sorts after World War II. It was held in the capital of a neutral European country. It concerned itself, among other matters, with Europe's postwar boundaries. It was held, however, not on the morrow of victory, as in 1815, but thirty years after the war had ended – in 1975. Its purpose was not to draw the boundaries of Europe but to ratify boundaries that had already been in force for three decades.

The 1975 Helsinki Conference did not, like the Congress of Vienna, create a postwar order. It simply acknowledged the existence of an order that had already been created by the outcome of the war, the subsequent maneuvering between the great powers,

---

[19] On the differences between worlds of two and of more than two great powers see Kenneth N. Waltz, *Theory of International Politics* (Reading, Mass.: Addison-Wesley, 1979), pp. 168–72.

and above all by their tacit restraint toward each other. The European settlement was so well established by 1975 that there seemed no point in pretending that it was merely temporary.[20]

The nineteenth-century managed balance of power system can usefully be compared not only with similar episodes in international history but also with something that is quite different in many ways but whose underlying logic illustrates the dynamics of the establishment and the disintegration of the Concert of Europe: the occasional behavior of individual firms in a single market. Both a market and the international system lack a supreme authority. Structure determines behavior in both cases, the relevant behavior being competition among the units of the system. Sometimes, however, firms in a market, like the great powers in the nineteenth century, modify their competitive behavior.

Firms ordinarily compete in terms of the prices they charge for their products or services. Each sets the price as low as it can while still making a profit; if it attempts to charge a higher price, its competitors will offer a lower one and take its business away. This lowest profitable price is known to economists as the market, or equilibrium, price. Sometimes, with some firms in some industries, however, this does not occur. Firms do not drive the price down. They receive a higher than equilibrium price.

Firms can improve their market positions – they can earn higher profits – by charging a higher than equilibrium price, just as sovereign states can be more secure if they mute their normal rivalry. Neither single firms nor single states are better off exercising self-restraint unless others do so as well. In both cases unanimity is required. Restraint is unusual, or at least "unnatural," in both cases. Economists call episodes of price restraint instances of "imperfect" competition. Similarly, writing three years after the collaborative arrangements that had been born at Vienna in 1815, Friederich Gentz, Metternich's secretary, said that "it would be contrary to the nature of man and of things that it [the Concert of Europe] should replace for a long time the condition of opposition and

---

[20] The United States agreed to take part in the Conference and acknowledge Europe's postwar borders in return for a Soviet agreement to protocols protecting human rights, whose terms the Soviet government did not subsequently honor.

struggle [among] a mass of independent Powers, each possessing its own character and system."[21]

The comparison between firms in an economy and sovereign states in the international system is useful because it provides another, larger universe of cases against which to evaluate the nineteenth-century balance of power system beyond the two other postwar periods. The comparison cannot be an exact one. There are vast and significant differences. But there are also parallels, which shed light on two of the most important issues concerning collective approaches to security: when they are undertaken, and how, once established, they break down.

Absent laws to the contrary, in theory firms in any industry could cooperate to keep their price above the equilibrium level. In practice, they do so only in industries in which a few firms are larger than the others. The reason is that the task of coordination is prohibitively difficult when many firms are more or less equal. Then none is large enough to have an independent effect on the industry-wide price and none has an incentive not to compete.

When a firm is large enough, when it produces a big enough share of the total output of a commodity to affect the industry-wide price, however, the situation is different. Then it has what is called "market power." By restraining itself it can make a tangible contribution to sustaining a price above the equilibrium level. But if it chooses not to practice restraint when other, similar firms are doing so, if it chooses to compete, its responsibility for pushing the price toward the equilibrium point will be apparent.[22] Where a few firms predominate, the industry may be said to have an oligopolistic structure. The higher price that can be obtained when powerful firms refrain from thoroughly competitive behavior is known as the oligopoly price.

There is a clear parallel with the managed balance of power system of the nineteenth century. The Concert of Europe was an affair of the great powers; it effectively excluded the numerous lesser states. At the Congress of Vienna and afterward the key decisions were the province of the strongest. The leading states

---

[21] Quoted in Hinsley, *Power*, p. 198.

[22] The effect of the concentration of power within a group like an industry or the international system on the prospects for and the costs of cooperation is discussed in Chapter 6, pp. 382–3.

had the political equivalent of economic market power. They could work out a settlement to a European question knowing that, having made it, they could enforce it. If all the great powers supported a measure, no other state could hope to overturn it. International inequality was a precondition for international order in the nineteenth century.[23]

Inequality does not make a collective approach to security inevitable. For while some industries are oligopolistic, having a few leading firms, and others are atomistic, with many firms of roughly the same size, the international system has always been marked by inequality. Some states have always been appreciably stronger and had much wider influence than the others. There has always been a small group of great powers among the members of the international system. But very seldom have collective approaches to the security problem been successfully established.

Not all industries with a few leading firms restrain competition to achieve a higher than equilibrium price for their respective products. An oligopolistic structure does not guarantee the oligopoly price. Whether it is achieved depends on circumstances particular to the industry and the time. To put the proposition in abstract terms, there is no necessary connection between one of the basic features of the system (defined here as the configuration of power within it) and the behavior of the constituent units.

Sometimes a deep, industry-wide recession leads to the restraint of competition among leading firms in that industry, and hence to an increase in their prices. They recognize that uninhibited competition will ruin them all. They realize that they must, in effect, hang together or they will be doomed to hang separately. The great wars that gave rise to the impulse for collaboration in 1815, 1919, and 1945 are the analogue in international politics.

Depressed industries, however, do not always restrict competition, and thriving industries sometimes do. Similarly, the perennial concentration of power within the international system and the periodic shocks of great disruptive conflicts have not always produced successful collective approaches to security. They are

---

[23] On the general subject of the relationship between equality and order in the international system see Robert W. Tucker, *The Inequality of Nations* (New York, Basic Books, 1977), Chap. 3.

apparently necessary, but not sufficient conditions for system-wide cooperation. Whether the impulse to prevent another war succeeded in yielding workable arrangements after the three great conflicts of modern history depended on the historical circumstances in each of the postwar periods. As with firms in an industry, structure did not determine behavior.[24]

If there is no general rule governing restraint or the lack of it among firms or great powers, there is an important feature of collaboration for the sake of restricting economic competition that is pertinent to international politics. Restraint is much more likely when firms cooperate explicitly, openly, and formally than when they do not. Formal organizations whose purpose is to arrange and promote the suppression of competition are known as cartels.[25] They address the need for universality in achieving the oligopoly price, a need that arises from the fact that no single firm can gain by restraining itself unless the others also practice restraint. By joining a cartel, each firm gives the others an assurance that it will exercise restraint. Cartels facilitate communication among firms. They serve both as vehicles for conveying the necessary assurances and as devices by which each firm can monitor the behavior of the others.

The Concert of Europe, with its formal meetings of the great powers, was the equivalent in the international system of a cartel. It was both a symbol that all the great powers accepted the need for inhibiting their normal competition and a forum for working out the details of their common restraint, that is, the resolution of issues that might otherwise have triggered conflicts. Without the more formal methods of the Concert of Europe, without the direct

---

[24] Students of economic competition have found that the "social structure" of industries – the informal norms and even the personal relations among the heads of the leading firms – count for something in determining whether competition is restrained. See F. M. Scherer, *Industrial Pricing: Theory and Evidence* (Chicago: Rand-McNally, 1970), pp. 82–4. In the same way, in the nineteenth-century managed balance of power system, the homogeneity of the diplomatic corps, the common backgrounds and attitudes of the diplomats and their personal networks, made cooperation easier.

[25] Some economists argue that price restraint is not possible over time without some sort of formal mechanism to police it. Only a working cartel, according to this analysis, can secure the oligopoly price for any extended period. See Oliver E. Williamson, *Markets and Hierarchies: Analysis and Antitrust Implications* (New York, Free Press, 1975), pp. 236–8.

contacts among the great powers and their explicit cooperation to settle complicated matters like Greek and Belgian independence and the Eastern Question in its various forms, the achievements of the nineteenth-century managed balance of power system would not have been possible.[26]

Cartels have another feature in common with the nineteenth-century international order in Europe. Their purpose is to restrict price competition. The aim of price competition for each firm is to obtain higher profits (or at least higher revenues) by acquiring larger shares of the overall market. One way to suppress competition, therefore, is to agree in advance on a fixed distribution of market shares. Cartels often arrange such a distribution.

Similarly, the purpose of international competition for each state in the nineteenth century was in some sense to increase its power and wealth through larger territorial holdings. The Concert of Europe, especially the Congress of Vienna, established a set distribution of territory in Europe for the purpose of suppressing competition among the great powers on the Continent. Each great power received the equivalent of a "share" of the European "market." The unwritten rule of the Concert was that none would seek to increase its share to the point of provoking another conflict of Napoleonic proportions.

Another feature of cartelized industries is analogous to Britain's special place in the nineteenth-century managed balance of power system. Some firms, lesser ones without market power, can disobey the cartel's rules. Rather than accept limits on their market shares, they can cut prices, or produce without restraint, or both. The larger firms, those with market power, ordinarily tolerate such competitive behavior, at least as long as the firms that engage in it are too small to affect the market as a whole. These truants are sometimes called "fringe firms." Whereas full-fledged members of

---

[26] Some economists have argued that, when only two firms dominate an industry, they will spontaneously coordinate their behavior to secure the oligopoly price. The larger the number of oligopolists, the more explicit their coordination must be (Scherer, *Industrial Pricing*, pp. 7–8). Transposed to international politics, this argument would help to explain the differences between the managed balance of power system of the nineteenth century and the international order after 1945, in which some cooperation has taken place without the formal mechanisms of coordination of the nineteenth century. See also Waltz, *International Politics*, pp. 168–72.

a cartel make sacrifices in the form of sales and market shares forgone in order to sustain the oligopoly price, fringe firms do not. They receive a benefit – in the form of the oligopoly price – without paying for it.[27]

Britain benefited in a similar way from the nineteenth-century balance of power system. The British were part of the Concert of Europe, of course, and took an active role in its deliberations. But the Concert's general rule of restraint did not really apply to them. The Continental powers had to rein in their appetites for territory in Europe. Since Britain had none, the system did not impose a cost on them in the form of potential benefits forgone as it did on its European members.

The parallel can be taken farther. The sacrifices that the members of a cartel must make can be seen as a kind of subsidy for the fringe firms. The potential benefits of competition that the firms renounce can be seen as costs that must be paid to keep the price above the equilibrium level. Fringe firms, like others in the industry, charge this higher than equilibrium price. Similarly, the managed balance of power can be seen as a kind of subsidy for British imperial expansion in the nineteenth century.

Britain added considerably to its overseas possessions (and its foreign influence as well) between the Congress of Vienna and the outbreak of World War I. There were a number of reasons for the growth of the British Empire: Britain's lead in the industrial revolution and its maritime supremacy were prominent among them. Also important, however, was the fact that the British did not have to devote resources to securing equilibrium in Europe and could direct them instead to imperial pursuits.

At the Congress of Verona in 1822 George Canning, Castlereagh's successor as foreign secretary, demonstrated his displeasure with French activities in Spain by recognizing the independence of several new republics in Latin America. Freed from Spanish rule, they could trade with whichever countries they chose, which worked to the advantage of Britain, the world's greatest trading power in the nineteenth century. Canning had, he said, "called

---

[27] Scherer, *Industrial Pricing*, p. 58. Fringe firms are instances of the more general phenomenon of "free riders." See Chapter 6, pp. 357–8.

the New World into existence to redress the balance of the old."[28] If a Continental power made a gain in Europe, Britain would compensate itself elsewhere.

Canning's policy can stand as the paradigm of the benefits Britain drew from the existence of the Concert of Europe. The exchange he claimed to have made was an unequal one. France got little in Spain, and in general the European powers made only modest gains on the Continent. It was, after all, the point of the managed balance of power system that they should respect the status quo there. Britain, by contrast, enjoyed a robust trade with Latin America and acquired a vast domain beyond Europe over the course of the century.

From this it follows that the balance of power was most useful to the British when they had least directly to do with it. In the half-century from the end of the Crimean War to the first Moroccan crisis of 1905, when the European balance became an issue in Anglo-German relations for the first time, Britain took only a modest part in European affairs. It was much less extensively involved than it had been during the preceding fifty years. In 1868 the House of Commons eliminated from the annual Mutiny Bill the traditional assertion that Britain maintained an army in part to secure the balance of power in Europe. This did not reflect a decline in the general importance of equilibrium there; rather it signified that the cost to Britain of sustaining the balance had decreased. Equilibrium remained a paramount interest; but Britain now had to do less to ensure it. It was the solidity and stability of the balance in Europe after 1871 that made possible the years of Britain's "splendid isolation." The British had the best of all possible worlds: equilibrium without exertion. It is little wonder that when the balance was challenged they worked energetically to prop it up.

Cartels do not last forever, and the ways they end have important points in common with the fate of the nineteenth-century international system. A cartel is always subject to cheating. A firm may violate its rules by producing beyond its assigned quota or offering a lower than designated price for its product. When the violator is a small fringe firm, the members of the cartel often tolerate its

---

[28] Quoted in Palmer, *Chancelleries*, p. 43.

behavior. But there is a limit to how much cheating any cartel can accept.

New firms that are not part of the existing cartel agreement may enter the market in any industry. To sustain the oligopoly price the new firm must be accommodated. It will want its own share of the market; that, after all, is the point of being in business. To keep the product's price high, other firms will have to relinquish parts of their shares that together equal what the new entrant receives. If they refuse to accommodate the newcomer in this way, its output will add to the total production in the industry as a whole. The increase in overall supply will, through the operation of the laws of supply and demand, lower the price toward the equilibrium level, undercutting the cartel.

The challenge to arrangements that support the price may come not only from a new entrant but from a firm that is already a member of the cartel. Over time the production costs within industries change. Some firms are more dynamic and become more efficient than others. These firms often come to feel short-changed by the cartel's rules, which, they believe, give them less than they deserve. They reckon that they can get larger market shares and higher profits without the cartel, in an environment of unrestricted competition. This gives them powerful incentives to cheat, to "defect" from the existing arrangements. The distribution of market shares within a cartel therefore tends to resemble what the balance among the firms would be without explicit agreements. The more dynamic the evolution of the production process (and hence the costs of production) in any industry, and the more uneven the changes this brings across the industry, the more fragile any cartel in that industry will be.

New entrants or dynamic, dissatisfied members of a cartel pose two threats. If the others do not relinquish enough market share to satisfy the challenger, it can lower its price, increase production, or both, to the point at which the oligopoly price no longer holds. The members of a cartel plainly have an interest in accommodating a challenger. But if they give up too much, if they reduce their own market shares too far, they will find themselves no better off, they will make no higher profits, than if there were no cartel at all. These firms may actually not fare as well as they would in unrestrained competition, at which point restraint has clearly become not merely pointless but actually counterproductive. In either case the dissatisfaction of one party can disrupt the cartel's arrangements and provoke the resumption of unchecked competition. The successful operation of a cartel requires the participation of all the relevant parties.

There is a suggestive although inexact parallel, once again, between the potential sources of instability in arrangements that restrict competition in a market and the final collapse of the international order of the nineteenth century with the outbreak of World War I in 1914. The arrangements for equilibrium were less formal in the second half of the century between 1815 and 1914 than in the first. The latter period was thus not as comparable to an economic cartel. There was, however, a stable balance of power on the Continent during the second period. This was partly the result of circumstances beyond the reach of diplomacy – the relative equality of the great powers, for example, and the consequent absence of a potential hegemonic state prepared to try to dominate the Continent. But the climate of tacit restraint and the vestiges of the managed balance of power that had carried over from the Congress of Vienna and its aftermath were also responsible.

The German role in the outbreak of war can be seen as an analogue of the challenges to a cartel. Germany was the equivalent of a new entrant in an industry. The Germany of 1914 differed so dramatically from the Prussia of 1815 as to qualify as a different country. At the end of the Napoleonic Wars, Prussia was the greatest of the several German states, all of which were equally sovereign, but the least of the five great powers. By 1871, the state of which Prussia was the core encompassed all the previously independent German states.

Still, Europe enjoyed almost a half-century of tranquility after the unification of Germany in 1871. It was not only territorial expansion that led to German restlessness and dissatisfaction with the status quo. It was internal expansion as well. In the last decades of the nineteenth century Germany industrial growth skyrocketed. Germany overtook Britain as the leading industrial nation in the Old World.[29] In this sense Germany was like a firm in a cartel that

[29] Statistics demonstrating this point can be found in Paul M. Kennedy, *The Rise of the Anglo-German Antagonism, 1860–1914* (London: Allen & Unwin, 1982;

is more dynamic than the others, that has decreasing production costs, and that calculates that it is receiving less than its due from the cartel's arrangements.

It was, in effect, a similar calculation that Germany made at the end of the nineteenth century and the first decade and a half of the twentieth. Germany's enormous growth was the disturbing element in European affairs. It was a development that could not be accommodated within the existing order. The Germans wanted more – more territory, more wealth, a greater share of the benefits that the Concert of Europe had originally apportioned. Their foreign policy was geared to obtaining more. It was an aggressive foreign policy, which can be seen as the equivalent of cheating by a dissatisfied member of a cartel. This restless, disruptive German foreign policy, the German challenge to the existing arrangements in Europe, was most responsible, although not solely responsible, for bringing on World War I.

The German grievance was very much like that of a dynamic, discontented firm. The Germans believed that they were receiving less than their due. Although surpassing the other powers in military and economic terms, they lagged behind in what were supposed to be the fruits, as well as the sources, of power: territorial possessions. The British Empire stretched to the four corners of the globe. France had staked out substantial holdings in North Africa and Indochina. Russia had expanded into Central Asia. Austria, although evicted from Italy, still ruled part of the Balkans. Beyond Europe, the United States had conquered the North American continent and reached into the Caribbean and across the Pacific to Hawaii and the Philippines. Even Japan had planted its flag on the Korean peninsula. Germany had nothing like any of this.

When the initial settlement had been made, what Germany received was appropriate to its size, wealth, and power. Circumstances had changed radically over the course of the nineteenth century, but the division of "market shares" in the international system had not been adjusted to take account of them. It hardly seemed fair to the Germans that Britain, in particular, could acquire

first published, 1980), p. 424, and A. J. P. Taylor, *The Struggle for Mastery in Europe, 1848–1918* (Oxford University Press, 1971; first published, 1954), pp. xxv–xxxii.

a vast empire overseas with scarcely a word of protest while Germany, as rich and powerful a country as Britain, should be denied even remotely comparable rewards. A term common in Germany after the turn of the century sums up this general feeling: *Gleichberechtigung* (equal entitlement).[30] The term expressed what Germany thought it deserved but was not receiving and what it became the aim of German foreign policy to achieve.

In pursuit of "equal entitlement" Germany provoked war. Its aim was to defeat its enemies before they became too strong, to expand its overseas possessions, and to create a sphere of economic and political predominance in Central and Eastern Europe.[31] A Balkan crisis in the summer of 1914 provided the occasion. The assassination of the heir to the Austrian throne at the end of June created a confrontation between Austria, which was Germany's ally, and Serbia, whose patron was Russia. Germany urged Austria to press its case rather than compromise, knowing that this would bring war with Russia. War did come in August 1914, a great European war that became a world conflict.

Of all the powers, Germany had the greatest responsibility for the outbreak of war. The Germans were the most willing to have it occur and did the least, given what was possible, to prevent it.[32] The other powers were not entirely without responsibility, but none was so dissatisfied with the existing state of affairs as to be ready to change it forcibly.[33] Germany's dissatisfaction had reached that point. As cartels can be broken by the cheating of a single firm, so the collapse of the late-nineteenth- and early-twentieth-century version of the managed balance of power system required the determination of but a single great power to bring it down.[34]

[30] Kennedy, *Anglo-German Antagonism*, p. 431.

[31] On German war aims see, among other works, Fritz Fischer, *War of Illusions: German Policies from 1911 to 1914*, trans. by Marian Jackson (New York: Norton, 1975; first published in German in 1969), pp. 470, 534–5; and David E. Kaiser, "Germany and the Origins of the First World War," *Journal of Modern History*, 55 (September 1983): passim.

[32] Kennedy, *Anglo-German Antagonism*, pp. 457–8.

[33] Austria might be regarded as an exception, but the Austrians would never have gone to war without German support.

[34] The question of which power was most responsible for the outbreak of war, a contentious one for fifty years, now seems more or less settled thanks in large measure to the exhaustive research of Fritz Fischer and others who have followed in his path. (Fischer's two major books are *War of Illusions* and the

What the Germans wanted the rest of Europe would not concede. What they sought, or at least what they would have achieved if they had won the war, was hegemony on the Continent. This the others could not accept. What was for Germany an effort to secure what it deserved was for the others a Napoleonic bid for master of Europe, and so had to be resisted. The predicament of the others was similar to that of firms in a cartel that faces a challenge to its distribution of market shares. Such firms are inclined to accommodate, but if their efforts toward accommodation go too far, they will subvert the very purpose of the arrangements. To permit the Germans to have what they sought would have undercut the security of the other powers by threatening their independence. Accommodation, the peaceful redistribution of "market shares" in Europe according to Germany's wishes, would have been self-defeating.

World War I was a familiar kind of European conflict despite its huge scale. It marked the resumption of the uninhibited competition among the great powers that had characterized the eighteenth

---

earlier *Germany's Aims in the First World War* [New York: Norton, 1967].) It is Germany that deserves, if not all the blame, certainly a larger share than the others. There is another, related issue that the origins of World War I raise and that the cartel analogy emphasizes. It is the question of whether the Germans' complaint that they deserved, and were being denied, "equal entitlement" did, in the end, have some merit. Why, after all, should Britain and Russia have had vast holdings, much of them acquired in the nineteenth century, while Germany did not? At least two things may be said in response to this question. First, the German bid for a domain beyond its borders comparable to those of the other great powers came at an inopportune time and in an especially inopportune place. Britain and Russia, and the United States and France for that matter, had expanded at the periphery of the international system, beyond Europe. Germany proposed to expand at its heart, in the center of the Continent. Where the British enjoyed strategic advantages, outside Europe, expansion was acceptable by the informal rules of the nineteenth century. Where Germany's natural advantages lay, on the Continent, similar behavior was not acceptable. German expansion there, justly or not, was bound to provoke resistance. Second, the question of German responsibility, or culpability, in this broader sense of the term cannot be resolved by an examination of the historical record in the way that the issue of responsibility in the narrower sense – that is, which country did the most to start the fighting in August 1914 – apparently has been. See Kennedy, *Anglo-German Antagonism*, pp. 427–30; David Calleo, *The German Problem Reconsidered: Germany and the World Order, 1870 to the Present* (Cambridge University Press, 1978), pp. 4, 5, 25, 52–3; Hinsley, *Power*, pp. 303–8.

century, this time with the technology of the twentieth. The war was fought to determine Germany's place in Europe, to decide whether Germany would hold sway over the entire Continent. In the end the German bid for mastery, like that of the French a century before and the Hapsburgs before that, was thwarted.

IV

If cartels and the nineteenth-century managed balance of power system have important elements in common, there are also crucial differences between them, which bear on the origins of World War I. German policy from the beginning of the century to the July crisis of 1914 did not arise from a cold-eyed, clear-headed calculation aimed at maximizing a single discrete, measurable benefit. Politics, after all, is not identical to economics. In many ways the two are not at all alike. In politics the goals are more diffuse, the connections between ends and means less clear, the influences to which policies are subject more numerous. The differences between politics and economics, the wide variety of forces and circumstances that are part of the life of sovereign states in the international system and that simple comparisons with idealized economic behavior necessarily leave out, are the subjects of the small library of historical studies that have been written on the origins of World War I. The war did not break out simply because Germany decided that its interest lay in defecting from the established international norms of Europe; nor was that decision, which the Germans did, in effect, make, a matter of simple straightforward, detached calculation.

By 1914 the managed balance of power system, even in the less explicit form that it had assumed after 1871, had been exhausted. The forces in European politics that had fostered restraint after the defeat of Napoleon had dwindled in importance or disappeared entirely. The memories of Napoleon and the Revolution, which had welded the great powers together in 1815, had long since faded away. The leaders of 1914 lived in another world. Their memories of war harked back to the Franco-Prussian conflict, which had been relatively short and decisive. Most people, by 1914, had no memory of any European war.

Colonial expansion had served as a kind of safety valve for European rivalries in the last half of the nineteenth century. The appetite for more territory could be satisfied beyond Europe's borders, in Asia and Africa. By the second decade of the new century most of the global real estate of any value had been snapped up. There were no worlds left for ambitious European powers to conquer that did not already belong to someone else. The focus of the competitive impulses of the great powers turned back toward the Continent.

Prevailing attitudes toward European territory, moreover, had changed; this was another instance of the disappearance of norms that had sustained the managed balance of power system. The growth of national feeling made it much more difficult for the great powers to exchange provinces and move borders, as in some giant board game, for the sake of equilibrium. Redrawing the map of Europe at Vienna in 1815 was regarded as part of the normal workings of international politics. The German annexation of the French provinces of Alsace and Lorraine in 1871 was not so regarded, at least not by the French. The loss of the provinces created lasting French enmity toward Germany that was not at all in keeping with the spirit of moderation and flexibility required by the operation of the managed balance of power system.

The relationship between domestic and foreign policy on which the system established at Vienna rested had also changed. It had in a sense been reversed. The fear of challenges to their internal orders had brought the great powers together to avoid conflict with one another after 1815. In 1914 the eastern empires of the Continent were still under pressure from the same forces that the French Revolution had originally created. It was the achievement of the Hapsburg, Romanov, and Hohenzollern monarchies to have survived for more than a century after Louis XVI had been dethroned. They had not, however, managed to eliminate the forces that threatened them; these forces in fact grew progressively stronger over the course of the century. As they did so, the regimes' tactics for holding them at bay shifted dramatically.

They began to conduct aggressive foreign policies with the hope of enlisting broader support within the societies they governed. Foreign adventures, or at least success abroad, came to seem a way of becoming popular and legitimate at home. In Germany's hybrid political structure, the emperor and his men were constantly trying to preserve the royal prerogatives against encroachment by the elected parliament. The policy of "world power" was a way of promoting popular and therefore parliamentary support for the Crown. This was one of the calculations that lay behind the decision to build a fleet to rival Britain's.

The role of domestic politics in shaping the external relations of the great powers in the years leading up to 1914 differed from one country to another and varied over time. At the least, however, internal considerations did not weigh on the side of international prudence and restraint as they had a century earlier. Peace, and therefore equilibrium, were no longer the indispensable allies of conservatism.[35]

To add to the instability of the early years of the century, the balance of power, in military terms, was increasingly difficult to gauge. It was a time of rapid change in military technology, as the fruits of the industrial revolution began to be harnessed in systematic fashion to the techniques of warfare. To the political reasons for conflict were added more strictly military motives. The powers spent more and more on armaments. They began to worry that they would be put in jeopardy by the military innovations of the others. Unease and uncertainty about the consequences of Russian military reforms contributed to Germany's decision to force a war in the summer of 1914.

The economic environment in which the great powers conducted their affairs was also changing. Competition for markets became more intense around the turn of the century. In response, the major states erected tariff barriers within which they staked out exclusive economic zones. Even Great Britain, long the champion of liberal economic practices, began to waver in its commitment

[35] The importance of the need to win support for the Reich in shaping Germany foreign policy is a theme of Fritz Fischer's two major books. See, e.g., *War of Illusions*, p. viii. On the political motives for building a battle fleet, the *locus classicus* is Eckart Kehr, *Battleship Building and Party Politics in Germany, 1894–1901*, ed., trans., and with an intro. by Pauline R. Anderson and Eugene N. Anderson (University of Chicago Press, 1975; first published in Germany, 1930). For the argument that the effort to preserve the old domestic order governed the policies that led to war in 1914 throughout Europe see Arno J. Mayer, *The Persistence of the Old Regime* (New York: Pantheon, 1981). It was Bismarck himself who began the practice of using foreign threats to buttress the position of the monarch. He was brought to power originally to do just that.

to free trade. The United States and Russia, with their home territories of continental scope, and Britain and France, with their considerable overseas empires, had larger potential economic domains than Germany.

The growing intensity of economic protectionism fed a more general social, intellectual, and political climate that permeated the workings of the European governments of the day and that make international politics seem more urgently and dangerously competitive than ever before. The economic competition reinforced the idea, for instance, that in the twentieth century only "world-states" of continental proportions like the United States and Russia, or with overseas empires like Britain and France, could hope to play leading roles in world affairs. The clear implication for Germany was the need to expand in order to remain a great power.

This geopolitical outlook was, in turn, buttressed by social Darwinist ideas. These were simplified versions of the discoveries of the nineteenth century about human evolution that were transposed to the social world. They held that world history was a struggle for survival and that while some nations and states prospered, others, the less fit and worthy ones, were destined to perish.

These ideas lent themselves to national and racial interpretations. Talk about the natural superiority of the German people, which was current before World War I, was carried to lunatic extremes in the Third Reich. But well before Hitler came to power, in 1916, in the midst of the war, Max Weber, who was certainly no lunatic, wrote that "a people of 79 million placed between such conquerors [as Russia and North America] has the *duty* to be a mighty state. It was necessary for us to be a mighty state, and in order to have a say in the decision of the future of the earth we had to risk this war. We would have had to do so even if we had cause to fear that we would be beaten."[36]

This mélange of ideas, prejudices, and superstitions formed the intellectual, political, and cultural climate, the "mental atmosphere," in which the European governments operated in 1914. The effect on the Germans was to make the international order seem more and more like a straitjacket, in which they would sink

[36] Quoted in Fischer, *War of Illusions*, pp. 457–8.

into mediocrity and decline unless they broke free. To the Germans, defection from the European order seemed not simply profitable, a method of adding to the power, wealth, and prestige of the empire, and not only justified, a way of obtaining what was rightfully theirs, but also urgent, indeed their only hope of avoiding national decay. Germany had "only one choice: to grow or waste away."[37]

The climate of opinion that made international politics seem much more fiercely competitive than ever before, the unease at the pace of change in weaponry and the pressure to make gains abroad to shore up the position of the government at home, were not confined to Germany. They affected the policies of the other great powers. They had the least effect on Britain, which was the most liberal and most stable great power, as well, of course, as the one with the greatest measure of geographic detachment from the Continent. British foreign policy in the period ending with the outbreak of World War I was determined chiefly by external rather than domestic considerations.[38]

The most important of these was the overextension of British power. By the end of the nineteenth century the British imperial reach spanned the globe. The Indian subcontinent was the jewel in the imperial crown. Most of North America had been lost at the end of the eighteenth century, but its upper tier, Canada, had remained British. To it were added territories around the rim of India from Tibet to Burma to Ceylon, possessions in the Antipodes and in Africa from Egypt to the Cape, and concessions along the coast of China. This was the empire upon which the sun never set.

It was glorious but expensive. Britain encountered increasing difficulty in maintaining it. In the nineteenth century, industrial productivity became the basis of wealth and military strength. The British enjoyed an industrial lead over the rest of the world that helped them build their empire. By the last decades of that century the lead was gone, making it much more difficult to maintain what

---

[37] Ibid., p. 33.

[38] Zara S. Steiner, *Britain and the Origins of the First World War* (New York: St. Martin's Press, 1977), pp. 2, 155, 164. On internal difficulties in Britain that were in some ways comparable to those on the Continent see George Dangerfield, *The Strange Death of Liberal England* (New York: Capricorn Books, 1961; first published, 1935).

had been acquired. It was more difficult as well because competing claims on the resources necessary for imperial governance were becoming ever more powerful. Politically influential forces in British society preferred to support domestic reform, social services, or tax relief. All this made the imperial role that Britain had assumed in the course of the nineteenth century difficult to sustain. In 1902 Joseph Chamberlain, a prominent Conservative political figure, called the empire a "weary Titan staggering under the too vast orb of his own fate."[39]

The Boer War of 1899 to 1902, in which subduing a small Afrikaaner force proved an unexpectedly long and costly chore, demonstrated the extent of Britain's international overcommitment. The British government therefore moved to lower the cost of its overseas position, chiefly by resolving or limiting conflicts with other great powers. To this end the British were prepared to compromise rival claims and even to make concessions. In the last years of the old century and the first years of the new, they conducted a policy of appeasement toward the other great powers.[40]

This was the policy that Britain adopted toward the United States, effectively abandoning any military role in North America. This state of affairs was confirmed by the Hay–Pauncefote Agreement of 1901. Britain also came to terms with Japan, the other newly risen non-European great power that, like the United States, was building a formidable navy. The Anglo-Japanese alliance was signed in 1902, enabling Britain to avoid any conflict with Japan in the Pacific and East Asia, which in turn freed the Royal Navy to concentrate its forces closer to home.

In the first decade of the twentieth century Britain also conciliated its traditional Continental rivals, France and Russia. The Anglo-French entente of 1904 and the entente with Russia that

---

[39] Quoted in Michael Howard, *The Continental Commitment* (London: Temple Smith, 1972), pp. 11. On British overextension see Paul M. Kennedy, "The Tradition of Appeasement in British Foreign Policy, 1865–1939," in *Strategy and Diplomacy, 1870–1945* (London: Allen & Unwin, 1983), p. 23.

[40] Paul Kennedy argues that the tradition of appeasement dates from the middle of the nineteenth century. Whether it was in force as early as 1865 is perhaps debatable, but it certainly predates the 1930s, as he notes, and was a prominent – if not the dominant – diplomatic tendency from the end of Britain's "splendid isolation" under Salisbury at the turn of the century until the beginning of the war. Kennedy, "Tradition of Appeasement."

followed in 1907 were arranged to settle colonial issues. They had, initially, nothing to do with European affairs. In the first of them, France conceded British primacy in Egypt while Britain promised France a free hand in Morocco. The terms of the second concerned Tibet, Afghanistan, and Persia. The British aim was to simplify the task of defending India. Both ententes were part of Britain's effort to bring more nearly into balance the expenses of its overseas activities and the resources that it would devote to them.

As the burden of empire grew heavier for the British, the equilibrium in Europe became all the more valuable to them. The "subsidy" that it provided was more useful than ever at the end of the nineteenth century. In straitened circumstances, after all, extra, "unearned" income is particularly welcome. Accordingly, Britain became increasingly active in trying to preserve the balance on the Continent. The desire to maintain the balance, to retain the benefits of equilibrium without exertion, had a pronounced effect on Britain's relations with Germany up to the moment that the cabinet voted for war.

Britain tried to conciliate Germany as well as the other great powers. The Kruger Telegram of 1896, a clumsy German effort to intervene in South African affairs against Britain, had aroused British suspicions of Germany almost for the first time. A colonial agreement in 1898 included a German pledge of abstention from the South African tangle. In 1902 Germany and Britain cooperated in collecting debts from Venezuela. The British gave their approval to Germany's Berlin-to-Baghdad railroad. As late as 1913 there was an abortive agreement between the two great powers to partition part of the Portuguese empire. These, however, were minor matters. The Anglo-German relationship in the years leading up to the war was dominated not by cooperation but by a naval rivalry.

The German decision to acquire a battle fleet aroused anti-German sentiment among the British public and alarmed the British government, which had on the whole regarded Germany as friendly. The British saw the new fleet as a direct challenge to them. They were correct.[41] It was indeed part of the German drive

[41] Admiral Tirpitz, the father of the German fleet, subscribed to the "risk theory," according to which Germany had to be able not actually to defeat Britain at sea, but merely to inflict enough damage to make the British navy vulnerable to the French and the Russians. The German capacity to do so, it was reckoned,

for world power on a scale comparable to that of Great Britain. It was one means of achieving the "equal entitlement" that Germany craved.

The British were not opposed in principle to accommodating German aspirations. There was even some sympathy for the German desire for a larger "place in the sun." But the British could not tolerate a *naval* challenge. The Royal Navy was, after all, the guardian of the empire's lifelines. Maritime supremacy was one of the two central pillars of British security policy. Still, it was not strictly true that Britain would tolerate *no* other naval power of any consequence. The British tolerated, indeed came to terms with, the United States and Japan, both of which had built fleets. The source of this tolerance, however, was the fact that the American and Japanese fleets were based on the other side of the world. Germany was next door. That made for an irresolvable problem.

It was an axiom of naval strategy that a fleet must control its home waters. The home waters for Britain and Germany were the same – the North Sea. Only one or the other could control it; they could not share control. The fleet of the lesser power would be at the mercy of that of the stronger. Given the importance of their navy, the British could not afford to be in the weaker position.[42] Unlike the colonial disputes with France and Russia, and even those with Germany that Britain was able to resolve to the satisfaction of both, the naval question was at once close to home, vital, and not subject to compromise.

Still, negotiations between Britain and Germany about ending the naval rivalry did take place. The talks did not yield an agreement, because the Germans were never willing to offer what the British would accept. They did offer to concede naval superiority to Great Britain. In return, however, they demanded a free hand on the Continent. Britain was asked to promise not to side with France or Russia in the event of a European war. Germany was

would give Germany leverage over Britain. These ideas proved to be mistaken. On this subject see Paul M. Kennedy, "Strategic Aspects of the Anglo-German Naval Race," in *Strategy and Diplomacy*.
[42] The naval rivalry was, to use a term that has come into use in contemporary discussions of military strategy, a "zero-sum game." See Mandelbaum, *Nuclear Revolution*, pp. 114–15; Kennedy, *Anglo-German Antagonism*, pp. 422–3; and Kennedy, "Strategic Aspects," pp. 155–6.

asking, in effect, that Britain sacrifice one of the two principal aims of its security policy in order to ensure the other. The British declined.

The outcome of the competition in capital ships was an anticlimax. The naval rivalry ended two years before the beginning of war. The German government concluded that it could not sustain an arms race both on land and at sea and decided to concentrate its resources on fortifying its army. Britain went to war against Germany in 1914 for the same reason that it had fought Napoleon: to preserve equilibrium in Europe, to prevent a single power from dominating the Continent. The German threat seemed especially menacing because Germany had a navy; but the German navy alone did not bring Britain into the war.

Britain went to war in 1914 to vindicate an interest well established and repeatedly emphasized over three centuries.[43] Britain joined a coalition to oppose a would-be European hegemon. Sir Edward Grey, the foreign secretary, warned the House of Commons on August 3, 1914, of the dangers of remaining aloof from the conflict: "I do not believe for a moment, that at the end of this war, even if we stood aside and remained aside, we should be in a position, a material position to use our force decisively to undo what had happened in the course of the war, to prevent the whole of the West of Europe opposite to us – if that has been the result of the war – falling under the domination of a single Power."[44] Yet up to the last moment, in the summer of 1914, Britain's ultimate role in the European conflict that was coming ever closer was very much in doubt.

British entry into the war did not come as a complete surprise. Britain had supported France in the two Moroccan crises of 1905 and 1911 and had issued private warnings to Berlin about German belligerence. British military planning had been reoriented to the

---

[43] The German violation of Belgian neutrality gave a basis in international law for British intervention in Europe. This helped to rally British opinion to the French and Russian cause. But the reasons for intervention were geopolitical. The cabinet decided to fight even if Belgium decided to *join* Germany. Steiner, *Origins*, p. 237. Michael G. Ekstein and Zara S. Steiner, "The Sarajevo Crisis," in F. H. Hinsley, ed., *British Foreign Policy Under Sir Edward Grey* (Cambridge University Press, 1977), p. 407.

[44] "Extract from Grey's House of Commons Speech on the Eve of War," August 3, 1914, in Bourne, *Foreign Policy*, p. 504.

Continent. Military conversations between the British and French general staffs had taken place, which laid the groundwork for the dispatch of the British Expeditionary Force to northern France once the war began.

Neither the warnings nor the results of the military conversations were made public, however. The British government insisted throughout the July crisis that it was bound to neither side nor to any particular course of action. In his August 3 speech to the House, Grey emphasized that he had given no promise to France of anything beyond diplomatic support.

The policy of avoiding any clear commitment before the outbreak of war carried with it, potentially, a serious cost. It is possible, or at least arguable, that had Britain declared earlier and more forthrightly that it would join the anti-German group German policy would have been different. Deterrence, the prevention of attack by the threat of response, is an ancient concept that has come to have unprecedented importance; the advent of nuclear weapons has made it the chief aim of the policy of the United States and the Soviet Union toward each other. Although it was not at the center of British policy in 1914 as it came to be for the great powers after 1945, it was entirely consistent with the aim of British policy, which was to prevent war. No matter who won a European war, Britain would be, in a sense, the loser. Others could fight with the hope of gaining territory on the Continent if they won. Britain would acquire none no matter what happened. Nonetheless, Britain would suffer more than any other power from the disruption of commerce that the war would bring.[45] Its distinctive set of national interests made Britain, by the summer of 1914, the great power most in favor of avoiding war. War was not, of course, avoided. But a more explicitly deterrent policy might have made this possible.

A clearer sense that Britain would fight might have given more weight in the first decade of the century to the argument of those within the German government who wanted reconciliation with Britain but were overruled by others, the kaiser among them, who insisted upon building a fleet, a policy that blocked accommodation.

[45] Paul Kennedy, "Strategy versus Finance in Twentieth-century Britain," in *Strategy and Diplomacy*, pp. 87–97.

Later, it might have prompted modifications of the Schlieffen Plan, the operational orders of the German army, which ensured that any war in Europe would be a war with France. Had Germany not attacked France, it is conceivable that the French would not have come to Russia's defense or, even if they had, that Britain would have chosen not to enter the war.[46]

None of this can be known. Indeed, the opposite argument – that Germany intended to wage a war regardless of what Britain did – also has support in the historical record. The Germans were certainly bent on overturning the status quo in Europe. World War I was, in this sense, hardly an accidental conflict. It is clear, however, that, given the nation's interests, one feature of British policy that requires explanation is the insistence of having a "free hand" and the consequent failure to align publicly and unambiguously with France and Russia.

Here an "inside-out" explanation – one emphasizing domestic forces – is germane. The British cabinet felt constrained by considerations of domestic politics. In the years before 1914 there was by no means a consensus in the country concerning support for France and Russia, especially if this risked causing war. Germany, a vigorous, commercial, Protestant nation, had admirers in Britain, despite its battleship program. France, in contrast, was Catholic and the traditional enemy. Russia was ruled by a backward, repressive autocracy. There was, as well, a current of opposition to the idea of war in general and of military ties with any power that might drag Britain into one. This point of view was strongly represented in the governing Liberal Party and indeed the cabinet. The Liberals were divided on foreign policy. The initial basis for the division had been imperial issues, particularly the Boer War. The split persisted between imperialists like Grey and H. H. Asquith, the prime minister, who were well disposed toward support for France and Russia, and "radicals" like Reginald McKenna, Herbert Samuel, and even, for a time, Lloyd George, who had opposed the South African conflict and were skeptical of entanglements with the Continental powers.

During the crisis of July 1914, several cabinet ministers threat-

---

[46] Kennedy, *Anglo-German Antagonism*, pp. 445–6. On German hopes for British neutrality see Fischer, *War of Illusions*, pp. 486, 512.

ened to resign from the government if it decided to go to war. Grey was eager to hold it together, not only to keep his party in power but also because he was resolved that the country be united if it did fight. In any event, the foreign secretary felt unable to give a pledge to France or Russia that the cabinet would refuse to support, and he did not believe, almost until the day that war was actually declared, that it would support a promise to fight on the Continent in a war begun over an issue as distant from Britain's central concerns as the fate of Serbia.

The cabinet, and Grey in particular, had other reasons for advocating the policy that Britain adopted in the July crisis. These other motives qualify as an "outside-in" explanation; they involve, that is, the influence of international circumstances on British conduct. They have their roots in the rationale for and the practices of the nineteenth-century managed balance of power system.

Britain was active in trying to resolve the crisis short of war. Grey gravitated toward the role of mediator. From the first he sought to bring the two opposing camps together. He certainly did not envision, until very late in the day, joining one of them in fighting the other. When, with the Austrian ultimatum to Serbia on July 23, 1914, he grasped the gravity of the situation, he went into high gear. On July 24 he proposed to the German ambassador in London that the four great powers not directly involved in the dispute work together to mediate it. On July 26 he made the proposal in a slightly different form: an ambassador's conference along the lines of the one that had helped to settle the Balkan War a year earlier. Two days later, with the Austrians unyielding in their demands, he floated a different sort of plan: Austria would occupy Belgrade as a pledge for the execution of Serbian promises but would take no other military action. And two days after that, on August 31, he reverted to the original proposal for mediation by the four disinterested (or less interested) great powers.

Serving as a mediator in the crisis was incompatible with aligning with one side or the other. Scrupulous neutrality was necessary for achieving any measure of success. Britain was not unambiguously neutral, but the ententes with France and Russia were all the more reason to make every effort to avoid overt alignment.

Grey's hopes for successful mediation were based on his own recent experience. He had helped to settle the Balkan War of 1912.

In October of that year Montenegro challenged Turkey. Other Balkan peoples joined the challenge, and Turkey's remaining positions in Europe were quickly destroyed. This raised the danger that Austria and Russia would clash to fill the void left by the disintegration of Ottoman rule. A conference was convened in London to address the various problems arising from the Balkan conflict. With Grey himself playing a leading role, the conference settled the most contentious issues in early 1913 without an expansion of the conflict. The London conference seemed to revive the Concert of Europe. It replayed, in lower key, the Congress of Berlin of 1878, with Britain taking the leading role instead of Germany. Lord Crewe, a member of the cabinet in 1914, said in retrospect of British policy during the July crisis: "All through the month we attempted to exercise a mediating influence; probably the whole cabinet, including Grey, were a little over-flattered by the success of the Balkan Conference the year before."[47]

Mediation had strong appeal to the British. Their overriding interest was that of keeping the peace. Mediation was a way of doing so while retaining the benefits of the nineteenth-century managed balance of power system – equilibrium without exertion. It promised, if successful, to keep the cost to Britain of maintaining a balance of power in Europe at a modest level. To have stood openly with France and Russia, to have attempted a policy of overt deterrence, would have meant conceding that equilibrium could no longer be achieved collectively, that an active British military role in European affairs, with all its attendant risks and costs and the inevitable drain on imperial resources, was necessary once more. It is not surprising that Grey preferred to try to keep alive the very much less expensive managed balance of power system.

The motives for British policy in the July crisis, with its emphasis on mediation, were in fact the same as those that had animated British support for collaboration against Napoleon. They were the same as those that prompted Castlereagh's and Palmerston's enthusiasm for the concert of Europe. British policy in 1914 was an unsuccessful effort to preserve the "subsidy" that collective arrangements in Europe provided.

Grey's diplomacy invoked not only the spirit but also some of

---

[47] Quoted in Ekstein and Steiner, "Sarajevo Crisis," p. 402.

the techniques of the managed balance of power system. His initiatives followed the model of Castlereagh's efforts to achieve collective action a century before. He bore the precedents of the past in mind, and even explicitly referred to them in 1914 and earlier. He regarded the London Conference of 1912–13 as the latest in a line of great-power meetings to resolve pressing European issues by conciliation and compromise that began with the Congress of Vienna.[48] His efforts can be seen as the last gasp of the system of achieving equilibrium in Europe by collective methods. They failed. The European powers returned to the older practice of international relations. Between 1914 and 1918 equilibrium on the Continent was the outcome of uninhibited competition among the great powers – that is, of war.

V

World War I and its aftermath were in many ways similar to the Wars of the French Revolution and the settlement that followed. A bid for dominance in Europe was thwarted in the second case as in the first. The Germans, like the French before them, were defeated after a long, bitter, and costly struggle. Once again the victorious powers assembled in one of their capitals – in Paris, rather than Vienna – to work out the details of the postwar order. The work of arranging the settlement belonged to the great powers. The lesser states were spectators. The leaders of the four victorious powers in 1919 – Britain, France, Italy, and the United States – corresponded to the representatives of the partners in the anti-Napoleonic coalition a century earlier.

The postwar settlement of 1919 had a number of features in common with the arrangements that emerged from the Congress of Vienna. The losing power on each occasion was made to relinquish its conquests but was otherwise left intact. A belt of territories was created around the defeated country to insulate it from the rest of Europe. Germany was surrounded by a *cordon sanitaire* that included the successor states of the Hapsburg Empire and a reconstituted Poland, just as the Netherlands, Switzerland, and

[48] Steiner, *Origins*, pp. 111, 115, 188; Holdbraad, *Concert of Europe*, pp. 182–3.

Prussia had been strengthened to help pin France within its designated borders. Both countries were partly occupied for a limited period after the end of hostilities. The occupying troops were soon withdrawn in both cases. Both France and Germany were made to pay indemnities to their conquerors. Both were given new governments. The victorious coalition installed a regime of which it approved and which, not coincidentally, was like the governments of the coalition's members. The Bourbons were restored to power in France; the Weimar Republic was established in Germany. The kaiser, like Napoleon before him, was sent into exile.

Both wars were traumatic for those who fought them. Each was longer and more destructive than anticipated. Each had unforeseen and generally unwelcome political consequences. Each, accordingly, gave rise to a widely shared wish to take steps to prevent another such conflict. After the Wars of the French Revolution the great powers took such steps. After World War I they did not. Instead of laying the foundation for a century of peace, the second settlement was destroyed by another great war only twenty years later. But the aftermath of World War I was, like the period following the defeat of Napoleon, one of those rare moments in international history when the great powers saw their safety as lying in cooperation, when a successful collective approach to security seemed possible. The Paris settlement did not establish a working collective system of security in Europe. For all its similarities to the work of the Congress of Vienna, it differed in two principal ways, which in turn account for the difference in consequences.

The settlement after 1815 was stable because all the great powers agreed to be part of it. It was a collective approach to security because it was the work of the entire international system, or at least of those of its members who had the most power. This was not the case with the arrangements that the members of the winning coalition made after World War I. The structure they erected was shaky from the outset because some of the main props were missing.

Russia was not part of the settlement. After the crushing Russian defeat on the eastern front in 1917, the Romanovs were overthrown. By the end of the war a small, radical group had seized power in the capital. The Bolsheviks were revolutionaries who wanted nothing to do with conventional diplomatic procedures or with the representatives of the capitalist powers. Ideology aside, they were scarcely in a position to take part in a new Concert of Europe. All their energies were devoted to consolidating power in Russia. The country was in chaos; the Bolsheviks by no means controlled all of it. Even if they had, the victorious powers would not have admitted the new Communist government to their councils. Indeed, several of the allied governments lent assistance to forces within Russia trying to dislodge the Communists. As a result, the largest European power, although temporarily not functioning as a presence in international affairs, was not a part of the European settlement.

In contrast to the prevailing attitude toward Russian participation in the peace process, the victorious French and British emphatically did want the United States to take part in the postwar European order. The American role in the war had been a minor but important one. Only in the last year had American troops joined the British and French in fighting the Germans. The American force on the Continent had been small in comparison with those of the Europeans. Still, the war could not have been won without the men, material, and financing that the United States had supplied. By 1919 the United States had become, in effect, the westernmost of the European powers. Its allies counted on using American resources and American leverage in the postwar period. Woodrow Wilson, the American president during World War I, also wanted his country to take an active role in the management of international affairs, although his idea of that role was not the one that most British and French statesmen envisioned.[49] His countrymen did not follow his lead. The United States Senate rejected membership in the League of Nations, the international organization that Wilson had helped to devise, which eliminated the United States from active participation in the political and military (although not the financial) affairs of the Continent for more than two decades.

The idea of equilibrium had been central to the proceedings at Vienna in 1815. It was an important goal of the great powers as they rearranged the map of Europe. Establishing a balance of power on the Continent was, they believed, the surest way to avoid an-

[49] See Chapter 2, pp. 80–2.

other catastrophic war. It was so important that Britain and Austria were prepared to join with their erstwhile enemy, France, against two of their partners in the anti-French coalition, Prussia and Russia, to enforce a settlement faithful to it. Such a tactic was unthinkable at Paris a century later. Equilibrium had no such status there. This was the second crucial difference between the two postwar settlements.

The men who gathered at Paris were as determined as their predecessors at Vienna had been to prevent another war. This they proposed to do – some of them, anyway – not by restoring the old European order but by transcending it. The spirit of the day no longer dictated a series of prudent, finely calibrated adjustments to the consequences of anarchy by a careful balancing of forces at the heart of the international system, which had been the achievement of the nineteenth-century managed balance of power system. In 1919 there was an effort to modify dramatically the anarchic character of the system itself through a new international organization. In this sense the Paris Peace Conference was much more ambitious and, as it proved, far less realistic than the Congress of Vienna.

Equilibrium had been the basis for conducting the main business at Vienna, the reallocation of the European possessions that France had been forced to give up. Pieces of the Continent were passed back and forth among the great powers. Who got what depended, in part, on how each addition affected the overall balance. Territory was fungible and could be traded like shares of stock or chips in a card game.[50] The men gathered at Paris also had to dispose of territory – sometimes the same territory. They could still resort to nineteenth-century methods in distributing lands outside Europe – the Ottoman possessions in the Middle East, for example. They followed a much different rule in reconstituting Europe, however.

They reset the Continent's borders not so as to strike a balance among the great powers but according to the principle of national self-determination. Distinct ethnic, linguistic, and national groups were declared to be entitled to their own sovereign states, an idea that had seemed dangerous to the extent that it was taken seriously at all in the aftermath of the Wars of the French Revolution. The

[50] See, e.g., Gulick, "The Final Coalition," p. 657.

differences between the leaders who assembled at the two postwar
meetings mirror the shift in the guiding principle of the two settlements. In Henry Kissinger's words, "Metternich, with his cosmopolitan education and rationalist philosophy, Austrian only by
the accident of feudal relationship, could be imagined equally easily
as the minister of any other state."[51] This was true as well of the
czar's representatives, none of whom was a Russian. It might even
be said of Bismarck, a Rhinelander serving a Prussian dynasty. It
was not true of any of the leaders who assembled at Paris. With
the demise of the multinational empires of Central and Eastern
Europe came the disappearance of the cosmopolitan class of leaders
who had guided their destinies.[52] Insofar as it was possible, and
with many exceptions, the map of Europe was redrawn along national lines. This turned out, in the absence of a balance among
the great powers, to promote instability in the postwar period.

The 1919 settlement was made, inevitably, at the expense of the
losing power. This had been the case in 1815 as well. On the earlier
occasion the participation of all the members of the victorious coalition in the settlement had served as a check on any effort by
France to overturn it. To reduce further the French incentive for
revenge, the Vienna settlement had been a moderate one. The
Concert of Europe quickly recognized France as having the rights
and prerogatives of a great power.

Since not all the great powers were represented in the settlement
after World War I, it was even more important to have the defeated
power, Germany, reconciled to it. Circumstances put a premium
on giving the Germans reasons to support the new dispensation
on the Continent, which meant treating Germany in a way the
Germans found acceptable.

Germany did not, of course, find the settlement acceptable. The
Germans' sense of having been unfairly treated was a continuing

---

[51] Kissinger, *World Restored*, p. 321.

[52] The leaders of the two great European adversaries of World War II might seem
exceptions to this rule. But Hitler, although born a Hapsburg subject, considered himself above all a German. Stalin, although a Georgian, identified with
Russia and liquidated most of the non-Russians in the upper ranks of the Communist Party (along with many who were Russians). The empire that he be-
queathed to his successors, a latter-day version of the departed multinational
empires, is dominated by Russians.

problem in the interwar period.[53] The heart of their grievance was Article 231 of the peace treaty they signed at Versailles. The article read, "The Allied and Associated Governments affirm and Germany accepts the responsibility of Germany and her allies for causing all the loss and damage to which the Allied and Associated Governments and their nationals have been subjected as a consequence of the war imposed upon them by the aggression of Germany and her allies."[54] The allied powers had inserted the clause in the treaty to justify the reparations they demanded of Germany. These were not without precedent. France had been made to pay reparations after 1815 and after 1871. Nor was the clause, on its face, unreasonable. The Germans had, after all, been more responsible than any other power for the outbreak of the war. On the western front the war had been fought almost entirely in northern France, great tracts of which had been ravaged and blighted. The Germans had deliberately done particular damage during the last days of the conflict as they retreated. As for the reparations bill itself, whether the Germans could ever have actually paid all that the original terms stipulated remains a debatable – and still debated – question. In the end Germany did not pay anything approaching the full amount.[55]

Whatever can be said in retrospect about the fairness of the treatment of Germany, the Germans themselves emphatically be-

---

[53] In accounts of the interwar period, German resentment of the Versailles Treaty tends to receive more credit for the undoing of the postwar settlement than the failure of two of the great powers to guarantee it. The Germans did resent the treaty, and their effort to evade its terms were a continuing theme of the 1920s and 1930s. But France had not been wholly pleased with the results of 1815 either (see Dakin, "Congress of Vienna," pp. 34–5). The Germans were able to violate the terms of the 1919 settlement because there was no full-fledged Concert of Europe to prevent this.

[54] Quoted in Martin Gilbert, "The Treaty of Versailles," in J. M. Roberts, ed., *Europe in the 20th Century: Volume 2, 1914–1925* (New York, Taplinger, 1968), p. 25.

[55] Turkey, also a defeated power in World War I, received harsher treatment in the Treaty of Sèvres. The Turks managed, however, to overthrow much of it. The harshest treaty of all was the one effectively ending the war on the eastern front that the Bolsheviks signed at Brest-Litovsk in 1917, which stripped Russia of virtually all the territories to the west and south of Russia proper that had been acquired since the time of Peter the Great. The German people took no apparent comfort from the fact that others were treated worse than they.

lieved that the Allies had dealt with them unfairly.[56] They did not consider themselves guilty of aggression.[57] The German government had gone to great lengths in 1914 to place the blame for starting the war on Russia. The Russians had in fact mobilized for war first, and in 1919 most Germans continued to hold them responsible for precipitating the conflict. The Germans expected a more lenient peace than they received. The principles that the Allies had announced in advance, particularly Woodrow Wilson's Fourteen Points, seemed to promise greater generosity to the vanquished than the Versailles Treaty reflected. The principle of national self-determination, for example, was not fully applied to Germany. German-speaking Hapsburg provinces were kept outside the German state, and a corridor was carved out of German territory to give Poland an outlet to the sea. Moreover, the Germans were given no say in the terms of the treaty. It was worked out by the victorious powers, who then told them to sign it. Germany was threatened with full-scale occupation if its leaders refused. In German eyes, therefore, the Versailles treaty was a harsh, hypocritical, and "dictated" peace.

In a larger sense the peace settlement was dictated by the character of the war, which was awful beyond all experience. With the help of railroads, larger armies were sent into the field than ever before. The generals on both sides believed in attacking the enemy directly. The new elements of waging war – the machine gun, the trench, barbed wire – gave the advantage to the defense. Commanders sent large waves of soldiers charging at enemy positions. The defenders cut them to ribbons. The result of these tactics, employed repeatedly by both sides on the western front, was carnage unparalleled in the history of warfare. Even at the remove of seventy years, the number of casualties has the power to appall: Russia, 1.7 million men dead and more than 5 million wounded;

---

[56] One thing that can be said in retrospect is that a more generous settlement, one the Germans might have accepted in good grace, would probably have had to concede to Germany some of the things the Allies were fighting to deny it. Such concessions, needless to say, would have been difficult to make.

[57] The German government actually offered at one point to accept the terms of the treaty as long as they made no mention of German "guilt." Gerhard Schulz, *Revolutions and Peace Treaties, 1917–1920* (London: Methuen, 1972; first published in German, 1967), pp. 169, 186–7.

Austria, 1.2 million dead and 3.6 million wounded; Germany, 1.8 million dead and 4.2 million wounded; France, 1.4 million dead and 3.6 million wounded; the British Empire, almost 1 million dead or missing and another 2.2 million wounded.[58]

Even these figures, large as they are, do not tell the full story of the war's impact on the states that fought it. It touched the lives of millions who never saw a trench or wore a uniform. Those who stayed home had friends and relatives killed and wounded. Millions of noncombatants were drawn into the war effort on both sides, working in the factories that were converted from civilian production to the manufacture of war material. The trend of mobilizing entire societies for war that had begun in France after 1789 was carried much farther in World War I.

There was an inevitable connection between the way the war was waged and the way the peace was made, a connection that helps to account for the failure to reproduce the Concert of Europe after 1918. The scope of the conflict, the toll that it took in death, injury, and the disruption of daily life, set the themes of the Paris Peace Conference. Because the war had been so terrible, those who endured it wanted not simply to avoid another but to abolish the conditions that made war possible in the first place. World War I discredited all the old ways of statecraft; even diplomacy itself was suspect. It had, after all, led to the great four-year cataclysm, or at least had failed to avert it. Woodrow Wilson, with his idea of the League of Nations, was hailed in Europe as the harbinger of an entirely new kind of international relations, which promised to transcend, not reform and restore, the system of the nineteenth century. It was widely believed that the world required nothing less.

The scale of the fighting led to a search for allies to share its costs, which in turn shaped the announced purposes of the war and so the goals of the settlement. Britain and France championed the cause of national self-determination in the hope that some of the national groups within the Hapsburg and Ottoman empires would rise up against their rulers.[59] The goal of national self-

---

[58] The figures for the United States were 115,000 dead and 205,000 wounded. All these figures are approximate and may well be low. They are from John Terraine, *The First World War 1914–1918* (London: Macmillan, 1965), p. 183.
[59] The tactic had little success. The peoples of Central Europe, although evidently

determination made their cause more attractive to the United States, whose help they sought to enlist almost from the beginning of the fighting. Woodrow Wilson was a staunch proponent of the principle. He believed that once put into practice, national self-determination would help to prevent future wars.

The belligerent countries required great exertion and enormous sacrifices from their own people. The postwar settlement was decisively affected by the need to justify these sacrifices. The need of governments to retain the confidence of those they governed was apparent from the beginning of the conflict. Each maneuvered to fix the blame for starting the war on others so that it could summon its own people to a defensive and therefore legitimate struggle. The Germans went to great lengths to induce Russia to mobilize first in the summer of 1914. Official sensitivity to the public mood continued throughout the conflict. The war saw the first widespread use of official propaganda on both sides to bolster public commitment to the struggle.

It was the popular experience of war that set limits on the peace that the victorious governments could make. In September 1914, when the initial German offensive had been stopped and it was becoming apparent that the war would not end quickly, the German chancellor Bethmann-Hollweg ruled out a compromise peace because such an outcome "would seem to the people an altogether insufficient reward for such tremendous sacrifices."[60] If the cost of war circumscribed the freedom of diplomatic maneuvers after a few weeks of fighting, it weighed all the more heavily after four terrible long years. The leaders of the four victorious powers had to devise a peace whose terms were commensurate with the sacrifices that their people had made to win the war. So great had been the sacrifices that it was hard to know what could justify them. At the very least the men of Paris had to make arrangements that would prevent future conflicts and so vindicate the four-year struggle as "the war to end all wars." The League of Nations was founded to guarantee this. The peoples of Europe had to be granted their

---

pleased to be rid of Hapsburg rule when the war was over, did not bestir themselves to overturn it while the fighting was underway. The British did help to organize a modest Arab rising against the Turks in the Middle East, but this had only a marginal effect on the outcome of the war.

[60] Fischer, *War of Illusions*, p. 545.

national rights. And the Germans, who had caused all the suffering, had to be forced to compensate those whom they had made to suffer but who had finally defeated them. The statesmen assembled at the peace conference could not have returned home to announce to the people who had sent them to Paris that their sons and brothers had died for equilibrium.

The relationship between the national leaders who made the Paris settlement and their home constituencies points to another, broader sense in which the character of the war was incompatible with peace terms whose aim was to restore the practices of the Concert of Europe. The war itself produced a revolution in each of the states that took part. It destroyed the old European order. The forces that the Continental opponents of Napoleon had fought to hold back finally triumphed in 1919. The eastern empires disappeared. Britain and France changed as well, although not quite as dramatically. The governments that survived the war, or were created in its wake, drew legitimacy from popular support, not dynastic lineage or aristocratic tradition. They were, perforce, dedicated to justice, to the fulfillment of national claims and individual rights. The goal of the nineteenth-century managed balance of power system did not sit comfortably on this new agenda. The balance of power did not fire the public's imagination. Its value might have been unmistakably clear to the cosmopolitan, professional diplomats of the nineteenth century, but they were no longer in charge. Those who were not in charge were beholden to a broader slice of society than their predecessors. Public opinion was sovereign, and the public demanded something better than equilibrium.

As in the Wars of the French Revolution, Great Britain was part of the victorious coalition in World War I. The British assumed a major role in the deliberations at Paris, as they had a century before at Vienna. Britain's approach to the settlement in 1919, as in 1815, differed from that of its Continental partners, on the later occasion most notably from that of France. The British were more interested in arrangements that would restore equilibrium to Europe. Their aims were closer than those of the French to the principles on which the settlement in 1815 had rested. These aims were not, in the end, achieved. The failure of the British representatives at Paris to achieve their goals reflects the more general failure to reconstitute the nineteenth-century version of the balance of power system after World War I.

Britain's strategic position was the same in 1919 as it had been in 1815. The war had changed many things, but not geography. The two main requirements for British security persisted: naval supremacy to safeguard the trade routes and imperial communications; and a balance of power in Europe so that no continental state could threaten the British Isles. The outcome of the war made it easier in some respects for the British to ensure their security. German military power was broken. The German fleet was scuttled at the end of the war. But the burden of security was in some ways heavier in 1919 than it had been in 1914. The British Empire had grown larger with the addition of some of the Middle Eastern possessions of the Ottoman Empire, including the province of Palestine, within whose borders lay the city of Jerusalem, and much of Mesopotamia to the north. The cost of maintaining the empire was raised, as well, by the beginnings of nationalist stirrings, particularly in India and Egypt. Britain was therefore in no better position than before to take a major military role on the Continent while carrying out its imperial responsibilities. The subsidy that a contrived European balance provided remained indispensable.[61]

As at Vienna, Britain was represented at Paris by an official of unusually high rank. Lloyd George, the prime minister, led the delegation. In the policies that he preferred as well as in the fact that he chose to be present at a Continental peace conference, he was the descendant of Castlereagh. Of all the leaders at Paris he was the one whose inclinations were closest to what the re-creation of the balance of power system of the nineteenth century required. He had inclinations rather than a coherent philosophy of specific plans. He was not a systematic thinker. At Paris, as elsewhere, he counted on his capacity for improvisation, which was considerable.

Lloyd George wanted to include the Bolshevik government of Russia in the deliberations at Paris. Just as Castlereagh had resisted Prussian demands for harsh treatment of France in 1815, so Lloyd George opposed French pressure for a settlement that, in his view,

---

[61] For the argument that it was the consistent, if seldom explicitly expressed, British purpose in the postwar period to find a substitute for the nineteenth-century balance of power system, see L. C. B. Seaman, *Post-Victorian Britain, 1902–1951* (London: Methuen, 1966), pp. 128–9.

was unduly harsh on Germany. He opposed ceding large parts of eastern Germany to Poland and the French scheme for occupying the left bank of the Rhine. He was skeptical about the demand for reparations, at least in the amount that France was determined to extract.

The British prime minister was afraid that a settlement that embittered Germany would sow the seeds of a revolution along Russian lines there.[62] He doubted the Germans' capacity to pay the reparations demanded of them and believed that the most important economic task before the Allies was not the collection of damages but the reintegration of Germany into a functioning European economic order. He was wary of the danger that the Germans would devote themselves wholeheartedly to overturning the settlement if they found it intolerable. Castlereagh had had the same fear about France.

Lloyd George was partly successful at Paris. Germany was not dismembered. In general, however, he did not get what he wanted. The settlement reflected less his sense of what was prudent and proper than the approach of those who disagreed with him.

He failed where Castlereagh had succeeded, in the first place, because he had less leverage at Paris than his predecessor had had at Vienna, and so could not overcome the French as Castlereagh had resisted the wishes of the Prussians. Britain had in fact made a much larger contribution to the victory over Germany in the twentieth century than to the defeat of France in the nineteenth.[63] The earlier contribution, however, came at just the right time to

---

[62] There were in fact Communist-led uprisings in Germany in 1919.

[63] The difference in the cost to Britain of the two wars is illustrated by the differences between two great battles of the respective conflicts in which British participation was central: Waterloo and the Somme. They were fought in the same corner of Europe a century apart. Each, as it happened, entered into the national consciousness as a symbol of the war and therefore of the legacy of the war for the peace settlement. At Waterloo, Wellington led an army of seventy thousand men, half of whom were foreign mercenaries. At the Somme, almost a million men saw action and more than four hundred thousand of them became casualties.

Waterloo was brief – it lasted only a day – and it was decisive; Napoleon's forces were routed. The Somme dragged on, after a frightful first day on which the British suffered 57,000 casualties, for more than five months. It changed nothing. The two battles are vividly described in John Keegan, *The Face of Battle* (New York: Vintage Books, 1977; first published, 1976).

give the British a role at Vienna that was disproportionate to the sacrifices they had made. The Continental powers realized that they needed Britain, and so made concessions to keep the British involved. Britain had the option, after all, of retreating into isolation. In 1919 it was the United States and Woodrow Wilson who enjoyed this status, and equilibrium was not uppermost in Wilson's mind.

Britain was not, of course, totally without influence at Paris; but Lloyd George could not use the leverage that Britain's role in the war had earned on behalf of the kind of settlement that he wanted. Opinion in Britain was more or less the same as that in France. The British government, like that of France and Germany, had launched a campaign of propaganda to arouse enthusiasm for the war. The British people, too, had suffered huge losses. They, too, therefore, demanded a settlement that would vindicate the price they had had to pay for victory.

The British public made its feelings known. A general election was held at the end of 1918. Lloyd George led a slate composed largely of Unionists, not his fellow Liberals, which won a large majority on a platform of a harsh peace. He had sounded this theme in his own campaign, promising to make Germany pay a heavy war indemnity. Whatever his private preferences, he had to continue to pay public homage to the need for a stringent settlement. When reports reached Britain that the peace conference was considering modifying the bill for reparations, the prime minister received a telegram signed by more than 370 Tory members of his parliamentary coalition warning against weakness toward Germany.

In 1815 the government and the then much smaller politically relevant public had wanted stricter terms for France than Castlereagh thought reasonable. The foreign secretary was able to ignore London. He occasionally acted without even consulting the cabinet because, as he later said, with the delays that consultation would have required "the whole machine of Europe would have been arrested."[64]

One hundred years later Lloyd George could not ignore the voices of Parliament and the country that were transmitted, in various ways, across the Channel. The revolutions in transportation

---

[64] Nicolson, *Congress of Vienna*, pp. 187, 236.

and communication in the intervening period were, of course, partly responsible for this. The prime minister could not claim that messages from London took too long to reach Paris for him to be able to act on them.

He was bound by the consequences of the political revolution that the war had brought as well. In Castlereagh's time, foreign policy was the preserve of a small elite in Britain. This was true in Palmerston's day. It was even true to a considerable extent for Grey. But the war swept away the basis for the detached, independent conduct of foreign policy in Britain. Nothing more aptly expressed the change than the presence at Paris of Lloyd George himself. With his own personal retinue and his spontaneous maneuvering, he completely eclipsed the traditional guardians of British foreign policy at the Foreign Office. His role, and the differences between him and the men who presided over British policy in the July crisis, symbolize the changes the war brought to the British as well as to the Continental political systems.

Grey, the sober Northumbrian squire, was a traditional leader. A member of a prominent Liberal family, he had virtually inherited his commitment to public life. By temperament and background his was a career based on duty, not ambition. He had in many ways more in common with his distant predecessor Castlereagh than with his cabinet colleague Lloyd George, a Nonconformist Welsh solicitor of the middle class. Energetic, brilliant, volatile, boundlessly ambitious, Lloyd George was a tribune of the people, not a representative of the gentry. Politics was for him, as it had been for Disraeli but not for Grey, a clamber up the "greasy pole." He had reached the top through his capacity to heed and capitalize on public opinion: Once there he could hardly ignore it.

The Paris peace settlement had the effect of returning Europe to the pattern of the eighteenth century, in which equilibrium was achieved not by conferences, mediation, and the great powers acting in concert but through alliances, arms competition, and above all wars. Twenty years after it was made there was another great European and world war.

In a sense the second great war of the twentieth century was a continuation of the first. The alignments were the same: Britain, France, the Soviet Union (as Russia had become), and the United States fought Germany. The issue at stake was the same – whether

Germany would dominate Europe. The outcome was the same: Germany was defeated. The leaders of the warring powers in the second war, with the exception of the Soviet leader Stalin, had taken part in the first one. Germany was led by Adolf Hitler, who had been a corporal in the kaiser's army. Pétain, the leader of Vichy France, was the great hero of Verdun, and de Gaulle, the head of the Free French forces, had fought in the first war, indeed had been taken prisoner by the Germans. The American president, Franklin D. Roosevelt, had been Woodrow Wilson's under secretary of the navy. The British prime minister, Winston Churchill, had served as first lord of the admiralty during the first year of the war and even had a personal connection with the larger pattern of which World War II was a part. His ancestor Marlborough had helped to thwart Louis XIV's bid for mastery of the Continent at the beginning of the eighteenth century.

After the end of World War II an equilibrium of sorts was reestablished in Europe. The settlement has some features in common with the work of the Congress of Vienna.[65] If the pattern of international relations harked back in part to an earlier time, however, if the great powers' roles were familiar, their parts were played by different actors. The changes that the two world wars brought to the international system confirmed the fears of the men of 1815. They had feared that uninhibited international competition would ruin them. So, in the twentieth century, it did. In 1919 the eastern empires disappeared. The Romanov Empire was reconstituted by the Bolsheviks, but it was governed by bureaucrats, many from the lower classes and the peasantry, not by the Russian aristocracy and the czar. The British and French empires survived the first world war, but the second dealt them a crippling blow. The metropolitan countries, although victorious in that conflict as well, had to liquidate their overseas possessions in the two decades following 1945.

This was not the only loss they suffered. Stripped of their holdings, battered and more or less defeated by the Axis powers, Britain and France – as well as Germany and Japan, which actually did lose the second war – were reduced to the second rank of the international system. They ceased to be great powers. When, after

---

[65] See above, pp. 28–31.

1945, something like the nineteenth-century managed balance of power system was established, it was the United States and the Soviet Union, not they, that were the members of what was the equivalent in the international system of an economic cartel.

This made for an ironic conclusion to three centuries of British security policy. With the end of empire, one of the two pillars of traditional British policy fell away. It was no longer necessary to concentrate on protecting the nation's overseas holdings. Britain was free to concentrate on helping to ensure equilibrium on the Continent. This the British did after 1945. For the first time a British military contingent was stationed there permanently in peacetime. But its presence was of minor importance for establishing the balance in Europe. British troops were welcome but not necessary. It was the United States that counted on checking the potential hegemonic power, the Soviet Union. Great Britain had ceased to be a great power.

2

France, 1919–1940

The Failure of Security Policy

I

A major purpose of the European settlement after World War I was to keep France secure against Germany. The French were convinced from the very outset of the postwar period, correctly as it turned out, that Germany posed a continuing threat to their security. The Paris Peace Conference of 1919, at which the victorious powers met to devise the postwar settlement, was the beginning, not the end, of French efforts to remain secure. Over the course of the next twenty years France tried first to preserve the terms of the settlement against German efforts to overturn it, then to resist another German bid for mastery of Europe, and finally simply to protect itself against the German army. The French search for security was one of the principal themes of European and world history during the years from 1919 to 1940, and it involved each of the major strategies for remaining secure.

The French had paid a high price for the victory of 1918. Their losses over four years, in men and material, had been heavy. The war in the west had been fought almost exclusively on their soil. In crafting the settlement, the French were more urgently concerned with the arrangements in Europe than the other members of the victorious coalition because, unlike its allies – the United States and Great Britain – France was geographically part of the Continent. The postwar deliberations took place in its capital. The

French were responsible for a series of measures intended to strengthen themselves and weaken Germany: the German obligation to pay reparations; the partial occupation for fifteen years and permanent demilitarization of the west bank of the Rhine and a fifty-kilometer strip to the east, the territory known as the Rhineland; international control of the Saarland; and strict limits on the size of the German army. France also took an interest in the eastern part of the settlement, which created a series of independent nation-states in territories that had belonged to the now vanished Hapsburg, Romanov, and Ottoman empires. The settlement gave birth, or rebirth, with French approval and encouragement, to a new, smaller, independent Austria, Hungary, Poland, Czechoslovakia, Rumania, and Yugoslavia.

The France of this period was neither a very strong nor a very weak power. It belonged to the large middle category of states that are roughly the equals of their adversaries. France was, to be sure, decidedly inferior to Germany in population and industrial production, which together form the basis of military might in the twentieth century. France was militarily weaker than Germany, and its relative weakness was central to the policies that it pursued. The unfavorable ratio of potential strength colored French diplomacy and military planning. France's security policies cannot be understood apart from this presumed inferiority to Germany.

The difference between the two neighboring countries, however, was not so great that France regarded resistance to a German attack by ordinary military means as hopeless. France was weaker than Germany, but it was not, as defined here, a weak state.[1] The French did not assume, as weak states do, that Germany would win any war the two might fight. France did not, like the People's Republic of China after 1949, rely largely on strategies appropriate to extreme weakness.[2] The French did not expect to be overwhelmed, as weak states do. When Germany attacked, in May 1940, they resisted. Their sudden, sweeping defeat came as a shock. France was not prepared to fight on in unconventional fashion, as weak states that aspire to remain independent without powerful allies

[1] See the Introduction and Chapter 4, pp. 193–4.
[2] See Chapter 4.

usually are. Nor did Germany win the battle of France because of superior strength. The Germans did not bring the full weight of their potential military resources to bear in the spring of 1940.[3]

Because their position in the international system is less constraining than are those of the strong and the weak, states that fall into the intermediate category have a wider range of choice than the other two types. Here, too, French policy between the two world wars was representative. France adopted each of the basic approaches to security available to sovereign states: collective policies, alliances, conciliation, and the use of force.

In the interwar period there were several attempts to address the security problem collectively – that is, through arrangements involving all the major powers in an effort to modify the basic anarchy of the international system that lies at the root of the security problem. The most extreme example of a collective approach would be the sacrifice of separate sovereignties to form a world government. The League of Nations, which was established as part of the peace settlement, seemed briefly, to some, to be a promising basis for such a global Leviathan. A less revolutionary collective approach to security, in which there was marked interest after World War I as there had been after the Wars of the French Revolution and World War II, is a world police force. It would involve, in effect, the persistence of the victorious coalition into peacetime. While retaining their sovereign prerogatives, the members of the coalition would jointly enforce order throughout the international system. The least demanding collective approach to security, one that was actually put into practice after 1815, is a managed balance of power system. It involves modest cooperation among the great powers to preserve a rough equilibrium of military strength among them and to avoid a major war.[4] Like world government and a global police force, it was briefly attempted in the interwar period.

None of the three collective approaches was, strictly speaking, a French security policy. Collective arrangements are a property of the international system, not of a single state. They necessarily involve all states, at least all the major ones. France was neither

<hr />

[3] See Section V.
[4] This is the subject of Chapter 1.

the prime mover behind each of the proposed collective arrangements nor even particularly enthusiastic about all of them. Nonetheless, each had some bearing on French security.

Successful collective arrangements are rare; unfettered anarchy is the norm in international politics. Most states therefore adopt self-help policies. These do not have to be carried out alone, however. Alliances are common features of international politics. The search for allies was an important part of French security policy in the 1920s and 1930s. But an alliance is not, by itself, a security policy. Singly or together, states must decide how to respond to potential adversaries. They have, very broadly speaking, two alternatives. They can choose conciliation or resistance. They can rely on diplomacy or force. With differing emphasis at different points over the course of two decades, the French adopted both approaches.

The French case is thus representative of the range of security policies available to sovereign states. All of the major approaches to security – world government, a world police force, a managed balance of power system, alliances, diplomacy, and war – were part of French policy between 1919 and 1940.

All of these efforts failed. The failure of French policies is often connected with the political and social shortcomings of France itself.[5] Such "inside-out" accounts, which emphasize the influence

---

[5] The most prominent recent version of this point of view is Jean-Baptiste Duroselle, *La Décadence, 1932–1939* (Paris: Imprimerie Nationale, 1979), the thesis of which is expressed in its title. Perhaps the earliest and probably the most influential book adopting this perspective is Marc Bloch's *Strange Defeat*, trans. by Gerard Hopkins (New York: Octagon Books, 1968). A widely read English-language version of the story is William L. Shirer, *The Collapse of the Third Republic: An Inquiry into the Fall of France, 1940* (New York: Simon & Schuster, 1969). This explanation has had considerable influence because it corresponds to the experience of those who lived through the interwar period, especially the 1930s. It has also suited partisan purposes. Both supporters and opponents of Vichy had an interest in blaming the Third Republic for what happened to France. Both saw the events of 1940 as a moral drama and the defeat as a fall from grace. Vichy presented itself as the necessary antidote to years of godless republicanism that had brought France to its knees. The regime claimed to be not a German puppet but the necessary foundation for the revitalization of the nation. The anti-Vichyites had no love for the fallen republic either. It had, after all, perished ignominiously. For them, however, Vichy was the continuation of the fall from grace. Salvation came not from Pétain and the Church but from the resistance.

of internal forces on security policy, impute France's downfall to deep divisions within French society, divisions of ideology and social class that fatally weakened the country in its struggle with Germany.[6] These accounts also indict the French political system, with its fractious political parties, because it produced weak, unstable governments that were unable to act decisively in moments of crisis.[7] The exhaustion of French society itself at every level, from the governing elite to the peasantry, and the general weakness of will after the trauma of the First World War are also invoked to explain France's fate in the interwar period and in 1940.[8]

The French defeat lends itself as well to an "outside-in" explanation, according to which the configuration of the international system and France's position in it doomed French security policies to failure. The responsibility for France's defeat, by this account, lies ultimately with the postwar settlement, which saddled the French with an impossible task: attempting to uphold arrangements that were unacceptable to Germany without receiving the help that was necessary for them to succeed. According to this interpretation, the settlement was, in the French phrase, "une paix trop douce pour ce qu'elle a de dur" – "a peace too mild for its severity." It compelled the French to enforce "Napoleonic conditions" by "Wilsonian methods."[9]

This task, not surprisingly, proved impossible for the French. Because of what they had suffered in the war and what they believed was therefore their due in peacetime, they were not willing to be generous to Germany at Paris;[10] nor were they able to get

---

[6] See, e.g., Felix Gilbert, *The End of the European Era, 1890 to the Present* (New York: Norton, 1970), p. 252; Anthony Adamthwaite, *The Making of the Second World War* (London: Allen & Unwin, 1977), p. 43; Anthony Adamthwaite, *France and the Coming of the Second World War, 1936–1939* (London: Cass, 1977), p. 14; D. C. Watt, "Diplomatic History, 1930–39," in C. L. Mowatt, ed., *The Shifting Balance of World Forces* (2d ed.), The New Cambridge Modern History, Vol. 12 (Cambridge University Press, 1968), p. 713.
[7] Adamthwaite, *France and the Coming*, pp. 9–10.
[8] Duroselle, *La Décadence*, p. 19; Bloch, *Strange Defeat*, p. 172.
[9] Rohan Butler, "The Peace Settlement of Versailles," in Mowat, ed., *The Shifting Balance*, pp. 221–2; Walter A. McDougall, *France's Rhineland Diplomacy, 1914–1924: The Last Bid for a Balance of Power in Europe* (Princeton, N.J.: Princeton University Press, 1978), p. 8.
[10] Nor is it altogether clear that greater French generosity could have reconciled

the assistance required to enforce terms that Germany considered not simply ungenerous but intolerable. The terms were imposed after a long, bloody war that had been won by a coalition of great powers. France could not have achieved victory by itself but had to try to sustain the victory alone.

Both types of explanation, both domestic and international considerations, are relevant to an understanding of France's failures. The French task does appear, in retrospect, to have been a formidable one. Difficult though it was, however, it was not impossible. Certainly the task of defending the metropolitan territory itself was not beyond France's powers.

The French failures were plainly related to their own flaws. At crucial moments in the interwar period the country's internal divisions and the resulting paralysis influenced the making of decisions, with adverse consequences. Ideological polarization, for instance, inhibited the formation of alliances in the 1930s.[11] When German forces marched into the Rhineland in 1936, in clear violation of the Versailles Treaty, France failed to respond in part because the government in Paris had just fallen and the caretaker cabinet had no mandate to take decisive action of any kind.[12] The most energetic French effort to enforce the postwar settlement,

---

Germany to the settlement. A reconstituted Poland, which had little to do with French demands, was a standing invitation to German revisionism.

[11] See Section III. An often cited example of the effect of internal divisions on foreign policy is France's approach to the Spanish civil war. Leon Blum, the Socialist prime minister, decided against sending aid to the Loyalists for fear of arousing the French Right. In 1936 "ideological affinities eclipsed national considerations." René Remond, *The Right Wing in France From 1815 to de Gaulle*, trans. by James M. Laux (Philadelphia: University of Pennsylvania Press, 1966; first published in French, 1963), p. 303. "Blum . . . was genuinely afraid that civil war in Spain might set the example for a civil war in France." James Joll, *Europe Since 1870: An International History* (Harmondsworth: Pelican Books, 1976), p. 354. Blum plainly did act (or more properly failed to act) with an eye toward the potentially explosive repercussions at home. But Franco's victory, although not irrelevant, was not decisive for French security. For the contrary argument, that the outcome of the Spanish civil war was of considerable significance for French security policy, see Adamthwaite, *The Making*, pp. 58–9.

[12] On the Rhineland episode, a crucial moment in the 1930s, see John Emmerson, *The Rhineland Crisis 7 March 1936* (London: Temple Smith), 1977; Robert J. Young, *In Command of France: French Foreign Policy and Military Planning, 1933–1940* (Cambridge, Mass.: Harvard University Press, 1978), pp. 119–29.

the occupation of the Ruhr in 1924 in order to compel Germany to pay reparations, was abandoned, according to one interpretation, because the French themselves could not muster the political and economic wherewithal to sustain the policy.[13] French policy can be seen as both a tragedy of malevolent fate and one of flawed character.

There is, in addition, a third way to understand French security policy between the two world wars. This interpretation connects the failures of the security policies that France pursued at least in part to pitfalls inherent in the policies themselves: These policies failed not because they were hopeless or because France did not carry them out properly, but rather because of difficulties to which all such approaches are subject. Although it does not emphasize France's position in the international system, this third interpretation is like the "outside-in" style of explanation in that it traces outcomes to conditions outside French society itself and not within France's control.[14]

Collective security policies require the participation of all major

---

[13] Stephen A. Schucker, *The End of French Predominance in Europe: The Financial Crisis of 1924 and the Adoption of the Dawes Plan* (Chapel Hill: University of North Carolina Press), 1976, argues that France's failure to set its economic house in order made the French government subject to financial pressure from Britain and the United States, which obliged France to quit the Ruhr. See also McDougall, *France's Rhineland Diplomacy*, p. 12. French society's refusal to exert itself affected military policy. The one-year term of service for conscripts, which the Assembly refused to prolong, circumscribed the nation's military options throughout the 1930s. Similarly, the failure to remove the government to North Africa in June 1940 and stage a "second Marne" there, a last-ditch effort to resist after the fashion of 1914, may be attributed to the demoralization of the French leadership and so to domestic infirmity.

[14] This third approach, like outside-in explanations, tends to put French society and France's leadership in a more favorable light than do most accounts of the interwar period. It therefore risks being unduly exculpatory. Robert J. Young's account of French military planning is in the spirit of this third type of explanation: "One need not be blind to the shortcomings of the fallen Republic to recognize within it a seriousness of purpose toward the perils at hand, a determination to resist German attempts at hegemony, a willingness to devote enormous care and effort to the cause of national defense." Young, *In Command*, p. 2. "All in all the military and diplomatic efforts of prewar France, of the fallen and discredited Third Republic, did not constitute a sparkling or brilliant national policy. . . . But it may be hoped that this volume will restore to France a greater measure of independence, of rational and coherent motivation, of sensible planning, of dignity, than hitherto has been the case." Ibid., p. 258.

states. Neither France alone, nor any other single power, could have made them work. The reluctance of others to take part undercut France's efforts to contrive collective arrangements in the interwar period. Similarly, the same difficulties that beset French alliance policies in the 1930s exist for all alliances, potential or actual. The French policy of conciliation foundered on the problem that any such policy faces: the refusal of the adversary to be conciliated. And when the French went to war, the failures that led to their defeat were the same as those to which any warring country is susceptible.

In this way France's security policies are, again, representative of a larger class of cases. The causes of France's failures can be found at other times and in other places. States with positions similar to that of France in the international system do not necessarily fail; if some states lose wars, after all, others must win them. When collective and self-help security policies misfire, they do not always do so for the reasons that France's initiatives in the interwar period did. But the French case does illustrate some of the general problems associated with the security policies available to all sovereign states.

II

In the aftermath of World War I the victorious powers, France among them, undertook several collective approaches to security. Such approaches have an obvious appeal. They address the security problem at its root – the structure of the international system. They propose to solve it by cooperation rather than force. Successful collective approaches are nonetheless both rare and rarely attempted.

They tend to appear in the immediate aftermath of great wars, when what is after all the most familiar self-help approach to remaining secure has produced personal suffering, economic destruction, and political dislocation. The years following World War I were just such a period. The great powers, including France, attempted to address the security problem by cooperative, collective methods. Their efforts did not succeed. The Paris Peace Conference of 1919 did not reproduce the work of the Congress of Vienna a century before. It did not create a twentieth-century version of the nineteenth-century Concert of Europe.[15] The peace conference was not the only occasion during the interwar period in which collective arrangements were considered. Nor was the managed balance of power system the only collective form that seemed plausible. Several of the collective schemes proposed going well beyond what the men at Vienna had achieved in modifying the anarchy of the international system. Versions of a world government and a world police force were, for a time, on the agenda of the great powers.

France was more closely involved in some of the collective efforts than in others. But each was to some extent related to French security policy. Each failed, moreover, for reasons that have relevance beyond the case of France.

The League of Nations, which was created after the war, looked at first as though it might be the kernel of a world government. It was intended to be the first universal peacetime international organization. The Concert of Europe had been more a series of customs than a formal body and had met only sporadically. The League, by contrast, consisted of several institutions that convened on a regular basis. It was organized to be a parliament of states. The expressed intention of its founders was to keep the peace in Europe and the rest of the world by replacing the pattern of international relations that had led to the cataclysmic world war.

The British and, even more so, the Americans (or at least the American president, Woodrow Wilson) were more favorably disposed toward the League than were the other powers. The idea of applying the rule of law to the jungle of international politics struck a responsive chord in Anglo-American political culture. To Americans the peaceful unification of their own thirteen original colonies seemed a precedent for the gradual amalgamation of sovereign states into a harmonious international order. The vision of the League as a substitute for the more familiar instruments of security policy – arms, alliances, and wars – appealed to the two English-speaking powers as well because they were both removed from the European continent, where these instruments had so often been used. The English Channel and the Atlantic Ocean promoted a certain faith in the use of conciliation, reason, and parliamentary

---

[15] See Chapter 1, Section V.

procedures in relations among sovereign states in the countries they sheltered. The French, who lived closer to the cockpit of international affairs, lacked this faith.

Any government, no matter how democratic, must be able to enforce its rules. On questions of enforcement the founders of the League were ambivalent at best. Article 16 of its charter prescribed sanctions against states that violated the League's basic precepts or flouted its decisions. Only by a unanimous vote of its members could the League authorize sanctions, however, and once authorized there was no way to enforce them. Although his intentions were far from clear, perhaps even to himself, Woodrow Wilson does not seem to have intended for the League to be able to act as a sovereign body. He told Lloyd George that the League would not have executive powers and assured the United States Senate that when the League voted sanctions it would not be mandatory for the member states to carry them out. However far Wilson was prepared to go in endowing the new organization with the means to enforce its will, moreover, no other leader was prepared to go farther.

The League's rules of international conduct were soon violated. Germany first evaded and then renounced the demilitarization clauses of the Versailles Treaty. The clauses were not part of the League's charter (although a commitment to the League was the first article in each of the postwar peace treaties), but the Germans certainly breached the spirit of the organization, the purpose of which was to uphold the postwar settlement. Japan and Italy explicitly violated the charter. Both committed forbidden acts of aggression. The League's response to both countries was ineffective.

In 1931 Japanese forces stationed in the Chinese province of Manchuria acted to bring the entire province under their control.[16] The League's response was to dither. Finally, almost two years later, it endorsed a report condemning the invasion. In 1935 the League voted sanctions against Italy for its invasion of Ethiopia, but only after prolonged haggling. The sanctions were limited in scope, and their imposition was delayed until Ethiopian resistance

[16] They had been concentrated along the main railway line. On September 18 they fanned out and occupied the main cities.

had virtually collapsed. In July 1936 they were lifted, signifying their failure. Japan and Italy responded to these measures by quitting the League, Japan in 1932 and Italy in 1937. Germany had left in 1933, and the Soviet Union withdrew in 1939 when the organization condemned its invasion of Finland. In each case, rather than obey the League's decisions, the miscreant power simply ignored them.

Even before the challenges of the 1930s made its shortcomings as a mechanism for keeping the peace unmistakable, the League's role in international affairs was a marginal one. One of its most notable achievements, the 1924 Geneva Protocol making the arbitration of international disputes compulsory, was, like the League's charter itself, a series of fine-sounding phrases with no power of enforcement behind them. The Hague Disarmament Conferences of the 1920s had little effect on the course of European affairs.

In truth, apart from Woodrow Wilson, the founders of the League did not have great expectations for it. They did not anticipate that it would blossom into a global Leviathan. Lloyd George thought it would be a useful forum for making adjustments in the peace treaties, especially the territorial provisions. The French did not, on the whole, believe that the League held even that promise, modest though it was. They feared that it would detract attention from the real business of postwar European affairs, which was to sustain the strength necessary to keep Germany from overturning the settlement. To them the League was the *idée périlleuse* – "the dangerous idea" – of President Wilson. The French went along with the idea to stay in the good graces of the Anglo-Americans.

The significance of the League for the history of security policy, therefore, lies not only in its failure to keep the peace, but also in the fact that it was never really expected to do so. It is not the failure to form a world government after World War I that is striking, but rather the modesty of the efforts to establish an overarching authority for the international system. Indeed, the League can scarcely be called a serious effort in that direction at all. In this sense the League of Nations brings to mind the passage in the Arthur Conan Doyle story "Silver Blaze" in which Sherlock Holmes draws Dr. Watson's attention to the curious case of the dog barking in the night. Watson replies that the dog did *not* bark. That, Holmes responds, is what is so curious.

After World War I conditions were more favorable for the creation of a world government than they had ever been before, and perhaps than they have been since. The idea of reconstructing international politics was popular among ordinary people throughout Europe, and it seemed evident that such people, and not only their leaders, would have a say in shaping the postwar world. The war had taken a terrible toll. There was broad-based interest in adopting radical measures to prevent another such conflict. To the two strongest powers, the United States and Great Britain, the rule of law in international affairs seemed natural.

Yet the League did not come close to being the embryo of a global state that would take the place of the anarchy of international politics. The war did not create the international equivalent of the circumstances that compel individuals in the state of nature, according to Hobbes, to form a commonwealth. The charms of sovereignty continued to outweigh the costs of maintaining it. The war did demonstrate that anarchy could have terrible consequences; but it did not demonstrate that it was unbearable. The powers had suffered great losses, but not so great as to make independence, and the insecurity that comes with it, intolerable.

In fact the war had, on balance, the opposite effect. It reinforced the impulse to divide the world into many independent sovereign jurisdictions, and so made world government an even more distant prospect than it had been before 1914 – when it had hardly been imminent. The national principle – the sovereign independence of national communities – was the basis of the peace settlement. The result was to multiply rather than decrease the number of sovereign states. World government, in that it deprives all national groups of their own independent political apparatus, was in a sense precisely what the war had been fought to prevent.[17]

---

[17] Wilson seems to have reconciled in his own mind the multiplication of sovereignty, of which he was a champion, with his vision of a harmonious postwar order on the grounds that self-determination, which he equated with democracy, would make states at last behave peacefully, under the pressure of public opinion. He assumed that on every contentious issue the public would have an opinion, that it would be formidable, and that it would compel governments

Keeping the winning coalition in existence to police the international system in the wake of a great war is a less taxing enterprise than creating a global Leviathan with the powers of an effective government. A joint European (or worldwide) police force is, like world government, a collective approach to security. It relies on cooperation among all the major powers. Unlike what they must do to form a world government, however, they retain their sovereign prerogatives while promising to act together to keep order. This is essentially what Metternich had envisioned in his version of the Holy Alliance after the Wars of the French Revolution.[18] This idea is also embodied in the Security Council of the United Nations, which was formed after World War II.

There was, as well, an effort to sustain the coalition that had won the first great war of the twentieth century. The French proposed that they, the British, and the Americans remain united after the war to enforce the settlement. This, not the League of Nations, was the postwar arrangement they preferred. France agreed not to occupy the German Rhineland permanently in return for a pledge that Britain and the United States would assist in making certain that the terms of the settlement were observed.[19]

The arrangement was not precisely like the Europe-wide police force that Metternich had envisioned or the mechanism for global order that the framers of the United Nations hoped the Security Council would be. In French eyes it was directed not against any breach in the postwar settlement that might occur, but against

---

to follow peaceful policies. Upon arriving in Paris on December 21, 1918, he said: "My conception of the League of Nations is just this: that it shall operate as the organizing moral force of men throughout the world, and that whenever, or whatever, wrong and aggression are planned or contemplated, this searching light of conscience will be turned upon them, and men everywhere will ask, 'What are the purposes that you hold in your heart against the fortunes of the world?' Just a little exposure will settle most questions. If the Central Powers had dared to discuss the whole purpose of this war for a single fortnight it never would have happened, and if, as should be, they were forced to discuss it for a year, war would never have been conceivable." George Scott, *The Rise and Fall of the League of Nations* (London: Hutchinson, 1973), p. 32. See also Sally Marks, *The Illusion of Peace: International Relations in Europe, 1918–1933* (New York: St. Martin's Press, 1976), p. 31.

[18] See Chapter 1, p. 22.

[19] Wilson concurred in the promise. The American guarantee was to stand until the League had become an effective substitute for it.

Germany. Metternich had feared the revolution; the French feared the Germans. Nor was what France wanted a fully collective approach to security. It did not encompass all the great powers. Germany and Russia were excluded. Nonetheless, the same logic underlay the French proposal: A group of states powerful enough to win a great war was powerful enough to keep the peace afterward. The habit of collaboration that the presence of a common enemy had fostered could continue after the enemy's defeat.

The coalition that won World War I ended as had those that had triumphed in 1815 and 1945. It disbanded. The British and the Americans did not provide the guarantee that the French expected. When the United States Senate refused to ratify American membership in the League of Nations, the commitment that Woodrow Wilson had made to France was voided. Britain did join the League but declined, for almost all of the interwar period, to conclude the formal military alliance that France sought.[20] As had happened at the end of the last great European war, and as was to occur after the next one, the coalition disintegrated after 1918 because the cause that held it together disappeared. Britain and the United States shared with France the aim of keeping Germany from dominating Europe, but their common interests did not extend much farther. Not only were the great powers not interested in surrendering their sovereign prerogatives to some international body; they were also unwilling to coordinate their policies except under duress, for a limited time, and for a specific purpose. In the absence of a mortal threat, their interests diverged. The United States wanted no part of European politics. The British were ambivalent. Although they could not ignore the affairs of the Continent, they were not prepared to make the commitment that the French sought and that membership in a scheme to police Europe would have required, just as they had declined to promise to involve themselves in Continental politics in the way that Metternich had proposed a century before.

Another collective approach to security, the managed balance of power system, requires a more modest change in the organizing

---

[20] See Section IV. The British commitment by itself would not, in any event, have been enough to form a global police force. The alliance with Britain that France sought qualifies, in the terms used here, as a "self-help" rather than a collective security policy.

principle of anarchy than does world government or a global police force. It is a much less radical departure from the normal workings of the international system and is therefore easier to establish. Unlike the other two collective approaches, it actually has been established. The conquerors of Napoleon established collective arrangements that contributed to the long peace between 1815 and 1914. Although the Paris Peace Conference did not replicate the work of the Congress of Vienna, it was not the only occasion in the interwar period when there seemed to be a chance of establishing a balance of power. At Locarno, Switzerland, a series of agreements were signed in 1925 that appeared to lay the foundation for a twentieth-century version of the nineteenth-century Concert of Europe. Four arbitration conventions between Germany and its neighbors – France, Belgium, Poland, and Czechoslovakia – were agreed to. The Treaty of Mutual Guarantee, also known as the Rhineland Pact, declared Germany's western frontier, as defined by the Versailles Treaty, to be permanent. If an "unprovoked attack" by Germany against France or by France against Germany occurred, the victim would be entitled to assistance from Britain and Italy, the other two signatories. Accords between France and Poland and France and Czechoslovakia stipulated that if Germany rejected arbitration these countries would assist each other, by force if necessary. Germany joined the League of Nations and received a permanent seat in its directing council.

Locarno inaugurated a period lasting to the end of the decade in which the foreign ministers of Britain, France, and Germany met regularly to address common problems. The men who held these positions for most of the period, Austen Chamberlain, Aristide Briand, and Gustav Stresemann, had a good working relationship. Locarno began, as well, a period in which European affairs were more tranquil than immediately before or afterward. Locarno and its aftermath resembled the Concert of Europe in several ways. There was a commitment to collective procedures, as there had been in the nineteenth century. Germany was admitted to the councils of Europe as a full participant. The territorial settlement received the endorsement of the European powers, and where it was not to be strictly maintained it would, according to the promises given at Locarno, be revised jointly and peacefully rather than unilaterally and by force.

The parallel between the Locarno era and the Concert of Europe can be taken farther. If the 1925 conference itself was the equivalent during the period after 1919 of the Congress of Vienna, which was the founding meeting of the nineteenth-century managed balance of power system, the Hague Conference of 1929 might be said to correspond to the periodic meetings of the great powers that followed the Vienna congress in the first half of the nineteenth century. The subject at The Hague was not the disposition of territory or the establishment of new independent states, as in the nineteenth century. It was, rather, the most contentious issue in European politics in the 1920s: reparations. A compromise settlement, the Young Plan, was agreed upon, which seemed to resolve the matter to the satisfaction, or at least without the immediately poisonous dissatisfaction, of the countries involved.

The parallel between Locarno and its aftermath and the nineteenth century has its limits. The parties to Locarno did not unanimously wish to re-create the Concert of Europe. The British *were* explicitly interested in solidifying the European equilibrium. Their aim in 1925, as it had been in 1815, was to minimize their own role in Continental affairs and thus be free to concentrate on imperial matters. As in the past they sought the best of both worlds: equilibrium without exertion.[21] The various treaties negotiated at Locarno were formally signed later in the year in London. For the occasion an official of the Foreign Office brought a portrait of Castlereagh, the British architect of the Congress of Vienna, out of storage and hung it in the room where the signing ceremonies took place.

Germany and France, however, had different purposes in mind at Locarno and thereafter. For the Germans the agreements were part of an ongoing strategy of modifying the postwar settlement. By 1925 they had made some headway. Most significantly, they

---

[21] In fact, the British were split between those, like Austen Chamberlain, who wanted to offer France an explicit security guarantee, and others, Churchill among them, who wished to avoid Continental entanglements. The great advantage of Locarno was that each side could regard it as consistent with its own preferences. Chamberlain considered the agreements the equivalent of an alliance with France. Others believed that they deterred Germany and reassured France without actually taking sides with either. Jon Jacobson, *Locarno Diplomacy: Germany and the West, 1925–1929* (Princeton, N.J.: Princeton University Press, 1972), pp. 17, 23, 37.

had avoided paying reparations in the full amount decreed at Paris. Locarno was a defensive maneuver, a way of consolidating the progress that had been made in revising the settlement. The Germans were wary of an Anglo-French alliance. The Rhineland Pact hedged against this possibility by putting Germany at least formally on an equal footing with France in relations with Britain. The Germans were able to sign the Locarno treaties without acknowledging the eastern provisions of Versailles as permanent, although they had to renounce the use of force to change them. In return for signing the agreements, the Germans were able to put an end to the Allied occupation of the Rhineland earlier than had been scheduled.

The French, by contrast, wished to uphold the Paris settlement. By 1925 their efforts to do so unilaterally and by force had come to a dead end. Locarno marked a shift in tactics. The French found the Rhineland Pact attractive because it was the closest thing to a security guarantee from Britain that they had managed to obtain since the end of the war. In theory the British had equal obligations to Germany. The French were certain, however, that they, and not the Germans, would be the victims of unprovoked aggression and would therefore be able to call on Britain for help.

The fact that the principal parties to Locarno harbored different motives did not necessarily doom the chances for establishing a working managed balance of power system. It is quite possible for states to follow common rules for different reasons and with different and even conflicting ultimate goals. The members of the Concert of Europe did not share a single vision of the future. France in the nineteenth century, like Germany in the twentieth, was unhappy with the terms of the settlement that it had to accept after its military defeat. The French did not provoke another major war, thanks in part to the procedures established at Vienna. It was not foreordained that Germany would resort to war to alter the work of the Paris conference. Stresemann did well for a time without using force. During his stewardship of German foreign policy, from 1925 to 1929, he obtained the effective termination of reparations, secured the Rhineland, negotiated the early evacuation of Allied troops from German territory, and presided over the formal readmission of Germany to Europe. For all his success, however,

Germany, unlike France, ultimately went to war to destroy the settlement.

Locarno differed from the Concert of Europe in other ways as well. It was not fully collective. It did not include all the major powers. The United States and the Soviet Union, as Russia had become, the two great non-European (or partly European) states that would dominate the Continent after the next war, did not take part. There was another difference. Locarno did not treat all parts of the European settlement uniformly. The various treaties did not guarantee the eastern part against revision as they did the western provisions. Germany promised to respect its western borders as defined at Versailles; it was not required to make this pledge for the east. It merely promised to refrain from changing its eastern frontiers by force. The difference was noted at the time and had the effect of weakening the eastern part of the settlement.

Locarno can be seen as an abortive effort to establish the kind of working relationship among the European powers that had been the hallmark of the long peace of the nineteenth century, an effort frustrated by Germany's refusal to be reconciled to the territorial and political arrangements that had emerged from the Paris Peace Conference. There was no long peace after World War I. Still, there was a short period of harmony in the second half of the 1920s, when Germany seemed to be observing balance of power norms. Locarno and its aftermath can therefore also be seen as a partial, short-lived, twentieth-century equivalent of the nineteenth-century Concert of Europe. Seen in this way there is another parallel with the nineteenth-century managed balance of power system. In each instance Germany brought about the end of equilibrium. The Germans would not follow the rules. Like a cartel, a managed balance of power system requires the cooperation of all the major powers. One defector can destroy it. In the 1930s, as at the beginning of the century, Germany defected. The Germans were unhappy with the existing distribution of power in Europe and acted to change it. In this sense, both world wars had the same cause.

If the long spell of peace after the Wars of the French Revolution and the brief period of harmony in the interwar period ended for the same reason, however, they ended in different ways. The nineteenth-century balance of power system eroded gradually; the Locarno procedures collapsed suddenly. In the last years of the nineteenth century and the first decade and a half of the twentieth the prevailing attitudes and practices of international politics slowly changed, until in 1914 the habits of cooperation and restraint among the great powers were finally overthrown. The comity of the second half of the 1920s disappeared much more rapidly. On the first occasion Germany gradually became disenchanted with the existing European order and finally resolved to break it. On the second the Germans were disenchanted from the outset and abruptly shifted their tactics for altering the postwar dispensation.

Collective approaches to security belong to the 1920s. They seemed then to have some promise of success. The period has the look, in retrospect, of a postwar decade. The memories of the trenches were still fresh. The sense of a common interest in preventing another great conflict was still more powerful in Europe than the particular interests of the separate states. The postwar settlement showed signs of being permanent, especially from 1925 to 1930. The 1930s appear, by contrast (and seemed increasingly to those who lived through them), a prewar period. Political differences overshadowed the common interest in keeping the peace. Hitler did not share this interest at all.

The turn of the decade is the line of demarcation between the time when collective approaches to security received serious attention and the years when self-help policies predominated. Collective approaches flourish in the wake of a major war, when the emphasis is on preventing another and when the common experience of warfare makes cooperation possible even among countries with competing interests. When the issues that divide sovereign states carry greater weight, when it is all too plausible to fight over them, when cooperation among the major powers is impossible, then states must defend themselves as well as they can.

The transitional event in the interwar period was the Great Depression. The economic slump made the international system more competitive. To cope with it, the European governments adopted policies that set them against one another. They erected tariff barriers, engaged in competitive devaluations of their currencies, and generally practiced "beggar-thy-neighbor" policies.[22] The Depression weakened all the governments that had to contend with it. It strengthened extremist parties that promised radical remedies for the economic distress, notably in Germany. The Depression helped to create the conditions in which Hitler, the dominant figure of the 1930s, came to power.

The French were not particularly enthusiastic about world government, as represented by the League of Nations, or a managed balance of power system, as attempted, perhaps halfheartedly, at Locarno and afterward. The proposed common front with Britain and the United States aside, the French did not count on collective measures to keep themselves secure. Collective approaches require the cooperation of all the major powers, and the French were never optimistic that Germany would cooperate. The failures of these collective efforts did not, therefore, surprise the French. Nor did the failures particularly disturb them. For all its difficulties, the decade of the 1920s was a relatively calm period in Europe. In the 1930s the world became more dangerous. France's security problem became more urgent, and the French fell back on the more familiar self-help approaches. These were not suddenly launched in the wake of the Depression. They were adopted in the first postwar decade, but they were put to the test in the 1930s. The self-help policies also failed, with disastrous results for France. These failures, like those of the collective approaches, were representative of setbacks to which many states are vulnerable.

III

Because they were dubious that collective approaches could contribute to their security, the French emphasized self-help policies from the moment of victory in 1918 to the moment of defeat in 1940. States adopt self-help policies in order to cope with the consequences of the structure of the international system rather than to change that structure. They accept the basic anarchy of world politics instead of trying to reform it, as efforts to establish a global Leviathan, a world police force, and a managed balance of power system do.

---

[22] See Chapter 6, p. 340.

Self-help policies are not necessarily undertaken alone. France did, however, act alone in the early years of the interwar period to try to enforce the settlement. In 1929 Germany fell behind in paying reparations. The French sent troops to occupy the Ruhr, one of Germany's major industrial areas, in order to collect what the Germans owed.[23]

The occupation of the Ruhr was the final stage in an intermittent effort, begun during the war, to weaken Germany by detaching the western part of the territory of the state that Bismarck had put together in 1871. Some versions of France's war aims called for the "amputation" of western Germany. At the Paris Peace Conference, French leaders sought to occupy the west bank of the Rhine and the bridges across the river permanently, and also proposed that the Rhineland be a buffer state between France and Germany. In the postwar period the French tried to encourage separatist tendencies in the Rhineland.

If successful, this French effort to deprive Germany of the heart of its iron and steel industries would have changed the balance of power in Europe. Without its western territories Germany's advantages over France in population and industrial production would have been greatly reduced, if not entirely eliminated. It did not, of course, succeed. The other great powers, notably Great Britain, did not approve of the French ambition to detach part of Germany or, later, of the French move into the Ruhr. Passive German resistance and British disapproval forced France to withdraw. (When the demilitarization clauses of Versailles were overturned, and especially after the remilitarization of the Rhineland in 1936, the French army could not easily return.) The Ruhr occupation marked the last time in the interwar period that the French tried to act alone to vindicate their security interests. For the next fifteen years France relied on others. At the heart of French security policy in the interwar period was the effort to form alliances.

Forming an alliance is a way to be both safe and sovereign. It goes with the grain of international politics. It represents an accommodation to the most powerful force in the international system and is therefore an old and familiar feature of relations among

---

[23] The French government intended to appropriate the production of the Ruhr's mines.

sovereign states. A state that forms an alliance pools its military resources with one or several other sovereign political communities and so enhances the strength at its disposal. By definition forming an alliance is not a unilateral security policy. It does qualify as a self-help approach, as the term is defined here, because it addresses the insecurity that anarchy confers on all sovereign states rather than trying to reconstitute the international system by modifying its organizing principle. Collective security policies involve cooperation, tacit or explicit, among all the important members of the international system. An alliance pits some states against others.

Seeking alliances was a sensible, logical approach to security for the French in the interwar period. Their aim was to keep Germany in check. Germany was stronger than France. The French had been able to prevail in 1918 only with the help of powerful allies. They therefore needed allies to win the next round or, better yet, to prevent another round from taking place.

At the heart of every alliance is a tension. The partners have some things – not everything – in common. Their interests partly overlap; that, after all, is the basis for any alliance. But the interests of two sovereign states are never identical. Goals and aspirations inevitably diverge. Sometimes they are opposed, even with alliance partners. There is invariably a tension between what is common between the parties and what is not. The tension takes two forms. There are two variants of the basic problem that every alliance poses, and both were relevant to France between the two world wars.

One variant is the problem of alliance formation. It revolves around the question of whether two states with partly overlapping interests will agree to make common cause, that is, whether they will agree to fight on behalf of each other. The problem appears when there are several roughly equal powers in the international system. When the system is "multipolar," each power has the choice of aligning with several of the others. Which will join which is an open question. Eighteenth-century Europe fit this pattern, and in that era occasional reshufflings of the alignments among the great powers did take place.

The second, related variant of the general alliance problem is that of execution. When the alignments in the international system are clear, when there is little room for maneuver, the question that states confront is not which side to fight on but whether to fight at all. It is obvious where the common interests lie. What is in doubt is whether these common interests are sufficiently powerful and intense to be worth making sacrifices and taking risks to defend. At issue is not whether an alliance will be formed but whether its terms will be honored in the moment of truth. This second variant of the problem basic to any alliance is common to "bipolar" international systems, like the one that emerged from the Second World War. Since 1945, there have been only two great powers, around which the lesser states have tended to cluster. There has been less choice, less flexibility, and less prospect for realignment in the bipolar system than in multipolar systems.[24] France's relations with Italy and the Soviet Union in the years between the two world wars revolved around the problem of alliance formation. In French relations with several of the newly formed states of Eastern Europe and with Great Britain in the same period, the issue was whether the terms of the alliances that had been formed would be carried out. The question was one of executing alliance commitments.

Italy was both a plausible and an attractive ally for France. The Italians had fought on the side of the winning coalition in World War I. The two countries had a common interest in preserving postwar Austria, the small core of what had been the much larger Hapsburg Empire, as an independent state rather than seeing it absorbed into greater Germany as many Germans and Austrians wished. An Italian alliance, moreover, would secure France's Mediterranean flank and give the French a bridge to the eastern countries to which they had made commitments. The French generals placed a high value on the Italian army – too high, as its inept performance in Southern Europe in 1940–1 was to demonstrate. In the 1930s Italy was believed in some quarters to be a formidable military power.

Successive French governments therefore tried to form an alliance with Italy, which for most of the interwar period was governed by Mussolini and his Fascists. For a brief period the French seemed

---

[24] The different consequences of bipolar and multipolar systems for the likelihood of war are analyzed in Kenneth N. Waltz, *Theory of International Politics* (Reading, Mass.: Addison-Wesley, 1979), Chap. 8. See also George Liskka, *Nations in Alliance* (Baltimore, Md.: Johns Hopkins University Press, 1962), p. 16.

to have succeeded: In 1934, relations between Germany and Italy were strained and a German move against Austria seemed imminent. Italy sent troops to the Austrian frontier. On January 7, 1935, French Prime Minister Pierre Laval signed a pact with Mussolini promising mutual assistance to protect Austria. In March, Hitler unilaterally declared the abolition of the disarmament clauses of the Versailles Treaty. In response, representatives of Britain, France, and Italy met at Stresa to reaffirm the Locarno accords. They made special mention of the need to preserve the integrity of Austria. The "Stresa front" was widely interpreted as a common stand against Germany.

In fact there was less anti-German solidarity than met the eye, and in any event the Italian invasion of Ethiopia changed the course of Franco-Italian relations. At first the French were disposed to tolerate it. The British, however, were opposed, and the French ultimately joined them in opposition. The rapprochement with Italy thus came to an end. Mussolini gravitated toward Germany. In 1937 he joined the "Anti-Comintern Pact" that Germany and Japan had signed the year before. In May 1939, the formal alliance between Germany and Italy, the so-called Pact of Steel, was concluded. The "Rome–Berlin axis" had little military import for the French. Italy held back when Germany and France went to war in September 1939. By the time Mussolini did declare war, on June 10, 1940, France had already been defeated.[25] The agreements did, however, signify the choice that Mussolini had made. He had chosen Germany, not France.

France's relations with the Soviet Union followed a similar pattern. Like Italy, the Soviet Union was a potential ally. Like Italy, Russia had fought on France's side against Germany during the First World War. The regime in Moscow had reason to fear German designs, as the course of the Second World War would vividly demonstrate. Stalin was wary of Hitler, who never tried to conceal his determination to stamp out Bolshevism everywhere. Whereas the military value of Italy as an ally tended to be overrated in France, the significance of the Soviet Union was underappreciated. In the 1920s the country was convulsed by a civil war. During the

---

[25] Mussolini decided to enter the war in large part because it was evident that France could no longer resist.

purges of the 1930s Stalin liquidated much of the army's high command. Some French military observers considered the Polish forces worthier allies. The skepticism about Soviet military prowess did not blind France to the existence of common interests with the Soviet Union, however, nor prevent the French government from tying to act on them. In May 1935 the Franco-Soviet Mutual Assistance Pact was signed, and the next year the French Chamber of Deputies ratified it. At the same time Stalin authorized European Communist support for anti-Fascist policies. The French Communist Party reversed its previous stance and endorsed rearmament.

The Franco-Soviet Pact was never implemented. Its terms were vague and hedged. It did not codify a firm commitment to mutual defense. It stipulated that the Council of the League of Nations would decide when the conditions for military cooperation had been fulfilled. Despite Soviet wishes, it did not include a military convention.

The Soviet Union, like Italy, had another option: alignment with Germany. In the immediate aftermath of the war and the Bolshevik revolution, with France and the other western powers trying to overthrow or at least isolate the Communist regime, the government in Moscow turned to the Germans. The 1922 Treaty of Rapallo with Germany established military and economic cooperation between the two outcasts of the Paris settlement. Hitler's assumption of power pushed Stalin back toward the west, but in the end the Soviet dictator chose the eastern option, which came to fruition on August 22, 1939, when the Soviet and German foreign ministers, Molotov and Ribbentrop, signed a nonaggression pact. Like Mussolini, Stalin chose the Third Reich over the Third Republic.

The French failures to form alliances with Italy and with the Soviet Union had several common elements. Each involved French domestic politics. "Inside-out" explanations apply to both cases. Although the French Right was unperturbed by the Italian invasion of Ethiopia, the Left opposed the move, and its opposition was an obstacle to good Franco-Italian relations. (Ultimately it was the need to keep in step with Britain that determined French policy.) The Left was, if anything, even more opposed to Italian policy in the Spanish civil war. Mussolini and Hitler supported Franco and his insurgents. The French Left was firm in its support of the

Loyalists. Although Leon Blum's Popular Front government, which was in power when the war broke out, did not send assistance to the Spanish government, it could not conceivably endorse Mussolini's actions.

In the case of the Soviet Union it was the French Right that blocked a full partnership. The Right was suspicious of the Soviet regime, especially in view of its close ties to the French Communists. Still, it was a conservative prime minister, Louis Barthou, who negotiated the Franco-Soviet Pact of 1935. The accord foundered in part on political changes within France. The Left made substantial gains in the next elections, bringing the Popular Front to power. The domestic strength of the Left gave the Right second thoughts about forming an alliance with the foreign patron of the Communists, who were part of the governing coalition. Although right-wing French deputies had generally favored the Franco-Soviet Pact when it was first concluded, in the ratification ballot nine months later, in February 1936, a majority of them voted against it.

There was another feature common to France's failure to secure the help of Italy and of the Soviet Union in its confrontation with Germany. Hitler's success in overturning the Versailles settlement influenced the two powers whose assistance France sought. In the contest between Germany and France it was Germany that was gaining the upper hand. Mussolini was impressed by Hitler's strategic coup in remilitarizing the Rhineland without firing a shot. Stalin could not properly be called an admirer of Hitler, but he certainly took careful note of what happened at Munich in 1938. The outcome of the negotiations among France, Britain, and Germany was a triumph for Hitler. Just as significantly, the French and the British did not include the Soviet Union in the deliberations. Stalin might reasonably have concluded that he could not rely on them. In joining Germany, Italy and the Soviet Union were climbing aboard a bandwagon that gathered momentum as the decade wore on.[26]

---

[26] Waltz argues that states tend to "balance" rather than "bandwagon," that is, to oppose rather than join other states whose power is rising. Waltz, *International Politics*, pp. 125–7. This is true in the long run, and when the ascendant state begins to threaten the independence of others. The Soviet Union did resist

There is yet another reason for the course of both Italian and Soviet policies in the 1930s, a reason rooted in the dynamics of alliance formation under circumstances in which choice is available. France and Germany were in effect bidding for the allegiance of the other two countries. This was literally the case with the Soviet Union: French and British representatives were in Moscow at the moment, in August 1939, when Ribbentrop arrived there to sign the Nazi-Soviet Pact. Germany outbid France for both because the Germans had more to offer. They had more to offer because they, like the Italians and the Soviets and unlike the French, were revisionists. France was committed to preserving the Paris settlement. Germany, Italy, and the Soviet Union believed that they had something to gain by overturning it. All had grievances against the postwar dispensation. Hitler, Mussolini, and Stalin were happy to put an end to the arrangements that the victorious powers had made in 1919 and to take more for themselves.

At the heart of Mussolini's foreign policy was the ambition to expand Italy's influence and imperial control. His aspirations ran parallel to Hitler's. What Germany wanted in the east Mussolini sought to the south – living space. His goal of *spazio vitale* was the equivalent of the German aim of *Lebensraum*. He dreamed of a Mediterranean empire encompassing Southern Europe and North Africa.[27] His efforts to create it began with his assault on Ethiopia in 1936. In 1940, after the fall of France, he launched an attack from Libya toward Egypt. In the Balkans his schemes against Yugoslavia compounded France's difficulties in cooperating with Italy. In 1939 he occupied Albania, a tiny state that was already under Italian influence. In October 1940 came the next step, an attack on Greece. Mussolini even harbored designs on French territory within Europe. When, in November 1938, his foreign minister Ciano referred in a speech in the Chamber of Deputies

Hitler. The other European powers did eventually unite to defeat Napoleon. But it is not necessarily the case in the short term.

[27] This is a major theme of McGregor Knox, *Mussolini Unleashed: 1939–41* (Cambridge University Press, 1982); see pp. 209, 286–9. German and Italian ambitions were partly in conflict, not just over Austria but in the Balkans as well. Mussolini was not pleased when Hitler marched into Rumania in 1940. He attacked Greece in part to avoid being shut out of that part of Europe.

to Italy's "natural aspirations," Fascist deputies rose and chanted "Tunis, Corsica, Nice, Savoy."[28]

Even apart from this most extreme version of Mussolini's aspirations, his ambitions were bound to bring him into conflict with Britain and France. The western powers were the patrons of the status quo in precisely the regions where he sought to expand. They held the strongest positions there, and it was they whom he would have to displace. Both had interests in the Balkans – Britain in Greece, France in Yugoslavia. Both had imperial possessions in North Africa. Both were Mediterranean powers, and neither was willing to concede dominance there to Italy. Mussolini's goals were much more compatible with Hitler's aims. Once the settlement was shattered, each could reckon, Germany and Italy could divide the spoils. So they did. When Hitler annexed Austria, he reserved control of the German-speaking South Tyrol region for Italy. His purpose was to compensate Mussolini for having done nothing to block the annexation; but the gesture also served as a symbol of the two countries' common revisionist ambitions.

The Soviet Union, too, had revisionist goals. Territories that the czars had accumulated over several centuries escaped Russian control in World War I and during the Revolution, although the Bolsheviks had recovered a considerable part of them by the end of the 1920s. The Soviet alliance with Hitler made it possible for the regime in Moscow to expand its holdings. In the wake of the Nazi-Soviet Pact it moved to bring under its sway the Baltic republics of Estonia, Latvia, and Lithuania, which had become independent in 1919. Soviet military bases were installed in 1939. Then, in 1940, the republics were forcibly incorporated into the Soviet Union. In November 1939, Stalin attacked Finland.

Secret clauses of the Nazi-Soviet Pact defined the spheres of influence of the two countries in Eastern Europe. They left open the question of whether Poland would remain independent. When it was clear that the Wehrmacht was conquering Poland, Soviet forces moved in from the east. The Russians and the Germans once again divided it between themselves. This partition of Poland was,

[28] Ibid., pp. 38–9; John Lukacs, *The Last European War* (Garden City, N.Y.: Doubleday, 1976), p. 33.

like the reservation of the South Tyrol for Italy while Germany swallowed Austria, a symbol of the common revisionist aims that had drawn the two revisionist powers together. Germany and the Soviet Union had combined to crush and divide Poland as Germany and Italy had, in a way, divided the formerly independent Austria. (There were notable differences, among them the fact that many Austrians favored what happened to their country; few if any Poles were happy with the fate of theirs.)

The Soviet Union made the greatest gains from the revision of the post–World War I settlement that emerged from World War II. In 1939, however, the Soviet government was not necessarily as eager to destroy the arrangements of 1919 as was Italy; or at least Stalin felt more threatened by Germany than did Mussolini and so was more willing to put aside his ambitions temporarily to check Hitler. It is arguable that Stalin was prepared to forgo his designs in Eastern Europe for a solid alliance with Britain and France. If this contention is accepted, it follows that if the western powers had been more forthcoming the partnership might have been sealed.[29] Without access to the Kremlin's archives there is no way of settling the question; but even assuming that Stalin was interested, the prospects for an alliance with the West foundered on the problem of Soviet revisionism.

The Soviets insisted that a military pact with the West would have to include a provision for the transit of Soviet troops through Poland. The demand was understandable; there was no other way to reach Germany. But the Poles adamantly refused. They were wary of Russian designs to the west. They knew that the Soviet government had not renounced the perennial Russian ambition to dominate in Eastern Europe. They feared, in short, Soviet revisionism, and rightly so, as the events of 1945 and afterward were to prove. France and Britain, as architects of the Paris settlement, were not willing to force the Poles to accede to the Russian terms. So a Franco-Soviet alliance was never truly formed.

In relations with both Italy and the Soviet Union, France was

---

[29] Contrasting views of Stalin's seriousness about an alliance with the western democracies may be found in Jiri Hochman, *The Soviet Union and the Failure of Collective Security* (Ithaca, N.Y.: Cornell University Press, 1985), and Jonathan Haslam, *The Soviet Union and the Search for Collective Security* (New York: St Martin's Press, 1984).

thus the victim of the wider difficulties inherent in alliance formation. When there are several great powers and at least some have the option of choosing which others to join, alignment is decided by a kind of competitive bidding. In the auction for the allegiance of the two powers with some freedom to maneuver, the French were at a disadvantage. They could offer less than the Germans. As usual, the higher bid was accepted.

When the range of choice is narrower, the question that states face is not which power will align with which; that is obvious. Instead, they must decide whether the common interests that underlie the obvious alignments will be strong enough for one country to go to war on behalf of another. At issue is not whether country A will side with country X or Y; its affinity for Y is evident. Rather, what is uncertain is whether A will fight at Y's side against X or remain aloof from the conflict. This problem of alliance execution produces two complementary fears, to which any ally is subject.

One is the fear of abandonment. It arises from the possibility that the ally will stand aside rather than fulfill a commitment to fight when the war actually begins. The other is the fear of entrapment. It stems from the prospect that one ally will entangle another in a quarrel in which the second has no substantial stake. The risk of entrapment is the risk of fighting an unwanted and unnecessary war.[30] The two fears are not necessarily equally distributed within an alliance. When one power is stronger than the other or less exposed to the threat they both face, the one more advantageously placed will be more concerned with entrapment than with abandonment. The weaker party, or the one more directly in the path of the aggressor, will be preoccupied with the danger of abandonment. The weaker party will worry that the alliance will not work. The stronger, more secure ally will worry that it will work, in effect, only too well.[31]

---

[30] On abandonment and entrapment see Michael Mandelbaum, *The Nuclear Revolution: International Politics Before and After Hiroshima* (Cambridge University Press, 1981), pp. 151–2.

[31] The Atlantic Alliance in the post–World War II period exhibited both concerns. The United States, the strongest, most secure member of NATO, generally worried about entrapment. The Western Europeans, who were more directly threatened, on the whole worried that the United States would abandon them. They encouraged the American government to multiply the tokens of its resolve to defend them against an attack from the east. Ibid., pp. 147–66. See also

In the interwar period France was subject to both anxieties. The French made alliances with several of the states that were carved out of the three eastern empires that had been defeated in World War I and had disappeared in its aftermath. Relations with these "successor states" were shaped by French wariness of being entrapped by them in an unwanted or at least premature war with Germany. (The eastern allies themselves worried, with good reason, about being abandoned by France.) France was also aligned, and finally firmly allied, with Great Britain. Of the two it was the British who were in the stronger position; they were less directly exposed to the threat from Germany. French policy toward Britain was driven by the need to avoid abandonment. For their part the British were leery throughout the 1930s of being entrapped by France in another great Continental conflict.

The French wariness of entrapment had its origins in the natural political affinity between France and the successor states of Central and Eastern Europe. The eastern countries owed their boundaries, and in some instances their existence, to the terms of the postwar settlement. Germany, the Soviet Union, and Italy objected to the lines drawn at the Paris Peace Conference. The newly formed or newly enlarged states therefore looked for support to France, the strongest Continental champion of the postwar order. France entered into what amounted to alliances with several of them.

The first of there arrangements came in 1921, when France concluded a treaty with Poland. This initial version of a Franco-Polish alliance was aimed as much at Russia as at Germany, and in 1934 the Poles actually signed an ultimately meaningless non-aggression pact with the Germans; but France and Poland drew closer in the latter half of the decade. The French affiliated themselves with the agreement among Czechoslovakia, Yugoslavia, and Rumania that came to be known as the "Little Entente." The terms of the French accords with these countries varied. None involved firm commitments of long standing. It was only in May 1939 that

Michael Mandelbaum, "The Luck of the President," *America and the World 1985: Foreign Affairs*, 64, no. 3 (1986): 404–6. The same distribution of concerns has been apparent in relations between Israel and the United States. The American side has been wary of being drawn into a conflict in the Middle East. The Israelis have been at pains to avoid losing American support. See Chapter 5, Section IV.

the French army held staff talks with its Polish counterparts, and it conducted no such discussions with Czechoslovakia at any time. Still, the alignments were clear and the common interests underlying them evident.

France did not, however, resist when Germany moved to overturn the European settlement at the expense of its eastern neighbors. The French did not come to the defense of their eastern allies. They stood aside while Germany conquered and occupied them or, in the case of Czechoslovakia, actually agreed to German occupation of part of the country without the need for conquest.

To protect its eastern allies France would have had to mount mobile offensive military operations in order to send help to countries under pressure from Germany or to open another front so that the Germans could not concentrate exclusively on fighting in the east. The French never developed the means to undertake such operations. (While the Rhineland was unprotected, French forces could have moved easily into the western part of Germany, even without special preparations. The German remilitarization of the area in 1936 made the task much more difficult. France never attempted it.) There was a contradiction between France's political goals and its military resources.

The French did go to war for Poland. They declared war on September 3, 1939, two days after the German attack on Poland began and a few hours after Britain had issued a similar declaration. But Poland was the exception that proves the rule. The impetus for offering a binding western guarantee to the Poles and then for declaring war when Germany attacked came from Britain, not France. The British dragged the French along with them, in a reversal of the relationship between the two countries for the entire interwar period until the second half of 1939.[32] Having declared war, moreover, France did nothing to help Poland. The French army stayed behind its lines while its ally was overrun.

Behind France's policy toward its eastern allies lay a wariness of entrapment. Given the choice between war with Germany and the defeat of their allies, the French chose defeat and – temporarily – peace. France's interests were the same as those of the successor states: the preservation of their independence, the integrity of the

[32] See Section IV.

Paris settlement, and the containment of Germany. But the French interest in the independence of Poland, Czechoslovakia, and the other eastern states was not powerful enough for France to fight to defend them. France was unhappy to see the successor states overcome and was itself worse off for their defeat; their armed forces ceased to be available to fight Germany, and with the Nazi–Soviet Pact, Hitler was free to concentrate on the west. Nonetheless, France itself was not fatally compromised by the German victories of 1938 and 1939. If the French could not hope to uphold the postwar settlement in its entirety, they could still hope to defend themselves. That is what they did hope, plan, and attempt to do.

The French did not believe that it was possible to defend themselves successfully without the help of Great Britain. Their supreme consideration throughout the 1930s was the need to ensure that when war came Britain would help to resist Germany. The fear of being abandoned by Britain, and the effort to prevent this, were in large part the basis of French security policy. France had good cause for this concern. On the British side of the Channel the complementary fear of entrapment was very much an influence on the making of foreign policy. It was in fact the combination of the French fear of being abandoned by Britain and the British concern about being dragged into an unwanted conflict that determined western policy toward Germany in the crucial years after Hitler came to power.

IV

As with the successor states of Central and Eastern Europe, France found in Great Britain an obvious partner against Germany. Both countries generally supported the existing order in Europe. Indeed, together they had been largely responsible for shaping it. Each had nothing to gain and a great deal to lose from its destruction. Whereas Germany, Italy, and the Soviet Union were revisionists, Britain, like France and the successor states, was a partisan of the European status quo. Britain was much more important for France than Poland, Yugoslavia, Czechoslovakia, or Rumania. It was much more powerful, and so a much more useful ally.[33]

[33] The United States was potentially as powerful an ally as Britain, proving, in

Britain continued to control the richest and most extensive empire on the planet. London remained the most important financial center in Europe. The French planned for a long war against Germany, in which they would draw upon the resources of their own empire. They hoped to have access as well to the men and material of the British Empire, which had contributed to the Allied effort in the last war. Even to make use of their own overseas possessions, the French needed secure sea lanes, for which good relations with Britain were indispensable. France needed allies and Britain was, all things considered, the logical, plausible, and ultimately indispensable ally. The French therefore made strenuous efforts to cement their ties with Great Britain. They were prepared to sacrifice a great deal to remain on good terms with the British. They ventured nothing that could lessen the chances that when war came Britain would stand at France's side.

As with France and its eastern allies, indeed as with all alliances, Britain and France had interests that were overlapping but not identical. The differences produced the complementary fears of abandonment and entrapment, which in turn shaped the way the two powers dealt with Hitler from the mid-1930s to the second half of 1939. Both were committed to the dispensation of 1919. France, however, was more committed than Britain, more reluctant to change it, and more inclined to see any change as threatening. Ultimately the differences could be traced to geography.

Britain's attention after World War I, as before, was directed not only to Europe but also to the requirements of controlling and managing its large empire. As before the war, Britain's foreign policy was pulled between the requirements of Continental equilibrium and the obligations of empire. The conflict between the two was acute because the cost of policing the empire had risen

fact, during World War II and especially after 1945 to be much more powerful. France recognized the American potential and hoped for eventual assistance from North America, as in World War I. But the French did not count on direct help from across the Atlantic in the short term. The United States could more readily keep its distance from Continental affairs than the British could; North America was separated from Europe by a wide ocean, not a narrow channel. In the 1930s most Americans wished to keep clear of European quarrels. Moreover, American military forces themselves would probably not, in the early stages of a European war, have been of much help to France. The United States had a powerful navy, as did Britain, but only a modest army, and the battle against Germany would take place primarily on land.

steadily. Britain was made poorer by the war, but the empire had grown larger and its inhabitants more restless. As in the past, British security required a balance of power in Europe. As had invariably been the case before 1914, the British wished to sustain the balance at the least cost to themselves. Britain's geopolitical choices came down to strategic and financial questions. The government had to decide where to prepare to fight. There was a limit to how much the British public would pay for defense, and throughout the interwar period the cabinet was persuaded that it could not afford to plan for both European and imperial wars. The decision in turn determined what kind of army Britain would have and where it would be stationed. For most of the period between the two wars the British army had a strictly imperial mission.[34] Similarly, the British fleet was largely committed to the Far East. The British government was therefore well disposed to measures that promised equilibrium in Europe without their having to incur any costs to sustain it.[35]

France's overseas empire was significant as well. But unlike the British, the French could not afford to give higher priority to imperial duties than to European threats. They lived in Europe. Germany was next door. The German threat was immediate, not, as for the British, indirect. Developments on the Continent were more urgent, serious, and potentially dangerous for France than for Britain.

There was another, related difference in the approaches of the two western powers to the 1919 settlement and to Germany. Britain favored German economic recovery and the resumption of Germany's trade and financial connections with the rest of Europe. As the world leader in finance and a country dependent on trade, Britain had much to gain from Germany's return to its prewar economic patterns. As the years after 1945 were to demonstrate,

[34] It was not until after Munich that the British army returned to the idea of fighting on the Continent. Michael Howard, *The Continental Commitment* (London: Temple Smith, 1972), p. 127.

[35] There was another reason that the British were anxious to avoid a Continental conflict. The dominions, which had supplied troops for the 1914–18 war in large numbers, made it clear that they would refuse to do so again. Australia, Canada, and New Zealand's reluctance counted with London. Adamthwaite, *The Making*, p. 70; Howard, *Continental Commitment*, p. 76.

German economic recovery held even greater potential benefits for France. But, again, for reasons ultimately of geography, France saw the prospect of renewed German economic strength principally in political and military terms. A more prosperous Germany might make Britain and France more prosperous; it would also make Germany stronger. France was more concerned with the second consequence than with the first.

These differences made for different views of the postwar settlement. Both Britain and France generally supported it; but on particular issues the French tended to favor harsher terms and stricter enforcement. The British were more sympathetic to German claims that the terms were unfair and ought to be modified.

The difference was a source of friction throughout the interwar period. It began with the drafting of the settlement itself and France's desire to amputate part of Germany and occupy the Rhineland. Britain disagreed on the grounds that such measures were unfair and would sow the seeds of German dissatisfaction with the settlement.[36] France insisted on reparations. Some in the British camp, Lloyd George in particular, were not sure that what the Allies were demanding was either fair or prudent.[37] British doubts about the wisdom of the settlement's economic provisions grew after the Versailles Treaty was signed. John Maynard Keynes wrote a polemic against the settlement in general and the reparations requirements in particular entitled *The Economic Consequences of the Peace*. In it, Keynes argued that Germany could not pay the indemnities without being ruined. It expressed, and itself helped to create, a view that was widely held in Britain. When France occupied the Ruhr, Britain was opposed. The divergence of perspectives on the settlement continued beyond the first half of the 1920s and was not confined to disputes about aspects of the settlement. In 1935, for example, Britain signed a naval treaty with Germany for the purpose of avoiding maritime challenges in Europe in order to concentrate on the Far East; the accord dismayed the French. When Hitler came to power, German demands for revision of the postwar settlement became more dramatic and in-

---

[36] The British prevailed, which did not, of course, reconcile Germany to the Versailles Treaty.

[37] See Chapter 1, pp. 66–7.

sistent. The response of the British was conditioned by their own attitude toward the postwar order, which in turn arose from Britain's own constellation of interests. Complementing the British attitude toward the settlement was a wish to avoid entrapment in a Continental conflict. Britain was therefore strongly disposed to try to satisfy Hitler's demands. The French were much less eager to accommodate him. But they did not want to resist his demands if they would then have to fight alone. They needed to keep in step with the British, to avoid being abandoned. The British preference for modifying the European settlement and the French requirement for harmony with Britain underlay the western powers' policy toward Hitler during the second half of the 1930s, the policy of appeasement.

Appeasement is one of two approaches an alliance may take toward an adversary. An alliance, by itself, is not a security policy. It is a more powerful, less coordinated presence in the international arena than a single sovereign state. It represents a promise that states make to carry out one particular policy, that of fighting a war, together. Once formed, peacetime alliances, like single states, must decide what policies to adopt toward potential adversaries. Singly or together, states may practice policies of resistance, relying on the use or threat of force, or they may choose conciliation, the principal tool of which is diplomacy.[38]

The aim of conciliation, or, as it is sometimes called, appeasement, is to resolve disputes without war. It is a sensible, inexpensive, and therefore attractive method of dealing with adversaries. It was Britain's preference, and so it became British and French policy toward Hitler. The Nazi leader moved to expand his power and the territory he controlled. Britain and France either did nothing to stop him or, as at Munich in 1938, cooperated with him.

The purpose of appeasement from the British standpoint was to satisfy German grievances and thus avoid war. When Hitler came to power, the postwar settlement had already been modified; the reparations issue had been settled, for example. He proceeded to assault what remained. In 1935 he renounced the limits on the

---

[38] No state pursues one of these two broad alternatives to the exclusion of the other. None is entirely conciliatory; all have some means of defense. This basic choice, which all states face, is the subject of Chapter 5. See especially Section I.

German army imposed by the Versailles Treaty; he ordered that it be enlarged and that conscription be resumed. Britain and France did nothing in response. In March 1936 Hitler put German troops into the Rhineland, again in violation of a provision of the treaty. Even beyond its symbolic significance, the measure had adverse strategic consequences for the Western powers. A demilitarized Rhineland had been hostage to France; it lay open to easy French occupation, and so gave the French government leverage over Germany. French forces could quickly penetrate German territory in support of their eastern allies. Once reinforced, the Rhineland became a potential staging area for a German attack on France. The French were alarmed, the British hardly pleased. Neither, however, did anything to stop Hitler, even though several months passed before German forces were strong enough to mount a defense against an Allied assault. On March 12, 1938, came the *Anschluss*, the German annexation of Austria. France was again alarmed, as was the Soviet Union; neither country, nor Britain, took any action. Finally, in September 1938, Britain and France accepted Hitler's demand that part of Czechoslovakia be ceded to Germany. The British government was, with the Third Reich, the principal architect of the arrangements by which Czechoslovakia was partitioned. France was also party to the Munich agreement.[39] The prime minister at the time, Edouard Daladier, joined the British prime minister, Neville Chamberlain, in signing it.

Western acquiescence at each stage seemed sensible to the British, with a few notable exceptions like Winston Churchill. Hitler gave assurances on each occasion that he would demand nothing more, that he would go no farther, that he would be satisfied. On renouncing the military clauses of the Versailles Treaty, for example, he declared support for its territorial provisions. When he sent troops into the Rhineland, he offered to return to the League of Nations and to negotiate nonaggression pacts with his neighbors. There was a strong disposition among the British to believe him. Chamberlain returned from Munich saying that the agreement had ensured "peace in our time."

What Hitler was demanding, moreover, although it always violated the letter or the spirit of the postwar order – or both –

[39] Mussolini attended the Munich conference as well.

invariably seemed reasonable, a way of righting a wrong done to
Germany in the angry aftermath of World War I. Hitler's policies
appeared to continue Stresemann's. The western powers had managed to live with Stresemann; indeed, they had cooperated with
him. The arms limits imposed by Versailles, which Hitler discarded
in 1935, did, after all, discriminate against Germany. German resentment at being denied rights others enjoyed was understandable, it was thought, and could be eliminated if the offending
restrictions were done away with. The same could be said of the
demilitarization of the Rhineland. The union of Austria with Germany seemed simply to be an application of the principle of national
self-determination to the German people. It was, in any event,
immensely popular with the Austrians. Hitler got an enthusiastic
welcome in Vienna in the wake of the *Anschluss*. Similarly, the
part of Czechoslovakia that Hitler received in September 1938 was
heavily populated by German speakers. German grievances
seemed to many in the west legitimate ones. Because they were
legitimate, it was assumed, once they were satisfied Europe would
enjoy tranquility. Appeasement was considered a way of perfecting
the map of the Continent and ensuring the peace.

Appeasement not only appeared to correct the mistakes of the
Paris Peace Conference, it was also a logical expression of Britain's
particular interests. It was a way of coping with the competing
demands of Continent and empire. Since British interests had been
more or less the same for several centuries, appeasement fit
squarely within the tradition of British foreign policy. The British
had practiced a successful policy of appeasement toward all the
other great powers except Germany before World War I and had
tried to conciliate the Germans as well.[40] Chamberlain drew an explicit parallel between Munich and the workings of the nineteenth-
century Concert of Europe.[41]

The British fear of entrapment was also the product of Britain's

---

[40] See Chapter 1, pp. 47–50; Paul Kennedy, "The Tradition of Appeasement in
British Foreign Policy, 1865–1939," in *Strategy and Diplomacy, 1870–1945*
(London: Allen & Unwin, 1983); Martin Gilbert, *The Roots of Appeasement*
(London: Weidenfeld & Nicholson, 1966), p. 97; Adamthwaite, *France and the
Making*, p. 23.

[41] Telford Taylor, *Munich: The Price of Peace* (Garden City, N.Y.: Doubleday,
1979), p. 65.

constellation of interests and thus contributed to the policy of appeasement. Britain had, with France, a common interest in preserving the European settlement and keeping Germany in check. But the British interest was less pressing. Britain was not willing to pay as high a price as France was to preserve it. Had the British been asked, when Hitler came to power, whether they were willing to see the European order overturned, they doubtless would have replied that they were not. But this was not the question that events posed for them. They were asked to yield parts of the settlement in order to preserve the whole. This they were willing to do rather than risk being entrapped in a costly, dangerous, and destructive war – which they were not, in any event, prepared to fight – in order to protect features of a settlement that they had convinced themselves were expendable.[42]

France had a different attitude toward the settlement, toward German objections to it, and toward Hitler's demands for changing it. The French did not believe that the terms set in 1919 were unfair. They were never sanguine that Hitler could be appeased by being given what he was demanding at the moment. Daladier is supposed to have scoffed at the cheering crowds that greeted him on his return from Munich, contemptuous of their belief that peace had been secured.[43] Still, the French were not anxious to fight. They, too, expected war to be costly.

When, between 1935 and 1939, Hitler acted or was threatening to act, and when resistance to Germany was in question, official French attitudes varied – both within each cabinet and from crisis to crisis. France recognized the implications of the remilitarization of the Rhineland, but no one in authority was prepared to try to evict the Germans. There was talk of decisive action. No official wanted to appear weak. But neither the politicians nor the generals were ready to attack. Similarly, the French request for British help in response to the *Anschluss* seems to have been made for the purpose of appearing resolute to France's own domestic audience. The French government did not intend to go to war for Austria. In September 1938, by contrast, a substantial fraction – although

---

[42] On the British army's reluctance to fight in Europe at the time of Munich, see Howard, *Continental Commitment*, pp. 119, 122; on the British reaction to the Rhineland crisis in 1936 see Shirer, *Collapse*, pp. 264, 275.

[43] Young, *In Command*, p. 215; Taylor, *Price of Peace*, p. 336.

not a majority – of the French cabinet was willing to fight to prevent Hitler from swallowing part of Czechoslovakia.[44] It was the reluctance of the British that proved decisive in creating the Munich agreement. Had the French government been willing to act alone it might have taken a stand on behalf of Czechoslovakia, a country with which, unlike Austria, it did have a treaty. The French were not, however, willing to stand alone. Their policy was dominated by the fear of abandonment. A war against Germany without British help seemed a hopeless proposition.

During each episode of appeasement, the French tried to draw closer to Britain.[45] They made it clear at each stage that they were willing to hold back from engaging Germany, to go along with the inaction or the concessions that Britain wanted, in exchange for a firmer British commitment to help defend France. In this sense French policy was ultimately successful. France did receive the guarantee that it had first sought, and believed that it had received, at the end of World War I. Although the terms were not fully worked out until 1940, when the second great European war of the twentieth century began in September 1939 Britain stood at France's side.[46]

The outbreak of war marked the failure of the policy of appeasement. That failure, like France's other failures in the interwar period, was not foreordained; it was not determined by the French position in the international system. Its causes, however, have relevance beyond the French case. Here again, the failure was representative of other national experiences.

The premise of any policy of appeasement is that the party being appeased will be satisfied with the concessions that it receives. If the demands of the country in question are limited, if they can be satisfied by concessions that do not amount to abject surrender, if the recipient country is placated by these concessions, then appeasement can pave the way for cordial relations. Hitler was not satisfied with his gains of 1935, or 1936, or 1938. Successful ap-

---

[44] Shirer, *Collapse*, p. 376; Adamthwaite, *France and the Making*, p. 222; Young, *In Command*, pp. 208–9.

[45] This was a theme of French policy throughout the interwar period. The French signed the Rhineland Pact at Locarno in part because it was the nearest thing to a security guarantee they could get. See p. 88.

[46] Joint war planning began in earnest in March 1939.

peasement requires accurate judgment of the other party's actions. The British judgment of Hitler was wrong. The error of the supposition on which they had been proceeding came into sharp relief six months after Munich. Hitler did what he had assured Chamberlain he would not do: He took over the rest of the Czech provinces of Bohemia and Moravia. He also recognized Slovakia as a separate entity. Hungary took the Carpatho-Ukraine. Czechoslovakia ceased to exist as an independent state. The British public was shocked. Its attitude toward Europe shifted swiftly and emphatically. On March 31, 1939, Britain gave a guarantee of support to Poland and began discussions on military coordination with France. When Hitler attacked Poland at the beginning of September 1939, Britain declared war and France followed.

The British had erred in supposing that Hitler would be satisfied with the concessions they were prepared to make. Indeed, of all the leaders of great powers in the twentieth century Hitler seems, in retrospect, the least likely to have been appeased.[47] If his aims were not utterly without limits – the debate about his ultimate intentions continues among historians[48] – they certainly went far beyond what France and Britain would have regarded as compatible with their security.[49] What he had in mind for Germany and Europe was foreshadowed in his 1925 book *Mein Kampf*. There was a tendency after he came to power to dismiss the book as an expression of the extreme and excessive enthusiasms of a youthful

[47] Indeed, of all the leaders of the modern period only Napoleon can be compared to Hitler in the extent of his ambitions and the determination to pursue them. In one way, moreover, this is unfair to Napoleon. Hitler deliberately caused many more innocent people to be killed. In the wickedness of his policies Hitler bears comparison only to Stalin. Perhaps, on this score, he has no historical parallel at all.

[48] See, e.g., Alan Bullock, "Hitler and the Origins of the Second World War," in Hans W. Gatzke, ed., *European Diplomacy Between the Two World Wars, 1919–1939* (Chicago: Quadrangle books, 1972); Adamthwaite, *The Making*, p. 40; Lukacs, *Last European War*.

[49] Hitler did hope to come to terms with Britain. His terms would certainly have included German mastery of Europe, which would have violated one of the two fundamental precepts of British security policy. If Britain had been willing to accept such terms, a deal might have been struck after June 1940. No doubt Hitler would have given assurances that he would respect Britain's imperial holdings. Just how much such assurances were worth was apparent from his performance in the 1930s, which was one reason (although far from the only reason) that Churchill had no interest in reaching any accord with him.

agitator, which the mature statesman had left behind. On the contrary, it turned out to be a faithful harbinger of the Nazi program.

A policy of appeasement not only may fail to improve the position of the sovereign state or alliance that undertakes it; it may also leave those who practice it in a worse position than they would have been had they never adopted it. A conciliatory approach by one state to another may, rather than make the other less hostile, convince the second power that the first is weak and that the time is right to press harder.[50] This, however, was not the case with Hitler. Appeasement did not create aspirations where none had existed before. They had always been present. Hitler brought with him to the Reichschancellery his guiding ideas – revenge on France, hatred of Jews, expansion to the east. Nor does the appeasement that the western powers practiced seem to have speeded his timetable for conquest and expansion.

Appeasement can have a more modest aim than the resolution of grievances in order to avoid war. It may be intended to stall, to buy time, to postpone a confrontation that seems ultimately unavoidable until it can be undertaken in more favorable circumstances. Some British officials saw the Munich agreement as serving such a tactical purpose. Because it was designed to secure an alliance with Britain, France's policy consistently had this aim.

Whether appeasement served this second purpose, whether it permitted Britain and France to oppose Germany from a stronger position than would have been the case if they had fought earlier, is a question that cannot be answered with any certainly. There is no way of knowing how the war would have turned out if it had begun in 1936 or 1938. It is possible to speculate, however, and a case can be made that the western powers did *not* improve their military prospects by appeasing Germany until 1939, that in fact the French and British position deteriorated as a result of the concessions to Hitler.

Had the British and French taken a stand against Germany in 1938, they could hardly have fared worse than they did in 1940, when Germany overran France in a matter of weeks. And France was obviously in a stronger position toward Germany in at least one important respect before the remilitarization of the Rhineland

[50] The danger of "temptation" of this kind is discussed in Chapter 5, p. 256.

in 1936.[51] As for 1938, it appears in retrospect that the Allies' chances against Germany were better at the time of Munich than the following year. They might have made use of the Czech army. How well it would have fought is difficult to say, but at least Germany could not have concentrated its forces on its western front as it was able to do in 1940. The Germany army had not firmly established plans for the blitzkrieg operations that brought swift victory in May and June 1940.[52] Germany would probably have had to fight a long war, for which it was not economically prepared.[53]

The recognition that appeasement was not the way to cope with Hitler led Britain and France to adopt the other principal self-help security policy that is available to sovereign states: They went to war. In September 1939, the final, disastrous episode in France's twenty-year effort to remain secure commenced.

V

War is the last, most costly, and usually most decisive of the major approaches to security. The war that came in 1939 was not a surprise to the French. They had suspected almost from the moment the Versailles Treaty was signed that they would have to fight Germany again. Their interwar diplomacy was designed to place them in the most favorable possible position from which to meet another German bid for mastery of Europe. Nor did French planning for war begin with the British agreement in 1938 to coordinate the military preparations of the two countries, or even with the rise of Hitler. How to defend the country against Germany was a preoccupation

---

[51] If the French had challenged Germany in March 1936, it is likely that the German forces would have been withdrawn. It is even conceivable that the resulting humiliation would have led to the overthrow of Hitler. Adamthwaite, *The Making*, p. 52. See also "An Exchange on Dominoes," *New York Review of Books*, Mar. 15, 1984, pp. 46–7.

[52] John Mearsheimer, *Conventional Deterrence* (Ithaca, N.Y.: Cornell University Press, 1983), Chap. 4.

[53] Williamson Murray, *The Change in the European Balance of Power, 1938–1939* (Princeton, N.J.: Princeton University Press, 1984), pp. 262–3, 352–3. The conclusion of Murray's book, the most careful study of the issue, is that Germany could *not* have done so well a year earlier. See also Taylor, *Price of Peace*, pp. 986–9, 995.

of the French from the Paris Peace Conference onward. They made many of the basic decisions in the 1920s. They discussed and debated their defense policy within the ranks of the army and in the Chamber of Deputies. They made extensive and costly preparations. Their final effort at remaining secure, however, the one that the French took most seriously, in which they invested the most time, energy, and resources, was in the end, like the others, in vain.

At the beginning of the war, in September 1939, the French army remained in place within France's borders while Hitler's forces conquered Poland. There followed nine months of inactivity, the period from October 1939 to May 1940 known as the "phony war."[54] Then, on May 10, 1940, Germany struck westward. The French believed that the brunt of the attack would come from the north and sent the major part of their defending force into Belgium. Instead, the attack came from the east. German forces moved through the Ardennes forest, crossed the Meuse River, and swept across the center of France. They trapped and routed the main French units. In ten days they had reached the Channel. In the Battle of France the French army was swiftly and decisively beaten. The British evacuated as much as they could save of the expeditionary force they had sent to the Continent, mainly through the port of Dunkirk. The French prime minister, Paul Reynaud, resigned. Marshal Pétain, a hero of the previous war, succeeded him and asked for an armistice on June 17. France's twenty-year effort to remain secure had come to a definitive and disastrous end.

The French defeat was a great and unexpected catastrophe. Like other historical catastrophes, it inspired a search for its causes that continued long after the event. An explanation that relies exclusively on external forces plainly does not fit the facts. The defeat was not a simple consequence of France's position in the international system. Nor can it be deduced from the difference in strength between Germany and France. Germany was indeed the stronger power. In a long war, unless France received assistance and with all other things being equal, Germany was bound to win. But the war of 1940 was a short one. It was much too brief for the German advantages in population and industry to have determined

---

[54] The French term for the period was *drôle de guerre*, the German, *sitzkrieg*.

the outcome. Nor did France fight alone. Britain was a full partner against Germany.

Since the very beginning of the ongoing attempt to determine the reasons for the defeat, explanations invoking features of French society, "inside-out" explanations, have had wide currency. The first and most influential effort to explain the French defeat, one that established a pattern for the many other studies that followed, blamed weaknesses within France itself for the downfall. The distinguished French historian Marc Bloch, who was in uniform in 1940 and was later executed for taking part in the resistance to the Nazis, wrote immediately after the collapse a book called *Strange Defeat*. The disaster, he argued, was the result of "errors for which every citizen was, in part, responsible."[55] He indicted virtually every sector of French society for defects that contributed to the calamity: the high command, the politicians, the workers, the intellectuals, and the country's system of education.

All deserved criticism. There is some validity to this explanation, but not, perhaps, as much as Bloch and those who followed him believed. The French nation did not fail to arm itself adequately before May 1940. The French military did not lack manpower or modern equipment. If anything, the order of battle of the two sides – the number of troops, tanks, artillery pieces, and airplanes that each could put into the field – favored France. Neither in strictly numerical terms nor in the quality of weaponry was the French side at a disadvantage. Successive cabinets during the interwar period had encountered resistance to spending money on defense; but it was not, in the end, the failure to spend enough that doomed France.[56]

Nor did France's troops fail to do their duty on the battlefield. Their morale did not collapse under fire. There were no large-scale mutinies as there had been in the trenches in 1917. If the French soldier of 1940 lacked the extraordinary tenacity that his prede-

---

[55] Bloch, *Strange Defeat*, p. 127.
[56] Barry R. Posen, *The Sources of Military Doctrine: France, Britain, and Germany Between the World Wars* (Ithaca, N.Y.: Cornell University Press, 1984), p. 82; Mearsheimer, *Conventional Deterrence*, p. 100: Robert Alan Doughty, *The Seeds of Disaster: The Development of French Army Doctrine, 1919–1939* (Hamden, Conn.: Archon Books, 1985), p. 183; Marks, *Illusion of Peace*, pp. 139, 141.

cessor had displayed on the western front in the last war, he could not fairly be accused of cowardice or weakness of will. It is true that many troops fled in confusion during the German offensive, but they did so after German units had overrun their positions or had cut off their rear. The French army perhaps fought patchily; but it did fight, and it was not poor battlefield performance by the rank-and-file soldiers that accounts for the outcome of the battle.[57]

The performance of the French high command was scarcely flawless. The army was poorly led. Here an "inside-out" account is relevant to the result of 1940; leadership is ultimately a feature of the society from which it comes. The high command made one great error. It sent the bulk of the defending forces in the wrong direction.[58] And having dispatched their troops in the wrong direction, the French military leadership proceeded to send them too far. In an attempt to reach a defensive position well north of the border between Belgium and France, the French found themselves engaging the German army not along a static front, dug in behind fortifications, as they had made ready to do throughout the interwar period, but in a fast-moving "encounter battle" for which the Germans were better prepared. These errors would have hindered French military efforts under the best of circumstances. They proved fatal, however, for a reason that cannot be traced directly to the singular features of French society.

For all their mistakes, the French might well have managed to stop the German advance if they had been able to fight the kind of war they had been expecting. They had planned and prepared to meet the German attack, stabilize the front, and settle down for a long struggle in which, over time, they could draw on men and material from Britain, from their own empire and that of the British, and perhaps ultimately from the United States. The plan was based on a series of assumptions about the way the battle would proceed and what would and would not work on the battlefield. These

---

[57] The German air attacks had a more serious effect on the French troops than the more familiar kind of artillery bombardment had had on the men in the trenches in World War I. Shirer, *Collapse*, p. 646; For a negative appraisal of the morale of French forces see Lukacs, *Last European War*, pp. 272, 274.

[58] Another error, this one of omission rather than of commission, can also be laid to the high command. Most French combat aircraft never saw action in the spring of 1940. Shirer, *Collapse*, p. 608; Posen, *Military Doctrine*, p. 84.

expectations and assumptions together formed France's military doctrine, its fundamental ideas about how to wage a war. They were the basis for the way France employed its personnel and equipment. They turned out to be wrong.

France was defeated in 1940 not because it was unprepared or because its forces would not fight, but because it was prepared for and did fight the wrong kind of war. The mistakes of military doctrine made the errors of the commanders fatal. The forces and calculations that determined France's military doctrine were those that generally shape the doctrine of any sovereign state. This final cause of France's downfall, therefore, was neither the product of the French position in the international system nor purely the expression of the character of French society and politics. Like the failures of the different forms of collective security and of appeasement, it arose from difficulties inherent in the approach itself, difficulties that therefore have relevance beyond the French case. France was thus the victim of a pitfall to which all states are susceptible.

French military doctrine emphasized defense. There was almost no provision for taking the offense. French military planners did envision ultimately attacking the German positions and moving the line of battle forward, as at the end of World War I, but only in the late stages of a long conflict during most of which the French forces would hold ground, not take it.

The principal method of defense on which France counted was the continuous front. They planned, that is, to defend all along the border, not simply at selected points. They wanted to avoid yielding any territory at all. The French fortified the northeastern part of their border opposite Germany. They built what came to be known as the Maginot Line, which was a series of elaborate trenches and reinforced positions. The frontier directly to the west of the Maginot Line was not fortified: Because it was thickly forested, it was considered impassable by large forces, a natural obstacle to enemy attack. The German attack did, however, proceed through the Ardennes region, along the eastern part of the Belgian border, proving the French planners wrong. The French–Belgian border from the Ardennes to the Channel also remained unfortified. When the Maginot Line was built, Belgium was a French ally. It was presumed that French troops would rush to the defense of the

Belgians if the Germans invaded. In 1936 Belgium declared itself
neutral, but the fortifications were not extended; and the French
did, of course, move into Belgium in 1940 when Germany
attacked.[59]

There was another crucial feature of French military doctrine –
the expectation that the war would be a static one, with the lines
of battle and armies shifting very gradually if at all. The French
command assumed that each side would concentrate its forces and
bombard the other with as much firepower as possible. The pace
of the war would be slow and measured. Battles would be me-
thodical set pieces, with time available for deliberation, the anticipation of the enemy's next moves, and the necessary adjustments.

Germany had a different and of course ultimately more successful
doctrine. It emphasized offense. Germany went on the attack. The
Germans made pivotal use of weapons that had first appeared in
World War I but had not been decisive in that struggle: the tank
and the airplane. France had tanks and airplanes as well, which in
1940 were as numerous and well engineered as Germany's. The
Germans used them in a different way and to much better effect,
however, than the French.

The French weapons were integrated into the army's defensive
battle plans. France's tanks were heavy and not mobile. They were
dispersed among infantry and artillery units, which were expected
to bear the brunt of the fighting.[60] By contrast, the Germans clustered their tanks together in special formations. These panzer units
served as the spearpoint of the German attack. In the campaigns
in the west in 1940 and in the east in 1941, they punctured the
adversary's line and rapidly penetrated deep into its rear, sowing
disruption and confusion. German tanks, with close support from
"dive-bomber" aircraft that served as flying artillery, launched a
swift, devastating attack on the defending French forces in May

---

[59] The French wanted the German attack to come through Belgium, because they
believed it would benefit them in two ways. First, they could fight Germany
on Belgian rather than French territory. Second, a German assault on Belgium
would bring Britain into the war, as they believed had happened in 1914.

[60] The French developed special motorized units, but these were to be employed
to ferry troops to what was expected to be a static front. Judith M. Hughes,
To the Maginot Line: The Politics of French Military Preparation in the 1920s
(Cambridge, Mass.: Harvard University Press, 1971), p. 224.

1940. The offensive had the effect of a drug that strikes the nervous system and so paralyzes the body.

Germany's blitzkrieg tactics defeated France in an astonishingly short time. The speed of the German assault was the key to victory. The French had not reckoned with the sudden rupture of their front. They could not adapt to the pace at which the battle unfolded. Their conception of the relationship between time and space on the battlefield was fatally obsolete. "From the beginning to the end of the war," Marc Bloch wrote in 1940, "the metronome at headquarters was set at too slow a beat."[61]

By the time the French high command recognized what was happening, it was too late. They were not well prepared to cope even if recognition had dawned sooner. Their internal communications were slow. They would have found it difficult to fight the war of movement that would have been required. The French army was not trained to fall back quickly to form new defensive lines once the front was broken or to attack the Germans on the flanks of their blitzkrieg column, where they were most vulnerable. It was not trained to be flexible, but even with greater flexibility the French commanders would have lacked adequate operational reserves.

France's doctrine was suited for a different, more measured war. The faulty preparation of the French was not, however, a simple mistake. It was not the result of incompetence or blunders. It had deep roots. It was sensible, logical, indeed almost inevitable.

Inferiority to Germany in the main categories of military potential imposed a defensive orientation on France. It is a historical axiom of warfare that to be successful the offense must have larger forces than the defense that it confronts. The experience of World War I seemed to vindicate this view: Offensive surges consistently failed, at great cost, in the face of the trenches, barbed wire, and machine guns on both sides. Technology appeared to have compounded the natural advantages of the defense. The French did not believe that they would have a larger army than the Germans, at least not in the early stages of the war. Their first task was to stop the initial German attack. They would wage a long war in which circumstances would gradually turn in their favor. They

[61] Bloch, *Strange Defeat*, p. 43; see also Young, *In Command*, p. 251.

could not afford the "Napoleonic luxury" of fighting beyond their borders, at least not initially.[62]

International political considerations also gave French military thinking a distinctly defensive cast. France's main political aim was, after all, defensive; it was to uphold the existing order in Europe. The French suspected, moreover, that they would get British help in a war only if it were clear that they were the victims of aggression. They had to make sure, therefore, that their military policies were strictly defensive.[63]

France's general commitment to the postwar settlement did not dictate an exclusively defensive military doctrine, however. To the contrary, some capacity for offense was necessary to enforce the settlement's eastern terms. A then-colonel in the French army, Charles de Gaulle, made the point in a 1934 book entitled *Vers l'armée de metier*.[64] He called for the creation of an elite corps of 100,000 men with the training and equipment to make swift offensive strikes beyond France's borders. It was to be a "mechanized system of fire [and] shock."[65] What de Gaulle prescribed had a good deal in common with the panzer units that Germany ultimately assembled. He anticipated some of the techniques of blitzkrieg warfare. Others also advocated the ideas de Gaulle espoused. They made no headway with the French authorities, however. Their ideas encountered opposition from the political Left on the grounds that they would require a separate elite group within the army that might prove politically troublesome.[66] There was a technical military difficulty as well. The manner in which France

---

[62] The phrase was Daladier's. Quoted in Adamthwaite, *France and the Making*, p. 62.

[63] There was another, more narrowly military reason for the French emphasis on defense. Offensive operations were more difficult to execute. They required considerable training to perfect. The French law of conscription provided only a one-year term of service. The high command considered this too short a time to train troops for offensive operations. Doughty, *Seeds of Disaster*, pp. 35, 38–9; Posen, *Military Doctrine*, p. 108.

[64] The English title, oddly, is *The Army of the Future*. A better (and more literal) translation would be "Toward a Professional Army."

[65] Charles de Gaulle, *The Army of the Future* (London: Hutchinson, 1940), p. 93.

[66] The high command did not like the notion of a "two-class" army either. Young, *In Command*, p. 180; Hughes, *Maginot Line*, p. 210.

planned to mobilize its reserves for a major war was incompatible with the establishment of a special striking force. The plans called for breaking up the professional standing army into small groups that would serve as the cores around which the much larger number of reserves would assemble. If the professionals were concentrated in a special mobile force within the larger army, they would not be able to form the skeleton of the mass army. The consequence of this system was that, in response to each challenge from Hitler, France had no military option between doing nothing and full-scale national mobilization. The absence of any intermediate course of action was another cause of French paralysis in the face of Hitler's demarches.[67]

The emphasis in French military doctrine on defending along a continuous front was as deeply rooted and as inherently plausible as the devotion to defense itself. France's industry, which was essential for fighting a modern war, was clustered in the northern part of the country. Much of northern France had been overrun in 1914. The French could not afford to have this happen again; to concede ground in the early stages of the war was to accept an even greater handicap against Germany than France had in the best of circumstances.

The French army did not follow the dictates of its doctrine with strict fidelity when the war began: The French command sent its forces north into Belgium. This maneuver did have its own logic, however. The French intended to establish a defensive line there, stretching, if possible, into the Netherlands. They anticipated that a Belgian front would have three advantages. First, the battle-ground of the war would be removed from France itself, which would thus be spared the destruction that combat would certainly bring. This was a consistent theme in French military planning. Second, if the French forces met the Germans at the point at which they planned to fight, the battle line would be relatively short, so the defenses could be thicker than they would be if the engagement took place on France's borders. Third, the procedure would allow

---

[67] L. Mysyrowicz, *Autopsie d'une defaite: Origines de l'effrondrement militaire français de 1940* (Paris: L'Age d'Homme, 1973), p. 273; Doughty, *Seeds of Disaster*, pp. 21, 37–8.

French forces to join troops from Belgium and the Netherlands, creating a larger and more formidable obstacle to a German advance than the French alone could pose.

By sending their best fighting divisions to the north, the French left themselves without an adequate reserve force to protect the home territory if the Germans broke through from that direction or if, as turned out to be the case, the attack came from elsewhere. This, too, was an error, and not a minor one. It was not necessarily catastrophic, however. Historians of 1940 are given to quoting the dictum of the elder Moltke that a single mistake in the initial deployment of an army cannot be made good during the entire course of the campaign.[68] This has not always been true. France stopped Germany at the eleventh hour, at the Marne, in 1914. The error of sending troops away from the axis of the main German attack might have been corrected. France might have staged a second Marne in 1940, but for the pace at which the German attack proceeded. The French could not shift their troops by rail as fast as the German forces could advance by road.

France's expectation of a slower-moving war was as basic to its doctrine as the commitment to defense and to a continuous front. It, too, was logical. It was based above all on French experience in the last war. After the initial German surge was checked, World War I became a protracted, grinding war of attrition. Between the fall of 1914 and the spring of 1918 the line of division between the two great armies on the western front scarcely moved. The various offensives that the two sides launched, almost all of them costly and futile, were preceded by elaborate preparations over weeks or even months. The war seemed to proceed in a kind of sanguinary slow motion. On the eastern front and in the last months in the west, the armies did move rapidly, but it was the first three and a half years that left the strongest impression. The French assumed that the next war would be fought in the same way. Their planning took place in the shadow of their memory of trench warfare.

Here, again, French security policy was part of a larger, older pattern. Armies perpetually fight the last war. This is often the

[68] Shirer, *Collapse*, p. 606; Alastair Horne, *To Lose a Battle: France, 1940* (Boston: Little, Brown, 1969), p. 517.

subject of retrospective criticism,[69] but it is, after all, the sensible thing to do. War is a grimly empirical enterprise. It is not surprising that those responsible for waging it should base their plans on the most recent experience. On what else would it be prudent to base them? Wars tend to make deep impressions on those who fight them and those who must think about fighting again. Because the stakes are so high, planning tends to be careful and conservative. Flights of imagination, experimentation, and procedures without the weight of accumulated precedent do not recommend themselves to the people charged with defending their fellow citizens.

The proposition can be put in a different way. Modern armies belong to the general family of large organizations. They are structured according to the principle of hierarchy and are characterized by specialization of function. The military is in fact the prototypical organization, the most "organized" of all. Like other organizations, such as private firms and government bureaus, militaries tend to be conservative. They resist outside influences. They prize stability and familiarity. They operate according to set routines – standard operating procedures – from which those who run them do not like to deviate. Organizations display pronounced inertia. They are difficult to change. In military organizations, as in others, innovations are rare; continuity is the norm.[70] French military doctrine during the interwar period conformed to this pattern. It was set soon after World War I and resisted efforts to alter it, efforts that, because of the political and military logic of France's guiding assumptions, were not particularly powerful.

In the twentieth century the technology of war has changed rapidly. Any army that refused to use the latest weapons would soon meet a disagreeable fate. France did adopt the most modern armaments, the tank and the airplane, and the French army did make use of them. But it incorporated them into existing plans. The tank was seen as an instrument of defense, part of the strategy of fighting a long war of attrition, and therefore to be used in a way compatible with familiar routines.

---

[69] Such criticism of the French army is common. Mysyrowicz refers to its "blind attachment to the past." *Autopsie*, p. 39. Bloch makes similar criticisms. *Strange Defeat*, p. 53.

[70] This is a major argument of Posen, *Military Doctrine*; see esp. pp. 38–46.

Germany had a different doctrine, the product of a different set of influences. The German army, which was also a large organization, did manage to introduce several important innovations, which brought victory in 1940. The sources of innovation in Germany were missing in France. The German blitzkrieg, a sharp departure from the World War I pattern of fighting, was the exception that proves the rule.

Germany was naturally attracted to offensive doctrines because it wanted to overthrow rather than maintain the European order. In addition, the Germans needed to win quickly. Although superior when matched against France alone, they could not assume that the French would fight without allies. In fact, they had to plan for a war on two fronts. If they had to fight in the east and the west simultaneously, as in the first war, their resources would be stretched thin and a long conflict would exhaust them. The style of attack of 1914 to 1918, with its emphasis on frontal assaults, was plainly unsuitable. It had proved costly and futile. World War I offered an example of the wrong kind of offensive doctrine.

The traditional alternative to a war of attrition was the flanking maneuver, in which the attacker went around the opposing defenses and encircled its adversary's forces. The enormous size of modern armies of the twentieth century seemed to make this impractical, at least on the front between France and Germany. The defensive line could be extended so far that there remained no room to get around it. The blitzkrieg accomplished the aim of the flanking maneuver by a different method. Instead of going around the enemy's line, the attacker punched a hole in the middle of it, poured its forces through the breach, and fanned out in the rear to disrupt and conquer. It was a way to take the initiative and win quickly and cheaply. The Germans sought and found such a method of fighting. The French, because of their different geopolitical position, did not, nor did they give thought to how to cope with it if it were used against them. They assumed that German plans for the next war would be based on the last one, just as theirs were.

A difference in political aims was not the only reason for the differences in military doctrine between Germany and France. Other pressures for military innovation affected the one but not the other. Organizational change often comes in the wake of failure. The German army had failed: It had lost the last war. Defeat provided a stimulus for reconsidering operational methods. The French, having won, had less impetus to abandon existing procedures. Often change is also imposed from outside an organization. Here, too, the German experience differed from the French. In part because it had lost the last war, the German army had less prestige, political power, and independence from civilian authority than its French counterpart. Hitler took a hand in military affairs. He played an important role in the adoption of the blitzkrieg approach. The French army enjoyed greater independence. Civilians had less influence on its doctrine. The lessons of the last war, if not entirely unchallenged, remained unshaken.

A wide range of factors produced the military strategy that guided France in its war against Germany in 1940: international political goals, domestic pressures, the lessons of the last war, and the inherent conservatism of modern armed forces. These are the determinants of all military doctrines. In the French case they reinforced one another, pushing military planning in the same direction. The doctrine turned out to be inadequate for coping with the attack that Germany mounted. The blitzkrieg triumphed. But it is difficult, in retrospect, to maintain that France *should* have been prepared for Germany's new tactics. As one historian of French military policy in the interwar period has put it:

> For the military leaders to have altered the doctrine and strategy successfully, France would have had to have abandoned or modified profoundly her doctrine of the methodical battle and firepower; relinquished many important resources crucial to fighting a war against Germany; surrendered a significant portion of her territory to the enemy; ended the fragmentation of her High Command; restructured her army solely on an abstract and unproven relation between new technology and concepts of combat; and rejected many of the lessons, traumas, and experiences of 1914–1918.[71]

The sweeping success of the German blitzkrieg came as a surprise, and a shock, to the French. It came as a surprise and a shock to others: Churchill confessed his astonishment at the conse-

---

[71] Doughty, *Seeds of Disaster*, p. 190. "She might have been able to do some of these," he concludes. "To expect her to have accomplished all, however, is perhaps to expect too much." Ibid.

quences of increased mobility on the battlefield.[72] The extraordinarily rapid progress of the panzer units in May 1940 came as a surprise even to the Germans themselves. No sooner had the three divisions commanded by Heinz Guderian crossed the Meuse than the high command ordered him to halt his advance. Had he done so the French would have had more time to organize a counterattack. He argued against stopping and received permission first to widen his bridgehead and then to undertake "strong reconnaissance." He interpreted both instructions liberally, pushed westward, and in a few days reached the Channel.[73]

To say that the blitzkrieg was an innovation that had startling and sweeping effects is to say that it marked a revolution in battlefield operations. It was, in Liddell Hart's words, "one of history's most striking examples of the decisive effect of a new idea."[74] Germany happened to be in a position to take advantage of this new idea; the French were not. France was the victim of the revolution that the blitzkrieg represented, Germany the beneficiary.

The defeat of 1940 was in this sense similar to the fates of the other approaches to security that France adopted in the interwar period. Like the failures to form a world government, a world police force, and a managed balance of power system, like the difficulties that France encountered in getting and keeping allies, and like the failure of the policy of appeasement, the French defeat on the battlefield had its roots in a pitfall inherent in the military approach to security. In this sense France was, again, unhappily representative.

[72] Shirer, *Collapse*, p. 680.
[73] B. H. Liddell Hart, *History of the Second World War* (New York: Putnam, 1970), pp. 72–3.
[74] He continues, "The effect of the idea of deep penetration by independent armored forces proved as decisive as other new ideas had been in earlier history – the use of horses, the long spear, the phalanx, the long-bow, the musket, the gun, the organization of armies in separate and maneuverable divisions. Indeed it proved more immediately decisive." Ibid., p. 66.

3

The United States, 1945–1980

The Natural History of a Great Power

I

World War II was longer, bloodier, and ranged over more of the planet than World War I. It had different consequences for one of the main determinants of the security problem, the distribution of power in the international system. In 1939 six states – Germany, France, Great Britain, Japan, the United States, and the Soviet Union – could be considered great powers;[1] each could conduct an independent foreign policy. By 1945 only two truly retained that status, and one was far more powerful than the other, so powerful as to be in a class by itself. The United States after 1945 is the exemplar of the strong state. The pattern of its international conduct has been characteristic of such states, and its security policies have been shaped by the forces that bear on the strongest members of the international system.

America's strength was in part the result of others' weakness. Germany and Japan had been conquered and occupied. Germany was ultimately divided, and Japan was given a constitution severely limiting the military forces that it could have. France had also been defeated and was included in the victorious coalition in 1945 by the courtesy of the powers that had won the war rather than because of the contribution the Free French forces had made to its outcome.

[1] Italy also considered itself a great power, and the others sometimes treated it as one.

Britain's contribution had been much larger, and the British enjoyed enormous prestige for having stood alone against Hitler for a year. In 1945 it was widely assumed that three great powers would dominate the postwar world. At the summit conferences at Yalta and Potsdam in 1945 the British prime minister, first Churchill, then Clement Atlee, joined the American president, Roosevelt in the first instance, Truman in the second, and the Soviet leader, Joseph Stalin. Britain's prestige masked a sharp decline in its power, which soon became evident. The country had been so weakened by the war that it spent the next decade and a half disencumbering itself of its vast empire.[2]

The Soviet Union was still a great power. It was one of the war's principal winners. Soviet power dominated Europe from a line in Germany west of Berlin to the Ural Mountains and controlled the stretch of Central Asia from the Urals to the Pacific that the czars had subdued and the Bolsheviks had retained. The huge Soviet army patrolled this expanse of territory. The country had earned wide respect for its heroic triumph over Hitler. Pockets of loyal Communists were scattered across Europe and throughout the rest of the world.

But the Soviet Union had paid a high price for victory. It had suffered casualties numbering in the millions, perhaps in the tens of millions. The German advance and retreat had devastated its western districts. The Soviet leaders faced an enormous task of reconstruction. And although they held sway over much of Eurasia, they had no way to project their power farther, beyond the Soviet army's line of advance.

---

[2] Long-term trends that culminated in the outcome of World War II were underway before 1939. Britain had been in decline, as measured by industrial production, since the latter decades of the nineteenth century. France had been in decline, by the same measure, even longer. As for Germany and Japan, their policies of conquest in the 1930s and 1940s arose in part from the belief that to survive as great powers they needed to control resources and territory comparable to those of Russia and the United States, two powers whose borders had expanded to continental dimensions in the nineteenth century. The history of the period since 1945 provides some evidence to support this belief. On national trends in industrial production in the past century and their implications for the distribution of power in the international system see Paul Kennedy, "World War I and the International Power System," *International Security*, no. 1 (1984): 7–40; and Paul Kennedy, *The Rise and Fall of the Great Powers* (New York: Random House, 1988).

The basis of American power, by contrast, had not been damaged by the war. The foundations of the nation's strength had been laid in the previous century. The republic spanned an entire continent, with access to the world's two great oceans. None of its neighbors, indeed no country anywhere in the Americas or anywhere in the world, could challenge the United States. Stalin might well fear that American forces in Europe would push eastward to invade Russia. The United States could not be invaded by any power from any direction. The war had increased American strength dramatically. Power in the international system is relative, so the decline of the other former great powers worked to the advantage of the United States as well as the Soviet Union.

The United States was one of the victorious powers in Europe. At the war's end, its forces were present in Italy, France, and the western part of Germany. America was also the victor in the Pacific war, where Britain had been very much the junior partner from 1942 onward. By September 1945 American forces had retaken the Philippines and occupied Japan, as well as holding many of the strategically situated islands between North America and the Asian mainland. The American navy patrolled the ocean surrounding them untroubled by any rival. The Pacific was as much an "American lake" as the Mediterranean had been a Roman one twenty centuries before. There was a strong American naval presence in the Atlantic and the Mediterranean as well.

Power is not only a matter of military force. It has an economic basis. In the modern era it springs particularly from industrial productivity. In 1945 the American economy towered over all others. The other principal industrial nations – which were, not coincidentally, the great powers of 1939 – had been shattered by war. Especially in Central Europe and Japan, agriculture had been disrupted and factories lay in ruins. Millions of workers were dead or had been displaced. America had suffered dislocations as well, but hardly on the same scale. The war had never touched the continental United States; it had in fact served as a tonic for the American economy. In 1945 an estimated 40 percent of the world's total industrial production came from the United States.

American power had yet another ingredient. The war with Japan had ended with the use of a new weapon, which was vastly more destructive than any previously invented. The weapon drew its explosive power from the energy locked in the heart of matter itself. Only the United States had mastered the technique of making the atomic bomb; in 1945, therefore, there was an American monopoly of the greatest weapon known to humankind.

All this gave the United States an enormous margin of superiority over its neighbors, over the former great powers, and over its future rival. The American advantage over others was comparable to, indeed probably greater than, that of France in the eighteenth century and Great Britain in the nineteenth. The United States after 1945 is as clear an example as is available in the modern period of a strong state.

Strong states, like others, have at their disposal a variety of security policies: collective approaches, alliances, appeasement, and war. Unlike states that are neither strong nor weak, such as France in the interwar period, the strong exhibit a common pattern of international conduct. They expand. They send their soldiers, ships, and public and private agents abroad. They fight wars, guard borders, and administer territories and people of different languages, customs, and beliefs far from their own capitals. They exert influence on foreigners in a variety of ways. The influence is not reciprocal. The strong do to others what others cannot do to them.

So it was with the United States after 1945. American power, American influence, and the American presence abroad expanded dramatically. To be sure, the power and influence of the United States were not confined within its borders before 1945. By 1941 the American republic was already a prominent and privileged member of the international system. Over the course of the nineteenth century the original thirteen colonies of the Atlantic seaboard had annexed the territory between Canada and Mexico all the way to the Pacific Ocean. In the first decade of the twentieth century American power reached farther, to the north, south, and west. The United States dominated the Western Hemisphere. Britain formally conceded American primacy in North America with the Hay–Pauncefote Accord of 1901. American forces intervened several times in the small republics of Central America and in 1898 came into possession of Cuba. The war with Spain in that year also marked the emergence of the United States as a power in the Pacific. One of the spoils of victory was the title to the Philippine archipelago, where American forces consolidated their control by putting down a guerrilla campaign over the next few years. The nation deployed a large Pacific fleet based in the Hawaiian Islands, an American possession 2,400 miles from the west coast of North America.

On the eve of its entry into World War II, then, the United States was both a great power and an imperial power. But it was only one among several, and not the one with the largest presence beyond its borders. The American presence was limited to the Western Hemisphere and the Pacific. In the postwar period it expanded dramatically. Ten years after the war's end there was scarcely a corner of the globe where an American interest was not reflected in some fashion. A detachment of American troops was stationed permanently on the European continent, largely in the western part of Germany, a development unprecedented in peacetime. There was an American military presence on the Asian mainland as well. American influence extended to the Middle East and to Africa, where the United States had hardly counted before 1945.

American expansion followed a pattern common to other countries similarly situated in the international system. The Soviet Union, which was far less powerful than the United States but still much more powerful than its neighbors, also expanded, although not as far. Nor was the expansion of strong states unknown before the second half of the twentieth century. Victorian Britain, the nineteenth-century power whose international position most closely corresponded to that of the United States in the twentieth, also enjoyed a margin of economic and military superiority over others, especially non-European peoples, and similarly extended its reach far beyond the British Isles.[3] Not only in modern states has strength been associated with expansion. There is a family resemblance between the United States, the Soviet Union, and Great Britain, on the one hand, and ancient Rome, on the other. The Romans in their day were also stronger than others. They too dispatched soldiers and governors far from the imperial city.

The influence that strong states have exerted has taken a wide

---

[3] For a further comparison between Britain in the nineteenth century and the United States in the twentieth see Chapter 6, pp. 347–54.

variety of forms, not all of them mutually exclusive: direct and indirect rule, economic exploitation, economic development, the imposition of a particular form of government, the formation of alliances with locally chosen rulers, and integration into a wider economic order. Although both the United States and the Soviet Union expanded after World War II, their presence was received in different ways. Revolts against Soviet dominance occurred in East Germany in 1953, Hungary in 1956, Czechoslovakia in 1968, and Poland in 1980–1. Nothing comparable took place in the western part of Europe, which played host to American forces. A great many people emigrated from the Soviet sphere of influence to countries where the United States was the most important foreign power. Migration in the opposite direction was sparse.

For all the differences among strong states, however, there is a pattern of international conduct that is common to them. Communist or capitalist, ancient or modern, the powerful do tend to expand; the United States after 1945 was no exception to this rule.

This common pattern of expansion raises two questions. First, what accounts for it? Why do the powerful project themselves beyond their borders? Second, what does this pattern have to do with the predicament common to all sovereign states, the security problem? In what sense can the expansion, in all its forms, of the most powerful members of the international system be itself considered a security policy?

The propensity of the strong to expand is one of the central features of the history of international politics. It has been frequently noticed and often accounted for. The explanations have often been of the "inside-out" variety, according to which it is the features of states themselves that drive them beyond their borders.

The impulse for expansion is inherent in all states, it has been suggested. In discussing the international struggle for power in his influential text on international politics, Hans J. Morgenthau refers to "those elemental biopsychological drives by which in turn society is created. The drives to live, to propagate, and to dominate are common to all men." "The tendency to dominate," he continues, "is an element of all human associations, from the family through fraternal and professional associations and local political organizations, to the state." He cites Thucydides: "Of the gods we know and of men we believe that it is a necessary law of their nature that they rule wherever they can."[4]

As a very rough approximation of the behavior of all sovereign states, the assumption of a steady disposition to push outward – the picture of states as "billiard balls" bumping against one another, with the largest having the greatest impact – may be useful. As an explanation of the way strong states behave, however, it is inadequate. It is not, in fact, truly an explanation. The location of the "natural" impulse for expansion has never been specified or persuasively described.

Perhaps the most familiar explanation of international expansion equates it with a particular form of economic organization – capitalism. Lenin, the most influential proponent of this school of analysis, held that the incessant search for enrichment in capitalist countries led to the export of capital, which required political control of the places to which the capital was sent. Capitalism, he argued, gave rise to an irresistible internal impulse to go abroad to conquer and dominate so as to be able to invest and profit. One useful feature of Lenin's theory is that it is specific enough to be tested. Historians and economists have tested it and have found it wanting. Direct political control in the nineteenth century was not necessarily associated with the export of capital. The British did not always expand where they invested, nor did they faithfully invest where they had expanded. Other capitalist states did not expand at all.[5] Expansion by the strong, moreover, is a very old feature of international politics. Full-fledged capitalism is relatively young and therefore does not account for the many episodes of expansion that occurred before it appeared.

Economic motives are not entirely irrelevant to the behavior of strong states. Some have expanded to enrich themselves. The Spanish acquired their holdings in America in the sixteenth and seventeenth centuries for this purpose. (The Spanish conquest of the

---

[4] Hans J. Morgenthau, *Politics Among Nations*, 3d ed. (New York: Knopf, 1965), pp. 33, 34, 35.

[5] See Tony Smith, *The Pattern of Imperialism: The United States, Great Britain, and the Late-Industrializing World since 1815* (Cambridge University Press, 1981), pp. 36–40. On this general subject see also Benjamin J. Cohen, *The Question of Imperialism* (New York: Basic Books, 1973).

New World was as much the work of individual adventurers as of the Spanish Crown.) Strong states, like others, prefer gain to loss in any undertaking. But profit is very far from being the master explanation for the ancient pattern they share.

Expansion does not always pay, and the strong expand even when they know this. Indeed, in the modern period foreign dominance has become less and less profitable. For neither of the two strongest states after 1945, the United States and the Soviet Union, has it been a paying proposition.[6]

The internal political and economic arrangements of strong states have varied. But each strong state has almost invariably been pleased with those arrangements, whatever they have been, and has sought to have others adopt them. The impulse to do so can

---

[6] Stalin stripped the European countries that the Soviet army occupied in 1945, especially the eastern part of Germany, of any assets that had potential benefit for the Soviet Union. In the 1970s, however, the Soviet empire in Central Europe apparently became a net economic liability. The subsidized oil that Moscow had pledged to make available to the other Warsaw Pact countries cost the Soviet Union a good deal, since it could otherwise have been sold on the world market at a considerably higher price. The Soviet dependents and clients beyond Europe, notably Cuba, were a drain on the Soviet economy. (See Charles Wolf et al. *The Cost and Benefits of the Soviet Empire* [Santa Monica, Calif.: Rand, 1986].) They were presumably valued by Moscow for political reasons. The Brezhnev Doctrine, the nearest thing to a charter for Soviet imperialism, arrogated to the Soviet Union the right to enforce political orthodoxy within its camp. Political rather than economic considerations lay behind this Soviet policy.

For the United States, the price of the wars in Korea and Vietnam could hardly have been offset by whatever profit might have accrued from having friendly governments in each place. It might be argued that the United States sent troops abroad to sustain the entire structure of capitalism. This certainly was one general aim of American foreign policy, although not necessarily the principal or decisive one. American forces were stationed mainly where the country's economic interests were greatest, in Western Europe and Japan; but they were not there to enforce free-market economic practices that, if they were removed, would disappear, depriving the United States of the economic benefits of having capitalist systems in these countries. American troops were in place to guard against external attack, not internal revolution. (Here they differed from the Soviet troops in the eastern part of the Continent.) Were the allied countries to assume full responsibility for their own defense, the United States would be able to enjoy the same economic benefits at lower cost. This was therefore the American preference. For the most part, the American troops stationed abroad remained where they were because the popularly chosen governments of the countries where they were stationed wanted them to stay. See also Section V, pp. 185–6.

be called by any one of a number of names: national or imperial or civilizing mission and ideology. A more awkward but accurate term is the "extension of the collective self."[7] It involves the state's wish to spread its domestic characteristics throughout the international system, its desire to make the world like itself. The impulse recurs among the powerful, including the United States after 1945. It is as common as expansion. It is, in fact, a cause of the characteristic expansion of strong states.

The impulse to extend the collective self is not, however, the only or even the principal cause of expansion. A state's desire to make the world over in its own image can reasonably be supposed to be more or less constant. The pattern of strong-state expansion is invariably irregular. The pace and direction of a strong state's expansion cannot be deduced simply from its power, even assuming, as is not the case, that power can be readily measured. "Inside-out" explanations cannot account for the *way* that strong states expand.

The alternative type of explanation, which traces the way states behave in the international system to the features of the system itself, the "outside-in" category, can account for when, where, and why expansion occurs. The strong are not simply pushed outward by their own self-esteem. They are also, and generally in the first instance, pulled beyond their borders by the way the international system is organized and by their own place in it.

The feature of the international system that draws the strong abroad is its peculiar interconnectedness. One thing can lead to another. There is a propensity for international chain reactions to occur. They are not inevitable, but in a system in which the members are in regular contact and in which there is no supreme authority to protect one state from another, there is nothing to prevent them. The outcome of a war far away may not bear directly on the fortunes of a strong state; but the victor may move on to further conquests, drawing closer and closer until the wisdom of earlier resistance becomes painfully clear. Trouble can gather momentum, like a boulder rolling down a

[7] Robert W. Tucker, *Nation or Empire? The Debate over American Foreign Policy* (Baltimore, Md.: Johns Hopkins University Press, 1968), p. 51.

hill. The person standing at the foot of the hill has an interest in what happens at the top.[8]

"If you don't pay attention to the periphery," the American secretary of state Dean Rusk once warned, "the periphery changes. And the first thing you know the periphery is the center. . . . [W]hat happens in one place cannot help but affect what happens in another."[9] The strong have often moved to stabilize the periphery while it is still distant, to stop potentially harmful chain reactions before they come closer. In 1954 President Dwight Eisenhower supplied a vivid metaphor for international chain reactions when he compared the likely consequences of the loss of one of the countries of Indochina to Communist rule to a row of falling dominoes. When the first domino in the row topples the rest follow in inevitable sequence.

The general principle to which the metaphor refers is a permanent feature of relations among sovereign states. Since the possibility of adverse chain reactions arises from the anarchic structure of the international system, the practice of reaching abroad to forestall them is as old as the international anarchy itself. As an explanation of international expansion this "domino principle" is therefore relevant to strong states from ancient Greece to the present, including the United States.

The domino principle also explains the irregular pattern of strong-state expansion. The powerful reach out to pacify the periphery, and extend their influence in doing so, when the periphery is turbulent and seems dangerous. Sometimes, however, it is calm. Troubles arise independently of the policies of strong states that feel obliged to respond to them. The powerful are drawn outward

---

[8] In one of the few passages in *Leviathan* in which Hobbes comments directly on the behavior of states rather than men he makes just this point: "And as small families did then, so now do cities and kingdoms, which are but greater families, for their own security enlarge their dominions upon all pretenses of danger and fear of invasion or assistance that may be given to invaders, and endeavour as much as they can to subdue or weaken their neighbors." Thomas Hobbes, *Leviathan*, ed. by Michael Oakeshott (New York: Collier Books, 1962), pp. 129–30.

[9] Rusk Press Conference, May 4, 1961, *Department of State Bulletin*, 44 (May 22, 1961), p. 763. Quoted in John Lewis Gaddis, *Strategies of Containment: A Critical Appraisal of Postwar American National Security Policy* (New York: Oxford University Press, 1982), p. 202.

by events whose origins they do not control and that do not occur in any predictable pattern.

The policy of preemption, of forestalling challenges, depends on an act of imagination by the strong. The powerful send their forces abroad not so much because of what is occurring at the moment as in anticipation of the possible consequences. They act because of what *could* happen. What they seek to avoid, however, is not purely the product of their imaginations. The dangers are not fantasies. Dominoes can topple; chain reactions do occur.

Nor is this pattern of behavior illogical or beyond the normal range of human conduct. It is simply an effort to establish a margin of safety. It is not unlike the precautions people take in their daily lives. They insure themselves against imaginable but unlikely disasters. They wrap packages with more padding than normal handling would require. They build houses to withstand greater shocks than are expected. They vaccinate their children against diseases that have all but died out. The world operates according to the principle that it is better to be safe than sorry. [10]

Safety never comes without cost. How much safety a person enjoys often depends on how much he or she can afford. The point is relevant to international chain reactions and the policies undertaken to preempt them. Since all sovereign states are part of the anarchic international system, every one of them can anticipate an unfavorable sequence of events that will ultimately place it in direct jeopardy. No particular turn of mind, no special national outlook is required to imagine a chain reaction beginning far away and advancing steadily closer. Each state is therefore equally susceptible to the impulse to extend itself in order to prop up wavering dominoes far from its borders. Only the strong, however, can act on this impulse. [11] It is the capacity of the strong to act in order to

---

[10] Another example is the Jewish custom of "building a fence around the law" – taking extraordinary precautions to avoid violating religious precepts. It is obligatory, for example, to refrain from work on the Sabbath, which begins when the sun sets on Friday. The time of the sunset is known in advance. Nonetheless, some observant Jews stop working an hour, or two, or even three before the designated time.

[11] This is also true of collective self-extension. Lesser states may be well pleased with their own internal arrangements, but they do not have the means to export

preempt events far away that distinguishes their international conduct from that of other states.

Taking preemptive measures to keep a row of political and military dominoes from toppling qualifies as a security policy in the sense that its motive is defensive.[12] To the world, such policies appear offensive. But strong states that are drawn abroad by unrest far away often do sense a genuine, if not a direct, threat. They are trying to protect themselves. Expansion is the byproduct, not the main purpose, of acting to reinforce shaky dominoes.

There is another sense in which the preemption in which strong states engage is a security policy. Preemption arises from the properties of the international system itself, the organizing principle of which is the source of the security problem. Anarchy makes chain reactions possible. The strength of a few states at different periods in the history of the system – and strength is also a property of the system because it is relative, having no meaning in absolute terms – enables those states to expand in order to forestall them. Preemptive expansion, the pattern of international conduct of the strong, is thus a product of the structure of the international system and a particular distribution of power within it.

Strong states can be usefully compared to firms that hold monopoly positions in markets. They are driven to expand, among other reasons, by the fear that a competitor may appear, gain a foothold, and increase its share of the market until the former monopolist is gravely injured. It is, again, the competitive environment that provides the incentive for expansion. But there is almost never a pure monopoly in any market in which one firm stands alone with no prospect of entry by others and no way for consumers either to forgo or to find a substitute for the product the dominant firm sells. There is almost always some potential or

---

them. Weak states generally try to spread their ideologies, if at all, by example rather than by force of arms.

[12] See George Liska, *Career of Empire: America and Imperial Expansion over Land and Sea* (Baltimore, Md.: Johns Hopkins University Press, 1978), pp. 4, 8. To act preemptively against a perceived threat is not the only reason that strong states expand. Preemption can complement other motives. A strong state may prize a foreign territory for its riches, for example, but once having acquired it worry that neighboring lands might be used as a base from which to assault the valuable possession.

actual competition with which a firm, no matter how powerful it is, has to contend.

Similarly, in the international system there has never been a single omnipotent state free from challenge. There has always been some source of countervailing power. Indeed, it is the counter-vailing power, the region or state or political movement outside the control of the powerful and so able to resist it, that makes the danger of a chain reaction plausible. A row of dominoes looks precarious when there is a force at the other end prepared to give it a push.

Even when its economic and military margin of superiority over others was at its zenith, the United States did not expand its in-fluence everywhere. The Soviet Union and the part of Europe that its armies had occupied by the spring of 1945 remained outside the American reach. The American government disliked Soviet imperial control at the center of Europe but never seriously chal-lenged it. The United States saw the Soviet Union as a challenge to its positions: It was the Soviet Union, its empire, and its allies that made the specter of dangerous chain reactions vivid. The American fear of falling dominoes and the consequent inclination to go abroad to steady them increased as the Soviet Union and its bloc seemed more likely to push outward.

The extent to which strong states expand depends in part, there-fore, on the power of the other states and groups they encounter to stop them.[13] It is the product of two opposing forces. But it is more than that. Expansion is discretionary for the mighty. How far abroad they go also depends on their disposition to expand. The language of economics is more appropriate here than the vocabulary of physics: A strong state's progress depends on both the cost of expansion and its willingness to pay.

The United States could have pushed Russia out of Central and Eastern Europe and perhaps even brought down the Communist regime in Moscow in 1945, or for a few years thereafter, if it had mobilized its resources and waged war with the same determination against the Soviet Union as it had fought against Germany. The cost would have been high, perhaps much higher than the price

---

[13] For a fuller discussion of the limits of expansion see Robert Gilpin, *War and Change in World Politics* (Cambridge University Press, 1981), pp. 146–8.

America had had to pay to defeat Germany and Japan. The United States never seriously considered paying it.[14] Willingness to pay depends on a state's domestic arrangements. It depends on the government's ability to muster its internal resources to propel itself abroad.[15]

Although strong states tend to expand, they do not expand in identical fashion. The direction and timing of their expansion in response to the fear of falling dominoes are shaped by the unpredictable outbreaks of threatening events beyond their borders. How far they expand their power, influence, and presence is determined by these external episodes and by their own particular domestic arrangements.

The security perimeters of the most powerful members of the international system are not fixed; nor do they move in only one direction. When countervailing forces are powerful enough, when the costs of sustaining the positions that the strong have staked out become sufficiently high, the perimeter contracts. This is another way in which the security policies of the strong differ from those of other states. Security for most countries involves assembling the resources necessary for self-defense. Security policy is the effort to do what plainly has to be done. Ends determine means. For strong states, means determine ends.[16] In security affairs, lesser states inhabit the realm of necessity; the strong live in a universe of discretion. For ordinary states security is an exercise in execution; for the strong it is a matter of definition.

The American definition of security after 1945 shifted back and forth. It expanded in two quantum leaps within five years of the end of World War II in response to the fear of toppling dominoes. It contracted modestly as a result of the war in Vietnam but expanded again, also very modestly, within a decade – again to forestall anticipated chain reactions far away. The United States therefore followed a pattern common to other, similarly situated

[14] There was no question of paying this price for most Americans in 1945, because they believed that the wartime cooperation with the Soviet Union could continue in peacetime and that the United Nations would resolve international disputes. But both illusions were dispelled well before the Soviet acquisition of nuclear weapons made an American attack so expensive as to be unthinkable.

[15] Gilpin, *War and Change*, pp. 96–8, 154.

[16] Tucker, *Nation or Empire?* pp. 45–6.

powers. That pattern, the security policy of the United States in the thirty-five years after 1945, is part of what Robert W. Tucker has called the "natural history" of great powers.[17]

II

The forces that bear on strong states – the fear of falling dominoes and the wish to spread their domestic arrangements to other countries – began to extend the security perimeter of the United States two years after the end of World War II. Together they created the first postwar definition of American security.

American expectations for the postwar world began with the assumption that the United States would demobilize and that life would return to normal for the millions whom the war had touched in one way or another. An international organization, the United Nations, had been established, which Americans hoped would keep the peace. It was to be a stronger version of the League of Nations. This time the United States would take part. American officials were aware that relations with the Soviet Union would be crucial in the postwar era. They hoped that the partnership against Hitler, or at least cordial relations, would continue.

The United States did begin to demobilize. The United Nations, however, proved to be of little use in keeping the peace. The policies of the two strongest powers counted for much more than the activities of the international organization, and relations between the United States and the Soviet Union deteriorated sharply. The American administration came to believe that Stalin was bent on conquest and expansion even beyond the lines that he had reached in 1945. The United States decided to resist him. The decisions about how and where to resist created the first American definition of security in 1947.

In that year a civil war was underway in Greece between Communist insurgents and a government supported by Great Britain. In February the British notified Washington that they could not afford to continue their aid. A Communist victory seemed imminent. The Americans decided to intervene. In May, President Harry Truman went before Congress to ask approval of a program

[17] Ibid., p. 51.

of aid to Greece and Turkey to thwart the Communist forces. "I believe that it must be the policy of the United States," he said, "to support free people who are resisting attempted subjugation by armed minorities or by outside pressures."[18] The policy came to be called the Truman Doctrine. In the same year, the European Recovery Program was launched. Through grants and low-interest loans it provided capital on a large scale to the countries in Western Europe to help them revive their economies, which the war had shattered. First proposed in a speech at Harvard University by Secretary of State George C. Marshall, the program came to be known as the Marshall Plan.

These two initiatives and the policies that followed from them constituted the first postwar definition of American security. It had a particular geographic focus. It specified Western Europe as the area whose fate was crucial for the United States. Western and Soviet forces had met in the middle of Europe in the spring of 1945. The line between them became the border between the two parts of a divided continent. This was the line, in Churchill's often quoted phrase, "from Stettin in the Baltic to Trieste in the Adriatic" along which an "iron curtain" had descended. Keeping the part of Europe that lay west of that line free of Communist control came, in 1947, to be defined as a necessary condition for American security.

The Americans saw a political threat to Western Europe. They worried that economic dislocation and social chaos there would enable indigenous Communist parties to take power. The Marshall Plan, rather than the North Atlantic Treaty Organization – which was not formed until July 1949 – was the centerpiece of American policy in Europe.[19] The American aim in 1947 was to encourage the consolidation of liberal political institutions in Western Europe and to warn the Soviets that the United States took an active

---

[18] Quoted in John Lewis Gaddis, *The United States and the Origins of the Cold War, 1941–1947* (New York: Columbia University Press, 1972), p. 351. The Truman Doctrine is discussed on pp. 346–52.

[19] American forces were never entirely withdrawn from Europe, and the Berlin blockade of 1948 certainly had military overtones. Nonetheless, the United States was not prepared to fight on the Continent, and its European policy from 1947 to 1950 was mainly, if not exclusively, an economic one.

interest in the region's fate. Washington was not bent on offsetting Soviet military forces on the Continent.

Official Washington began to suspect the Soviet Union of having aggressive designs on Europe even before the announcement of the end of British aid to Greece. A series of events, of which the Greek civil war was by no means the first, convinced Americans of the Soviet threat. The forcible imposition of a Communist regime in Poland and the Soviet rejection of the Baruch Plan for placing the newly harnessed force of atomic energy under the jurisdiction of an international authority preceded it, as did the Soviets' demand for a share of control over the Dardanelles and their grudging withdrawal, after American prodding, from the northern part of Iran. Even as American wariness of the Soviet Union grew, however, the dismantling of the American war machine continued. The anticipation of the imminent collapse of anti-Communist forces in Greece was required to galvanize first the American government and then the public. It was in response to the Greek crisis that the American consensus on the dangers to the nation's security was recast and new measures deemed necessary to protect it were adopted.

Underlying American policy in Europe in 1947 was the fear of falling dominoes. The United States supported anti-Communist governments to forestall an unfavorable chain reaction. When the British announced their intention to withdraw from Greece, the State Department worried that a Communist victory there would push Iran and Turkey, and perhaps even France and Italy, as well as Greece into the Soviet orbit. Dominoes would topple, they feared, in both the Near East and Western Europe. In appealing to a group of Congressmen to support the Truman administration's proposal to assist the Greek government, Under Secretary of State Dean Acheson used a different but equally vivid metaphor – contagion. In his memoirs he recalled what he said:

> In the last eighteen months, I said, Soviet pressure on the Straits, on Iran, and on northern Greece had brought the Balkans to the point where a highly possible Soviet breakthrough might open three continents to Soviet penetration. Like apples in a barrel infected by one rotten one, the corruption of Greece would infect Iran and all to the east. It would also carry infection to Africa

through Asia Minor and Egypt, and to Europe through Italy and France.[20]

The president himself invoked the specter of a chain reaction:

> It is necessary only to glance at a map to realize that the survival and integrity of the Greek nation are of grave importance in a much wider situation. If Greece should fall under the control of an armed minority the effect upon its neighbor, Turkey, would be immediate and serious. Confusion and disorder might well spread throughout the entire Middle East. Moreover, the disappearance of Greece as an independent state would have a profound effect upon those countries in Europe whose peoples are struggling against great difficulties to maintain their freedom.[21]

He offered the same justification for the economic assistance to Western Europe:

> We'll either have to provide a program of interim relief aid until the Marshall program gets going, or the governments of France and Italy will fall, Austria too, and for all practical purposes Europe will be Communist.[22]

The first definition of security followed a previous American pattern. Twice before 1947, in both World War I and World War II, the United States had intervened in Europe to keep a single power – Germany in both cases – from achieving primacy on the Continent. Through the first half of 1950, the emphasis of the postwar American security policy in Europe was economic. This, too, followed the pattern of the past. Only after initially making clear its political sympathies and then sending economic assistance and military supplies to the countries with which it sympathized did the United States become a full-fledged combatant in the two world wars.

The purpose of both previous interventions had been the forestalling of an adverse chain reaction.[23] Had Germany become the

---

[20] Dean Acheson, *Present at the Creation: My Years in the State Department* (New York: Norton, 1969), p. 219.

[21] Quoted in Smith, *Imperialism*, p. 194.

[22] Quoted in Daniel Yergin, *Shattered Peace: The Origins of the Cold War and the National Security State* (Boston: Houghton Mifflin, 1977), p. 328.

[23] Each was also undertaken to defend democracy, a goal that received major public emphasis in 1947 as well. See p. 152.

master of Europe it could have used the Continent as a base from which to challenge American maritime interests and perhaps, ultimately, to assault the United States itself.

American administrations from the early postwar years through the next two decades bore the recent past in mind. What most impressed them was not what their country had done in the 1940s but what Britain and France had failed to do in the 1930s. The two European powers had failed to respond quickly enough to a disastrous sequence of events. They had let Hitler go too far. Their mistaken policy of appeasement had allowed him to gather so much strength that he almost succeeded in bringing the entire continent under his control and did succeed in conquering France and isolating Britain. Had they acted when he renounced the demilitarization clauses of the Versailles Treaty, or marched into the Rhineland, or annexed Austria, or partitioned Czechoslovakia, the western powers might have stopped him at tolerable cost.[24] Instead, because of their timidity and delay, a massive, ruinous, six-year war was required to bring him down.

In the postwar political vocabulary of the West, appeasement became a term of abuse. It came to stand for a craven, willful disregard for the plain facts of international life. The experience of the 1930s, in the American view, demonstrated that a state ignored the peculiar interconnectedness of the international system at its peril.

Simple observation of the character of the system suggests that dangerous chain reactions are possible. The experience of the 1930s convinced American officials that such unfavorable sequences were not just possible but likely if allowed to proceed unchecked. The impetus for the expansion of the American presence to Europe in order to keep the western part of the continent from falling under Communist control came not only from the imaginations but also from the memories of those in charge of American policy. A fool, it is said, learns from experience, whereas a wise person learns from other people's experience. In moving to stop the European dominoes from toppling, the United States was influenced by what it took to be the pertinent and baleful British and French experience with Nazi Germany.

[24] On this subject see Chapter 2, Section IV.

What came to be called the "Munich analogy" – the application of the perceived lessons of the 1930s, especially the surrender of part of Czechoslovakia to Hitler at Munich in 1938, to the problems of the postwar period – may not have been accurate in all or even in most details. The differences between Stalin in 1947 and Hitler in 1933 may have been more important than the similarities. It is open to question whether the imposition of Communist rule in Eastern Europe in the 1940s would have threatened France, or the Communist attack on Indochina in the 1960s and 1970s would ultimately have menaced Japan, if the United States had not responded in either case. But the Munich analogy did rest on an incontrovertible truth. The international system was the same after World War II as before in at least one important respect: It remained anarchic. Chain reactions, of the sort that Hitler had begun in 1934 and that had ended only after a long, bloody, bitter decade, were still eminently possible.

The three American interventions in European affairs in the twentieth century followed not only an American but a British pattern. Great Britain had played the part of "offshore balancer" on the Continent well before the United States assumed the role. The practice was the core of Britain's traditional balance of power policy. London threw its weight on the scales of European politics when they tilted too far in one direction – that is, when one country, like Napoleon's France, became too powerful for Britain's comfort.[25] The balance of power policy was based on the fear of a dangerous chain reaction. Britain sought to keep the Continent out of the hands of a single state, lest, once having united it, the hegemonic power would turn its attention to the British Isles. Napoleon's "continental system" and Hitler's abortive plan for a cross-Channel invasion, "Operation Sea Lion," demonstrated that Britain's fears were not groundless.

The domino principle has had relevance beyond the European balance of power. It was chiefly responsible for British expansion in Africa in the latter part of the nineteenth century. It is testimony to the power of the fear of adverse chain reactions that it drew

---

[25] See Chapter 1, pp. 15–16. There is a further parallel between the American and British European policies. Both countries preferred to intervene indirectly, through financial support of particular Continental powers. Dispatching their own troops to fight in Europe was for both a last resort.

Britain into governing part of that continent despite the pro-nounced disinclination of the government in London for imperial rule there, in the face, in fact, of a widely held conviction that Africa was simply not worth having.[26]

In the nineteenth century the heart of the British Empire was India. Its wealth, size, and location made the Indian subcontinent the key to the British position in the world.[27] Maritime commu-

---

[26] The interpretation that follows is taken from Ronald Robinson and John Gallagher with Alice Denny, *Africa and the Victorians: The Climax of Imperialism* (New York: Doubleday, 1968; first published, 1961). See, e.g., pp. 7–8, 11, 14–15, 16, 18, 463.

[27] Ibid., pp. 11–13. Control of India was not necessary for the physical safety of the British Isles in the way that avoiding the dominance of a single power in Europe was. Distance did, in the end, make a difference. When forced to choose, in 1914 and in 1939, the British threw their resources into the support of their allies on the Continent rather than husbanding them for imperial defense and staying aloof from the quarrels between France and Germany. After the second war, of course, Britain gave up India and virtually all of its other imperial possessions without imperiling the independence of the home islands themselves.

The importance of India to Britain before 1947 is similar to the significance of Western Europe for the United States after 1945. As with Britain and India, the loss of Western Europe to a hostile power would not have jeopardized the physical safety of the North American continent. In the nuclear age, neither the Soviet Union nor any other power could launch a successful invasion of the United States. Nuclear weapons secure the integrity of the home territory of their possessors in a way that no other armaments ever have (see Chapter 4, pp. 246–9). Its commitment to Europe made the United States in some ways *less* secure than it would have been in isolation from the politics of the Continent. The chief threat to American safety came not from an amphibious assault on the east or west coasts or an overland attack from Canada or Mexico, but rather from intercontinental aerial bombardment by the Soviet Union. A Soviet attack, insofar as it was likely at all, was likely to arise from a Soviet–American conflict begun elsewhere. Europe was the most plausible location for such a conflict. Thus, while the British and American interventions on the Continent before 1945 followed the logic of the domino principle, and so could be seen as making an attack on the homeland less likely, the American commitment to Europe after 1945, or at least after the mid-1960s, when the Soviet Union had developed a full-fledged nuclear arsenal, arguably *increased* the chances of damage to the United States itself. Europe was, after all, the great stake in the geopolitical contest between the two great nuclear rivals. If the United States gave up its claim to that stake, little would remain to fight about (see Tucker, *Nation or Empire?* pp. 149–50).

Without congenial governments in Western Europe, however, the world would have been a very different and altogether less comfortable place for the United States. The loss of the western half of the Continent would have drastically reduced the American role in the world. The global position of the United

nications between the subcontinent and the home islands formed a kind of lifeline for the empire. Africa drew its importance from the fact that that line ran along its coasts. The Suez Canal and the Cape were crucial points on the sea routes between the two citadels of British power. The African continent was significant not for what it was but for where it was. Its location was significant enough to provoke a series of events that brought much of it under British rule.[28]

The Suez Canal ran across Egypt's northern border. The British had no interest in ruling Egypt themselves. They simply wanted to keep it out of unfriendly hands so as to preserve their own unimpeded access to the passage between the Mediterranean and the Indian Ocean. But in 1882 the indigenous government in Cairo collapsed. The British tried to prop it up or persuade other European powers to join in stabilizing it. They did not want to intervene alone; indeed, they did not want to intervene at all if they could avoid it. They feared, however, that if nothing were done the French would step in, putting the Suez Canal in the grasp of a rival European power and thus endangering India. They feared, that is, that the disintegration of local rule would start an unfavorable chain reaction. They moved to prevent it by assuming control of Egypt themselves.[29]

Turbulence at the periphery of the British security frontier, which had local causes, provoked preemptive expansion. The British went farther. Having taken control of Egypt, they had to protect

States has depended on Europe since 1945. This is essentially what the loss of India meant for Great Britain. It marked the end (or the beginning of the end) of Britain's status as a great world power.

In one way, Europe has been more important for the United States than India was for the British. Although Britain ceased to be a strong state after 1945, the world remained a relatively hospitable place because the United States sustained the kind of international order that British power had promoted. The United States assumed some of the military burdens and economic duties that Britain had undertaken in the nineteenth century and through the first four decades of the twentieth (see Chapter 6, pp. 347–54). If the United States had faltered, there was no plausible successor to step into its shoes.

[28] In the scramble for Africa in the 1880s France, Germany, and Portugal also acquired parts of that continent.

[29] "The security of the routes to the East was the one interest with which British cabinets could not afford to gamble. It was the *sine qua non* of the British movement in Egypt." Robinson and Gallagher, *Africa and the Victorians*, p. 159; see also pp. 84, 97, 100, 116, 157–8.

it. They felt compelled to secure the neighboring Nile Valley and the territories to the south and east between Lake Victoria and Lake Tanganyika. For the sake of Egypt, Britain ultimately came into possession of a large part of East Africa, including Uganda, Kenya, and the Sudan.

The same rationale drew the British into the internal affairs of South Africa. The southern tip of the continent commanded the Cape route between Europe and the east. When it appeared that the descendants of the seventeenth-century Dutch settlers, who were not considered reliable friends of Britain (and who were in fact thought to be potential allies of Germany), would consolidate their power there, the government in London moved to stop them. The result was the Boer War and the preemptive expansion of the British Empire to an area not regarded as important or valuable itself in order to forestall a development inimical to an interest that London *did* deem supremely important.

Developments on the border of the sphere of security that the British had defined for themselves drew them outward. Their motive in Africa was "essentially defensive and strategic."[30] India was vital to Britain; therefore, the route to India was vital; therefore, Egypt and South Africa, which sat astride this route, were important; therefore, the adjacent territories mattered – the British had to take an active interest in how they were governed and by whom. Britain expanded into Africa in the latter part of the nineteenth century to steady swaying dominoes. Robinson and Gallagher use another, similar metaphor: "The Mediterranean and Indian interest, like a driving wheel in some vast machine, was now engaging the lesser wheels of eastern-central Africa and connecting them one by one to its own workings."[31]

The domino principle is not a recent feature of international politics. It was in effect centuries before the heyday of the British Empire. It was partly responsible for the expansion of ancient Rome. The anticipation of an adverse chain reaction was one of the causes of the Punic Wars of the third and second centuries B.C. The Romans sought to control southern Italy and Sicily to prevent Carthage from establishing itself where it could threaten the im-

[30] Ibid., p. 472.
[31] Ibid., p. 289.

perial city. They expanded into Greece and Egypt to preempt Macedonia and Syria, which might otherwise, they feared, exclude them from the eastern Mediterranean. The Romans moved into Northern and Eastern Europe in the same fashion. They went to war for territories whose importance, like Africa for Victorian England, lay in their location. Armenia was situated between the borders of the empire and those of a powerful rival, Parthia. Rome conquered Armenia to keep Parthia from doing so. The purpose of the earlier Rhineland campaigns had been the same: to erect barriers to Rome's enemies at a distance from the boundaries of the empire itself. The same rationale underlay the conquest of Dacia, which was situated between the Danube and the Carpathians.[32]

The specter of dominoes ultimately crashing across the ocean to North America was not the only reason that the United States intervened in Europe in 1947. The impulse for collective self-extension was also at work. The Americans wanted to preserve and strengthen the European political systems that were similar to their own. Truman portrayed the Soviet threat as a conflict "between alternative ways of life":

> One way of life is based upon the will of the majority and is distinguished by free institutions, representative government, free elections, guarantees of individual liberty, freedom of speech and religion, and freedom from political oppression. The second way of life is based upon the will of a minority forcibly imposed upon the majority. It relies upon terror and oppression, a controlled press and radio, fixed elections, and the suppression of personal freedoms.[33]

The American commitment to Western Europe was a way of ensuring that civil liberties and popular sovereignty continued to flourish there, just as they did in the United States.

Since the Truman administration was seeking to preserve rather than install congenial political systems, in its public discussions of

---

[32] Rome exercised various degrees of influence over these peripheral territories but often did not govern them directly or tax their people. See Edward Luttwak, *The Grand Strategy of the Roman Empire: From the First Century A.D. to the Third* (Baltimore, Md.: Johns Hopkins University Press, 1976), pp. 22–6, 53–4, 101, 110.

[33] Quoted in Gaddis, *Origins of the Cold War*, p. 351.

the policies to this end it emphasized the Soviet threat to democracy. American efforts at extension of the collective self were cast in terms of what Americans opposed. Anticommunism was the postwar American version of the tendency of strong states to try to make the world over in their own image. It was the international mission, arising from domestic arrangements, particular to the United States. Preventing the imposition of alien and opposed beliefs and institutions is simply another way of promoting congenial, familiar, indigenous ones.

The American impulse for collective self-extension had deep roots. The early European settlers in North America, the Puritans, sought to establish ideal communities in the wilderness that would stand as beacons of godliness to the rest of the world.

One of their leaders, John Winthrop, spoke of his community as a shining city on a hill, to which all could turn for inspiration. The tradition of America as the exception to the ills, mistakes, and conflicts of the Old World and therefore an example to others became a powerful one in the nation's history, a tradition renewed by successive waves of immigrants from Europe. Still, the conviction that they had a worthy civic culture to offer others was not peculiar to Americans. The Victorians believed that it was their duty to spread the blessings of their own civilization to the rest of the world, a belief that encouraged the expansion of their empire. The Romans, too, considered their own rule a great source of benefit to those who came under it. American exceptionalism is not, perhaps, historically exceptional. But if the American impulse for collective self-extension after 1945 was not necessarily deeper or more potent than that of other strong states at different moments in international history, it was certainly no weaker.

The protection of democracy had a particular appeal to Americans in 1947 because they had just fought a great war in its defense. In its ideological aims the Cold War was a continuation of World War II. American leaders stressed these aims. They wanted to persuade the American public of the importance of supporting friendly governments in Europe. They were not at all certain that they would be able to do so. They were preoccupied with the danger of a chain reaction, but they worried that if the prospect was too remote, abstract, and hypothetical they would be unable to convince the average citizen to support preventive measures. So Americans were not simply asked to oppose Communism in order to support the establishment of an equilibrium of power in Europe – or to prop up swaying dominoes. They were summoned to foster democracy.

The invocation of American values also followed a familiar pattern. American soldiers had been sent to Europe twice in the twentieth century in the name of liberty, not the balance of power. In the nineteenth century, Britain's concern about international chain reactions had been similarly confined to a narrow group of people with responsibility for managing the empire's security policies. The domino principle had little currency among ordinary citizens.[34]

For the American definition of security in 1947, inner push and outward pull were complementary. The domino principle and the impulse for collective self-extension reinforced each other. The fear of an adverse chain reaction and the urge to make the world more like itself propelled the United States in the same direction – squarely into the middle of the politics of the European continent.

III

The outbreak of the Korean War changed the way that the United States conceived of the threats it faced. It was one of those precipitating events on the periphery, like the British withdrawal from the Greek civil war in 1947 and the collapse of the local regime in Egypt in 1882, that draws strong states outward. It set in motion a shift from the first to a second distinct definition of American security.

The war began on June 25, 1950, when troops from Communist North Korea attacked the non-Communist South. The South Korean government appealed to the United States for help. The Truman administration decided to send it. Formally the military effort to defend South Korea was undertaken by the United Nations. In fact, it was an American and South Korean war.

The tide of battle shifted back and forth several times. The north-

---

[34] There is an English saying that war is either a crusade or a crime. It captures an attitude that is also widespread in the United States. In liberal societies the extension of the collective self has a greater public appeal than the domino principle. Perhaps this is so in all societies, but in politically liberal countries the public has ultimate power over official policy.

ern forces initially overran Seoul, the southern capital, driving the Southerners back to the tip of the Korean peninsula. There the allied forces regrouped under the command of General Douglas MacArthur. He staged an amphibious landing at Inchon, far behind the northern lines. The northern forces were routed and retreated back across the thirty-eighth parallel, which had been the prewar line of division between North and South. When American forces pursued them, troops from the People's Republic of China entered the war and again the balance shifted. The American and South Korean armies retreated south, counterattacked, and the two sides fought to a stalemate over the next two years. Finally a truce was signed in 1953.

The second postwar American definition of security differed from the one that had crystallized in 1947 in three ways. Whereas the initial definition took shape gradually, the one that followed was put in place almost overnight after the outbreak of the war.[35] The Truman administration could act quickly because it did not have to convince the American public that the Soviet Union posed a threat. The only issue was the size of the threat. Here there was a second difference between the 1947 and the 1950 definitions of security. The second was broader in scope than the first, reaching beyond Western Europe to the Asian mainland. It included Korea, which juts out into the Pacific from Asia's eastern edge. It included China as well. Mao Zedong's Communists had driven Chiang Kaishek and his followers from the mainland to a refuge on the island of Formosa in 1949. On the day that war broke out in Korea, Truman ordered the American Seventh Fleet into the Formosa Straits between the island and the mainland. His purpose, as Secretary of State Dean Acheson later explained it, was "to prevent any attack from either Chinese side upon the other . . . to quarantine the fighting within Korea."[36] The order had the effect of making the island an American protectorate, a relationship that

---

[35] On the significance of the Korean War as the catalyst of a shift in American security policy see, inter alia, Hans J. Morgenthau, "Arguing About the Cold War: A Balance Sheet," *Encounter*, 28, no. 5 (1967): 39; Robert J. Art, "America's Foreign Policy: A Historical Perspective," in Roy C. Macrides, ed., *Foreign Policy and World Politics*, 5th ed., Englewood Cliffs, N.J.: Prentice–Hall, 1976), p. 361; Tucker, *Nation or Empire?* p. 28.

[36] Acheson, *Creation*, p. 369.

was sealed in the fall of 1950 when Chinese Communist troops entered the war in Korea. Mainland China came to be seen as an aggressive adjunct of the Soviet drive for world supremacy, an Asian arm of the Communist movement, or, more properly, the junior partner of the "Sino-Soviet bloc." The new American definition of security encompassed Indochina as well. In July, Truman requested an increase in aid to the French, who were trying to reestablish their imperial control in Southeast Asia. When added to the responsibility that the United States had already assumed for Western Europe, this made the scope of that definition very broad indeed.

The nature of the threat that the Americans believed they faced had changed as well. This was the third difference between the first two postwar conceptions of security. Before June 1950, the principal danger to American interests in Western Europe was deemed political. The purpose of economic assistance was to restore prosperity and so undermine the appeal of local Communists. With the outbreak of war in Korea the threat became, in American eyes, a military one. "The attack upon Korea makes it plain beyond all doubt," President Truman said on June 27, 1950, "that Communism has passed beyond the use of subversion to conquer independent nations and will now use armed invasion and war."[37] This new situation necessitated the deployment of military forces in threatened countries rather than simple economic assistance.

The American government acted accordingly. It dispatched an army to the Korean peninsula. Simultaneously, it launched a program to increase the nation's military strength. The defense budget grew dramatically. President Truman had originally requested $13.5 billion for the fiscal year 1951. Ultimately the Congress authorized $48.2 billion.[38] Within three years of the beginning of the war, American defense expenditures had quadrupled. Not all the money was spent in Korea, or even in Asia. Much of it went to Europe. From a simple guarantee pact NATO became a full-fledged military alliance with an army drawn from the member nations and

---

[37] Quoted in Harry S. Truman, *Memoirs, Volume II: Years of Trial and Hope* (New York: Doubleday, 1956), p. 339.

[38] Paul Y. Hammond, "NSC-68: Prologue to Rearmament," in Warner R. Schilling, Paul Y. Hammond, and Glenn H. Snyder, eds., *Strategy, Politics and Defense Budgets* (New York: Columbia University Press, 1962), p. 351.

led by an American commander. By the end of 1951 American priorities in Europe had changed. The goal of economic revival had taken second place to the aim of increasing military strength. NATO had replaced the Marshall Plan as the keystone of American policy.

Shortly after the outbreak of the war the Selective Service Act was extended and conscripts were sent to fight in Korea. The act was to remain in force for another two decades. The number of overseas military installations increased; by the middle of the 1960s there were an estimated 375 major American military bases and 3,000 lesser facilities all over the world. They supported a declared policy of being prepared to fight in both Europe and Asia. The American military adopted a policy of planning for two and a half wars. It was to be ready to wage major conflicts simultaneously in Europe and Asia, as in World War II, and to prosecute a lesser war somewhere else as well. Before June 25, 1950, the United States had not really been prepared to fight a major war anywhere.

Just as the first postwar American definition of security had precedents in American history, so the second, to which the Korean War gave rise, was partly implicit in the first. The Truman Doctrine was cast in universal terms. It pledged American assistance to free peoples everywhere, not only in Europe. (It was criticized in some quarters for exactly that reason.)[39] Any alliance, like NATO, is potentially a military partnership. The increase in the forces deployed on the Continent could be seen simply as the fulfillment of the pledge at the heart of the North Atlantic Treaty.

Nor was the United States entirely uninvolved in Asian affairs when the North Korean attack occurred. American forces occupied the islands that they had conquered in the Pacific campaign as well as Japan itself. Chiang Kaishek had received American aid on a large scale between the resumption of the Chinese civil war in late 1945 and his defeat and escape to Formosa in 1949. The Truman administration had sent modest help to the French in Indochina before June 25, 1950. When the attack from the north came, American troops were actually stationed in Korea, having arrived after the Japanese surrender in August 1945.

[39] Walter Lippmann, *The Cold War: A Study in U.S. Foreign Policy* (New York: Harper & Row, 1972), pp. 16, 18, 46.

In June 1950, moreover, an effort was underway within the American government to broaden the scope of the nation's definition of security, an effort that found expression in a document prepared for the president in April 1950 entitled NSC-68. The implication of its analysis was that American interests required opposing Communist expansion worldwide, not only in Europe, and that the Communist threat was a military as well as a political one. It recommended both nuclear and nonnuclear rearmament.[40] The study represented the thinking of a number of people in the upper echelons of the Truman administration.

The transition from the first to the second postwar definition of security, however, was neither smooth nor automatic. It would not have occurred as it did, and might not have occurred at all, but for the outbreak of war. The extension of the scope of American security to Asia was not at all certain in June 1950. The drift of events was not in that direction. The Truman Doctrine may have had global implications, but the Truman administration was at pains to deny that it would act on them. Congressional opinion was wary of stretching American commitments. Acheson testified that "it cannot be assumed . . . that this government would necessarily undertake measures in any other country identical or even closely similar to those proposed for Greece and Turkey."[41] Although present in Korea in June 1950, the United States was a reluctant trustee of the southern part of the peninsula, interested chiefly in ridding itself of the burden of occupation and with no inclination at all to fight on any account.[42] In a speech in January of that year Secretary Acheson had more or less said that the United States would not fight there, describing the American "defense perimeter" as stretching from the Ryukyus to the Philippines, a circumference that conspicuously excluded Korea.[43]

---

[40] Hammond, "NSC-68: Prologue to Rearmament," pp. 91, 99.

[41] Quoted in Joseph M. Jones, *The Fifteen Weeks (February 21–June 5, 1947)* (New York: Viking, 1955), p. 190.

[42] Ernest May, *'Lessons' of the Past: The Use and Misuse of History in American Foreign Policy* (New York: Oxford University Press, 1973), pp. 52–4, 59–60, 64.

[43] Acheson, *Creation*, p. 357. Although Acheson was later charged with inviting the North Korean attack by this omission, he was only stating the obvious. A few weeks later Congress rejected a bill granting a small amount of aid to Korea.

As for China, the American government had washed its hands of responsibility for future developments there, pointedly accepting the outcome of the civil war. This was the theme of the State Department's China White Paper, which was transmitted to the president on July 29, 1949. In January 1950 the administration declared that "the United States will not provide military aid or advice to Chinese forces on Formosa."[44] In Indochina, the assistance to the French had as much to do with winning their goodwill in Europe as with resisting Communists in Asia. It was modest, scarcely betokening the large part the United States would come to play – ultimately assuming most of France's war costs – let alone the direct involvement of American combat forces a decade and a half later. American officials drew no specific connection between the fate of Korea or Formosa or Indochina and the future of Europe. It was the Korean War that forged – or revealed – this connection.[45]

Nor could the Congress or the public be counted on to approve funds for the programs that NSC-68 urged, even for Europe. American officials did not count on this. They had deliberately downplayed the military implications of the Truman Doctrine. NSC-68 was not made public and the administration was not acting on its recommendations in June 1950. The president had declined to

In his memoirs Acheson calls the charge that his speech tempted North Korea "specious" and adds: "If the Russians were watching the United States for signs of our intentions in the Far East they would have been more impressed by the two years' agitation for withdrawal of combat forces from Korea, the defeat in Congress of a minor aid bill for it, and the increasing discussion of a peace treaty with Japan." Ibid., p. 358.

[44] Ibid., p. 351. See also May, *'Lessons,'* p. 65.

[45] Japan was an exception to the general pattern of American indifference to the future of Asia. There the shape of things to come was apparent before the Korean War. In theory American forces might have withdrawn, but in retrospect this never seems to have been likely. Japan's ultimate political status had not been decided when the war broke out. The Japanese–American Peace Treaty was signed afterward, its conclusion hastened by the war (Akira Iriye, *The Origins of the Cold War in Asia* [New York: Columbia University Press, 1977], p. 182). The war itself had a major impact on Japan's postwar economic history. The country became an important supplier of the American war effort in Korea. But the outline of the relationship between the two countries was already plain (ibid., pp. 174, 176). The anticipation of the Japanese–American alliance, George Kennan has speculated, may have induced Stalin to encourage, or at least assent to, the North Korean attack. George Kennan, *Memoirs, 1950–1963* (Boston: Little, Brown, 1967), p. 39; Iriye, *Cold War in Asia*, p. 177.

approve the extra defense spending that the study had suggested. Acheson later expressed doubt that rearmament on the scale that ultimately occurred could have taken place but for the war in 1950.[46] The attack on Korea made the world look suddenly different to American officials and the American public, and the American security definition changed accordingly.

The reason for fighting in Korea and extending the definition of American security to include commitments to defend Indochina and Formosa as well was the same as that for providing economic assistance to Europe: the fear that the failure to do so would start a sequence of developments, a chain reaction, unfavorable to the United States. The domino principle made the task of blunting the North Korean attack seem imperative to the Truman administration.

On its face, South Korea was a far less consequential place for the United States than Britain, France, or Germany. It was farther away. It neither grew nor produced anything that anyone other than Koreans needed. The United States had no historic ties to the country. Since there was no industrial production there, Korea could not produce military forces that, in unfriendly hands, could threaten American interests.[47]

Nor did the attack in Korea directly threaten Europe. There was no common border between the country where American troops went to fight in 1950 and the region that the United States had declared vital in 1947.[48] The chain reaction that American officials feared, and fought in Korea to prevent, was not, strictly speaking, geographic in character, as was the one the British were afraid the

---

[46] " . . . it is doubtful whether anything like what happened in the next few years could have been done had not the Russians been stupid enough to have instigated the attack against South Korea and opened the 'hate America' campaign." Acheson, *Creation*, p. 374.

[47] This was George Kennan's criterion for deciding whether a region mattered to the United States. The list of important places included North America, Britain, Germany and Central Europe, the Soviet Union, and Japan – but not Korea, China, or Indochina. Gaddis, *Strategies*, p. 30. On the significance of Korea see also Lippmann, *The Cold War*, p. 20, and May, 'Lessons,' pp. 79–80.

[48] The fate of Korea did have direct implications for Japan because of its proximity. But the United States was not yet as formally committed to Japan as to Western Europe; the Japanese archipelago was separated from the Korea peninsula by water, so an overland attack was not in prospect; and in American eyes Korea was urgent because of the perceived connection with Europe, not Japan.

domination of Egypt by an unfriendly power in the 1880s would set in motion. Korea was dangerous for its potential as a pernicious example. North Korean success in conquering the South could, Washington believed, encourage other aggressors elsewhere. Truman wrote in his memoirs that in June 1950 he had "felt certain that if South Korea was allowed to fall Communist leaders would be emboldened to override nations closer to our own shores."[49]

Korea was connected to Europe by the "demonstration effect" that its conquest might have there. Chain reactions can occur by the power of example. Regimes or groups in one part of the world can be encouraged by the success of others far away, or so it is often feared. Preventing the domino effect by example has the same rationale as the deterrent theory of crime prevention: If one person, or state, is permitted to escape punishment for violating the civil or international order, then others will be tempted to follow suit. If, however, the violator is suitably punished, would-be imitators will be discouraged. In the geographic version of the domino principle, one success makes a challenger better *able* to mount another assault. Once conquered, a territory becomes the base for an attack on a neighboring region. In the psychological version, one success makes a challenger – not necessarily the party that has just succeeded – more *inclined* to mount another attack somewhere else.

The power of a strong state includes its prestige, which is its reputation for using its power. The greater the reputation, the less likely it is that the state will have to act, because it is less likely to be challenged. Others will be intimidated by the presumption that their challenges will be firmly repulsed. Those responsible for American security policy in June 1950 had this very much in mind: "To back away from this challenge," Acheson later wrote, "would be highly destructive of the power and prestige of the United States. By prestige I mean the shadow cast by power, which is of greater deterrent importance."[50]

The conquest of South Korea seemed to the Americans likely to be a particularly powerful example, because of the image they had

[49] Quoted in Samuel F. Wells, Jr., "The Lessons of the War," *Wilson Quarterly*, Summer 1978, p. 122. See also May, 'Lessons,' pp. 76–8; Gaddis, *Strategies*, pp. 109–10.

[50] Acheson, *Creation*, p. 405.

of international Communism. They conceived of Moscow as the hub of a worldwide movement, its spokes reaching everywhere, that was prepared to conquer vulnerable territories. They had little doubt that Stalin had ordered the North Korean attack on the South and that Mao and China were in league with the Soviet Union. The conclusion followed logically that if the Communist movement enjoyed success in one place it would be encouraged to strike elsewhere.

The suspicion that dominoes can topple by example has taken on particular force in the twentieth century, when networks of rapid transportation and instantaneous communication have linked together every part of the planet. The fear of the power of adverse examples has driven the imperial policy of the Soviet Union. The Soviets intervened to keep Communist regimes in power in Hungary in 1956, Czechoslovakia in 1968, and indirectly in Poland in 1981 for fear that once one of the governments that they had installed was overturned the others would come under pressure.[51] The same motive was at work in the Soviet invasion of Afghanistan in 1979.[52]

The psychological version of the domino principle predated the electronic inventions of the twentieth century. Britain fought a series of small wars on the periphery of its empire in the nineteenth

---

[51] Charles Gati has argued that the Soviet leaders sent troops and tanks to crush the Hungarian uprising in 1956 because of "their sense of threat... their fear of vulnerability" and "their concern about the reputation and hence the power of the Soviet Union." He cites a statement that Khrushchev made at the time: "If we let things take their course, the West would say we are either stupid or weak, and that's one and the same thing. We cannot possibly permit it, either as communists and internationalists or as the Soviet state." "This rings true," Gati comments; "fear is a great inventor. By saying 'if we let things take their course' Khrushchev seemed to be alluding to what *might happen*. More lynchings [of Communist officials]? Capitalism? Neutralism today, NATO tomorrow? What then of the Soviet sphere in Eastern Europe, who's next to go? Whether these developments were or were not likely to happen did not really matter; what mattered was that they might." Charles Gati, "Imre Nagy and Moscow, 1953–1956," *Problems of Communism*, May–June 1986, p. 49.

[52] An official Soviet communiqué said: "To deny support to the Afghan revolution, to leave it face to face with the forces of international reaction and aggression, would have been to doom it to defeat, which would have been a serious blow to the entire Communist and national liberation movement." Quoted in Raymond L. Garthoff, *Detente and Confrontation: American–Soviet Relations from Nixon to Reagan* (Washington, D.C.: Brookings Institution, 1985), p. 930.

century in order to maintain its reputation for firmness. The British habit of engaging in brief naval interventions far from home to restore order or enforce the payment of debts, a practice known as "gunboat diplomacy," had the same purpose: to discourage others elsewhere from performing similar misdeeds.

The fear of the dangerous effects of reverses far away predates not only the television and the jet airplane, but the telegraph and the steamship as well. It is as old as international politics. It was a feature of imperial Roman policy. The elaborate Roman operation undertaken to crush the last remaining Jewish rebels at the fortress of Masada, south of Jerusalem, from 70 to 73 A.D. may have been intended to demonstrate to the whole Roman world the terrible and inevitable consequences of rebellion.[53] The fear of the power of adverse examples is older even than the Roman Empire. It was at the heart of the encounter between the Athenians and the Melians five hundred years before, as recorded by Thucydides. The Athenians insisted upon bringing Melos into their empire rather than allow it to remain independent, because, they said, if they let the Melians do as they pleased "our subjects would regard that as a sign of weakness in us." Since it was widely believed that "those who still preserve their independence do so because they are strong, and that if we fail to attack them we are afraid," they told the Melians, "by conquering you we shall increase not only the size but the security of our empire." The Melians, as Thucydides tells it, refused to give in and met the fate of the Jewish zealots at Masada.[54]

In Asia as in Europe the impulse for self-extension reinforced the imperatives of the domino principle. North Korea was a particularly oppressive Communist regime. The South Korean political system was itself not a model of democratic procedures, nor were

[53] This is Luttwak's surmise. *Grand Strategy*, p. 4; see also pp. 33, 49.
[54] Thucydides, *The Peloponnesian War*, trans. by Rex Warner (Harmondsworth: Penguin Books, 1972; translation first published, 1954), pp. 402, 403. The fates of the Melians and the Jews were not identical. Both were besieged. The Athenians subdued the Melians and, according to Thucydides, "put to death all the men of military age whom they took, and sold the women and children as slaves" (ibid., p. 408). When the Jewish resisters saw that they were about to be overcome, they killed themselves and their families rather than be captured. Flavius Josephus, *The Jewish War*, ed. by Mary E. Smallwood; trans. by G. A. Williamson (Harmondsworth: Penguin Books, 1984).

those of South Vietnam and Formosa. All were autocratically governed. But if their political practices were less liberal than those of Britain, France, and the Federal Republic of Germany, they were decidedly more so than those of their Communist neighbors, which aspired to replace them. The Asian regimes that came within the scope of the second American definition of security had market economies and belonged to the international economic system. A substantial part of the population of each was Christian. If they were not just like the United States, they were similar enough to kindle a spark of recognition in the American public. In 1950, as in 1947, the impulse to which domestic considerations gave rise led to policies that officials wanted to adopt on the basis of strategic calculations.

IV

From a vague hope for a return to something like prewar isolation and great expectations for the United Nations as an instrument for keeping order in the postwar world, the United States moved to a position of political and economic engagement in Western Europe and then to global military responsibilities that rivaled those of the British Empire at its zenith, all within five years. With the initial expansion of the American definition of security, President Truman and his advisers feared that the American public would not support the commitments they had made. The critics of the administration's programs, who included some of the most prominent congressional Republicans, charged that they would be costly and dangerous.

Their opposition was overcome. The administration launched a public campaign to win support for the Truman Doctrine and the Marshall Plan. It insisted that the costs would be modest. And, in fact, they were not high. They took the form of loans to Western Europe, which hardly strained the American economy and were sensible even on purely economic grounds. The European countries had a skilled labor force, managerial expertise, and available markets. They lacked only capital to become productive. This the United States provided. The Marshall Plan was a success. The recipients of aid soon became important trading partners, and the European recovery enriched the United States.

Because it stretched beyond Europe to Asia and included military preparedness as well as economic assistance, the second definition of security was much more expensive than the first. It began with the costliest security commitment: a war. Like most modern wars, the Korean conflict rapidly consumed weapons, ammunition, and supporting equipment, all of which had to be replaced. Like all wars, it also used up soldiers. Human casualties are more than economic losses. Countries are far less willing to sustain them.

Even in peacetime, the military commitments the United States had undertaken were expensive. The need to maintain overseas bases, to recruit and train large armed forces and to provide them with the most up-to-date weapons, not to mention the competition in nuclear armaments with the Soviet Union that began in the 1950s, placed an unprecedented burden on American society. In its fullest dimensions it turned out to be a burden the American people were not, in the end, willing to support.

With the Korean War, the American definition of security expanded dramatically, but the war also set the limits of that definition. The outbreak of fighting activated the domino principle and the impulse for collective self-extension, which drew the United States outward. But during the course of the war, social and political forces appeared both within and outside the country that imposed limits on American expansion.

The war demonstrated the existence of countervailing power, which raised the cost of the American presence abroad. The resistance that the United States encountered was part of a universal trend. There is a general tendency for the differences in power among sovereign states to diminish over time.[55] The ever broadening distribution of the methods of commercial industrial production is a familiar part of modern life. Once automobiles were made only in Europe and North America. Then they were produced in Japan. Now they are assembled in Korea, Mexico, Brazil, and India. Warfare is also an industrial enterprise. After World War II modern weapons came to be distributed all over the world, including the Korean peninsula. They were not made everywhere, but like automobiles, they were everywhere available.

[55] Carlo Cipolla, "Editor's Introduction," in Carlo Cipolla, ed., *The Economic Decline of Empires* (London: Methuen, 1970), pp. 5–6; Gilpin, *War and Change*, pp. 176–9.

The peoples of Asia and Africa learned how to use these weapons. The techniques of political and military organization also spread. People with exposure to Western culture used the idea of nationalism as a vehicle for mobilizing peasants who had previously been politically inert or had risen up spontaneously in uncoordinated rebellions that were easily crushed. Their energies were channeled into mass movements, guerrilla forces, and formidable regular armies.

In the nineteenth century Britain conquered India and Egypt, France subdued Indochina, Japan occupied Korea, and the European powers carved out protectorates in China, all at very low cost. The difference in military power between the strong and the weak was enormous. This huge difference made possible the rapid growth of European overseas empires. In the twentieth century the gap between the most powerful members of the international system and the others narrowed. The diffusion of power and the consequent reduction of the advantage the powerful enjoyed, in conjunction with the shift in the distribution of power among the industrialized countries that World War II produced, brought to an end the formal empires that the Europeans and the Japanese (as well as the Americans) had assembled. The same trends limited the scope of the expansion of American influence in the postwar era.[56] In 1950 North Korea and the People's Republic of China, with assistance from the Soviet Union, put up stiffer resistance to the United States than their forbears had been able to mount against Japan and the Europeans. They were able to make the price of the expansion of American influence higher than the cost of imperial control had been in the previous century.[57]

---

[56] This leaves aside nuclear weapons, which, for a variety of reasons, the United States did not use in Korea or Vietnam.

[57] After 1945 power diffused most visibly from the United States to the other capitalist industrial countries. Western Europe and Japan gained primarily in economic terms. They could have translated their wealth into political and military power, which could in turn have been used to circumscribe the expansion of the United States. But they chose not to acquire military power commensurate with their economic standing. They continued to depend heavily on the United States to ensure their security. The military gap between the United States and the Soviet Union narrowed after 1945 through the creation of a Soviet nuclear arsenal that, by the 1970s, was roughly the equal of the American one. This, too, had only a modest effect on the American definition

If the price of expansion for the great powers was higher in the second half of the twentieth century than in other periods of history, the willingness of the United States to pay it, in comparison with other strong states, was low. The American people refused to bear the cost of an extended conflict in Korea. As it continued, as it became costlier, as American and South Korea forces failed to win a decisive victory, the public became disenchanted. The war's popularity was directly tied to its most politically sensitive cost – the number of American casualties. The Chinese entry into the war sharply increased the number of American soldiers killed or wounded and thereby increased as well the number of Americans who believed that fighting in Korea was a mistake.[58] As the war became unpopular, so did the president responsible for its conduct. Truman's prospects for reelection in 1952 dimmed. He declined to run. The nominee of his party, Adlai Stevenson, was defeated.

The response to the Korean War reflected several enduring features of the American political system and of American society. Every country must decide how to apportion its resources between public and private goals. It must choose between guns and butter, between defense and welfare (which can be both private, in the form of individual consumption, and public, as in social programs). American society has a powerful bias in favor of consumption and welfare. The United States is sharply tilted toward the primacy of domestic over international concerns.

The bias is built into the nation's ethos. Its founding document dedicates the country to "life, liberty, and the pursuit of happiness." None of these has anything directly to do with foreign interests. None is a public goal. All are individual purposes. Chateaubriand once said, "Give the French glory and they will

of security, however. The United States did not try to encroach on the Soviet sphere of influence in Europe in the postwar period, but was as reticent in 1947, before the Soviets had any atomic bombs at all, as four decades later, when they had achieved nuclear parity. The Soviet Union affected the scope of the American security definition chiefly by arming Communist regimes in the Third World that fought the United States. Here, too, however, the growth of Soviet military power was not crucial. Moscow was no less effective in sponsoring opposition to the United States in the early 1950s in Korea than it was twenty years later in Indochina.

[58] John Mueller, *War, Presidents and Public Opinion* (New York: Wiley, 1973), Chap. 3.

forget gold." Americans have generally displayed the opposite preference.

Their government is so constructed as to ensure that that preference dominates public policy. The American political system is designed to weaken the instrument of the public purpose. Power is fragmented. It is divided among the national government, the fifty states, and thousands of municipalities. At the federal level it is further divided among the executive, legislative, and judicial branches. The executive branch, headed by the president, is the agent of security policy. President Truman and his associates were the driving force in the expansion of the American presence abroad. But the president's freedom of maneuver is circumscribed by the prerogatives of the Congress. A quarter-century before the Marshall Plan was adopted, the Senate kept the United States from an active role in European affairs, against the wishes of the president, Woodrow Wilson, by rejecting American membership in the League of Nations. The executive's capacity to convince the public to sacrifice private goals for particular policies, except in extreme circumstances, is more limited than in other political systems.[59] The United States has been constitutionally disinclined to provide generous support for international expansion.

A feature of American society also affected the spread of the country's influence abroad. All states weigh the costs of expansion in blood and treasure. The United States has traditionally counted the moral costs as well. Americans have worried since the eighteenth century that engagement with other countries would subvert the republican virtues and corrupt the liberal practices on which their political order was founded. The first president, George Washington, warned the American people as he left office against becoming entangled in the sordid political affairs of Europe. A

---

[59] On this score the United States after 1945 may be compared with nineteenth-century Britain. Both were democracies, with an executive partly responsible to the legislature. There were limits to the latitude that British cabinets enjoyed in the conduct of foreign policy, but it was broader than in the American case. The management of the nation's overseas interests remained the preserve of the British elite, as it had been when the franchise had been more restricted and the political class smaller. Foreign policy, in Robinson and Gallagher's words, was "still made at house parties, not by the man in the street or the man in the Stock Exchange" (*Africa and the Victorians*, p. 23). The watershed for the democratization of foreign policy in Britain was World War I.

strong aversion to a standing army runs through the nation's history. Eighteenth-century Americans, especially, feared that professional soldiers would be tempted to seize power. The acquisition of an American overseas empire in Cuba and the Philippines in 1898 gave rise to protests that good republicans had no business ruling other people without their consent.

The costs in lives and taxes of security policies have generally been more salient politically than their potentially corrupting effects. Concern for each has on occasion reinforced worries about the other. Every American war since 1898 – the two world wars mainly before American entry, the wars with Spain and in Vietnam and Korea chiefly afterward – has provoked opposition, both from a substantial fraction of the population (which became the majority in the case of Korea and Vietnam), on the grounds that the conflicts were (or would be) too costly, and from a much smaller but more vocal group that found the particular war's aims or its conduct, or both, inconsistent with American political values.

The concern with the corrupting effects at home of the American presence abroad has its roots, like the impulse for collective self-extension, in the powerful sense of American exceptionalism. Americans have embraced both expansion to make the world more like themselves and isolation to keep themselves from becoming more like the world.[60]

With the Korean War and the second expansion of the postwar American security perimeter, a gap opened between the security definition to which the American government had committed the country and the resources necessary to sustain it, which the American public was reluctant to authorize. The history of American security policy in the four presidencies following Harry Truman's can be seen as a series of efforts to bridge that gap. Those efforts

---

[60] Yet another variation is possible. Eugene V. Rostow, a former under secretary of state and director of the Arms Control and Disarmament Agency, has argued that the American presence abroad is necessary to preserve the liberal order at home: "I like to turn [Woodrow] Wilson's remark around: Wilson talked about making the world safe for democracy – we need a world in which American democracy would be safe at home. I don't think we could survive as a democratic nation if we were alone and isolated in a world of hostility, chaos, and poverty." William Whitworth, *Naive Questions about War and Peace* (New York: Norton, 1970), p. 20.

ultimately failed, and in the 1970s the American definition of security contracted.

The man who succeeded Truman as president, Dwight D. Eisenhower, accepted the dimensions of the definition of security that the Korean War had created. He gave some of the Korea-inspired commitments a formal status, signing several pacts patterned after, although generally not as binding as, the North Atlantic Treaty. The Southeast Asia Treaty Organization (SEATO) that was formed in 1955 and the security treaty with Taiwan of the same year, along with the treaty with Japan that Truman had signed in 1950, gave formal expression to the American security interest in Asia. The Eisenhower administration even pushed the nation's security perimeter into regions where the American interest had previously been muted or equivocal. Through bilateral accords, the United States associated itself with the members of the Central Powers Treaty Organization (CENTO) – Turkey, Iran, and Pakistan. Turkey was already part of NATO, but the tie to Pakistan drew the United States into Southwest Asia, which the British had just vacated after a century as the predominant power. The connection with Iran brought the United States officially into the Middle East, a region where the British presence had also been important, particularly after World War I. The United States was not entirely disinterested in this part of the world before the 1950s. The discovery of oil in the Arabian peninsula in the 1930s had attracted American attention (most of it from private firms), and American warnings had encouraged the Soviet Union to leave the northern provinces of Iran, which Soviet forces had occupied during the war, in 1946.[61]

---

[61] The United States replaced Britain in a number of regions, including, of course, on the European continent as the "offshore balancer." In some places the succession was deliberate. The United States stepped in to play a political and military role that Britain could no longer manage in Greece in 1947. There was, however, no conscious American strategy of assuming the duties of the British Empire. The United States did not rush in to every place that Britain had left, like India proper, and went some places that the British had not been, such as Indochina and Korea. Nor did the two countries cooperate everywhere. They were commercial rivals in Arabia and the Persian Gulf. Franklin D. Roosevelt's disapproval of European overseas rule was a point of contention between him and Churchill during the war, and in the immediate postwar

Eisenhower was acutely aware of the cost of the definition of security that he endorsed. He had, after all, been elected because that cost had risen too far. As a presidential candidate he had promised to end the war, and as president he did end it. The division of the Korean peninsula was made official. South Korea remained free of Communist control. The goal for which the United States had fought was achieved.

Notwithstanding this success, however, one plain lesson of the Korean War was that no administration could afford another such conflict, and even without a shooting war underway the price of the definition of security with which the United States had emerged from Korea was high. Eisenhower worried that the American people would simply refuse to pay for the far-flung commitments their government had assumed. He was concerned, as well, about the consequences if the public *did* pay for them. He feared that this would crush the American economy and distort American society. He thought it all too likely that the international responsibilities the United States had accepted would produce huge deficits and chronic inflation – the standard experience in wartime – or crippling levels of taxation. The result would be the erosion of the nation's liberties and the transformation of a free society into a "garrison state."[62] When he warned, at the end of his presidency, of the possibility that a "military–industrial complex," born of the heavy burden of defense the United States had assumed, would exercise

period the American government occasionally hinted that its generosity in providing economic assistance to Britain would depend on the dispatch with which the British freed their colonies. The ongoing difference of view between the Atlantic allies on this general issue culminated in the Suez episode in 1956, when the United States forced Britain and France to relinquish control of the Suez Canal, which they had seized after the Egyptian leader Nasser had declared it nationalized. By this time, American policy was driven not so much by the disapproval of Western European rule outside Europe, which was in any case fast disappearing, as by the fear that persisting vestiges of imperialism would enhance the local appeal of Communism and clear the way for Soviet influence. Although the United States did not deliberately succeed Britain in the Middle East, or France in Indochina, or Japan in Korea, however, the expansion of the American definition of security to those parts of the world was not entirely coincidental. In each place the departure of the imperial power set in motion forces that produced political unrest, which in turn appeared to the United States to be the beginning of an adverse chain reaction.

[62] Gaddis, *Strategies*, p. 134.

undue influence over American life, Eisenhower was sounding the theme of George Washington's farewell address: the danger that engagement abroad would subvert liberty at home.

To carry out the terms of the post-Korea definition of security, the Eisenhower administration chose an approach to defense that emphasized nuclear weapons. At the heart of the New Look, as it was called, was the threat to launch a devastating nuclear attack in response to Communist aggression against friends of the United States the world over. The prospect of such a response, of massive retaliation against a probe of the American security perimeter, it was thought, would discourage aggression. Threatening to deliver a few powerful nuclear explosives along the frontiers of Europe and Asia that the United States had pledged to protect would certainly place far less strain on the American economy than raising, equipping, and deploying the divisions of American troops that would be required to police them.[63]

There is a parallel between the New Look and Roman grand strategy during the first century A.D. The Romans, too, had to enforce order along a lengthy frontier. Nor could they afford to patrol or fortify every mile of their security perimeter. Their solution to the problem was to establish a group of special legions, based near Rome itself, that served as a mobile strike force, moving around the empire wherever they were needed. The Roman authorities might not respond to every minor provocation, but they could send the legions to crush any specific uprising. They depended on the prospect of punishment to deter mischief on their periphery, just as the New Look, with its threat of massive retaliation, was intended to do. The demonstration effect, after all, can work both ways: If successful defiance of a strong state can encourage others to mount further challenges, as the United States believed in the 1950s and as the Athenians feared two and a half millennia before, then the prospect of a challenge being crushed can also have a discouraging effect.[64]

---

[63] Michael Mandelbaum, *The Nuclear Question: The United States and Nuclear Weapons, 1946–1976* (Cambridge University Press, 1979), pp. 46–54; Gaddis, *Strategies*, pp. 148–9; 167–8.

[64] There is also a parallel with Great Britain's naval strategy in the days when its empire was most extensive. The British kept most of their fleet in their home

In keeping with the basic principle of the New Look, American military planners in the Eisenhower years assumed that nuclear weapons would be used in a wide variety of conflicts. On occasion, the American government issued veiled threats of nuclear attack, which may have helped to persuade the Communist side to negotiate an end to the Korean War and the Chinese to discontinue the shelling of the Taiwan Strait later in the decade.[65] The American threats were never carried out. Nor, however, did the United States fight any wars like the one in Korea during the remaining years of Eisenhower's term. Whether the emphasis on nuclear retaliation actually discouraged challenges that, if made, the United States would have felt obliged to meet is impossible to say.[66] In any event the costs of security did not rise in the Eisenhower years. They fell. Measured as a fraction both of gross national product and of federal expenditures, the largest expense for security, the defense budget, declined.[67] From the end of the Korean War to the end of the decade the costs of the extended American definition of security proved manageable.

John F. Kennedy, who succeeded Eisenhower in 1961, accepted the definition of security that he had inherited from his two predecessors. But he gave it his own expansive interpretation. He was convinced that the new nations of Africa and Asia and the long-independent countries of Latin America that shared many of their economic characteristics would form the crucial battleground in the struggle between the West and international Communism. Newly released from European rule, these countries, Kennedy believed, were poised between the two camps. The side that could offer the better prospects for economic success would, he thought, win their allegiance.

The chief danger that the West faced in the Third World, in his view, was the exploitation of economic backwardness and unful-

waters, occasionally dispatching a squadron for an exemplary punitive episode of "gunboat diplomacy." On Rome see Luttwak, *Grand Strategy.*

[65] See Chapter 4, pp. 244–5; also Gaddis, *Strategies*, pp. 168–71.

[66] The United States did not send combat forces to Indochina to relieve the French in 1954 not because nuclear threats were effective but because Eisenhower refused to send them. Leslie H. Gelb with Richard K. Betts, *The Irony of Vietnam: The System Worked* (Washington, D.C.: Brookings Institution, 1979), pp. 56–60.

[67] Gaddis, *Strategies*, p. 164.

filled hopes for prosperity by Communist insurgents who would try to capitalize on local grievances to seize power. They had succeeded in China in 1949 and had won half of Vietnam in 1954, but non-Communist forces had thwarted them in the Philippines and Malaya in 1954 and 1960. In 1961 Nikita Khrushchev, the Soviet leader, made a speech proclaiming support for such "wars of national liberation" that seemed to some Americans a declaration of war for the Third World.[68]

In the new nations, the United States faced the tasks that each of the two postwar definitions of security had presented. American security required both fostering economic development, as the Marshall Plan had been organized to do, and resisting military assaults, although of unorthodox kinds, as the United States had done in Korea. In the view of the Kennedy administration, the nuclear weapons on which the Eisenhower security policy relied were inadequate for both tasks. They were irrelevant to the sources of political unrest in what came to be called the developing countries. Weapons could not grow food or build factories. Nor could nuclear weapons, powerful though they were, prevent the infiltration and subversion, the ambushes and tactics of terrorism with which the Communists waged their wars of national liberation. The American nuclear arsenal had not, after all, prevented North Korea from attacking the South, or the Communist Viet Minh from defeating the French, or Mao's forces from conquering all of China.

A nuclear-weapon-based strategy seemed inadequate for protecting American interests even where economic development was well underway, where insurgency was a very remote danger, but where American stakes were highest – in Europe. The growth of Soviet nuclear might in the 1950s had, Kennedy and his advisers believed, made the nuclear threats upon which the New Look depended far less convincing than they had been when the Eisenhower administration had first adopted the policy. In particular, these threats could no longer be counted on to offset the Soviet superiority in nonnuclear forces in Europe. The United States could no longer credibly threaten to destroy the Soviet Union in response to a nonnuclear Soviet assault on Western Europe, because the Soviets could themselves respond by devastating North

[68] Ibid., p. 208.

America with their own nuclear arsenal. A nonnuclear war in Europe would force the United States to choose between accepting defeat and using nuclear weapons, which could provoke a nuclear attack on the United States. It was a choice, in the phrase used at the time, between humiliation and holocaust. To avoid the choice and prevent a Soviet attack on Europe, Kennedy concluded, the Western allies would have to be able to thwart it without resorting to the use of nuclear weapons. The Atlantic Alliance would have to field more tanks, airplanes, and troops on the European continent. This would be expensive. The new administration's preference implied the kind of expense that Eisenhower had sought to avoid, even though outlays for nonnuclear arms had risen during his presidency.

Kennedy was less daunted than Eisenhower by the costs of strengthening NATO's nonnuclear forces, because he came to office prepared to put into practice new techniques of economic management that promised to expand the nation's overall output. The great lesson of the century's most influential economist, John Maynard Keynes, Kennedy's economic advisers believed, was that stimulating the economy through increases in government spending and reductions in taxes could, if properly calibrated, produce not deficits but sustained economic growth. Although his security policies were more expensive than Eisenhower's, Kennedy was confident that with sophisticated economic management he could acquire more resources with which to pay for them.[69]

For the challenge to the United States in the Third World as well, the Kennedy administration believed techniques to be available upon which its predecessors had failed to capitalize. From the trial and error of the battle against Communist insurgencies in Malaya and the Philippines had emerged successful methods of counterinsurgency. Training programs to teach these methods to similarly threatened countries were needed, but huge investments of men and material were not. Guile and sophistication could help to sustain the Kennedy version of the second definition of security.

---

[69] Ibid., p. 204. The difference in practice between Eisenhower and Kennedy on defense spending was not so great as the difference in principle. Eisenhower did not favor a buildup of nonnuclear forces, but these did increase during his presidency. Kennedy favored such a buildup but found that Congress and the European allies would not spend as much as he wanted.

Once he had ended the Korean War, Dwight Eisenhower had avoided another conflict like it. Kennedy and the man who succeeded to the presidency upon his assassination in November 1963, Lyndon Johnson, did not. The Kennedy administration believed that the insurgency against the government of South Vietnam could be defeated by the same methods that had brought victory in Malaya. Local troops were to bear the burden of fighting Communist guerrillas while the Saigon authorities received American economic and military assistance and counsel from a handful of American advisers schooled in the ways of counterinsurgency. As the United States became more deeply involved, however, the conflict took on a different shape. It became a more familiar kind of American war, fought by a large regular army that included conscripts and that numbered half a million by 1968.

The Vietnam War was a logical outgrowth of the second postwar definition of American security. It was undertaken in a part of Asia that had come within the American security perimeter in the immediate aftermath of June 25, 1950. The American aim was to protect a government friendly to the West from a Communist insurgency. The United States was also fighting, at the outset at least, to block the expansion of China, which had been a goal in the Korean conflict as well.

The fear of falling dominoes weighed on the calculations of the officials responsible for sending American forces to Vietnam. Eisenhower had originally coined the phrase to describe an unfavorable chain reaction in Indochina, and it was subsequently invoked by others. American authorities feared that a setback there would set a dangerous example for those hostile to Western interests everywhere.[70] At the beginning of the war American policymakers saw it as a potentially powerful example because it would test the techniques of counterinsurgency. If they succeeded in Indochina, they believed they could defeat – or better yet discourage – similar assaults in other reaches of the Third World. Later, when the war

---

[70] On the use of the domino theory by American officials, see Gelb and Betts, *Irony*, pp. 31, 197–8, 366; May, 'Lessons,' pp. 93, 103–4; Gaddis, *Strategies*, pp. 238, 241, 265, 267; Godfrey Hodgson, *America in Our Time* (New York: Vintage Books, 1978; first published, 1976), pp. 233, 238, 239; Whitworth, *Naive Questions*, pp. 45, 106.

had ceased to be a guerrilla campaign, it was the very scope of American participation that made the demonstration effect of its outcome, especially if that were unfavorable, seem likely to be potent. "The commitment of five hundred thousand Americans has settled the issue of the importance of Vietnam," Henry Kissinger wrote in 1968, shortly before entering the government. "For what is involved now is confidence in American promises. However fashionable it is to ridicule the terms 'credibility' or 'prestige' they are not empty phrases; other nations can gear their actions to ours only if they can count on our steadiness."[71] If the United States exerted itself in Vietnam to the extent of sending half a million troops and then did not prevail, those disposed to challenge American positions elsewhere would be heartened and emboldened, while friends of the United States would be rattled and uncertain. The shock that the fall of South Vietnam would cause would set dominoes elsewhere to trembling.

As in Korea, the cost of the American military effort in Vietnam increased. It rose more slowly, but it continued to rise for a longer time because the Vietnam War went on longer than the Korean conflict. In the end the United States suffered more casualties in Vietnam than in Korea. Vietnam differed from Korea in another way: It gave birth to an antiwar movement that opposed American participation not on the grounds of expense but because the war violated American values. Though their number was relatively small, the movement's members were vocal and politically active and they made Washington's conduct of the war more difficult.[72]

Ultimately, Vietnam had the same political effect within the United States as had Korea. Public support fell as American casualties rose. The public decided that the price was too high and in the political year 1968 repudiated the policy of the incumbent president.[73] Like Harry Truman, Lyndon Johnson decided not to seek reelection. The Republican candidate, Richard Nixon, who

---

[71] Henry Kissinger, "The Vietnam Negotiations," in *American Foreign Policy*, expanded ed. (New York: Norton, 1974), p. 112.

[72] Michael Mandelbaum, "Vietnam: The Television War," *Daedalus*, 111, no. 4 (1982): 163.

[73] Popularity is measured in both cases by the response to the question "Do you think the war was a mistake?" Mueller, *War*, pp. 43, 52, 60.

had been Eisenhower's vice-president, promised, without speci-
fying how he would fulfill his promise, to end the war. He was
elected.

Like Eisenhower, Nixon searched for ways to reduce the cost of
sustaining the definition of security that he had inherited. In Indochina, he withdrew American ground troops, but not American
naval and air forces, replacing them with local soldiers. This policy
was called "Vietnamization." It was designed to reduce the highest
cost of the war to the United States – American casualties – while
keeping South Vietnam free from Communist control, which was
the reason American troops had been sent there in the first place.
For a time, Vietnamization succeeded.[74]

The Nixon administration sought to ease the burden on American
society and the American economy of the extended American definition of security in another way. It adopted a policy of providing
support to friendly states to help them keep order and defend
American interests in their regions while minimizing the presence
of the American military. The policies of 1947 had aimed at helping
the nations in the strategically crucial region of Western Europe
to help themselves through the provision of American economic
aid. The would-be regional powers in the Third World in the 1970s
received mainly military assistance. The United States sold armaments on a large scale to Iran, for example, which the Nixon
administration hoped would serve as a surrogate for the United
States in the Persian Gulf.[75]

At the same time Nixon undertook to relax tensions with America's chief adversary, the Soviet Union. The policy of détente had

[74] Eisenhower had reduced the cost of the Korean commitment by stopping the
war without withdrawing American ground troops. A contingent of these troops
remained in Korea three decades after the truce was signed. The price proved
tolerable to the American public. Nixon endeavored to reduce the cost of
Vietnam by withdrawing combat forces without ending the war. Whether the
American public would have paid the price that this required over the long
term is impossible to say. The South Vietnamese forces were not able to defend
their country against the armies of the North without the help of American
combat troops. The southern army was overrun, and the South conquered, in
the spring of 1975.

[75] The arms sales to Iran after 1973 had another purpose. They helped to offset
the American balance-of-payments deficit, which had worsened after the huge
increase in the price of oil. As a major oil producer, Iran benefited from the
increases and had cash to pay for the weapons.

a complicated history. It emerged from the negotiations, begun in the late 1960s, to normalize interstate relations in Europe. It was bound up with the stage that the competition in nuclear armaments had reached: The Soviet Union had, by the time the Nixon administration came to office, drawn more or less even with the United States. Détente was intended to serve a variety of purposes. The Soviet Union sought recognition of its status as the international equal of the United States and hoped to reap economic benefits from more cordial relations with the West. The Nixon administration wanted to make the rivalry less taxing and the measures necessary to ensure American security, as its requirements had come to be defined in the wake of the Korean War, less burdensome. The administration anticipated that the two arms control agreements it signed in 1972 – one a treaty effectively prohibiting systems of ballistic missile defense, the other a freeze on offensive weapons – would make the arms race less costly.[76] The economic agreements were intended to curb the Soviet appetite for challenging American interests around the world and so make it less costly to defend those interests. The Nixon administration also hoped that the Soviets would help to promote a settlement in Vietnam consistent with the purpose for which the United States was fighting.

At the end of the nineteenth century the British, finding their resources stretched dangerously thin in maintaining their empire, moved to conciliate the other great powers. They signed a series of agreements to resolve contentious issues of the moment or avert potential disputes with the United States, Japan, France, and Russia. They tried but failed to conciliate Germany as well. A similar purpose animated the Nixon policy of détente with the Soviet Union.[77]

Like Eisenhower's New Look, the Nixon policies of Vietnamization, détente, and support for regional powers were attempts to lower the costs of security to the United States. And like the New

---

[76] Insofar as it forestalled a competition in the deployment of complicated and expensive systems of missile defense, the 1972 treaty did make the arms race less expensive.

[77] On Britain see Chapter 1, pp. 49–51. On détente see Gaddis, *Strategies*, pp. 289–96. There is a particular resemblance between the effect of the Boer War on British policy and the impact of the Vietnam War on the United States.

Look, they did lower it. As a proportion of the nation's output and of the federal budget, spending on defense declined during the Nixon as during the Eisenhower years. Nixon differed from Eisenhower, and from Truman, Kennedy, and Johnson as well, however, in one important respect. He presided over a contraction of the boundaries of the sphere that the United States defined as crucial to its security and the creation of a third, slightly more modest postwar definition of security.

V

The third definition of postwar American security emerged more gradually and tentatively than the first two. It was never as clearly defined as the first, which was expressed in the Truman Doctrine and the Marshall Plan, or the second, which was embodied in the series of measures taken immediately after the outbreak of war in Korea. Nor was it dramatically different from the definition of 1950. The United States was as committed to the defense of Western Europe after Vietnam as before. NATO remained the integrated military alliance that it had become in 1950. American troops continued in place on the Continent. In 1971 the leader of the Democratic majority in the Senate, Mike Mansfield of Montana, sponsored a resolution calling for a reduction of the American forces in Europe. The Nixon administration opposed the Mansfield amendment and prevailed.

The United States maintained many of its commitments beyond the western edge of North America, too – but not all of them. The American role in Asia did change. It was there that the nation's definition of its own security contracted. The Korean War had extended it to the mainland. By the middle of the 1970s the American military presence there, once formidable, was practically gone. In 1975 Cambodia, Laos, and South Vietnam came under Communist control. The last redoubt of American military power on any scale was the site of the first foothold – South Korea.[78]

Although it excluded the mainland, the third American security

---

[78] There was talk of removing American troops from Korea as well. As a presidential candidate in 1976, Jimmy Carter promised to withdraw them, but once in office he declined to do so.

definition encompassed the Pacific. The Philippines and Japan (as well as Hawaii, which had become one of the states of the American Union in 1959) remained outposts of American sea and air power. The American promises to protect them remained in force. Its pattern of military deployments suggested that the United States was prepared to defend those parts of Asia that happened to be surrounded by water. This was in line with American military strength. In a battle for control of an island, or an archipelago like Japan and the Philippines, the defender ordinarily enjoys a greater advantage over the attacker than it does in land warfare. Amphibious assaults are more perilous than invasions over land because interdiction is easier. Sea and air power dominate struggles for islands. The United States still had, after Vietnam, the strongest navy and air force in the world. The defense of islands requires sophisticated military equipment rather than vast reserves of manpower. It depends more on technological competence than on a willingness to sustain losses on the battlefield. Here the United States had a comparative advantage over its rival, the Soviet Union. American troops were, to be sure, stationed in Korea as well; but Korea, although not an island, is the closest thing to it: a peninsula.

The post-Korea requirement to be prepared to fight two and a half wars gave way, in the wake of Vietnam, to a "one and a half war" policy. The American Department of Defense planned for a "major contingency of the magnitude that could arise in Central Europe,"[79] but not for a similar conflict in Asia. If such a war broke out, moreover, it would have to be fought, at least initially, by American volunteers. In 1972 conscription was abolished.

The United States left the Asian mainland because it was forced to do so. The Vietnam War ended in defeat. This alone does not account for the contraction of the American security perimeter, however. The shift from the second to the third postwar definition of security had begun well before May 1975, when the last helicopter ferrying American personnel to waiting ships in the South China Sea lifted off from the American embassy compound in Saigon as North Vietnamese troops entered the city. It was announced, or at least foreshadowed, by the Nixon Doctrine, the name given

---

[79] Department of Defense, *Annual Report, Fiscal Year 1980* (Washington, D.C.: U.S. Government Printing Office, 1979), p. 100.

to a pronouncement made on the island of Guam, where the President had stopped on the way to Vietnam in 1969.

The Nixon Doctrine was vague. It announced that the United States would keep its existing commitments but that America's allies would have to do more for their own security. The United States would continue to provide a nuclear shield, but in nonnuclear conflicts others would have to assume the principal responsibility for defending themselves.[80] If it lacked specific references, the theme of the pronouncement was clear. It was contraction. The place in which the speech was delivered emphasized the part of the world where the United States was prepared to do less than before.[81]

An important part of the transition from the second to the third definition of security was the rapprochement with the People's Republic of China orchestrated by the Nixon administration. Since the Communist victory on the mainland in 1949 and the entry of Mao's troops into the Korean War against the United States the following year, the two countries had not established formal diplomatic relations. When Nixon came to office in 1969, he and the Chinese government began to exchange hints of interest in better relations, which turned into messages passed through intermediaries and then secret meetings between high officials. Finally, the president made a dramatic visit to Beijing in February 1972.[82]

Deteriorating relations with the Soviet Union kindled China's interest in moving closer to the United States. On the American side, the war in Vietnam had the same effect. The Nixon China policy reduced the cost of American security by conciliating one of the nation's adversaries. The outcome of the Vietnam War that both countries anticipated made conciliation possible. The Chinese,

---

[80] Henry Kissinger, *White House Years* (Boston: Little, Brown, 1979), p. 222; Gaddis, *Strategies*, p. 298.

[81] The Nixon Doctrine had an odd history. The president held a press conference on Guam and made a number of informal statements about the American role in the world. He did not intend to offer an authoritative description of that role. His remarks, however, were portrayed by the press as just that and received worldwide attention. The Nixon administration thereupon rushed to embrace what he had said in order to make sure that what the press had proclaimed a doctrine was named for its author rather than for the island on which it had first been expressed. Kissinger, *White House Years*, p. 224.

[82] The details are in Chapter 4, pp. 223–5.

who were supporting North Vietnam, agreed to proceed once they were persuaded that the United States was bent on withdrawing at least its ground forces from Indochina. The conviction had taken root in Beijing by 1972, well before the forcible eviction of all Americans three years later.

The People's Republic having been declared friendly rather than hostile, one of the principal aims for which the United States was fighting in Vietnam evaporated. It was no longer a pressing American task to contain China. To the contrary, the United States had acquired an interest in strengthening that country so that it could serve as a counterweight to the Soviet Union. It was a chain reaction of *Soviet* successes with which American officials were concerned. Rather than an agent of Soviet expansion, China came to be seen as an obstacle to it.

The rapprochement with China brought the two impulses that propelled the United States outward into conflict with each other. The Nixon China policy served American strategic interests by reinforcing a barrier to Soviet expansion in Asia and by easing the burden of the security commitments that the nation had to support. But the People's Republic was, in 1972, a full-fledged Communist country. It repressed rather than protected and promoted the liberal values on which the American republic was founded. In Europe both the impulse to promote American values and institutions and the need to prevent adverse chain reactions led to the policy of opposing the Soviet Union. The two driving forces had been in harmony in Asia as well for two decades following the Korean War. But an alignment with the government in Beijing hardly served to make the world more like the United States. Faced with the choice between the strategic and the ideological, the international and the domestic interests of the United States, the Nixon administration chose the first over the second. It put the task of checking adverse chain reactions ahead of the cause of liberty beyond North America.

In addition to its higher cost, the eventual American defeat, and the rapprochement with China, there was another reason that the war in Vietnam led to the contraction of the American definition of security. By the time the American involvement in Vietnam had reached its peak, the fixed costs of the second American definition of security had been accumulating for almost two decades. These were substantial even apart from the special burden of fighting in Indochina. Historically, the costs of sustaining the expansive policies of strong states tend to rise. More troops are sent abroad. More military assistance is distributed to clients and allies. Weapons become more expensive. The costs rise as well because the diffusion of the basis of military power makes others stronger and better able to mount challenges.[83]

While the cost of the post-Korea definition of security increased, the disposition of the American people to pay it did not. The inbuilt preference for butter over guns became, if anything, more pronounced.[84] A new series of social programs, in addition to the public obligations the nation had assumed in the 1930s, were created in the 1960s. But the American people, through their elected representatives, declined to tax themselves to cover the full cost of the second postwar definition of security, which included the mounting expense of the Vietnam War, as well as the New Deal and Great Society programs.

The inflation that resulted is a familiar feature of strong states whose commitments exceed their willingness to support them.[85] The gap between commitments and publicly mobilized resources also put a strain on the international monetary system, in which the American dollar played a special role.[86] The economic dislocations in the United States helped to create a political backlash, which in turn encouraged the reduction of the American presence overseas. An important political moment in the contraction of the definition of security came at the beginning of 1968, when the voters of his own party repudiated Lyndon Johnson in the early presidential primary elections. The first of these came in New Hampshire, where Senator Eugene McCarthy, who opposed the Vietnam policy of the Johnson administration, received an unexpectedly high percentage of the vote – although not a majority.

[83] Gilpin, *War and Change*, pp. 162, 177–83.
[84] This, too, is a familiar historical tendency. See ibid., pp. 163–4.
[85] Ibid., pp. 164–5, 188.
[86] David Calleo argues that the United States first broke the rules of the monetary order that had been established at Bretton Woods in 1944, and then dismantled the Bretton Woods system altogether, rather than reduce the gap either by cutting back on military or welfare commitments or by taxing itself more (and thus consuming less). This is the theme of his book, *The Imperious Economy* (Cambridge, Mass.: Harvard University Press, 1982).

Surveys showed that more McCarthy voters were unhappy with inflation than with the president's conduct of the war. A vote against inflation, however, was in effect a vote against the war that had helped to ignite it. Johnson's successor interpreted it, as well, as a vote against the security policies that underlay it and acted accordingly.

Still, the continuities between the second and the third postwar definitions of American security are striking. The contraction of the nation's security perimeter in the wake of Vietnam was modest. After the Nixon Doctrine, after the abandonment of the policy of containing China, after the eviction from Southeast Asia, most of the commitments undertaken in 1950, not to mention those dating from 1947, remained in place. Those commitments were expensive, but the United States was still well equipped to pay for them. The country was politically steady and economically prosperous. The gap between it and others, which was unnaturally large at the end of World War II, had narrowed over three decades. But the American economy was still robust. In the 1980s it grew faster than those of most of the other industrial capitalist states.

The cost of an expansive definition of security remained manageable for the United States as well because of the character of the American presence abroad. American influence differed from the kind that previous strong states had exercised. Rome and Britain had controlled empires. They had governed others against their will, or at least without their consent. Ultimately those whom they governed resisted, raising the price of maintaining an empire until the metropole would not or could not sustain it. If imperial rule is defined as a relationship in which "a weaker people cannot act with respect to what it regards as fundamental domestic or foreign concerns for fear of foreign reprisals that it believes itself unable successfully to counter,"[87] then the United States after 1945 was not an imperial power. It was present abroad by the consent of the established authorities in the host countries. In the most important of them, those authorities were popularly chosen and therefore broadly legitimate. They welcomed, indeed encouraged rather than resisted, the American presence. Imperial power is the power to command; the United States did not command others. The pre-

---

[87] Smith, *The Pattern of Imperialism*, p. 6.

dominant form of American influence was a network of alliances with other sovereign powers, not an imperial domain like those of the past.[88]

The people of Western Europe and Japan paid in various ways to support the American presence in their countries. There was an ongoing dispute about how much they should pay; the United States wanted them to pay more. But there was no doubt of the principle that they drew benefit from the American presence and therefore should pay something.[89] The United States was generally reluctant to remain where its presence was actively unwanted, a reluctance that reduced the costs of its security policies.[90]

Moreover, one of the forces that had propelled the United States outward after 1945 continued to make itself felt. The impulse for collective self-extension remained potent. Neither the disastrous experience in Indochina nor the rapprochement with the People's Republic of China extinguished the urge to foster congenial regimes abroad. To the contrary, the Nixon administration came under attack from both the political Right and the Left for what they considered its cynical disregard of American values in drawing closer to the two Communist giants.[91] The two succeeding presi-

---

[88] Here the postwar role of the United States stands in contrast to that of the Soviet Union after 1945. While American military forces were deployed in Western Europe to defend the Continental subscribers to the North Atlantic Treaty against external attack, Soviet troops were stationed to the east to keep unpopular Communist regimes in power.

[89] The Western allies contributed direct subsidies and purchases to help sustain American overseas military operations. They also contributed in more round-about ways. The Europeans, especially the Germans, cooperated in the American policy of evading the requirement that dollars be convertible into gold so as not to jeopardize the American commitment to their security (see Chapter 6, p. tk). Their cooperation involved accepting dollars they would otherwise not have wanted. Imperial powers of the past extracted resources from local populations to support troops dispatched to keep them in order. Like other features of imperial rule, the support was involuntary and a source of resentment and resistance. See, e.g., Robert W. Tucker and David C. Hendrickson, *The Fall of the First British Empire: Origins of the War of American Independence* (Baltimore, Md.: Johns Hopkins University Press, 1982), Chap. 5.

[90] American forces left Indochina, although not until a great deal had been invested to keep them there; and the United States did not fight to keep a friendly regime in Iran in 1979, as a traditional imperial power probably would have done and as the Soviet Union did for a time in Afghanistan.

[91] Michael Mandelbaum and William Schneider, "The New Internationalisms," in Kenneth A. Oye, Donald Rothschild, and Robert J. Lieber, eds., *Eagle*

dencies, of opposed political views, attempted in different ways to put liberal values at the center of the nation's relations with the rest of the world. The administration of President Jimmy Carter placed great emphasis, at least rhetorically, on the promotion of human rights – meaning liberal institutions and procedures – in other countries. The administration of Ronald Reagan portrayed the rivalry with the Soviet Union as a conflict of creeds and stressed the threat that Soviet political practices as well as Soviet military power presented to the West.[92]

The other, more important force that drove the American security perimeter outward in 1947 and 1950, the one lodged in the international system rather than in American society, also continued to operate after the Vietnam period. In December 1979 the Soviet Union invaded Afghanistan. For the first time in the postwar period, Soviet troops moved across a border into a country in which they had not previously been stationed. The invasion had an effect on the United States similar to the British withdrawal from Greece and the outbreak of the Korean War. It triggered a series of events that extended the American security perimeter, not to Afghanistan itself but to the oil-rich countries of the nearby Persian Gulf.

In response to the invasion, Jimmy Carter declared in his January 1980 State of the Union Address:

> Any attempt by any outside force to gain control of the Persian
> Gulf region will be regarded as an assault on the vital interests

---

Entangled: U.S. Foreign Policy in a Complex World (New York: Longman, 1979), p. 65.

[92] Robinson and Gallagher describe British expansion into Africa as the product of weakness, doubt, and a sense that the tide of events in the world was going against them (*Africa and the Victorians*, pp. 3, 369, 471). Because the power and especially the economic vigor that had made Britain's informal influence pervasive in the first half of the century were ebbing, Victorian leaders believed that they had to secure formal control of the African territories. The experience of Vietnam did not undermine Americans' confidence in their political values quite so dramatically. It did divide the American political elite on how best to promote them abroad. Advocates of human rights wanted to put pressure on illiberal regimes within the American camp. Those favoring an emphasis on opposition to Communism held that the worst regimes by the standards of American values were Communist ones and that American pressure on friendly but undemocratic governments risked bringing Communists to power. Communist rule was all the worse, they argued, because it was not susceptible to change in a liberal direction as non-Communist "authoritarian" regimes were. A well-known statement of this position is Jeane J. Kirkpatrick, "Dictatorships and Double Standards," *Commentary*, November 1979, pp. 34–45.

of the United States of America and such an assault will be repelled by any means necessary, including military force.[93]

This policy was called the Carter Doctrine.[94] The administration proposed some concrete military programs to carry out, if need be, the new American commitment to defend the Gulf region. It authorized the creation of a Rapid Deployment Joint Task Force to be earmarked for dispatch to the area in case of an attack. It began an effort to acquire bases or basing rights both in the region itself and in neighboring countries.[95] The Carter administration initiated, and the Reagan administration continued, an across-the-board increase in defense spending. Just as the new forces after 1950 did not go exclusively to Korea, so the equipment authorized in the wake of 1979 was not mainly designated for the Gulf.

The United States was not entirely new to the region in 1980, just as the American interest in Western Europe predated 1947 and an American presence in Asia and the Pacific had been established well before 1950. American oil companies had had a large stake in the area since the 1950s. The American government had developed close ties with the two largest oil-producing countries, Iran and Saudi Arabia. In the western part of the Middle East, the United States had forged a particularly close relationship with Israel, had played an ever larger role in the Arab–Israeli wars of 1956, 1967, and 1973, and had served as broker and guarantor of the peace accord between Egypt and Israel that followed the third conflict.[96]

Official concern in Washington about the Gulf had been growing before the Soviet invasion of Afghanistan, just as the Truman administration worried about political stability in Europe before 1947. An oil embargo imposed by the Arab oil-producing countries

---

[93] Quoted in Zbigniew Brzezinski, *Power and Principle: Memoirs of the National Security Adviser, 1977–1981* (New York: Farrar, Straus & Giroux, 1983), p. 426.

[94] Carter's national security adviser, Zbigniew Brzezinski notes in his memoirs that the Carter Doctrine was patterned after the Truman Doctrine. Ibid., pp. 444–5.

[95] See Thomas McNaugher, *Arms and Oil: U.S. Military Strategy and the Persian Gulf* (Washington, D.C.: Brookings Institution, 1985), pp. 13–15. Military and economic assistance to Pakistan were also increased. See also Garthoff, *Detente*, p. 974.

[96] See Chapter 5, pp. 297–310.

in the wake of the 1973 war had sent the world price of petroleum soaring. With the fall of the Shah in 1979, control of Iran passed from a government friendly to the United States to a group of rabidly anti-American Muslim clerics led by the Ayatollah Khomeini. Plans were circulating within the United States government for increasing American attention to the Gulf before December 1979, even as NSC-68 had recommended a military buildup before June 25, 1950.

This third extension of the American definition of security changed American policy far less dramatically than the first two. The interest of the United States in the Gulf region was clearer and less equivocal before 1980 than was the commitment to Europe before 1947 and to Asia before 1950. The Carter Doctrine departed less sharply from the patterns of the past than had the Truman Doctrine or the engagement of American troops in the Korean War. The military measures undertaken for the defense of the Gulf added little to existing capabilities. The Rapid Deployment Force involved no new troops; it merely reorganized existing units.[97] The new basing facilities were modest, and many were located outside the Gulf region itself.

Still, the Carter Doctrine did put the world on formal notice, as had no previous policy or pronouncement, that the United States would fight to defend the Gulf. The general increase in resources devoted to defense that the Afghan invasion launched ultimately became, in sheer number of dollars, the largest ever in peacetime. And it was unlikely that the declaration would have been made or the buildup undertaken, at least with the same emphasis or at a comparable pace, but for the dispatch of Soviet troops to the Afghan capital.[98] The invasion was a precipitating event, one that changed the American image of the threat the Soviet Union posed and the measures necessary to meet it, like the British withdrawal from Greece and the North Korean attack on the South.[99]

As on the two previous occasions, the United States acted in

---

[97] More capacity for lifting these troops to the region was obtained. McNaugher, *Arms and Oil*, p. 14.

[98] Garthoff, *Detente*, p. 975; McNaugher, *Arms and Oil*, p. 13, n. 18.

[99] In January 1980 Carter said: "In my own opinion . . . the Soviet invasion is the greatest threat to peace since the Second World War. It's a sharp escalation in the aggressive history of the Soviet Union." Garthoff, *Detente*, p. 972.

1980 to prevent what loomed as a dangerous chain reaction. American officials feared that the Soviet Union would use Afghanistan as a platform for an assault on the countries surrounding the Gulf. "There is no doubt," Carter said, "that the Soviets' move into Afghanistan, if done without adverse consequences, would have resulted in the temptation to move again and again until they reached warm water ports or until they acquired control over a major portion of the world's oil supplies."[100] Like Egypt for Britain in the 1880s, Afghanistan was significant for a great power a century later not for what it was but for where it was. Although it was unimportant itself, its neighbors were consequential for the United States.

The significance of the countries of the Persian Gulf, in turn, was not military or political but economic. Their importance stemmed from the presence within their borders of the largest readily accessible deposits of oil on the planet. The Western world, especially Western Europe and Japan, came in the 1970s to rely so heavily on petroleum from the Persian Gulf that their economies could scarcely have functioned without it. The American commitment to protect these countries became a commitment to protect their foreign sources of energy as well. The United States had fought in Korea to forestall danger to Europe by the power of invidious example. The connection between Western Europe and the Persian Gulf, by contrast, was tangible. Although the significance of the Gulf states was largely economic, however, the American motive for preparing to defend them was ultimately political. Washington feared the political consequences of Soviet control of the region.[101]

The third extension of the American definition of security differed from the previous two in at least one conspicuous respect. It had nothing to do with the promotion of American values and institutions abroad. The Carter Doctrine pledged the United States to ensure that oil from the Persian Gulf would continue to be available for use in Western Europe and Japan. It made no mention, as had the Truman Doctrine, of free institutions and free

---

[100] Ibid., p. 972.

[101] The United States did not make military preparations to seize the oil fields itself when the price rose sharply in 1974 and 1979, events that inflicted economic damage on the West as the invasion of Afghanistan did not.

people. Nor did it commit the United States to protecting democracy in the region. There was none to protect.

The Europeans and Japanese were more dependent on oil from the Gulf than was the United States. Japan and most of the European nations had no petroleum of their own and so had to import all that they used. The United States still had many working wells in the Southwest, in Alaska, in the Gulf of Mexico, and off the coast of California. America's allies might therefore have been expected to involve themselves more deeply in the defense of the Persian Gulf. In response to the Soviet invasion of Afghanistan they did nothing.[102] Their passivity testified to one other feature that the events of 1947, 1950, and 1979–80 had in common: the position in the international system of the United States.

The world changed in the thirty-five years between the end of World War II and the proclamation of the Carter Doctrine. One of the notable changes was the economic recovery and subsequent prosperity of countries that had suffered widespread damage in the war, particularly Japan and Germany. By 1980 they had become substantial economic powers. They had not, however, gone very far to convert their wealth into military power. They had not undertaken full responsibility for defending their own territories, let alone regions beyond their borders. The United States still had a major share of this responsibility.[103] Western Europe and Japan still came within the perimeter of American security.

World War II had redistributed power in the international system. The United States had gained at the expense of, among others, Great Britain. The British were no longer powerful enough to respond to the fear of toppling dominoes, a point made clear by the outcome of the Suez affair of 1956, nor were the French, the Germans, or the Japanese. As a consequence of the reallocation of

---

[102] They were, in fact, unhappy at the punitive measures the American government wanted to take. Washington called for a boycott of the 1980 Olympic Games, which were scheduled to be held in Moscow. Most of the Western countries complied, but only reluctantly, and athletes from Great Britain (a country that, perhaps coincidentally, had its own oil) did participate.

[103] See Michael Mandelbaum, *The Nuclear Revolution: International Politics Before and After Hiroshima* (Cambridge University Press, 1981), pp. 166–75. The erosion of the American margin of economic superiority had greater consequences for the international economic system than for the political order. See Chapter 6, pp. 365–9.

strength, the United States *was* susceptible to the pull of the domino principle. The American government acted in 1947 and 1950 to prevent adverse chain reactions because it *could* act. Thirty-five years later the United States continued to act in the same manner because it was still the only country, with the exception of its chief adversary, that could do so.

Despite all that had changed, the rank ordering in the international system remained the same. The American margin of superiority over others had eroded, but it had by no means disappeared. The United States had the same position in the system in 1980 as it had had thirty-five years before.

A state's tendency to expand arises from both the character of the international system and the state's place within it. In 1980, as in 1945, the system was anarchic; at the later time, as on the earlier occasion, the United States was a strong state. Global economic, military, and political trends since 1945 had diminished but had not eliminated the American capacity to act on the impulse to expand that is built into international politics. The United States was still in a position to be drawn outward by distant disturbances that raised the specter of falling dominoes.

4

China, 1949–1976

The Strategies of Weakness

I

World War II redistributed and concentrated power in the international system. The United States and the Soviet Union emerged from the conflict considerably stronger than all other countries. The dissolution of the European colonial empires and the formation of many more independent political communities multiplied the number of lesser states. Although they were far less powerful than the two countries that would become nuclear giants in the postwar period, these new members of the international community were not necessarily weak states.

Strength and weakness are always relative. Where a particular state stands on the spectrum of power depends on what other countries it has to confront. Most of the numerous lesser powers after 1945 confronted one another rather than either the United States or the Soviet Union. One of them, however, had to contend with both. That country was the People's Republic of China. China's security policies between 1949 and 1979 were those of a weak state.

At first glance, China does not seem to belong to the category of weak states. It is certainly not by any standard a *small* state. It covers a larger expanse of the planet than any member of the international system except the Soviet Union, Canada, and the United States. It is by far the most populous of all sovereign political communities, numbering more than 1 billion people by the end of the 1970s.

For the purposes of security, however, it is not size that counts but strength, the capacity for self-defense. Although size is not irrelevant, it does not automatically determine how well a sovereign state can protect itself. Self-defense depends on military power. A state is powerful not in the abstract but in comparison with its potential adversaries. Many small or thinly populated states or ones that have feeble military establishments are not weak in the sense in which the term is used here, because they do not confront clearly superior enemies.

The People's Republic of China did muster considerable military might. It assembled a large army, which defeated the rival Guomindang in 1949 and got the better of the Indian army in border skirmishes in 1962 and Vietnamese troops in a short war in 1979. Compared with most of its immediate neighbors, China after 1949 was certainly not weak.[1] Compared with the United States and the Soviet Union, however, China was a weak state.

What made it weak was not simply inequality of power. Between every pair of sovereign states there is some difference in strength. What made China distinctive was the margin of superiority that its two great adversaries enjoyed and the Chinese policies to which this large disparity gave rise. Both countries were so much stronger than China that the outcome of a war between either and the People's Republic in which the stronger brought all its military resources to bear was certain. China would lose. Chinese security policies were a response to that commonly understood fact. They were a response, that is, to China's position in the international system.

Like strong states, the weak do not necessarily carry out security policies per se at all. In fact, most weak states do not at-

---

[1] In comparison with the peoples on their periphery – the Tibetans, Mongols, Manchus, and the peoples of Southeast Asia – the Han Chinese historically behaved as a strong state, in the pattern of the United States after 1945, Britain in the nineteenth century, and imperial Rome at the zenith of its power. See Chapter 4 and Michael H. Hunt, "Chinese Foreign Relations in Historical Perspective," in Harry Harding, ed., *China's Foreign Relations in the 1980s* (New Haven, Conn.: Yale University Press, 1984), p. 17.

tempt, by themselves, to conduct independent security policies. They either go along with the wishes of their stronger adversaries or affiliate themselves with third parties that are powerful enough to offset these much more powerful opponents. Each is a policy of submission; in neither case can the weak state act on its own. By choice or under compulsion it exchanges independence for security. Occasionally a weak state does seek to retain freedom of action in international affairs. After 1949 China was such a state.

The Chinese were resolved to chart their own course in the world. They were determined to maintain their independence as far as circumstances would permit. It is not surprising that they should place such emphasis on controlling their own destiny. Theirs was the oldest continuous political community in existence. They were the heirs of a great civilization and a vast empire. The Chinese people had always thought of their country as being at the center of creation.

Its history alone, however, does not explain China's distinctiveness as a weak state after 1945. Other countries could invoke precedents, if less ancient and glorious ones, for independence. In any case, precedents were hardly necessary. The impulse for independence became practically universal after World War II. The obvious differences between China and other weak states were related to the Chinese devotion to remaining independent. Its size, its population, and its potential for economic self-sufficiency gave China a weight in international politics that others lacked and made Chinese independence from the great powers more feasible. Compared with the United States and the Soviet Union, China was weak; as weak states go, however, it was strong. As a relatively strong weak state, it could aspire to independence; as a weak state, it had to adopt certain characteristic measures to remain free of foreign domination.

Markedly weak states are like very strong ones in that their position in the international system decisively influence their conduct. Both have less freedom to maneuver, and their policies are therefore more uniform and predictable, than states whose adversaries are neither much more nor much less powerful. In both cases, the state's position in the system imposes a particular pattern of conduct. So it was with China after 1949. Its security policies followed the logic of weakness.[2]

To impute the security policies of the People's Republic after 1949 to China's position in the international system is to employ an "outside-in" explanation. It is more common for accounts of Chinese foreign policy in this period to take the opposite, "inside-out" approach, with the emphasis on features of China's society, political system, and leadership. The country has often been portrayed as a revolutionary Communist state, seeking to overturn the world's existing order and reconstruct it along Marxist–Leninist

---

[2] A comparison between the different positions that states occupy in the international system and the basic variations in the structure of markets helps to account for the uniformity of the security policies of the very strong and the very weak and the broad differences among the security policies of states that are neither. A market characterized by monopoly is dominated by a single firm; in an oligopolistic market there are several large dominant firms; and where there are many firms of roughly equal size, there is said to be perfect competition. Strong states can be compared to monopolies, the position of weak states to that of firms in a perfectly competitive market, and states in the large in-between category to firms belonging to oligopolies. Both monopolies and firms facing perfect competition find themselves in "single-exit" situations (Spiro J. Latsis, *Method and Appraisal in Economics* [Cambridge University Press, 1976], p. 16). Each adopts a particular pattern of behavior, which can be predicted on the basis of its position in the market. In each case "the internal structure and characteristics of the decision-making unit [the firm] constitute merely irrelevent noise" (ibid., p. 25). So it is, in some measure, with the strong and the weak in the international system. Position determines behavior. The behavior of firms in an oligopolistic market varies much more widely and cannot be deduced from the market's structure. This is also the case for states that are neither strong nor weak. Both confront "multiple-exit" situations. The reason is similar. Both find themselves in "strategic" circumstances, in which the sensible course of action for each party depends on what the others choose to do. Each member of an oligopoly has some power over the market; states that are neither strong nor weak similarly affect the environment in which the others operate. There is greater freedom of maneuver and so greater uncertainty in each. In the cases of monopoly and perfect competition, and correspondingly for very strong and very weak states, by contrast, the environment does not vary because no other firm or state can shape it. Since the environment is fixed, the optimal way of coping with it is always the same. In "multiple-exit" situations, "the agent's internal environment, i.e. his decision and information-gathering rules, his psychological and social psychological characteristics etc., become central components in the explanation" (ibid., p. 16). Translated into the terms of international politics, this means that for states that are neither very strong nor very weak – and most states are neither – domestic considerations have an important bearing on policy.

lines, and above all as a Maoist state, governed by the beliefs of the supreme leader from 1949 to 1976, Mao Zedong.

Mao and his ideas were certainly important. He was not, perhaps, as consistently dominant a figure as he appeared to the rest of the world to be. Rivals contested his authority. At some times he was less powerful than at others. But his grip on foreign affairs seems to have been particularly strong. In China's dealings with the outside world, the available evidence suggests that Mao was in command.[3] Of course, very little evidence is available. That is another reason for emphasizing Mao's personal influence. The case of China in this sense differs from the others in this book. Since 1949, China's has been a closed political system. There are few documents or candid sources that reveal how decisions were made and why. Interpreting China's international policies after 1949 remains to a great extent an exercise in decoding esoteric pronouncements and inferring motives from behavior. Although the relevant calculations and jockeying for power were hidden from view, Mao's words were broadcast everywhere and with great fanfare. The Chinese said that these were the basis for understanding what they were doing. The student of Chinese foreign policy may doubt this assertion but has little else on which to form a judgment.[4]

Mao had a profound impact on Chinese domestic affairs. He appears to have been personally responsible for the wild swings in policy represented by the Great Leap Forward of the 1950s and the Cultural Revolution of the 1960s. In the international arena China's policy was much more tightly circumscribed. All governments have less room to maneuver abroad, where there are other sovereign powers, than at home, where they enjoy a monopoly of legitimate force. The governments of weak states find themselves even more narrowly circumscribed abroad than others. In fact, although it paid rhetorical homage to ideologically inspired goals, China did not seriously pursue them after 1949.[5]

[3] Joseph Camilleri, *Chinese Foreign Policy: The Maoist Era and Its Aftermath* (Seattle: University of Washington Press, 1980), p. ix; see also Donald S. G. Goodman, "Review of Michael Yahuda, *Towards the End of Isolationism: China's Foreign Policy after Mao*," *Times Literary Supplement*, May 18, 1984, p. 554.

[4] See James Pinckney Harrison, *The Long March to Power: A History of the Chinese Communist Party* (New York: Praeger, 1972), p. xiv.

[5] See Hunt, "Chinese Foreign Relations," pp. 39–40.

Mao endorsed the idea of revolution throughout the world, but under his tutelage China did almost nothing to promote it. The Chinese Communists may have been dissatisfied with the existing international order, but they made no significant efforts to overturn it. Their policies toward other countries were aimed chiefly at making themselves more secure. Mao's regime did not even run large risks to capture and incorporate the island of Taiwan, which it claimed as part of the People's Republic. That claim was in any event more a nationalist than a Marxist or Maoist one, and the Chinese were willing to set it aside in order to move closer to the United States when this served the interests of their security. Mao is reported to have said that the liberation of Taiwan could wait a thousand years.[6]

Mao said a great many things, not all of them consistent with one another. His pronouncements were numerous and Delphic enough to offer an authentically Maoist sanction to almost any policy. He and other Communist leaders often glorified flexibility.[7] On several occasions before 1949 they undertook to form a united front, making common cause with any group or foreign power whose support would enhance the party's position. They even made overtures to the archcapitalist Americans long before Richard Nixon's 1972 visit.[8] Their maneuvers were consistent with the simple aim of survival. This was the basis of party policy. Survival is, after all, the first task of any group or individual and necessarily the preoccupation of the weak. And survival was consistently in doubt for Mao and his colleagues.

In the 1930s and 1940s the Communists sought to survive within China in order to win power. Then, having gained control of the

---

[6] Taiwan was an issue of security as well as ideology. Chiang Kaishek's government there also claimed the right to govern all of China. Beijing therefore regarded the island as a base for a potential attack on the mainland.

[7] See, e.g., Robert G. Sutter, *China-Watch: Toward Sino-American Reconciliation* (Baltimore, Md.: Johns Hopkins University Press, 1978), pp. 75, 91; John Gittings, *The World and China: 1922–1972* (New York: Harper & Row, 1972), p. 242; Camilleri, *Chinese Foreign Policy*, p. 12; Jonathan D. Pollack, "China's Agonizing Reappraisal," in Herbert J. Ellison, ed., *The Sino-Soviet Conflict: A Global Perspective* (Seattle: University of Washington Press, 1982), p. 66.

[8] Sutter, *China-Watch*, pp. 4, 12, 16, 17; James Reardon-Anderson, *Yenan and the Great Powers: The Origins of Chinese Foreign Policy, 1944–1946* (New York: Columbia University Press, 1980), esp. pp. 168ff.

country, they found themselves subject to the same pressures on a larger scale. Retaining power meant surviving in an international system as hostile and threatening as China itself had been before 1949. The party's policies were similar before and after 1949 because the circumstances were similar. In both cases it was these circumstances more than political ideas drawn from Marx, Lenin, Mao, or anyone else that determined what the party did.

The Chinese Community Party and Mao himself were not, however, hypocritical, mouthing lofty ideals of social justice while seeking only to amass and retain power. One of the central principles on which the Chinese based their revolution was the need to be free of foreign control. Independence was part of their ideology. Mao and his colleagues were nationalists as well as Communists. They set out to remake China's relations with the rest of the world as well as its economic institutions and social structures. From its beginnings the party denounced the twin evils of "feudalism" and "imperialism." The two were deemed equally nefarious; the Communists' opposition to both helped them win support in China.[9]

The promise to overthrow the older order in the countryside, to loosen the grip of large landlords on Chinese agriculture, attracted peasants to the Communists' banner. It was the Communists' pledge to relieve the humiliation of foreign domination, their promise to abolish the coastal enclaves controlled by foreigners, and especially their willingness to resist when the Guomindang remained passive in the face of the Japanese occupation that won converts to the Communist cause among the urban population and the intelligentsia.[10] Nor was this promise only tactical, based solely on the calculation that it would help the party in its struggle for mastery of China. The humiliation inflicted by foreigners was deeply felt in all regions of the country and at every level of Chinese society. Independence from the imperialist powers was basic to the Communist program. "Hegemonism" replaced "imperialism" as the principal term for foreign domination in the 1970s, but the

---

[9] Harrison, *Long March*, p. 272; Maurice Meisner, *Mao's China: A History of the People's Republic* (New York, Free Press, 1977), p. 42; Reardon-Anderson, *Yenan*, p. 172.

[10] On the debate on the sources of the party's popularity see John Dunn, *Modern Revolution* (Cambridge University Press), 1972, p. 70; see also Meisner, *Mao's China*, pp. 37–8.

resistance to domination continued to form part of the basis for the regime's legitimacy both for the Chinese people and for itself. National independence was at the heart of the Chinese revolution. Although his successors repudiated much of Mao's legacy after his death, the substance of his foreign policy, with its emphasis on independence, remained.

China sought to maintain its independence in particular ways. Its diplomatic course was to navigate between the two great nuclear powers, trying to use their strength to its own advantage while avoiding binding ties to either. The principal episodes in the history of Chinese foreign policy between 1949 and 1979 – the Friendship Treaty with the Soviet Union in 1950, the Sino-Soviet split a decade later, the hostility to both the United States and the Soviet Union during the 1969s, and the shift toward the Americans in the 1970s – can be seen as responses to the changing international circumstance of a weak state trying to preserve its independence.

China's military policies were based on the assumption that it could not defeat either of its great adversaries in an all-out war and thus would have to raise the price of conquest to the point at which it would seem more expensive than it was worth to the enemy. The Chinese acquired and deployed military force to make certain that, if war came, the American or Soviet victory would be a Pyrrhic one.

A pattern of conduct that arises from the logic of weakness, like that of the Chinese, will appear wherever weak states strive to retain their independence. There is in fact a group of states whose security policies after 1945 resembled those of the People's Republic: the group of neutral countries in Europe – Finland, Sweden, Switzerland, Austria, and Yugoslavia. The neutrals differed from China in certain obvious respects other than their location. All were much smaller; all were wealthier; each was part of the industrial world. They had different cultural, social, and political traditions; all save Yugoslavia were liberal democracies, and the Yugoslav political system, although nominally Communist, was much more Western than that of any other Communist country.

For all their differences with China, and indeed among themselves, however, the position of the European neutrals in the international system was comparable to that of the People's Republic. Each of the European states was neutral. None belonged to either of the world's two main military and political blocs. None, however, was isolated from the conflict between those blocs, because each was located near the heart of the confrontation between them. Europe is the place where the United States and the Soviet Union confront each other directly. The neutrals' common international position, therefore, was the same as China's, and they responded to their situation in similar fashion.

The diplomacy of the European neutrals after 1945 was far less active than China's but can be seen nonetheless as the equivalent of the maneuvering of the People's Republic. The neutrals' military strategy and their preparations for war have pronounced affinities with those of China after 1949. Their common policies were the product of common circumstances, that is, of the same position in the international system. China and the European neutrals adopted the strategies of weakness.

II

Complete independence from all foreign powers means isolation from other members of the international system. This is not possible in the twentieth century. No state can wholly ignore all the others. Strong states are like powerful magnetic poles; weaker ones can seldom entirely evade their fields of force. Independence, therefore, must be redefined as equidistance among – or between – the most powerful states in the international system. Even this position is not always feasible. If the pull of one pole is stronger than that of the other, if one of the great powers is more threatening than the other, then independence requires not equidistance but closer association with the orbit of the other to offset the threat from the first. Weak states seek to use the power of stronger ones to offset their more formidable adversaries. The principle at work is obvious and common. It is the basis of alliances. It is therefore a tactic that compromises the independence of the weak state that employs it. Still, the kind of alignment that the weak state facing a powerful adversary will feel obliged to practice is not quite the same as a formal alliance.

An alliance carries with it the promise of assistance. Allies pledge to fight on each other's behalf. Alignment implies but does not guarantee assistance and generally does not specify what form it will take. Its purpose is not to create certainty in the mind of the potential aggressor that a powerful patron will come to the aid of the weak victim but rather to suggest that the patron *might* come. The difference between alignment, as it is defined here, and alliance is one of degree. A weak state whose diplomacy brings it nearer to one great power than to the other has greater freedom to maneuver but receives less protection than a lesser power tied to a stronger patron through a formal alliance. A weak state that emphasizes independence is sometimes obliged to surrender part of its liberty in the international system. Total independence makes for complete vulnerability, whereas total security leaves no latitude for diplomatic maneuvering. The diplomacy of the weak, when menaced by a much more powerful country, involves striking a balance between security and independence.

After 1945 the European neutrals were in fact more threatened by one great power than by the other. A concerted effort by the Soviet Union to conquer or subvert them or to control the workings of their political systems was much more likely than a comparable effort by the United States.[11] Menaced by one great power, they received a measure of protection from the other. The neutrals have a pronounced affinity for the Western coalition that the United States leads. All of them are tied economically to the West. All but Yugoslavia have liberal political regimes. That which is important in providing to the neutrals the indirect use of the weight of American military power to counterbalance the Soviet Union is not, however, something that is within their control. It is their location. Despite the absence of formal treaties, they are in effect aligned with the United States and the West because of where they are.

---

[11] Finland has a Treaty of Friendship, Cooperation, and Mutual Assistance with the Soviet Union, which the Finns interpret as a guarantee of their neutrality and take to justify their armed forces. These forces would ostensibly be used to prevent an attack on the Soviet Union through Finland. Although the Finns do not say so, they would also be used against the Soviets if needed. See Erling Bjol, "Nordic Security," Adelphi Paper No. 181 (London: International Institute for Strategic Studies, 1973), pp. 13–14. The Swedes, in candid moments, have admitted that the threat for which they must prepare comes from the east, not the west. Ibid., p. 19; William Taylor, "The Defense Policy of Sweden," in Douglas Murray and Paul Viotti, eds., *The Defense Policies of Nations* (Baltimore, Md.: Johns Hopkins University Press, 1982), p. 300.

To change the European neutrals' political status by force would upset arrangements that have lasted for a generation in a part of the world about which both the United States and the Soviet Union are sensitive and where they are both heavily armed. A Soviet attack on a neutral would establish a dangerous precedent. More to the point, it would set in motion events that might not remain confined to the countries in which they began. The United States has not pledged to defend Finland, Sweden, Switzerland, Austria, or Yugoslavia. But the Soviet Union knows that the Americans would not accept the conquest of any of these countries with equanimity, if only because they are so close to countries that the United States *has* pledged to defend. The Soviets could not be certain that a war initiated by an attack on Helsinki or Belgrade would stay within the borders of Finland or Yugoslavia. This uncertainty, fostered by geography rather than active diplomacy, contributes to Finnish and Yugoslav security. The European neutrals have received the benefits of alignment not because of what they have done but because of where they happen to be.[12] Their location is the equivalent, for the purposes of their security, of China's size. If gives them leverage against the strong that other weak states do not have. It thus gives them the prospect of conducting strategies of weakness with some hope of success.

Like the European neutrals, the Chinese valued their independence. Like them, China was considerably weaker than the powers it confronted, the United States and the Soviet Union. The threat to China, however, was not fixed for thirty years, as it was for the neutrals. The Chinese were not consistently in more danger from one than from the other great power. The United States and the Soviet Union alternated as China's principal threat. Unlike the

---

[12] The European neutrals are "free riders" in the sense that they have received the benefits of a collective good, in this case protection afforded by NATO, without contributing to its cost (see Chapter 6, pp. 357–65). In general, they spend a smaller fraction of their gross national product on defense than do the European members of the Atlantic alliance (which in turn spend proportionately less than does the United States). They do incur some costs for defense, however, and their defense burdens are heavier than the fraction of the GNP that they devote to it suggests. All have reserve armies, which require all able-bodied men up to a certain age to devote some part of each year to active duty. See John L. Clarke, "NATO, Neutrals, and National Defense." *Survival*, November–December 1982, p. 262.

European neutrals, moreover, the People's Republic did not receive protection from either great power simply by dint of its geography. Alignment with one great power or the other was not automatic; it required active diplomacy. The history of Chinese foreign policy in the three decades after 1949 is in part, therefore, the history of diplomatic initiatives to move closer to one than to the other, with an intervening period of detachment from both. At all times the Chinese were responding to what they judged to be the greatest threat to their security at the moment. Their diplomacy was the product of a deeply felt impulse for independence tempered by the need to remain secure.

Almost immediately after consolidating power in China, the leadership of the Communist Party aligned the country with the Soviet Union. Their Treaty of Friendship, signed in Moscow on February 14, 1950, established a number of programs for economic cooperation, including a low-interest Soviet loan to the Chinese. It included a pledge of mutual assistance in response to an attack by Japan or any of its allies.

The Sino-Soviet treaty was inconsistent with a policy of strict independence. It put the People's Republic in the camp of one of the two great powers. The new rulers of China had a predilection for the Soviet side in the global struggle. They were, like the Soviet leaders, Communists; that counted for something. The Soviet Union was the senior and most powerful member of the world Communist movement, the cradle of the revolution, and the motherland of socialism. Ideological solidarity was not irrelevant to China's international conduct in the years immediately following the Communist victory.

Mao and his colleagues no doubt valued fraternal ties not merely for their own sake, however, but also for what they might bring China. The new leaders sought economic assistance on a massive scale. The country they had conquered was poor. The disruptive four-year civil war had come on the heels of a harsh Japanese occupation, which had in turn been preceded by a long period of political disintegration and economic stagnation. The new Communist government faced an enormous task of reconstruction. Its leaders hoped that the Soviet Union would help with it. They certainly understood that they would get no help elsewhere.

An equally powerful motive for China's alignment with the Soviet

Union was security. As well as an act of Communist solidarity, it can be seen as the logical response to a perceived threat from the United States. The Friendship Treaty made reference to Japan but was aimed at Japan's conqueror and occupier.[13] In the first half of the 1950s the North American colossus, the strongest nation in the world, was to send troops to China's borders, fight a bitter war with the People's Liberation Army in Korea, surround China with bases, and in effect declare the Communist government in Beijing illegal and transitory. All of this was set in motion by the Korean War. The treaty with the Soviet Union, it is true, was signed four months before the war began. American officials had washed their hands of the Chinese civil war, asserting that the outcome had, all along, been beyond their power to change. Before June 25, 1950, the Truman administration was actually resisting any role for the United States on the Asian mainland.[14]

The new rulers of China, however, seem to have given a different interpretation to American intentions in Asia at the beginning of 1950: They felt threatened. The United States had given considerable support to the Guomindang during the civil war. The Communists may well have doubted that the Americans were prepared to write off completely so substantial an investment.[15] Ominously from the Chinese point of view, the United States was consolidating its position in Japan.[16]

If the Chinese Communist leaders suspected the United States of wishing to dominate China even after Chiang had retreated to the island of Taiwan, the Korean War confirmed their suspicions. The American commander, General Douglas MacArthur, moved his troops within fifty miles of the Manchurian border. The Amer-

---

[13] This interpretation can be found in Allen S. Whiting, *China Crosses the Yalu: The Decision to Enter the Korean War* (New York: Macmillan, 1960), p. 28.

[14] See Chapter 3, pp. 158–60.

[15] Mao denounced the State Department's *China White Paper* of 1949. Ironically, its purpose was to distance the United States from the Chinese conflict, a policy that was entirely in the interests of the Communists. Camilleri, *Chinese Foreign Policy*, p. 7.

[16] Mao and his colleagues were perhaps aware of a historical precedent for American intervention on the heels of their victory. The Ming dynasty was toppled in the seventeenth century by rebels from within China. But before the rebels could consolidate their hold on the country, foreigners from Manchuria stepped in, defeated them, and took control. John K. Fairbank, *The United States and China*, 4th ed. (Cambridge, Mass.: Harvard University Press, 1979), p. 93.

ican air force bombed power plants along the Yalu River, which divided Korea from China. In response, the Chinese dispatched "volunteers" to fight the American and South Korean forces that had swept up the peninsula. After initial success, the fighting went badly for the Chinese. Poorly equipped compared with their adversaries and employing tactics of frontal assault that were alarming to the defenders but also extremely costly to themselves, they suffered enormous casualties. In several major battles their losses were proportional to those sustained by the armies at Verdun and the Somme in World War I.[17] For the Chinese, one plain lesson of the war was their vulnerability to American firepower. Their only source of modern weapons was the Soviet Union.

The most modern and powerful weapon in 1950 was the atomic bomb. The Chinese did not have one. The United States issued oblique but unmistakable threats to use its atomic weapons against China both during the Korean War and afterward.[18] The only other country with nuclear weapons was the Soviet Union. However unreliable a source of protection the Soviet Union may have been – and neither Stalin nor his successors ever showed any inclination to fight on behalf of China – it was the only one available. And if the Chinese could not be certain that the Soviets would respond to an American nuclear attack against them, the Treaty of Friendship at least served to instill doubts in the minds of the Americans that the Soviets would *not* respond.

The Korean War triggered the expansion of the American military presence in Asia and the Pacific. The war itself ended in a standoff. The peninsula remained divided. The basic Chinese goal was achieved; there was no hostile state on the Manchurian border. But South Korea remained in the hands of a regime friendly to the United States, and American troops stayed there in force. The American association with Japan was made formal by the security pact signed by the two countries in 1951, which confirmed Japan's status as a base for American naval and air power. At about the same time the United States began assisting the French in their struggle against Communist insurgents in Indochina. Most impor-

---

[17] Drew Middleton, *The Duel of the Giants: China and Russia in Asia* (New York, Scribners, 1978), p. 72.

[18] Gittings, *World and China*, pp. 202–3.

tant, Chiang Kaishek became an American ally. Washington signed a security treaty with him in 1955. His forces were supplied with American weapons. American nuclear-tipped intermediate-range Matador Missiles were dispatched to Formosa in 1955. The American Seventh Fleet patrolled the Taiwan Strait. The American-sponsored Southeast Asia Treaty Organization, also created in 1955, was in effect an anti-Chinese coalition of Asian countries. All of this seemed to bespeak a determination to retrace the path the Japanese had followed in the 1930s, to reverse the verdict of 1949 and restore Chiang to power on the mainland.

The Chinese alignment with the Soviet Union lasted less than a decade. By the end of the 1950s, the relationship between the two had soured and the programs of cooperation had ended. In 1960, the Soviets abruptly withdrew the economic and technical advisers they had sent to help build Chinese industry.[19] At roughly the same time, the two ruling parties began trading charges of bad faith and ideological deviation. At first these exchanges took place privately. They soon became public but were couched in the particular argot of international Communism. Finally, the hostility between them burst into the open. An article entitled "Long Live Leninism" appeared without a byline in China in April 1960 but was widely attributed to Mao himself. It denounced those who were bent on revising "the truths revealed by Lenin," especially the truths that applied to relations between socialist and capitalist nations. The target of the author's ire was plainly the Soviet Union.[20] The Soviet leader, Nikita Khrushchev, responded by attacking the Chinese, directly but secretly at Communist Party meetings in Bucharest in June 1960 and in Moscow in November of that year, then openly but indirectly at the Soviet party's Twenty-second Congress in October 1961.[21] He leveled harsh criticisms at China's ally, Albania, but his real target was obvious.

[19] For a useful chronology of Sino-Soviet relations from 1949 forward see Harry Gelman, *The Soviet Far East Buildup and Soviet Risk-Taking Against China*, R-2943-AF (Santa Monica, Calif.: Rand, August 1982), pp. xxii–xxvi.

[20] O. Edmund Clubb, *China and Russia: The "Great Game"* (New York: Columbia University Press, 1971), pp. 440–1; see also Meisner, *Mao's China*, pp. 248–9.

[21] Nikita Khrushchev, *Khrushchev Remembers*, with an introduction, commentary, and notes by Edward Crankshaw; trans. and ed. by Strobe Talbott (Boston: Little, Brown, 1970, p. 475), esp. nn. 11 and 12.

The Sino-Soviet rift was at least partly an ideological split: It involved different views of social organization and international politics. "Inside-out" explanations are especially pertinent to Mao himself, who played a major role on the Chinese side. The Chinese were appalled by the bureaucratic ossification that afflicted the Soviet Union only four decades after the October revolution. The Soviets, in turn, were aghast at the disruption caused by China's "Great Leap Forward" and by the torrent of criticism that the Chinese Communist Party permitted during the "Hundred Flowers" movement. The Chinese were also scornful of Soviet reticence in confronting the West, while the Soviets were alarmed at the rash Chinese attitudes toward the prospects of nuclear war with the United States.[22]

The two Communist powers conducted their rhetorical dispute in ideological terms.[23] This was because these were the terms of public discourse in use in the Communist world, rather than because ideological grievances were the sum and substance of the quarrel. The use of certain political categories was indispensable because both regimes based their claims to power on the particular world view from which these categories arose, with its universal class struggle and its designation of the Communist Party as the arbiter of the proper method for prosecuting it. By abandoning this rhetoric they would have forfeited the basis for the legitimacy, such as it was, of Communist rule in Russia and China.

Another interpretation of the Sino-Soviet rift is that it was not simply a dispute over the means of putting the principles of

---

[22] The pioneering work on the subject, Donald S. Zagoria's *The Sino-Soviet Conflict, 1956–1961* (Princeton, N.J.: Princeton University Press, 1962), imputes the rupture chiefly to ideological differences. For a summary and analysis of the principal Western interpretations of the dispute see Donald W. Treadgold, "Alternative Western Views of the Sino-Soviet Conflict," in Ellison, ed., *Sino-Soviet Conflict*.

[23] Mao was particularly prone to charging that China could not get along with the Soviet Union because the Soviet leadership had been taken over by "revisionists." With his passing, China itself became much more "revisionist" – that is, more tolerant of Western economic practices and institutions – than the Soviet Union had ever been during his lifetime, but relations between the two countries did not revert to the friendship of the 1950s. Jonathan D. Pollack, *The Sino-Soviet Rivalry and Chinese Security Debate*, R-2907-AF (Santa Monica, Calif.: Rand, October 1982), p. 5; Harry Gelman, "The Sino-Soviet Dispute in the 1970s: An Overview," in Ellison, ed., *Sino-Soviet Conflict*, p. 357.

Marxism–Leninism into practice, but also a contest of national aspirations of the sort familiar throughout history.[24] The alignment with the Soviet Union was both artificial and fragile because it violated the strong Chinese preference for independence. For the Chinese regime, the Sino-Soviet Treaty of Friendship was not merely an arrangement of convenience, a way of getting economic reconstruction off to a good start with the aid of a friendly neighbor. It was also a matter of necessity, part of the price of survival in an international system whose most powerful member was hostile to Communist rule in China.

Alignment with the Soviet Union proved not to be convenient. The Chinese did not receive the benefits for which they had hoped. When it was no longer necessary, when the threat that had called it into existence had abated, the Chinese struck out on their own, as they had always preferred to do. They acted to assert their independence. The alignment did not end amicably. It proved to be worse than simply inconvenient. The Chinese came to see it as a threat to their independence. They came to believe that the Soviets had tried to use the Treaty of Friendship to dominate China, to subvert the very principle of independence the Chinese had aligned themselves with the Soviet Union in order to protect.

The Chinese were suspicious of the Soviets even when their relations were warmest. The 1950 treaty was not, after all, the culmination of a long pattern of friendly ties between the two Communist parties. In the 1920s, the Soviets had ordered the infant Chinese party, while retaining its own identity, to join the Guomindang, which proceeded to turn on the Communists and massacre them. Harassed and driven from the cities by Chiang Kai-shek's forces, they established themselves in rural China under Mao's leadership. The Russians criticized Mao's strategy of basing the revolution on the peasantry rather than on the urban proletariat.

---

[24] Gelman, "Sino-Soviet Dispute," p. 368. Jonathan Pollack has argued that over time the national aspects of the dispute came to take precedence over its ideological features. The death of Mao and the demise of the Gang of Four count as turning points in the process. China's public assertions, beginning in 1963, that the Soviet Union occupied territory that was rightfully Chinese, were also significant; territorial disputes are unmistakably national rather than "socialist" issues. Pollack, *Sino-Soviet Rivalry*, p. vi. The argument here is that the rift was largely a national one, even during Mao's lifetime.

Stalin was conciliatory toward the Japanese while they were ravaging China. In 1939 he negotiated an armistice with Japan and in April 1941 signed a neutrality pact. The Soviet Union finally declared war, a few days before the Japanese surrender in August 1945, then proceeded to march into Manchuria and strip the province of much of its industrial equipment before withdrawing.

The Soviets provided little assistance to their Chinese comrades in the civil war that erupted after the Japanese defeat. Stalin urged the Chinese Communists to compromise with the Guomindang and partition the country between them. Soviet representatives accompanied China's retreating government southward in 1949 when most other foreign emissaries had abandoned it; in May 1949 the Soviets even extended an agreement with the Guomindang for joint rights in Xinjiang for five additional years. Stalin's policies were evidently designed not so much to promote a Communist victory in China as to keep the country divided and weak.

After the victory, the Treaty of Friendship took two months to conclude. The negotiations were apparently difficult. For part of that period Stalin reportedly kept Mao waiting in Moscow to see him, to the displeasure of the Chinese leader.[25]

The benefits of alignment with the Soviet Union, apart from the measure of protection against the United States that it afforded, were meager and disappointing to the Chinese. They did receive shipments of armaments from the Soviets during the Korean War, but these did not start arriving in significant number until the late summer of 1951, long after China had entered the conflict. They were, moreover, of poor quality and came in limited quantity. The Chinese had to pay for them and resented having to bear the entire

---

[25] According to Mao: "In 1950 I argued with Stalin in Moscow for two months. We argued about the Treaty of Mutual Assistance and Alliance, about the Chinese Changchun Railway, about the joint-stock companies, about the border question." Quoted in Camilleri, *Chinese Foreign Policy*, p. 48. The report that Mao was kept waiting comes from Krushchev. The former Soviet leader was hardly a disinterested party: In his memoirs he blames Stalin for almost everything that went wrong in Soviet foreign policy, including the rift with China. Still, the period Mao spent in Moscow was unusually long, and no evidence that he was doing anything except waiting for Stalin has come to light. Nikita S. Khrushchev, *Khrushchev Remembers: The Last Testament*, intro. by Edward Crankshaw and Jerrold Schecter; trans. and ed. by Strobe Talbott (Boston: Little, Brown, 1974), p. 240.

burden of defending, as they saw it, the entire socialist camp against an assault by the American imperialists.[26]

The Chinese had to pay, as well, for the loans, the imported technology, and the factories that Soviet advisers helped to construct.[27] They had to produce goods for export to the Soviet Union in payment for this assistance – another source of Chinese resentment of the Soviets. The scale of Soviet assistance did not meet Chinese hopes.[28] In the late 1950s the Chinese reportedly advanced the idea that socialist solidarity required an equitable distribution of resources among the members of the socialist camp, equality being defined in per capita terms. During his 1957 visit to Moscow, Mao suggested a massive transfer of resources from both the Soviet Union and Eastern Europe to speed the industrialization of China. The Soviets refused.[29]

An important aim of the Communist leaders was the conquest

---

[26] Michael B. Yahuda, *China's Role in World Affairs* (New York: St. Martin's Press, 1978), pp. 55, 171; Gittings, *World and China*, p. 153; Clubb, *China and Russia*, p. 391; Camilleri, *Chinese Foreign Policy*, p. 54. According to Jonathan Pollack, however, the Chinese repaid only 20% of the costs of the military assistance they received from the Soviet Union during the war. "China as a Military Power," in Onkar S. Marwah and Jonathan D. Pollack, eds., *Military Power and Policy in the Asian States* (Boulder, Colo.: Westview Press, 1980), p. 81.

[27] In his memoirs Khrushchev describes an episode that can serve as a parable for the mutual disappointment and distrust that Soviet economic assistance provoked among the Chinese. It was agreed that a road would be built from Beijing to Soviet Kazakhstan. Each country was to build the road on its own side of the border. The Soviets did so. The Chinese did not and asked the Soviets to build the road on the Chinese side as well. Krushchev cites this as an example of Chinese duplicity and determination to exploit the Soviets. *Khrushchev Remembers*, p. 466. The issue may well have looked different from the Chinese point of view. Their country was poorer, its revolution was more recent, it was saddled with the burden of confronting the United States, and it had been the victim of a century of imperialist exploitation to boot. So the Chinese may well have believed that the Soviets should have been willing to do more for China than China should have been expected to do for the Soviet Union.

[28] It has been suggested that the Chinese received only 10% of what they requested in aid from the Soviets. David Floyd, *Mao Against Krushchev* (New York: Praeger, 1964), p. 12. If true, this may, of course, say as much about Chinese expectations as about Soviet generosity.

[29] It was during this visit that the Soviets promised the Chinese a sample atomic bomb, perhaps in an effort to assuage the anger that their rejection of Mao's economic demands had provoked. Clubb, *China and Russia*, p. 420–5.

– or, as they saw it, the liberation – of Taiwan, the last Chinese
province remaining outside their control. They failed to enlist Soviet help in this. They wanted Soviet military might to offset Chiang
Kaishek's protector, the United States. The Soviets refused. Mao's
public pronouncements in the latter part of the 1950s about imperialism, which he branded a "paper tiger," and about the balance
of forces in the world, which he took to favor the East over the
West, can be read both as efforts to prod the Soviets to oppose
the United States more actively and as jibes at the Soviet leaders
for shirking their socialist duty in confronting the imperialists, especially when Sputnik had given them a decisive military
advantage.[30]

The year 1958 marked a turning point in the People's Republic's
campaign against Taiwan and in Sino-Soviet relations in general.
The Beijing government precipitated a crisis by shelling a group
of small islands close to the mainland that the Guomindang controlled and had fortified. This was not, in all likelihood, intended
to be the beginning of an attack on Taiwan itself. It was more likely
aimed, rather, at driving the Guomindang forces off the smaller
islands, exposing the helplessness of the United States in preventing this, and beginning a process of demoralization on Taiwan
that would eventually lead to the collapse of Chiang's regime. The
United States responded forcefully, issuing stern warnings and
veiled nuclear threats and assisting in the resupply of the offshore
islands.[31]

The Soviets made it clear that they would not take part in the
campaign. They, too, issued stern warnings, cautioning the United
States against invading the mainland. But they did so in a way that
made it plain that, in harassing the islands, the Chinese Com-

---

[30] Zagoria, *Sino-Soviet Conflicts*, pp. 217–18; Camilleri, *Chinese Foreign Policy*,
p. 11. In his memoirs Khrushchev registers his alarm at Mao's cavalier attitude
toward confronting the United States and says that he undertook to explain the
elementary facts of life in the nuclear age to the Chinese leader. There is no
independent confirmation that the conversations that he describes took place
as he recounts them. But Khrushchev's inclusion of such accounts suggests that
he was disturbed by Mao's proclamations and defensive about Soviet policies
on this issue, which was perhaps just what Mao intended. Khrushchev, *Khrushchev Remembers*, pp. 467–70; Krushchev, *The Last Testament*, pp. 257, 261.
[31] Zagoria, *Sino-Soviet Conflict*, p. 215.

munists would have to rely on themselves. It is reasonable to suppose that Mao and his colleagues concluded that the Soviets would not help them win control of Taiwan. In fact, the Soviets more or less said so. Khrushchev's visit to Peking the next year went badly; Chinese disappointment with the Soviet performance in the 1958 crisis may have had something to do with this.[32]

The Chinese seem to have concluded from the events of 1958 that the United States was determined to protect Taiwan but not to invade the mainland.[33] Once the Communist shelling stopped, the Americans withdrew their air escorts from the Straits. An American official told the Chinese directly, through ongoing ambassadorial talks in Warsaw, that the United States had no intention of attacking the mainland or of supporting any effort by Chiang Kaishek to recapture it. If the Communists were prepared to leave Chiang in possession of Taiwan, the United States would not try to undo their revolution.[34]

If the Americans were not going to follow in Japan's footsteps, if they were not going to use Taiwan as a base from which to launch an assault on China itself, then the Chinese alignment with the Soviet Union was unnecessary. If the Soviets were resolved to be ungenerous in providing economic assistance and reluctant to help drive Chiang from Taiwan, then the alignment forged in 1950 was,

[32] Ibid., pp. 213, 214, 216; Camilleri, *Chinese Foreign Policy*, p. 57. Khrushchev describes the visit and its difficulties briefly but does not refer to the events of the year before. *Khrushchev Remembers*, p. 472.

[33] Sutter, *China Watch*, p. 63.

[34] Allen S. Whiting, *The Chinese Calculus of Deterrence: India and Indochina* (Ann Arbor: University of Michigan Press, 1975), pp. 68–9; Jonathan D. Pollack, *Security, Strategy and the Logic of Chinese Foreign Policy*, Institute of East Asian Studies, Research Papers and Policy Studies 5 (Berkeley: University of California, 1981), p. 23. The assertion that the Chinese concluded after 1958 that the United States posed no threat to them and that they were therefore free to abandon their alignment with the Soviet Union is not beyond challenge. They may have reached this conclusion as early as 1953, at the time of Korean armistice. On the other hand, they may have feared an American assault as late as the early 1960s, when the United States was reportedly still sponsoring anti-Chinese activity in Tibet. To the extent that the Chinese leadership did not feel confident that they would not face an American assault, the split with the Soviet Union and its willingness to confront both great nuclear powers simultaneously must be understood in "inside-out" terms. It becomes the expression of ideological precepts, a policy *not* fully compatible with the logic of weakness.

from the standpoint of the Chinese Communists, useless. It was, in fact, worse than useless. The Soviets, the Chinese came to believe, were bent on dominating them.

The Soviet Union trespassed on China's sovereign prerogatives. At the end of World War II they occupied Port Arthur and Dairen, ice-free ports on the Yellow Sea. Stalin agreed to withdraw after the Chinese Communist victory in 1949 but used the outbreak of the Korean War as an excuse to remain. In 1950, Soviet–Chinese joint stock mining companies were established to exploit China's mineral resources. Because they gave the Soviet Union a measure of control over China's resources, these arrangements came to offend the Chinese sense of national integrity.[35] After Stalin's death, his successors agreed to withdraw from the two ports and dissolve the joint stock companies, but a residue of bitterness and suspicion among the Chinese remained. The Soviets meddled in internal Chinese politics. They tried to arrange the Chinese leadership to their own liking, which usually meant supporting Mao's opponents.[36] After 1949, the Soviets established independent relations with Kao Kang, the party leader in Manchuria, whom they seem to have tried to build up as a rival to Mao. No doubt at least partly for that reason Kao was purged in 1953.[37] The issue of Soviet influence may also have been involved in the purge of three principal military leaders of the Maoist era – Peng Dehuai, the defense minister, in 1959; Lo Jui-ching, the army chief of staff, in 1965; and Lin Biao, the defense minister and designated successor to Mao, in 1971. The circumstances surrounding the fall of each man were complicated; in each case personal ambition and jockeying for position within the Chinese leadership were at least as significant as, if not more so than, differing attitudes toward other countries. But Peng and Lo and perhaps even Lin did seem to favor

---

[35] Khrushchev makes this point, blaming the mistake in offending Chinese sensibilities on Stalin. *Khrushchev Remembers*, p. 463; *The Last Testament*, p. 240.

[36] On the period before 1949 see Harrison, *Long March*, pp. 212–13, and Meisner, *Mao's China*, p. 34.

[37] Robert R. Simmons, *The Strained Alliance: Peking, P'yongyang, Moscow, and the Politics of the Korean Civil War* (New York: Free Press, 1975), pp. 57–8; Clubb, *China and Russia*, pp. 405–6; Meisner, *Mao's China*, p. 32. In his memoirs Khrushchev strongly suggests that Kao was Moscow's man in China. *The Last Testament*, p. 243.

closer ties with the Soviet Union than Mao and others would countenance.

Moscow's offers of military cooperation during the 1950s appeared to the Chinese to be pretexts, at best, for the use of Chinese territory and Chinese military forces for Soviet purposes and, at worst, for exercising the kind of control the Soviet army had established in Eastern Europe. The Soviets requested bases in China to communicate with their submarines in the Pacific. The Chinese refused. Khrushchev records Mao as saying, "We've had the British and other foreigners on our territory for years now, and we're not ever going to let anyone use our land for their own purposes again."[38] The Soviets also proposed a joint naval command in the western Pacific, which would have given them control over the Chinese navy and China's coastal waters. This, too, the Chinese refused. The proposals probably reinforced the Chinese view of the Soviets as the latest in the line of European imperial powers that had seized pieces of China's territory, dominated and distorted its economy, and in general trampled the country's national integrity.

Even contentious issues between the Soviet Union and China that seemed clearly related to Marxist–Leninist principles were at least partly conflicts of national ambition. Krushchev's denunciation of Stalin in his secret speech to the Twentieth Party Congress in 1956 shocked the Chinese. They were taken aback not so much by the smashing of an icon of world Communism – they could hardly have been uncritical admirers of Stalin – nor even because the attack on Stalin's cult of personality could be interpreted as an oblique attack on Mao. Rather, they were indignant because the speech marked a major shift in Communist orthodoxy, which Krushchev had undertaken without consulting them. The Chinese were offended at the idea that the Soviet Union could act unilaterally on behalf of the entire socialist camp. After Stalin's death, Mao considered himself the senior Communist leader. Neither he nor his colleagues were content to be the junior partner of the Soviet Union.[39]

---

[38] Khrushchev, *Khrushchev Remembers*, p. 473; Khrushchev, *The Last Testament*, p. 259.

[39] Khrushchev asserted that Mao sought primacy in the international Communist movement. The Soviet leader apparently assumed as a matter of course that

Similarly, China's Great Leap Forward of 1958, an effort to promote rapid economic growth by mobilizing the Chinese population and building industrial plants in rural as well as urban areas, was more than simply shocking to the Soviets because it deviated sharply from the Soviet pattern of economic development. It was also threatening to the Soviets because it was an effort to dispense with their economic assistance and to vault past them in economic terms. The Soviets did not relish the idea of the Chinese becoming richer and more powerful than they.

One of the basic causes of the Sino-Soviet rift, which at the same time symbolized the forces that drove the two powers apart, was the issue of nuclear weapons. When Mao journeyed to Moscow for the second and last time in 1957, the Soviets promised to provide China with a sample atomic bomb. When, in 1960, they withdrew their economic advisers, they reneged on this promise. In 1961 the Chinese declared that they would build their own bomb. In 1963 the United States and the Soviet Union signed the Limited Test Ban Treaty, which prohibited atomic testing in the atmosphere, in outer space, and in the oceans. One of its purposes was to complicate the task of developing atomic weapons for those countries that had yet to acquire them. Without testing, a country could not have full confidence in the nuclear weapons it had assembled. The test ban was intended to discourage, if only indirectly, the spread of nuclear weapons.[40] The Chinese, who did not have atomic weapons in 1963, saw the treaty as an attempt to keep them from getting any, as indeed it was. The signing of the treaty demonstrated that the Soviet Union would cooperate with the United States to advance what it defined as its own interests even at the cost of Chinese displeasure. The Chinese refused to sign the treaty and made their bitterest and most overt public denunciation of the Soviet Union to date, putting it on the same footing as the

this was something to which the Soviet Union alone was entitled. *The Last Testament*, p. 283; William E. Griffith, *The Sino-Soviet Rift* (Cambridge, Mass.: MIT Press, 1964), emphasizes the contest for leadership of international communism as the basis for the conflict between the two countries. On the difficulties each regime had in deferring to the other see Benjamin Schwartz, *Communism in China: Indeology in Flux* (Cambridge, Mass., Harvard University Press, 1968), Chap. 5, esp. pp. 144–8.

[40] See Michael Mandelbaum, *The Nuclear Question: The United States and Nuclear Weapons, 1946–1976* (Cambridge University Press, 1979), Chap. 7.

United States. They accused the two great powers of conspiring with each other against China.

To the Chinese, the atomic bomb was yet another benefit that the Soviet Union had promised but failed to deliver. Moscow's refusal to provide them with a sample bomb was another instance of Soviet duplicity and selfishness. Once again the Soviets were insisting on remaining superior to China. They appeared determined to keep China weak and thus subject to their influence. For their part the Soviets were undoubtedly alarmed at the prospect of a nuclear-armed China, considering the self-inflicted disruptions of the Great Leap Forward and Mao's loose talk about atomic war with millions of casualties. But for the Chinese the atomic bomb became a symbol of the kind of relationship Europeans had imposed on them and that the revolution had been made to overthrow. The bomb was the most powerful weapon of self-defense and therefore the ultimate guarantor of independence. The Chinese decision to acquire it was part of their determination to be subservient to no one.

III

In the 1960s, having broken with the Soviet Union, China adopted a position in international politics aloof from and hostile to both great powers. It branded both of them imperialist; it said both were seeking hegemony; it asserted that both had to be resisted. If there was no need to remain aligned with the Soviets, neither was there any reason to modify the decade-old hostility to the Americans.

China's position was not an entirely comfortable one. It did not receive protection, even indirect protection, from either of the two great nuclear powers. It was at odds with both of them. But the position was not so dangerous as to force the People's Republic to align itself with either. It was not untenable. Neither great power was as actively menacing as the United States had seemed during the Korean War and would be again in the eyes of some Chinese officials at the height of the Vietnam War or as the Soviet Union came to be seen after the invasion of Czechoslovakia in 1968. Moreover, although the People's Republic was independent, Beijing did not see itself as standing alone. The Chinese affiliated themselves rhetorically with the part of the world that belonged to neither

camp. Their place, they said, was in the "intermediate zone" between the two. The boundaries of the intermediate zone were never
permanently specified; they were constantly being redefined. They
generally encompassed the poorer nations of Asia, Africa, and Latin
America, those that together are commonly called the Third World,
many of them recently released from colonial rule. In the Chinese
view, these countries shared with China a history of imperial exploitation and an interest in breaking the grip of the two great
powers on the international system. On occasion, however, Beijing
seemed to count Europe, too, as part of the great space between
the United States and the Soviet Union. Almost any country other
than the two great powers seemed at some point eligible for membership in the intermediate zone.

In the history of the Chinese Communist Party, the idea of
standing in the vanguard of a third force in international politics
predated the break with the Soviet Union. It was another version
of the policy of united front, of making common cause on the basis
of a common adversary, which the party had championed before
1949. As early as 1946, Mao proposed the existence of a vast zone
between the United States and the Soviet Union. Zhou Enlai
played a prominent part in the celebrated meeting of the nonaligned nations at Bandung, Indonesia, in 1955.[41] In the 1960s,
however, it became a central theme of Chinese foreign policy. It
conformed to the spirit of independence.

Still, the Chinese did very little to advance the cause of the
world's intermediate zone. In the first half of the 1960s they provided modest support to a few Third World countries. They made
loans to some African nations, and in December 1963 and January
1964 Prime Minister Zhou Enlai and Foreign Minister Chen Yi
toured Africa. They competed with Moscow for the allegiance of
Communist parties outside Europe. Although they could offer less
economic and military assistance than the Soviets, they nonetheless
enjoyed some success. The Indian party split into two factions, one
of them supporting Beijing. Relations with the Indonesian Communists also became close.

---

[41] At the time the Chinese claimed that the nonaligned movement was simply an
adjunct to the socialist camp because the objective interests of the two groups
coincided. Yahuda, *China's Role*, p. 75–6.

On the whole, however, Chinese assistance to revolutionary movements in Africa and Asia was largely rhetorical. Often, it is true, Chinese rhetoric gave the opposite impression. In 1965 Lin Biao published an article entitled "Long Live the People's War" asserting that Mao's revolutionary strategy of organizing China's countryside and then surrounding, strangling, and capturing its cities had metaphorical relevance for the whole world. The Asian, African, and Latin American "countryside" should, he said, adopt similar tactics against the European and North American "cities." The article aroused considerable unease in the West. One of its purposes, however, was to distance China from these revolutionary struggles. Lin's message was that the people of the intermediate zone would have to wage their campaign against the global urban bourgeoisie on their own, without help from China. Such military and economic assistance as the Chinese did give was geared almost exclusively to the security requirements of the People's Republic rather than to the promotion of revolution the world over. As national aspirations had been central to the Sino-Soviet split despite the ideological terms in which it was conducted, so national interest rather than Communist ideology governed the distribution of Chinese foreign aid.[42] The Chinese would do their duty to the oppressed peoples of the world by serving as an inspirational example. By the light of that example others could find their own way.

In the middle of the decade, China's Third World policies, modest though they were, suffered serious reverses. In 1965 the Chinese attempted to organize a meeting similar to the Bandung Conference, this time in Algiers. They emphatically disputed the right of the Soviet Union to attend. A few days before it was scheduled to begin, the Algerian leader, Ben Bella, was overthrown and the meeting was never held. Shortly afterward an attempted coup in Indonesia touched off an assault on the Indonesian Communist Party and on ethnic Chinese living in the country. In its wake, hundreds of thousands of people were dead and a military government hostile to Beijing was firmly established in power.

[42] Ibid., p. 162; Camilleri, *Chinese Foreign Policy*, p. 95. See also Peter Van Ness, *Revolution and Chinese Foreign Policy: Peking's Support for Wars of National Liberation* (Berkeley and Los Angeles: University of California Press, 1970), p. 169.

In 1966 the Great Proletarian Cultural Revolution erupted. Chinese society was turned upside down. Bands of teen-aged Red Guards roamed the country wreaking havoc. Institutions were thrown into chaos. Industrial and agricultural production plummeted. Members of the elite were disgraced, imprisoned, banished to the countryside, even murdered. Red Guards fought pitched battles with local militia and even detachments of the People's Liberation Army in almost every province. With its society in turmoil and its economy in ruins, China withdrew from the world. Chinese ambassadors were recalled from almost every capital.[43]

China's identification with the vast third force in the international system was important not for its effect on other countries – it had none – but for what it expressed about the Chinese view of the world and China's place in it. It demonstrated the value that China placed on independence. Standing apart from both the United States and the Soviet Union was a position in which the leadership felt comfortable. The Chinese did not abandon the rhetoric of independence even when they ceased, in the 1970s, to stand equidistant between the two great powers. Although the official emphasis that the policy received varied considerably, from the 1960s onward the Chinese officially counted themselves part of the great mass of the world's people struggling against the dominance of the two hegemonic powers.

So compelling was the impulse to remain free from the influence of the great powers that the Chinese did not try to repair their relations with the Soviet Union even when, in 1965, they had every reason to do so. In that year the United States began to pour troops into Vietnam in order to bolster the government in Saigon, which was under attack from Communist forces supported by China. As part of their effort to prevent a Communist victory, the Americans began bombing North Vietnam, bringing the war, as in 1950, to China's borders. The Vietnam War re-created the circumstances in which China had aligned itself with the Soviet Union. Important Chinese officials, led by Defense Minister Lo Jui-ching, sought to restore the policies of 1950. Mao resisted this approach. He carried

---

[43] Harlan W. Jencks, *From Missiles to Muskets: Politics and Professionalism in the Chinese Army, 1945–1981* (Boulder, Colo.: Westview Press, 1982), p. 94ff. Meisner, *Mao's China*, p. 361.

the day; Lo was dismissed from office. China continued to defy both great powers even when American participation in the fighting in Indochina was most intense

China did abandon the stan.. of equal detachment from each of the great powers. The shift came in the late 1960s. Despite the American presence in Vietnam, Beijing moved closer to the United States because of the threat posed by the Soviet Union. The Sino-Soviet relationship deteriorated even further, from rhetorical hostility to military confrontation.

The shift was probably set in motion by the Chinese claim, first advanced in 1963, that the Soviets were occupying more than 1 million square miles of territory that the Russian czars had wrongly taken from China in the nineteenth century. The border between the two countries, the Chinese said, had to be redrawn. This placed a concrete object of dispute, of the sort over which nations have frequently gone to war, squarely at the center of a relationship already marked by suspicion and ill will.[45] In 1965 the Soviets began to augment their forces along the border with China, both in Central Asia opposite Xinjiang and in the Far East on the frontier with Manchuria.[46]

Both sides were extremely sensitive about their border regions. Each felt that these territories were vulnerable to the other side. The Soviet eastern territories were potential sources of great wealth because they were rich in minerals and timber. They were vulnerable, in Soviet eyes, because they were large, sparsely populated (few of the inhabitants being ethnic Russians upon whose

[44] The Chinese did not ignore the United States. They took steps to discourage an American attack on China, which Mao was confident could be accomplished without Soviet assistance. He was proved correct. See Whiting, *Chinese Calculus*, Chap. 6. President Lyndon Johnson conducted the bombing campaign so as not to provoke Chinese intervention along the lines of 1950. It is at least conceivable that, if the bombing had seemed more threatening to China itself, the Chinese leadership would have tried to repair relations with Moscow.

[45] Gelman, *Soviet Far East Buildup*, pp. 16–17; Camilleri, *Chinese Foreign Policy*, pp. 75–6. Khrushchev says that the Soviets were at first willing to negotiate seriously but that the Chinese demands turned out to be unreasonable (*Khrushchev Remembers*, p. 474) and also admits the Soviet concern that "if we started remapping our frontiers according to historical considerations, the situation could get out of hand and lead to conflict." *The Last Testament*, p. 284.

[46] Gelman, *Soviet Far East Buildup*, pp. vii–viii, summarizes the Soviet deployments.

loyalty Moscow could count), and situated several thousand miles from the European heart of the Soviet Union. Vladivostok is much closer to Beijing than to Moscow: Defending it and the rest of the eastern part of the Soviet Union was a military planner's nightmare. Communication with the capital was poor, and transportation across Russia and Soviet Central Asia was difficult. In a Sino-Soviet war in the east, China's lines of supply would be short, those of the Soviet Union thousands of miles long.[47]

The Chinese, too, had reason to consider their border provinces vulnerable. Xinjiang was the home of people who were not ethnic Chinese and thus of dubious loyalty to the regime. Manchuria had been occupied first by Japan and then by the Soviet Union, both within recent memory. Still, China showed no particular reaction to the increase in Soviet strength for the first four years that it was underway – perhaps because for much of that period the country was consumed by the Cultural Revolution.

In the second half of 1968, however, the Soviet deployments suddenly seemed ominous. The Soviet invasion of Czechoslovakia changed the Chinese estimate of the danger from the north, es-pecially since it was justified by the so-called Brezhnev Doctrine, which arrogated to the Soviet Union the right to intervene in order to enforce orthodoxy in Communist countries that Moscow pro-nounced deviant. It was surely not difficult for the Communist leaders in Beijing to imagine a Soviet attack on them, perhaps with the aim of installing in power a faction of the Chinese party more congenial to Moscow.

The Chinese responded sharply to the Soviet threat. They de-nounced Soviet violations of their airspace. They warned the So-viets against aggressive behavior. They began patrolling the disputed borders vigorously, leading to frequent incidents between the border guards of the two sides. In March 1969, the patrolling erupted into two battles on a small strip of land in the middle of the Amur River that the Soviets called Damansky Island, which formed the border between Manchuria and the easternmost Soviet territory in the Far East. A Chinese detachment seems to have ambushed a Soviet patrol on March 2 and to have gotten the better

---

[47] Khrushchev alleges that the Chinese had designs on Siberia even when Sino-Soviet relations were relatively harmonious. *The Last Testament*, p. 250.

of the engagement. On March 15 the Soviets returned with larger forces and thrashed the Chinese. Although the battles on Damansky Island were the largest and bloodiest clashes between the two countries, they were not the only ones. Others followed over the next few months on the borders of both Manchuria and Central Asia.

The polemics from the Chinese side grew sharper. The Soviets accelerated the pace of their military deployments, assembling armored divisions configured for a thrust into China. The firepower they amassed far exceeded what was necessary merely to defend their own territory. It exceeded the level of force the Chinese could hope to repel. As the increase in their forces continued, the Soviets issued veiled hints that they might launch attacks, even nuclear attacks, on China.[48]

By the end of the 1960s China thus found itself in the same position as it had been at the beginning of the 1950s: threatened by one of the two strongest states in the international system. The Chinese again followed the logic of weakness. They turned to the other great power. They moved closer to the United States not out of ideological affinity but in order to counterbalance the growing danger from America's adversary, the Soviet Union.

The rapprochement between the United States and the People's Republic developed over three years. It was a political version of a courtship ritual, with expressions of interest begun in secret and then becoming ever more public and direct.[49] The domestic politics of both countries made secrecy necessary. Two decades of animosity had created constituencies in both countries opposed to better relations between them.[50] Neither government wished to make public its wish for reconciliation until it was certain that the other's terms were acceptable.

[48] Gelman, *Soviet Far East Buildup*, p. 17; Sutter, *China Watch*, pp. 86–7.

[49] Kissinger calls the process "an intricate minuet between us and the Chinese so delicately arranged that both sides could always maintain that they were not in contact, so stylized that neither side needed to bear the onus of an initiative, so elliptical that existing relationships on both sides were not jeopardized." Henry Kissinger, *White House Years* (Boston: Little, Brown, 1979), p. 187.

[50] This may have been an issue in the fall of Lin Biao in 1971. Jonathan D. Pollack, "China and the Global Strategic Balance," in Harry Harding, ed., *China's Foreign Relations in the 1980s* (New Haven, Conn.: Yale University Press, 1984), pp. 153.

The trend of Sino-American rapprochement began with symbolic gestures intended as signals of interest in improving relations. Almost as soon as Richard Nixon assumed the presidency in 1969, he made it clear that the United States wanted to resume the ambassadorial talks in Warsaw between the two governments that had been suspended after the onset of the Cultural Revolution. In November of that year regular patrolling of the Taiwan Strait by the American Seventh Fleet was terminated. On the Chinese side, the Lushan Party Plenum of 1970 revived the slogan of "peaceful coexistence among peoples of different social systems."[51] In the spring of 1971, the Beijing government invited the American table tennis team, then competing at the world championship tournament in Nagoya, Japan, to go on from there to visit China. The invitation was accepted. At about the same time, the American journalist Edgar Snow, who had had close ties to the Chinese Communists since their days in Yenan in the 1930s, revealed that Mao had offered to receive Nixon in Beijing. Since neither side formally recognized the other, they lacked the usual means of diplomatic communication. So they established private channels, first through intermediaries – Rumania and, most important, Pakistan – then directly. The result was a secret trip to Beijing by the president's national security adviser, Henry Kissinger, and several associates in July 1971. Kissinger arranged the dramatic visit of the president to China in February 1972, which publicly affirmed that the hostility of twenty years had been set aside.[52] The People's Republic had moved from the intermediate zone of the international system to the edge of the American field of force.

The sequence of events enhanced Chinese security because it complicated Soviet strategic calculations. The Soviets could not be certain that if they attacked China the Chinese would *not* receive help from the United States, just as, after the Treaty of Friendship of 1950, the American government had had to reckon with the possibility that, in a war with China, the Soviet Union might intervene. As in the earlier period, alignment created uncertainty, giving Beijing a measure of safety. The Shanghai Communiqué,

---

[51] Meisner, *Mao's China*, p. 367.

[52] The two trips are described in detail in Kissinger, *White House Years*, Chaps. 18, 19, and 24.

which the two sides signed at the end of the Nixon visit, included a suggestive statement of their common opposition to any effort to seek hegemony in East Asia.[53] The Nixon visit inaugurated a period during which, in Kissinger's words, "America and China reinforced each other while almost never coordinating tactics explicitly."[54] Through active diplomacy the Chinese had acquired what the European neutrals enjoyed automatically: a measure of protection provided by the shadow of American power. China also acquired insurance against the United States actually doing what Chinese rhetoric had sometimes accused it of doing: collaborating with the Soviet Union against the People's Republic. The rapprochement relieved any lingering military pressure on China to the south from the American forces still fighting in Indochina.[55] The Chinese were able to shift forces from the south and the east to the north, to confront the Soviets.

The parallels between China's rapprochement with the United States and its alignment with the Soviet Union two decades earlier are striking. Both were undertaken for the sake of security. For the Chinese, reconciliation with the United States was, as Kissinger put it, a matter of "dire necessity."[56] Again China faced the threat of attack, including nuclear attack, from a power far stronger than itself. The Soviet Union, in fact, posed a greater threat than the United States because it was so much closer. For American troops to be in position to invade China, they would have to be transported thousands of miles from home. Soviet troops in position to invade *were* at home; they were deployed in their own country.

The entente with the United States was the product of security calculations, at the expense of ideological precepts, which distinguished it from the earlier Chinese alignment. The Treaty of Friendship of 1950 joined two Communist countries. The Shanghai Communiqué of 1972 was signed by leaders of regimes constituted according to different – indeed opposed – principles. The alignment with the United States represented as clear a triumph of interna-

---

[53] Nixon and Kissinger had in fact planned to help China in the event of a Soviet attack. Ibid., p. 764.

[54] Ibid., p. 1089.

[55] The rapproachement became possible when the Chinese were convinced that the United States was determined to withdraw from Indochina. Ibid., p. 689.

[56] Ibid., p. 1055; see also p. 1073.

tional over internal considerations, of security over ideology, as has occurred in the twentieth century.[57]

But there were further parallels between the two periods in Chinese security policy of alignment with a great nuclear power. The Chinese had fought the Americans in Korea in the earlier period, and they battled with the Soviets, on a much smaller scale to be sure, along the borders between the two countries in the late 1960s. Just as the Korean War had led to the deployment of American military forces around China's borders, so too after the skirmishes of 1969 the Soviets surrounded the Chinese. They fortified their borders with northern China. A 1966 treaty brought Soviet troops to Mongolia, leaving them poised to strike at Beijing. India, which had been hostile to China since the skirmishes between the two countries in 1962, signed a friendship treaty with the Soviets in 1971. In the second half of the decade, the Soviets began deploying mobile intermediate-range nuclear-equipped ballistic missiles of the SS-20 class in Asia, which were evidently aimed at Chinese targets. The Soviet Pacific Fleet was expanded and strengthened, and an agreement with the victorious Communist government of Vietnam gave Moscow the use of naval facilities on the South China Sea that the United States had built and abandoned. At the end of 1979, the Soviet Union invaded Afghanistan, putting 100,000 troops into a country on the western border of the People's Republic.

There is even a parallel, in the events of the 1950s, with China's later border dispute with the Soviet Union. The United States never claimed any Chinese territory but did support the Guomindang regime on Taiwan, which asserted its right to govern all of China. Between the Korean War and the Nixon visit, this was one of the most contentious issues in Sino-American relations. The Shanghai Communiqué drew much of the sting from it. The United States acknowledged that the governments on both sides of the Taiwan Strait considered that there was only one China, not two (thereby sidestepping, for the moment, the question of which was the legitimate one), and that this was an assertion the American

---

[57] " . . . the Chinese leaders were the most unsentimental practitioners of balance-of-power politics I have encountered." Ibid., pp. 1087–8; see also p. 1074. It was also a triumph of external over internal considerations for *American* policy. See Chapter 3.

government did not contest. The communiqué advocated a peaceful resolution of the matter. The Americans thus pledged that they would neither countenance an invasion of the mainland nor endorse a permanently independent status for Taiwan. By contrast, in *their* dispute with the Chinese, the Soviets did not admit that the territory that China claimed had been taken illegally by the czars was in fact part of China, at least not publicly. The Soviets' military preparations suggested that, unlike the United States on the issue of Taiwan, they did not expect the matter to be resolved peacefully.

There is a final point of similarity between China's hostility to the United States and its later confrontation with the Soviet Union. In the 1950s, China tried to goad the Soviet Union into adopting a more aggressive policy toward the United States, which would have helped the Chinese achieve some of their goals. In the 1970s, they urged the Americans and their European allies to do more than they were doing to offset Soviet military power. The world's most dangerous region, the Chinese said, was Europe. It was there, consequently, that the West should increase its military strength. Larger military forces on the Soviet Union's western borders would, of course, work to the advantage of its eastern neighbors, conspicuous among which was the People's Republic of China.

During both periods China tried to get one strong state to bear the burden and pay the costs of opposing the other, which would in turn have lightened the burden and lowered the cost of security to the Chinese themselves. These efforts are sometimes cited as modern versions of the imperial Chinese tactic of setting one "barbarian" against another.[58] No doubt this practice was part of the Chinese past. Chinese history is long and rich enough to serve as the repository of any and all diplomatic tactics. If the tactic recurred, it did so because the force of logic stood behind it. It is logical for weak states to enlist the strength of more powerful ones. Indeed, this is a logical course for *any* state. Preparing for war, not to mention fighting one, is costly and dangerous. All states prefer that others, not they, do it.

The Chinese made no pretense of ideological solidarity with the

---

[58] Clubb, *China and Russia*, p. 382; Harry Gelber, "Nuclear Weapons and Chinese Policy," Adelphi Papers No. 99 (London: International Institute for Strategic Studies, 1973), p. 3; Hunt, "Chinese Foreign Relations," p. 8.

United States, however, as they had with the Soviet Union in the 1950s, even when internal political changes and the expansion of commercial contacts with the West followed the death of Mao and the fall of the "Gang of Four." Nor did they show interest in a formal alliance with the United States along the lines of the 1950 Treaty of Friendship, even after Washington withdrew formal diplomatic recognition from Taiwan and extended it to Beijing in 1979.

Cooperation between the People's Republic and the United States, including the exchange of military information, did increase after 1972. Following Nixon's startling journey to Beijing, visits by important American government officials became routine. In 1979, after Mao's death, Deng Xiaoping began to open China's economy to the West. Beijing's reasons for maintaining good relations with the United States thus came to have a domestic as well as an international basis. The rapprochement ceased to be the pure product of security calculations. The ties with North America, Western Europe, and Japan multiplied. But China continued to insist that it was nonaligned, that it belonged to the vast third force that was gathering strength in the international system. Deng told the United Nations in 1974 that the socialist bloc had ceased to exist and that China was part of the Third World.[59] China's task, its official rhetoric insisted, continued to be resistance to the hegemonic designs of the two great powers, although the Soviet Union was branded the more ambitious and dangerous of them. Independence remained the ideal to which Chinese foreign policy aspired.

IV

When weak states are threatened by more powerful ones, alignment with another strong state is not alone sufficient to ensure security. Diplomatic maneuvers do not guarantee protection in case of actual attack. An independent weak state must be prepared to defend itself. Like most states, it ordinarily prefers not to have to fight, especially since in a contest in which a stronger adversary brings its full weight to bear the weak state is certain to lose. Fighting is not always necessary. Sometimes the prospect of re-

[59] Meisner, *Mao's China*, p. 377.

sistance can keep even a more powerful adversary from attacking. The threat to fight may make it unnecessary to carry out the threat. It may deter aggression.

Deterrence is the strategy of the hedgehog, whose sharp quills discourage other animals from molesting it. Any state whose aim is defensive will prefer deterring an adversary to having to fight. Strong states deter others by virtue of their strength. They do not, however, always have strictly defensive goals. When confronting a strong state, a weak one by definition has a defensive aim. Its preferred policy is therefore deterrence.

Deterrence affects the intentions of the adversary. It bears on the other's calculations as well as its capabilities. Those calculations concern not only the likelihood of success, but also the price that the attacker will have to pay to succeed. The calculations by one side in a conflict turn on its estimate of the other's military capacities and determination to use them.

Determination is an especially relevant issue when the weak try to deter the strong, because the weak have no hope of victory. The threat to resist carries less weight when resistance is certain to be overcome eventually. The strong may not believe that the threat will ever be carried out. Successful deterrence requires making it credible. Weak states that seek to retain their independence, including the People's Republic of China, have devoted considerable effort to trying to persuade their adversaries that they would indeed defend themselves despite the odds against them.

The simplest way for one state to try to persuade another that it will fight is to say so. All of the European neutrals have declared that they will defend themselves. It is a clear, settled, often repeated Swedish, Finnish, Swiss, and Yugoslav policy to resist any intruder no matter how powerful. After 1949 the Chinese also frequently declared that they would defend their own territory. Their rhetoric was often colorful and always emphatic. A typical passage was contained in Lin Biao's report to the Ninth National Congress of the Chinese Communist Party in April 1969, when the People's Republic was at odds with both great powers: "We must . . . on no account ignore the danger of U.S. imperialism and Soviet revisionism launching a large-scale war of aggression. . . . Chairman Mao said long ago that we will not attack unless we are attacked: if we are attacked, we will certainly counter-attack. If they insist on fighting we will keep them company and fight to the finish. The Chinese Revolution was won on the battlefield."[60] "The key to putting off war lies not in holding talks and concluding agreements, as is vociferously preached by some people," a Beijing *People's Daily* editorial of 1977 said, "but in the united struggle of the peoples of all countries against hegemonism."[61]

Words alone are not enough for successful deterrence. There must also be visible preparations to fight. All of the neutrals have national armed forces that are recruited, trained, and equipped to defend their territory. All have reserve armies, which depend on the mobilization of civilians to fill their ranks in case of war. The popular character of these armies is a sign of the national resolve to carry out self-defense. Sweden and Finland have air forces and coastal navies as well.[62] All have operational plans for resisting attackers alone, without direct assistance from any other country.[63] The Swiss have undertaken to protect their civilian population against aerial bombardment with underground shelters located throughout the country, which are reinforced against attack and stocked with food.

The Chinese, too, constructed air raid shelters, especially after 1969 when the Soviet threat loomed large. From 1949 onward, the People's Republic assembled a large army – in sheer number of soldiers, the world's largest. Its task was to defend Chinese territory. The People's Liberation Army, unlike the armed forces of Sweden, Switzerland, Finland, and Yugoslavia, was on occasion deployed outside China's borders. In 1965 a detachment of fifty thousand troops was sent to North Vietnam. A few antiaircraft battalions actually engaged in combat against the American air force, and Chinese engineering battalions repairing North Vietnamese bridges and roads came under fire. Their main purpose, however, was to deter an American attack, to warn the Americans

---

[60] Quoted in Kissinger, *White House Years*, p. 176.
[61] Yahuda, *China's Role*, p. 271.
[62] On Sweden see Taylor, "Defense Policy," p. 315. On Finland see Tomas Ries, "Finland's Armed Forces: Isolated but Unbowed," *International Defense Review*, 17, no. 3 (1984): 269–70.
[63] Sweden has taken another step toward self-sufficiency by building its own defense industry. Bjol, "Nordic Security," p. 18. The Swedes also aim at overall economic self-sufficiency to permit them to stay out of any European conflict.

by their presence that China would fight if American troops invaded North Vietnam, just as the People's Liberation Army had in Korea in 1950.[64]

By saying that it will fight and being prepared to do so, a weak state can convince its adversaries that it will indeed resist an attack. The best way for such a state to acquire a reputation for being willing to defend itself, to make credible the threat to fight resolutely, is to use its forces in combat. The most convincing support for the credibility of a threat to do something is a record of already having done it.

The European neutrals have not had occasion to wage war since 1945. The Swiss have not fought since 1815. Finland and Yugoslavia did fight, tenaciously and with some success, against much stronger adversaries in World War II, the Finns against the Soviet Union in 1939 and 1944, and the Yugoslavs against the occupying Germans between 1941 and 1945. Their enduring reputations as peoples ready to resist invaders even against long odds made each country's policies of deterrence in the postwar period all the more credible.

The Chinese felt more threatened than the European neutrals in the postwar period, no doubt rightly. The task of deterrence was more urgent and more difficult for them. China did fight on several occasions after 1949. Allen Whiting has argued that the full-scale wars and lesser skirmishes in which the People's Republic has been engaged were undertaken in response to perceived threats for the sake of deterrence.[65] They had a number of features in common. The entry into the Korean War in 1950, the attacks on Indian outposts along the border between the two countries in 1962, and the clashes with Soviet forces on the Ussuri River in 1969 were all preceded by warnings from Beijing, as was the dispatch of troops to North Vietnam in 1965.[66] Each operation had

---

[64] This is the argument of Whiting, *Chinese Calculus*, Chaps. 6 and 7.

[65] Whiting makes this general argument in *China Crosses the Yalu* and particularly in *The Chinese Calculus of Deterrence*, a pioneering work in that it considers Chinese international behavior in comparative perspective. The book's premise is that "comparative foreign policy need not exclude China as an idiosyncratic actor which is only susceptible to understanding through the esoteric analysis of Sinologues" (pp. xix–xx). That is also the premise of the present chapter, on which Whiting's work has exercised a more extensive influence than the citations may suggest.

[66] In some respects the Chinese incursion into Vietnam in 1979 fits this descrip-

limited goals. In none of them was China seeking to capture territory. The People's Liberation Army left Korea after the armistice.
Nor did it press its advantage after routing the Indian forces. It
withdrew from Vietnam a few months after the 1979 occupation.
When the American bombing of North Vietnam ended, the
Chinese forces that had been sent to support the regime there in
1965 were withdrawn. Each operation, according to Whiting, took
place during a period of Chinese weakness, which the Chinese
feared the great powers would exploit by attacking.[67] China's purpose on each occasion was to warn the great powers – either the
United States or the Soviet Union, or both – that it would resist
an invasion. Each was intended to be a demonstration of China's
resolve. Each engagement was fought, that is, for the purpose of
deterrence.[68]

Neither the United States nor the Soviet Union attempted to
invade China and dislodge the Beijing government. To what extent
Chinese belligerence contributed to the great powers' reluctance
to do so is not easy to say. The demonstrated Chinese willingness
to fight certainly affected American policies. American casualties
influenced the conduct of the war in Korea, and the memory of
Korea defined the limits of the military effort in Vietnam.[69] It seems
reasonable to suppose that China's pugnacity affected Soviet plans
in the 1960s and 1970s as well.

No doubt internal factors had some bearing on the effectiveness
of Chinese deterrence. Ideology was one. Mao emphasized the
power of the masses to overcome material and social obstacles to
political and economic goals. He launched sweeping, disruptive

---

tion. *The Chinese Calculus of Deterrence* was published in 1975 and so does
not include an analysis of the 1979 operations.

[67] Whiting argues that in 1962 the Chinese feared an American attack from Taiwan,
which contradicts the argument of this chapter that the Communist regime
concluded in 1958 that it need not fear such an invasion. (*Chinese Calculus*,
pp. 67ff). The general proposition is difficult to test because China was in almost
constant turmoil. At virtually any time after 1949 the Chinese government might
reasonably have considered itself weak at home and therefore vulnerable to its
foreign enemies.

[68] The shelling of the offshore islands in 1958 had a different purpose. It was part
of the campaign to capture Taiwan. See above, p. tk, and Zagoria, *Sino-Soviet
Conflict*, pp. 207–8.

[69] John Mueller, *War, Presidents and Public Opinion* (New York: Wiley, 1973),
p. 197; Whiting, *Chinese Calculus*, pp. 182, 192–5.

public campaigns in pursuit of such goals. The Great Leap Forward and the Cultural Revolution shook the institutions of the People's Republic. They did serious damage to the Chinese economy. They deliberately produced the kind of chaos that ordinarily occurs in the wake of unplanned and unwanted events such as wars, revolutions, and natural disasters. They demonstrated that the Chinese leadership would go to great, painful, and costly lengths to put its revolutionary principles into practice. If Mao and his colleagues were willing to make such huge sacrifices for the sake of transforming Chinese society, which was one of the two pillars of the Communist revolution, it was all the more plausible that they would do so to preserve the country's territorial integrity from foreign encroachment, which was the other pillar.

Mao appeared to the international community to be rash, impulsive, and not altogether rational. Such a man might be more readily expected to fight against hopeless odds than one who was more moderate, reasonable, and generally conventional.[70] If Maoism ruined China – and a good many Chinese seemed, after the chairman's death, to believe that it had – it also contributed to the protection of the country against its enemies, thus ensuring that only the Chinese themselves would have the opportunity to ruin it.

Deterrence may fail. Threats, especially by the weak to resist the strong, may not be convincing. If a weak state has failed to dissuade an adversary and is attacked, and if it wishes to remain independent, it must have some means by which to defend itself. And it must have decided in advance how it will fight. Military plans are part of successful deterrence. To impress the strong the weak need a plausible strategy for self-defense. Yet by definition, they cannot prevail against a more powerful adversary that is determined to win. How then can they plan to fight?

They can proceed on the assumption that third countries will influence the military plans of their adversaries so as to minimize their own disadvantages. They can assume that in the political context of a war they will not, in fact, be weak. The Swedes, for example, assume that they will be the object of a "marginal" or

---

[70] He seemed especially irrational on the subject of nuclear weapons. See the quotes on p. 244.

"peripheral" attack by a strong state that will reserve most of its forces for confronting another great power. Sweden will be a secondary theater of war. Its stronger enemy will commit only a small fraction of its forces there. Through total mobilization Sweden will, the Swedish government assumes, be able to cope with them.[71]

A weak state may assume that a stronger opponent will be interested only in ensuring that a rival great power does not occupy its territory. The Germans claimed that they moved into Norway in 1940 merely to keep the British out. It is a principal aim of Switzerland's security policy to avoid appearing to be a "power vacuum" into which a stronger country might be tempted to move preemptively, not because it covets Swiss territory but because it fears that if it does not do so another will. The Finns have declared this to be the purpose of their military preparations and so, too, on occasion, have the Swedes.[72] For a weak state to avoid becoming a power vacuum it does not have to have the capacity to defeat a stronger one; it simply needs to demonstrate that it can put up a fight.

Or the weak may assume that, while the strong state may concentrate enough of its forces to overwhelm the resistance it meets, another strong state will intervent. The Finns held out against the Russians in the hope that others would come to their aid. A weak state may hope for the benefits of an alliance without formally having made one.

An illustration of such a policy can be found in the history of naval strategy. At the beginning of the twentieth century Germany built a fleet of capital ships to challenge the British navy, which for centuries had been the master of the world's oceans. The Germans reckoned at the outset of their challenge that they did not need a fleet large enough to defeat the British, but only one formidable enough to inflict sufficient damage to make the Royal Navy

---

[71] Ingemar Dorfer, "Nordic Security Today: Sweden," *Cooperation and Conflict*, 17 (1982): 279; Adam Roberts, *Nation in Arms: The Theory and Practice of Territorial Defense* (New York: Praeger, 1976), pp. 77, 92; Taylor, "Defense Policy," p. 302.

[72] On Finland see Kari Mottola, "The Politics of Neutrality and Defense: Finnish Security Policy Since the Early 1970s," *Conflict*, 17 (1982): 299, 301. On Sweden see David Vital, *The Inequality of States: A Study of the Small Power in International Relations* (New York: Oxford University Press, 1967), p. 153, and Roberts, *Nations in Arms*, pp. 41–3.

vulnerable to France and Russia after an engagement with Germany. (It should be noted that the German "risk theory," as it was called, was designed to extract concessions, not simply to deter attack. Although the fleet was built, the strategy failed; the British made no concessions.) The principle underlying the risk theory is a logical and therefore a common one for the military strategies of weak states. It is analogous to their diplomatic strategies. It aims at taking advantage, without a direct alliance, of the military might of third parties.

Weak states cannot always count on help from third countries when fighting stronger adversaries, however, and certainly not swift and decisive help. Chinese diplomatic maneuvering after 1949 aimed at making use of the power of one of the world's nuclear giants to inject a dose of caution into the policies of the other. But the Peoples' Republic did not count on either the Soviet Union or the United States coming to its rescue in the event of attack by the other. The Chinese relied on themselves. The weak must generally confront the prospect of fighting alone against much more powerful adversaries. They cannot hope to overcome the opposing forces. A strong state is assured of victory if it is willing to pay a high enough price. That is the source of the weak state's leverage. It must try to affect the *price* of victory for the strong. Its goal in fighting must be to make the cost of victory higher than the gains of victory can justify. Preparations for fighting in this way may thus dissuade a stronger adversary. Deterrence can, and in the case of a weak state must, be based on the threat not to win a war in the conventional sense of the term but simply to wage one.

All states must choose between an emphasis on offensive and defensive military operations. The choice is straightforward for the weak. The European neutrals and the Chinese necessarily chose the defense. They did not have the resources to conquer and hold territory beyond their borders; it was all they could do to defend what they already had. Another, less familiar distinction is equally important for the military policies of the weak. It is the distinction between defense by denial and defense by *punishment*. Denial involves preventing the adversary from achieving its goal, which is occupying territory. Punishment aims at making the achievement of that goal more costly than it is worth. The two modes of defense imply different kinds of military operations.

Defense by denial centers on what is at the heart of most wars, the battle between two armies that confront each other directly, arrayed more or less opposite each other on terrain that becomes the battlefield. They fight until one of them breaks or retreats, or until both are ready to stop. Battles are contests for the control of territory – the aim of most wars. The general form that a battle takes has a long history, which doubtless begins with the first combat between organized communities.

Armies tend to resemble one another. They are as large and well equipped as the size and resources of the communities from which they come and the state of military technology permit. In the modern period they have become increasingly complex organizations, composed of infantry, artillery, and supporting air forces, whose missions reinforce one another. Their preparations to fight battles are compatible with a strategy of denial by punishment. A strong state may calculate that it could prevail over a weaker one in a series of formal engagements but that the casualties and loss of equipment that it would suffer in doing so would be too great to justify the capture of the territory in question. This was the calculation that Germany tried to impose on Britain in naval terms with the risk theory. It is the basis for the formal defense plans of the European neutrals. Or the stronger power may launch an attack, discover the cost of battle to be higher than anticipated, and so desist. If the strong state is determined to overcome formal resistance, however – and the weak can seldom be certain that this will not be the case – and if the weak cannot count on other forces arriving in time to take part in the battles it must fight, then a different kind of military approach is necessary to increase the cost of victory.

The alternative military approach abjures formal battles, in which the weaker side is bound to be overcome, its army smashed and rendered useless. Modern integrated armies, once defeated, ordinarily cannot function; they can neither deny nor punish. The alternative military strategy of the weak concedes to the stronger party that which battles are fought to decide – the control of territory. It concedes the penetration of foreign forces and their occupation of the sovereign territory of the weak. It concedes what is ordinarily thought of as victory. But it seeks to exact a high price for occupation by harassing the occupying forces. It attempts to inflict casualties through piecemeal, scattered attacks on the flanks and outposts of the invader rather than hurling it back along a front.

The terrain of the occupied country plays an important role in such an approach. The rougher and more forbidding it is, the greater are the country's opportunities. The more protection it affords harassing forces so that they can hide, strike, and retreat without being crushed, the better suited it is to the kind of hit-and-run tactics on which this approach relies.

Harassing forces are organized in a different way than armies whose task is to fight battles. Their units are small, so that they can move rapidly, strike suddenly, and conceal themselves easily, even disbanding when necessary and then reforming. Their organizational structure is simple. The units tend to resemble each other. Each is capable of operating independently regardless of the fate of the others. By contrast, when a major part of a formal modern army is knocked out of action, the entire army usually ceases to fight.[73]

There is a modern naval version of the strategy of defense by punishment. Its instrument is the submarine. Submarines cannot fight full-scale battles with fleets of capital ships for control of the sea, which is the maritime equivalent of the control of territory. Their task is to harass opposing fleets and sink larger ships. The environment is favorable. The sea is vast and opaque. Submarines are smaller, simpler, and less expensive than battle groups, which are the basic units of main fleets. They operate in decentralized fashion. Battle groups consist of many ships of different types traveling together; submarines operate alone or in small packs. They practice hit-and-run tactics, striking suddenly, then escaping to hide in the ocean's depths.

The land equivalent of submarine warfare, the military approach that lends itself to the strategy of punishment and relies on small, decentralized harassing forces, is guerrilla warfare. Guerrilla campaigns, such as the resistance to Napoleon's armies in the peninsular campaign of 1812 and the Yugoslav partisans' harassment of the Germans during World War II, are exercises in punishment.

---

[73] The functional differentiation of the French army made possible the triumph of the German blitzkrieg tactics in 1940. The Germans knocked out the "brain" – the command mechanisms – of the French forces, which fell into disarray and surrendered. See Chapter 2, Section V.

The weaker party cannot defeat the stronger one, it cannot prevent the occupation of its territory, but it can make occupation costly over time.

A guerrilla war is a contest in competitive punishment. The occupier can inflict punishment as well as absorb it. In this contest the two sides are unevenly matched, but in ways that sometimes offset each other. The strong can do more damage to the weak than the weak can do to the strong. But the weak state is likely to be more willing to absorb punishment than its stronger occupier. It ordinarily has the greater stake in the conflict, particularly when the war is being fought on its territory. It has a greater interest in evicting the occupier than the occupier has in staying. The weak state is often willing to pay a higher price to liberate its territory than the strong will want to pay to occupy it. But the stronger state can inflict greater punishment. It holds the weak state's population hostage, whereas the weak state, with its guerrilla fighters, can strike only the armed forces, as distinct from the society, of the strong.

The Vietnam War illustrates the point. North Vietnam was able to win control of the South by making American participation in the war more costly than the American public was willing to underwrite, although there were many more North Vietnamese than American casualties, and the United States did extensive damage to North Vietnam whereas the war never reached North America. The North Vietnamese were willing to take more punishment than the Americans. In order to win the war, they had to take more punishment.

Sweden, Switzerland, and Finland all have defense strategies whose aim is to deny an invader control of their territory. Their military doctrines call for "perimeter" or "forward" defense. They plan to fight battles to stop the invading enemy. Their capital cities and most of their population centers are located near their borders. Their troops are concentrated nearby because the countries cannot afford simply to abandon these cities.[74] They are also prepared, however, to fight in guerrilla fashion. This is a secondary but none-

---

[74] On Finland see Ries, "Finland's Armed Forces," p. 266. The Finns may also station troops around Helsinki to guard against a Soviet-inspired coup there. Bjol,"Nordic Security" p. 14. On Switzerland see Roberts, *Nations in Arms*, p. 53.

theless important element of their defense strategies. Finland has troops prepared for guerrilla warfare. They are trained to operate independently for months, striking at the enemy from the rear. The Swiss are well aware of the possibilities of guerrilla fighting and are ready for protracted resistance should their first line of defense be breached. In the 1970s the Swedes actually debated making guerrilla tactics their principal method of self-defense. The policy of forward defense remained in place, but Swedish military planning does allow for harassing tactics, which are called "free warfare."[75]

The organization of the neutrals' armed forces lends itself in each case to guerrilla campaigns. The Finns plan to mobilize in a decentralized way so that if the army is disrupted in one part of the country it can still fight elsewhere. The Swiss also have decentralized mobilization procedures, and their tactics emphasize dispersion, mobility, and harassment. Each male citizen has his own weapon, which he keeps with him.

The terrain of all three countries is favorable for guerrilla operations. Much of Switzerland, especially outside the main cities, is mountainous. Alpine redoubts are available to shelter those who will fight after the cities have been overrun. The northern part of Sweden, Upper Norland, is hospitable country for guerrillas. Invading troops would have to use the roads, where they would be vulnerable to the specially trained Swedish Northern Brigades. Finland is a harsh country. Only 10 percent of it is suitable for armored operations, in which a powerful invader could bring its strength fully to bear. The best form of transportation for much of the year, and the only form in some places, is the ski.[76]

Of all the neutral countries of Europe the one that relies most heavily on guerrilla tactics is Yugoslavia. "General people's war" is the primary means of defense. The entire country is organized

---

[75] Dorfer, "Nordic Security," p. 279; Roberts, *Nations in Arms*, p. 115.
[76] Ries, "Finland's Armed Forces," p. 268. Sweden and Finland have plans for coastal defense. Although the aim is to protect territory, such operations resemble guerrilla tactics more than conventional battles because the defender can maneuver, strike, retreat, and evade retaliation. A seaborne invader is vulnerable to land-based forces just as main forces on land are vulnerable to guerrilla harassment. Sweden also has a number of submarines. Taylor, "Defense Policy," p. 315.

to harass and punish an invader.[77] Not coincidentally, of all the European neutrals Yugoslavia is the one that most closely resembles the People's Republic of China. Like China, Yugoslavia is a former member of the Soviet camp, which broke away as the result of a bitter political dispute. Like China, it remained Communist and so has been an alternative model for other Communist countries, a standing reproach to the Soviets, as well as a renegade. Yugoslavia has been perhaps the most threatened of the European neutrals. Although it does draw some measure of protection from the existence of the Western alliance, it has had the least reason to expect assistance from the Western camp, with which, because it has remained Communist, it has had fewer economic ties and a weaker political affinity than Switzerland, Sweden, and Finland. Yugoslavia has not counted on outside help in defending itself as have the other three.

Like China, Yugoslavia is larger than the other three neutrals, with more space to maneuver, attack, retreat, and hide. Finally, guerrilla warfare is central to the history of the Yugoslav state, just as it is central to the history of the Chinese Communist regime. The Yugoslavs waged their war of liberation against the German occupiers in World War II in guerrilla fashion, as did the Chinese Communists against the Japanese from 1937 to 1945.

The Chinese Communist Party's history as a guerrilla force is well known. Both before and after 1949, however, Communist armies were as often formal military forces fighting set-piece battles as bands of guerrillas launching hit-and-run raids. During the climactic years of the civil war, from 1945 to 1949, the Communists fought large-scale engagements with Chiang Kaishek's Guomindang armies. The new Communist regime sent large infantry units into battle against the United States in Korea. Throughout the 1950s, under the influence of Soviet advisers, the People's Liberation Army became an increasingly professional force. Neither the border skirmishes with India in 1962, nor the clashes with Soviet forces in 1969, nor the invasion of Vietnam in 1979 was a guerrilla campaign. The Chinese mounted frontal attacks in each instance, with the aim of gaining at least temporary control of territory, although perhaps for the ultimate purpose of deter-

---

[77] Roberts, *Nations in Arms*, pp. 155, 172ff.

rence.[78] In the 1970s the main forces of the Chinese army were deployed in strength in the Beijing and Shanghai regions (not directly along the borders) to guard against a Soviet thrust through Manchuria or Mongolia.

Even when the emphasis was on formal military organization, however, the guerrilla tradition, the style of fighting the Chinese called "People's war," did not disappear.[79] There was always a civilian militia. Millions of Chinese civilians received some military training and had access, at least in theory, to weapons.[80] China also maintained regional forces that were separate from the main army units and were descended from anti-Japanese guerrillas. Their purpose was to take advantage of the sheer mass of the Chinese population. If foreign armies penetrated Chinese territory, whether because they were deliberately lured deep into China or succeeded in overcoming forward resistance, they would, according to the doctrine of people's war, be drowned in an ocean of soldiers.

From the arrival of the Communists in Yenan at the end of the Long March in 1937 until 1945, and intermittently from 1959 to the death of Mao in 1976, first the party and then the country were committed, at least rhetorically, to a strategy of defense through people's war. A common political pattern is associated with these two periods. In both Mao defeated rivals and dominated Communist political affairs. The Long March solidified his grip on the party. In 1959 and 1965 Peng Dehuai and Lo Juiching, respectively, were purged. Mao's power was being challenged on both occasions. It was especially shaky in the wake of the failures of the Great Leap Forward. Both Peng and Lo preferred a more formal style of warfare than Mao favored.[81]

Guerrilla warfare fit Mao's view of the world. In the performance of any social task, he believed in the importance of ideological fervor – "redness," as it was sometimes called because red was

---

[78] The March 2 attack on Soviet forces on Damansky Island was an ambush but was carried out by border guards, not guerrilla fighters.

[79] In the 1970s official doctrine called for a combination of people's war and forward defense. Jencks, *Missiles to Muskets*, p. 151.

[80] The militia were evidently very poorly equipped. Ibid., pp. 169, 171.

[81] Harlan Jencks argues that the two of them and Lin Biao "were all purged when they lost out in struggles for political power, and only incidentally, if at all, because they advocated particular military lines." Ibid., p. 253.

the color of the Communist revolution – as against the claims of technical expertise. He valued enthusiasm and what he viewed as the correct political convictions above competence in all things, including warfare. Modern weapons, he declared more than once, were less powerful than the will of the masses.[82] Guerrilla warfare requires commitment, perseverance, and the willingness to suffer punishment. Formal warfare, especially in the contemporary period, demands technical expertise. The guerrilla fighter is an ideologue; the officer of a formal army is a professional.

An emphasis on guerrilla warfare was associated with periods of maximal independence as well as with Mao's political ascendancy. The party had no real friends or allies in the 1930s. In 1959 and again in 1965 when military strategy was being debated, so too was the question of reconciliation with the Soviet Union. Both Peng and Lo favored improving ties; Mao was opposed.

The independence from the Soviet Union on which Mao insisted resulted in a weakened China. Standing alone, the Chinese could not hope to defeat either the United States or the Soviet Union. This made guerrilla warfare an attractive method of defense, indeed perhaps the only feasible way in which China could defend itself. Soviet assistance in the 1950s gave the People's Republic access to relatively modern weapons, with which the People's Liberation Army could face the Americans in formal battles. Without Soviet help, the Chinese would have been hopelessly outgunned. One reason Mao was prone to dismiss the worth of modern armaments was that he had none. When the Chinese Communists were most independent, they were also most isolated; when they were most isolated, they were weakest; and when they were weakest, they placed greatest reliance on guerrilla warfare.[83]

---

[82] Ibid., pp. 73–4.

[83] The differences between formal and guerrilla warfare recall a distinction central to the work of one of the great figures in the history of social thought, Emile Durkheim. He distinguished between two bases for social cohesion in human societies. One of them, organic solidarity, stems from the interaction of differentiated but interdependent parts. Like the organs of the body, none can function without the others. Organic solidarity, according to Durkheim, is a property of societies whose complicated economies are based on an extensive division of labor (Emile Durkheim, *The Division of Labor in Society*, trans. by George Simpson [New York, Free Press, 1933], Book 1). The formal approach to warfare operates in the same way. Large armies consist of functionally distinct

On land, weak states wage guerrilla warfare against more powerful enemies to raise the price of victory beyond what the strong state will pay. At sea, the ideal weapon of the weak is the submarine, the maritime equivalent of the guerrilla lying in ambush. In the twentieth century the skies have become a third theater of war. In air warfare one particular weapon has some of the same properties as the submarine and guerrilla warfare. It is an instrument of punishment. The punishment it can inflict is so great that the threat to use it has a powerful deterrent effect, which is the preferred strategy of the weak. In the 1960s and 1970s it came to play an important role in the security policies of the People's Republic of China. The weapon is the atomic bomb.[84]

V

For the first fifteen years of its existence, the People's Republic of China did not have nuclear weapons, whereas the United States and the Soviet Union did. This was one of the reasons for China's

parts connected by ever more complex systems of communication and control. None of the separate parts can win without the others. Infantry without air power will be overcome by an opposing army with a supporting air force.

Mechanical solidarity, Durkheim's other basis of social cohesion, is a property of societies having simpler economies with very little diversity. Instead of doing different jobs, their members tend to have the same tasks; they are farmers or herdsmen. None needs the others to survive (ibid.). Similarly, guerrilla units both resemble and operate independently of each other. The history of social life, in Durkheim's view, is the history of the evolution from mechanical to organic solidarity as the basis for social cohesion.

The parallel may be carried a step farther. "Organic" societies are more capable but less resilient than "mechanical" ones. Economies based on an extensive division of labor are more productive but are also more easily disrupted than simpler ones. Similarly, formally constituted armies can muster far greater firepower than can bands of guerrillas; they can conquer and hold territory as guerrilla forces cannot. But a modern army can also be decisively defeated by an equally large and well armed military force, especially if its mechanics for coordination are disrupted. German blitzkrieg warfare reduced the French army to impotence in 1940 in this way. A guerrilla army is not vulnerable to a comparably sudden and sweeping defeat. When one unit is stopped, the others fight on without it and continue to punish the occupier.

[84] The nuclear explosives carried by land- and submarine-based missiles are not pure instruments of air warfare. They are the space-age versions of artillery and naval guns. But their range and power are such that they are most useful for punishing societies, not, like conventional artillery, for defeating opposing armies.

relative weakness. Both great powers threatened China with nuclear attack simply by virtue of having these weapons. Sometimes they went farther, hinting that they would actually use them.

These nuclear threats inspired a rhetoric of determined resistance. Chinese statements on the subject, Mao Zedong's in particular, were hair-raising for their evident disregard for, and even ignorance of, the terrible realities of the nuclear age. In 1946 Mao called the bomb "a paper tiger which the reactionaries use to scare people. It looks terrible but in fact it isn't. Of course, the atom bomb is a weapon of mass slaughter, but the outcome of a war is decided by the people, not by one or two new types of weapons." In 1958 he said, "I don't see the reason for the atom bomb. Conventional weapons are still the thing."[85] He claimed to be unconcerned about the prospect of an American nuclear attack. "If they are going to do it [start a nuclear war] they'll just do it. It will sweep the world clean of imperialism, afterwards we can rebuild again, and from that time onwards there can never be another world war."[86] Mao's apparently cavalier attitude alarmed Khrushchev, and the Soviet leader was not the only person who took it as evidence that the chairman was a dangerous madman.[87]

Mao's statements were, however, what the leader of a weak state threatened by a stronger one equipped with nuclear weapons might be expected to say in order to show that he was not intimidated. Under similar circumstances in the aftermath of Hiroshima and Nagasaki, Stalin had declared that nuclear weapons frightened only those with weak nerves. Mao was determined to show that China's nerves were strong.

Even as the Chinese sounded defiant in the face of nuclear threats, they adjusted their policies in response to them. It was the danger of nuclear attack from the other great power that helped to push China into alignment first with the Soviet Union and then with the United States. Despite the defiant rhetoric of the Chinese, moreover, nuclear threats made them more accommodating. After the United States had hinted that nuclear weapons might be used

[85] Jonathan D. Pollack, "China as a Nuclear Power," in William H. Overholt, ed., *Asia's Nuclear Future* (Boulder, Colo.: Westview Press, 1977), pp. 36–7.
[86] Gittings, *World and China*, pp. 230–1.
[87] Khrushchev, *Khrushchev Remembers*, p. 471; Clubb, *China and Russia*, p. 443.

in Korea, China, along with North Korea, began the negotiations that finally produced an armistice in the Korean War. During the crisis triggered by the artillery barrages that Beijing launched against the Guomindang-controlled offshore islands in 1958, the United States again hinted that it might bring its nuclear arsenal into play. The shelling stopped.

Similarly, following the border clashes of 1969, the Soviets floated the rumor that they were contemplating a nuclear strike against China. The Chinese toned down their anti-Soviet rhetoric and agreed to begin negotiations on the disputed boundaries. The incidents along the borders tapered off. The Chinese discontinued the aggressive patrolling that had produced the border incidents.

China remained both independent of and unoccupied by foreigners for fifteen years without having nuclear weapons. The bomb was not an absolute necessity for Chinese security. Still, the Chinese decided to obtain it. In October 1964 they detonated their first nuclear explosion. In June 1967 the People's Republic successfully tested a fusion, or hydrogen, bomb. In 1969, at the time of the clashes with the Soviets, the Chinese had bombs mounted on ballistic missiles of medium range – about six hundred nautical miles – as well as carried by a fleet of bombers that had been acquired from the Soviet Union in the 1950s.[88] By the late 1970s they had added between sixty and eighty-five missiles with longer ranges, of about eighteen hundred miles, to the forty or fifty medium-range missiles already deployed and were working on prototypes of intercontinental range.[89] China's missiles were deployed along the borders with the Soviet Union in the north and northwest and in Tibet, and were apparently aimed at Soviet targets.[90]

Although its stockpile of bombs grew steadily from the mid-1960s to the late 1970s, China remained, in nuclear terms, decidedly inferior to the United States and the Soviet Union. Its public positions on the use and control of these weapons stemmed from this disparity. The Chinese proclaimed that they would never be the first to use them in a war.[91] This was sensible: In a nuclear conflict

---

[88] Cited in Gelman, *Soviet Far East Buildup*, pp. 43–4, n. 20.
[89] Cited in Jencks, *Missiles to Muskets*, pp. 158, 295–6.
[90] Ibid., p. 159.
[91] Whiting, *Chinese Calculus*, pp. 242–3.

either of the great powers could do much more damage to the People's Republic than China could inflict on either of them. (Through the late 1970s, in fact, China could do no direct damage to the United States, having no ballistic missile capable of reaching North America.) As for arms control negotiations, the Chinese rejected such talks as a form of collusion between the hegemonic powers, a thinly disguised effort to perpetuate their international privileges. China called for total disarmament by all nations, which, in the unlikely event that it ever came to pass, would strip the United States and the Soviet Union of important sources of strength and make the Chinese less weak in comparison.

Nuclear weapons can be used as instruments of denial. They can be employed in battles to stop the advance of opposing armies. The two European neutrals that gave serious thought to acquiring nuclear weapons, Switzerland and Sweden, considered incorporating them into their plans for forward defense, that is, for protecting their borders.

Nuclear weapons are also weapons of punishment. They can inflict enormous, unprecedented damage. They are so powerful, in fact, that it would be difficult to employ them strictly for the purposes of denial. The use of nuclear weapons almost anywhere, on almost any scale, would kill civilians and damage property as well as destroy military targets.[92] The bomb, therefore, conforms to the logic of weakness. It is the equivalent of guerrilla and submarine warfare. Guerrilla fighters and submarines can inflict punishment on the armed forces of a strong state. Nuclear weapons, because they can be delivered through the air, make the *societies* of strong states vulnerable to punishment by the weak. Nuclear weapons give weak states the means to do what, in the past, could be done only by the strong as the result of occupation.

Nuclear weapons lend themselves to the tactics of punishment. They are in this sense like guerrilla forces and submarines. They are complicated to assemble. A substantial number of highly trained people is required to make them; the task lies beyond the competence of a majority of sovereign states. Once assembled, however, bombs can be deployed and used in decentralized fashion.

---

[92] The design and deployment of nuclear weapons vary according to the mission they are assigned. Some are intended to strike military targets, others to pulverize cities. But even those with strictly military missions would in all likelihood cause civil damage as well.

Like guerrilla units, each bomb in a country's nuclear arsenal can be delivered more or less independently of all the others. One airplane carrying a bomb can fly even if the rest of a national air force is crippled. In theory, at least, one missile can be launched when all others are grounded. But one bomb, whether delivered by airplane or missile, can do much more damage by itself than a handful of guerrilla fighters or a single submarine with nonnuclear torpedoes; and it can inflict the damage on the home society, not only on the occupying army or the navy of the enemy.

Because a single bomb can do so much damage, the threat to use nuclear weapons has a powerful deterrent effect on a potential aggressor, even one much more powerful in military terms. Nuclear weapons give a state the means for a credible policy of deterrence through the threat of punishment against a far more powerful adversary when defense by denial – that is, by preventing occupation – is not feasible. Indeed, the bomb is the single most effective source of protection from a stronger adversary available to a markedly weaker state. None of the European neutrals has chosen to acquire the bomb, but one European power that is not neutral but is weak in comparison with its principal adversary does have it: France has pursued just such a nuclear strategy.

The French aim is to deter the Soviet Union by threatening to inflict nuclear punishment in retaliation for a Soviet attack. In a nuclear war with the Soviets, France would be overwhelmed and destroyed. A state that resists a stronger nuclear-armed adversary runs the risk not only of occupation but also of annihilation. But in such a war the Soviet Union would probably suffer grievously as well. Moscow or Leningrad (or both) might be destroyed. The Soviet Union as a functioning political community might survive and, in that sense, prevail over France; but the price of victory would be far steeper than the benefits Moscow could achieve by crushing France would be worth. The French calculate that their threat to "tear an arm off the bear," even if they cannot be certain of mortally wounding it, will keep the Russian bear at bay.[93]

Although never stated quite so graphically, this was also the nuclear strategy of the People's Republic of China. In fact, the

---

[93] On the principles of French strategy see Pierre Gallois, *The Balance of Terror: Strategy for the Nuclear Age,* trans. by Richard Howard (Boston: Houghton Mifflin, 1961).

People's Republic had to place greater reliance on its capacity to injure the Soviet Union because it had considerably less assurance than France – which was, after all, part of the Western alliance – that the United States would come to its defense. Although the Chinese increased their nuclear stockpile, they did not match the Soviet nuclear arsenal weapon for weapon. Nor did they need to do so. In a nuclear exchange, the Soviets could not be certain of destroying before launch or deflecting in flight all the nuclear explosives that China could hurl at them. Even one bomb striking a Soviet target would inflict catastrophic destruction. As the Chinese arsenal grew, the Soviets had less and less reason to believe that they could avoid damage in a nuclear battle. In any event, only a few explosives were required to instill the doubts on which the deterrence of the strong by the weak depends. Mao is reported to have said in 1965: "All I want are six atom bombs. With these bombs I know that neither side will attack me."[94]

Because the bomb can be used in decentralized fashion and because it is so destructive that the prospect of being the target of even a single one will have a powerful deterrent effect, it is the ideal weapon of the weak.[95] Many states face potential threats from others that are stronger and could certainly defeat them. Very few states, however, have nuclear weapons. Many cannot get them; they cannot make them, and others refuse to provide them. Others follow the familiar pattern of the weak; they find shelter in the shadow of the strong. Most European countries are either protected by the American or covered by the Soviet nuclear arsenals.[96] In this sense they do not conduct independent security policies. The European neutrals have been aligned, although not allied, with the United States and so draw some benefit from its nuclear shield.[97]

[94] Gelber, "Nuclear Weapons," p. 19.

[95] On this point see Michael Handel, *Weak States in the International System* (London: Cass, 1981), p. 198. The book includes useful discussions of a number of the problems of security associated with weakness.

[96] See Michael Mandelbaum, *The Nuclear Future* (Ithaca, N.Y.: Cornell University Press, 1983), pp. 89–97.

[97] Moral objections have played a role in the refusal of the neutrals, especially Sweden, to acquire nuclear weapons. The Swedes might not have been so firmly resolved to do without these weapons, however, if NATO were not firmly implanted in Western Europe.

Not only do most weak states not have nuclear weapons; most nuclear weapons have been in the possession of the strongest members of the international community – the United States and the Soviet Union. These weapons have added to the strength of the two major powers but have not been the basis for it. In a world free of nuclear armaments, neither would have to rely on defense by punishment. Both would be able to defend their borders. Nuclear weapons increased the gap in strength between the great powers and all those without these armaments. There was, as well, a gap between the nuclear might of the great powers and that of China. But there were also striking similarities in nuclear strategy among the three. If China's diplomacy and its preparations for nonnuclear war resembled those of the European neutrals, its nuclear strategy was close to the policies of the two countries that in other ways were China's opposite. The bomb produced a convergence of the strategies of the United States and the Soviet Union, on the one hand, and China, on the other. The paradoxical effect of these most powerful of all armaments was to endow their possessors with some of the characteristics of lesser states. The bomb is the weapon of the weak not only in the sense that it lends itself to the logical strategy of weak states that wish to remain independent – deterrence through the threat of punishment – but also in that it compels its possessors, no matter how powerful they are in other terms, to pursue strategies of weakness.

American and Chinese strategies were not identical. The United States had considerably more nuclear firepower. That made a difference. The difference was summarized by the concept of "assured destruction." The term refers to a nuclear arsenal resilient enough to survive in all-out assault, even a nuclear attack, in sufficient strength to devastate the attacker. The capacity for assured destruction provides as firm a guarantee of successful deterrence as is available, because an attack on a country that possesses it amounts to an act of suicide. Assured destruction means that its possessor can inflict enormous punishment under *any* circumstances, no matter what the adversary does to try to prevent this. It guarantees the result that guerrilla and submarine warfare seek.

What ensures assured destruction for the United States and the Soviet Union is the size of their nuclear stockpiles. The larger one state's nuclear arsenal is, the more difficult it will be for another to knock out all of its bombs or defend against them. Assured destruction can also be achieved through concealing, protecting, and making mobile retaliatory weapons. Submarines carrying nuclear explosives do all three.

The United States and the Soviet Union had many more nuclear explosives than China. But the Chinese took steps to reduce the vulnerability of their arsenal to preemptive attack. They concealed and moved their bombs in order to complicate Soviet plans to destroy them in a surprise attack. They reportedly hid some in caves.[98] Both great nuclear powers could be certain that a large enough fraction of their nuclear stockpiles would survive an attack to destroy the attacker in a retaliatory strike. China did not enjoy such certainty; but China's adversary, the Soviet Union, could not be certain that China could *not* retaliate in a devastating manner following an attack.[99] Effective Chinese retaliation was perhaps less than absolutely certain, but it was distinctly possible. That possibility promoted doubt in the Soviet calculations about the wisdom of attack, which contributed to deterring one.[100] The difference between the policies of deterrence of the United States and the Soviet Union, on the one hand, and China, on the other, was one of degree.[101]

---

[98] Gelber, "Nuclear Weapons," p. 15; Gelman, *Soviet Far East Buildup*, p. 44.

[99] On the difficulties for the Soviets in launching a preemptive strike against Chinese nuclear forces see Gelber, "Nuclear Weapons," p. 34.

[100] The case against the acquisition of nuclear weapons by weak states rests in part on the difficulty of acquiring enough invulnerable armaments to make retaliation certain. See Handel, *Weak States*, pp. 199–200, and Vital, *Inequality*, p. 173. But nuclear arsenals that fall short of the standard of assured destruction, although not as desirable as larger, more resilient stockpiles, are far from worthless. Even a handful of bombs, even the six that Mao said were all that he needed, have some deterrent effect. The difference is that a nuclear force capable of assured destruction makes it certain that an attack will fail (in that it will provoke retaliation): A lesser nuclear stockpile makes it *un*certain that an attack will *succeed*.

[101] The Chinese nuclear forces on the Soviet border were vulnerable to nonnuclear attack. There was a risk that with a Soviet thrust across the border they would either be fired so as to be kept out of enemy hands, thereby touching off a nuclear war, or else be captured, depriving China of the means of punishing the Soviet Union. This vulnerability, however, reinforced Chinese deterrence. The Soviets had to reckon with, or at least worry about, the possibility that faced with a choice of "using or losing" their nuclear armaments, the Chinese

Moreover, and here is the important point of similarity, their common capacity for assured destruction put the United States and the Soviet Union in the same position in relation to each other as China's position in relation to each of them. Chinese, American, and Soviet strategies were parallel. Each great power's nuclear arsenal made the other in effect a weak state. Neither could disarm the other: That is the meaning of assured destruction. Neither, therefore, could defend itself by denial from a nuclear attack by the other. In a war between the two, each homeland would be vulnerable to the other, whatever preventive measures the other took. Each side, that is, could punish the other. Because the United States had the capacity for assured destruction, it could punish the Soviet Union under any circumstances; because the Soviet Union had the capacity for assured destruction, it could punish the United States under any circumstances. The capacity was mutual. Since neither side could defend itself against attacks by the other, each had to practice deterrence through the threat of punishment. That is precisely the policy of the would-be independent weak state confronting a much stronger adversary.

The United States and the Soviet Union were the strongest imaginable weak states because the punishment they could inflict was enormous. But they were still weak in the sense that they could not protect their societies against enemy attack. Their huge nuclear stockpiles simply meant that deterrence through the threat of punishment was likely to be successful. Their weapons did not relieve them of the need to practice the strategy of weakness.

A nuclear war between the United States and the Soviet Union would be an exercise in competitive punishment, like the occupation of a weak state by a stronger power. It would be a contest not for the control of territory but in inflicting and enduring civilian destruction. In this sense it would take the same form as a guerrilla war, except that both sides would find themselves in the position

would use them. The Soviets had to consider the danger, that is, that a non-nuclear war that they initiated would become nuclear (Jencks, *Missiles to Muskets*, p. 159). The Chinese did work to develop missiles with long enough ranges to be located well behind the border and still be able to strike deep into the Soviet Union.

of the occupied country and both could punish the civilians as well as the soldiers of the other. In waging a nuclear war, each side would hope that the other would decide that the punishment it was suffering was not worth the goal for which it was fighting and give up, which was the Chinese strategy against the Japanese occupiers in the 1930s and 1940s, the Yugoslav strategy against Germany in World War II, and the Vietnamese Communist strategy against the United States in the 1960s. Neither the United States nor the Soviet Union wanted to fight a nuclear war against the other. Each attempted to deter an attack by threatening punishment in response, which was precisely the rationale for the military preparations of the European neutrals and for China's military plans and operations after 1944.

All other things being equal, to be successful a policy of deterrence must be credible. A country with a nuclear arsenal that has the capacity for assured destruction will find it less difficult to make credible a threat to retaliate in response to an attack than will one with a smaller nuclear stockpile, such as China's. It was easier for the United States and the Soviet Union to persuade each other of their determination to retaliate for an attack than it was for China to persuade either of them of the same intention – although the Chinese threat evidently proved sufficiently persuasive.

The United States did encounter difficulty in making deterrence credible, however, and so had a further element of policy in common with China. The United States pledged to defend not only its own territory but also that of its allies located thousands of miles away. The credibility of this pledge was subject to doubt, not because, as with China, the American nuclear arsenal was small, but because what it was being used to defend was not American territory. In both cases there was a disproportion: In the American case it was between the aim of the policy – the protection of others – and the possible penalty for carrying it out – the annihilation of the continental United States. In the case of China the disproportion was between the punishment the country could inflict and the damage it would suffer through defeat and occupation.

Not coincidentally, therefore, the measures the United States adopted to persuade the Soviet Union that it would defend Western Europe were similar to those the Chinese took to convince the United States and the Soviet Union that they would defend themselves. Like the Chinese, the Americans repeatedly declared that they would fight. American troops were stationed on the Continent to reinforce this assertion, just as China sent soldiers to North Vietnam as a symbol of its determination to resist an American invasion. And just as the Chinese did fight – in Korea, on the Indian border, and along the frontiers with the Soviet Union – to warn the great powers of the cost of attacking them, so the United States fought – in Korea and Vietnam – to reinforce the credibility of its promise to defend other countries, especially in Europe.[102]

Because nuclear weapons are instruments of punishment, they blur, although they do not eliminate, the distinction between the strong and the weak. China's nuclear weapons policies, like its diplomacy and its other military initiatives, were those that states similarly situated, confronting much more powerful adversaries, would have been, and were, driven to adopt. Its maneuvers between the two strongest powers in the international system, its military engagements outside its borders, and its preparations to cope with invasion can be understood as responses to the particular international predicament of weakness. China's nuclear strategy was also characteristic, in important ways, of *all* nuclear strategies, because nuclear weapons, with their special, revolutionary properties, place all states at which they are aimed in the same position as that of the People's Republic of China after 1949.

[102] See Chapter 3. The United States also attempted to bolster the credibility of its pledge to protect Europe by the size of its nuclear arsenal. It had many more weapons than were necessary simply for assured destruction.

5

Israel, 1948–1979

The Hard Choices of the Security Dilemma

I

Of all the sovereign states of the postwar period, Israel was the most threatened. Tiny and awkwardly shaped, only nine miles wide at its narrowest point and with long, vulnerable borders, it was surrounded by larger and far more populous countries that objected not to Israel's size, its political system, or its policies, but to its existence.

Although beleaguered and vulnerable, Israel was not a weak state in the sense that the People's Republic of China was weak after 1949.[1] It did not face certain defeat in a war with its adversaries, as China did in a war with the United States or the Soviet Union. Indeed, Israel fought four wars with its Arab adversaries in twenty-five years and won them all.[2] These victories did not, however, make Israel a strong state like the United States after 1945. In none of the conflicts was the outcome assured. The Israelis fought by conventional, not guerrilla, methods. They expanded their territorial holdings but could not compel their Arab neighbors to accept their country as a legitimate, permanent part of the Middle East. Despite the victories, the Arab threat persisted. Israel belonged to that large middle category of sovereign states that are

---

[1] See Chapter 4, Section I.
[2] The Israelis counted the artillery duel with Egypt across the Suez Canal in 1969–70 as a fifth war, the "war of attrition."

roughly comparable in power to their would-be adversaries. Like France after 1918, Israel was neither much stronger nor much weaker than its enemies.[3]

Its position in the international system did not determine Israel's security policies. It had a wider choice than the very strong or the very weak. It faced one choice, in particular, that is universal in international politics. After 1967, although not after 1948, Israel confronted a particularly acute version of the security dilemma.

The security dilemma is based on the fact that threats, and preparations to meet them, are interrelated in unpredictable and contradictory ways. It is a byproduct of the anarchy that is the organizing principle of the international system. Anarchy makes war between sovereign states possible but not certain.

Each state's security depends in part on what other states decide to do. Security is a hybrid of the tangible and the intangible. It depends on a state's own capabilities. But it also depends on others' intentions, which are not uniform or always easily anticipated; for each state's security is the product of its own means and others' ends. These are interrelated, but – and here is the crux of the security dilemma – they are interrelated in unpredictable ways.

A state can control its own capabilities. It can decide, within limits, how powerful it will be. It cannot control how its power will affect the disposition of other states to treat it. No state can be certain in advance how others will decide. All will set their capabilities – they will make themselves more or less strong – so as to make themselves more secure; but their policies can have the unintended effect of making them less so. This is true no matter what course a state chooses. Any course involves some risk. So the choice of security policy presents any sovereign state with a dilemma.

The security dilemma is not central to relations between every pair of states in the international system. But those that are in regular contact with each other, that have some prospect of military rivalry, that are roughly equal in strength, and that wish to preserve the status quo do face the choice that it imposes. The choice is depicted in Table 1.

Fredonia wishes to maximize its security in dealing with its

[3] See Chapter 2.

Table 1. *The security dilemma*

Sylvania's intentions	Freedonia's capabilities	
	More	Less
Less hostile	Deterrence	Conciliation
	1	2
	4	3
More hostile	Provocation	Temptation

neighbor Sylvania. It has two broad alternatives. It can increase its military capabilities. This decision, in turn, will affect Sylvania's intentions in one of two ways. Sylvania may become less hostile. It may, that is, be deterred from attacking. Or it may become more hostile than it would have been if Fredonia had not made itself stronger. It may perceive a threat where none existed before. Sylvania may thus be provoked. Fredonia can also choose to make itself less strong.[4] This, too, can affect Sylvania's intentions in ways that increase Fredonia's security, but it can also make Fredonia *less* secure. Sylvania may become less hostile than before. The result can be conciliation between the two countries. But Sylvania may also become either more hostile or no less so and more inclined to act on its hostility now that Fredonia is weaker than before. This second alternative may therefore tempt Sylvania to undertake offensive action rather than coax it into conciliation.

The security dilemma is rooted in the anarchic structure of the international system, of which every sovereign state is part. All states thus confront the security dilemma in some form. In any relationship between any two of them, the four alternatives that comprise it are present. Yet the choice that it embodies has not

---

[4] States rarely make themselves weaker by giving up military might. They may weaken themselves in relation to others by refraining from becoming as strong as they might be.

been a prominent part of the security policies of most states. Its influence on the history of international politics, even under a different name or under none at all, is extremely modest. The reason is that there is a powerful and virtually universal impulse for states to increase their military strength. Deterrence is to some extent the policy of almost all of them. Almost all have armed forces of some sort, and many adopt diplomatic strategies that add to their capacities to defend themselves.

It is rare for any state to be decisively influenced by the prospect that its preparations for war will have the unintended and undesired consequence of making war more likely.[5] The idea that there is such a thing as too much national strength has not been influential in the history of international politics.

Most states have believed that greater strength will bring greater security. They have not necessarily been correct. An increase in national strength can produce a provocative effect. It can make an adversary at first warier, then more hostile, and, when it acts on its hostility, ultimately more threatening than it would have been had there been no increase in strength. If Fredonia acts on the impulse to be stronger, if Sylvania feels threatened by this and responds by strengthening itself, and if this makes the military balance less advantageous to Fredonia than it was in the first place, then by strengthening itself Fredonia has become *less* secure.

Episodes of provocation have occurred from time to time, or so students of international politics have believed. Germany's aggressive diplomacy in the years leading up to World War I, it has been argued, unnecessarily alarmed the other European powers. The German decision to build a fleet of capital ships pushed the British into alliance with France and Russia. Similarly, some have contended, the Chinese dispatch of troops to Korea to fight the United States in the fall of 1950 provoked twenty years of avoidable animosity and conflict. The competition in nuclear armaments between the United States and the Soviet Union has also been interpreted as involving unintended provocation, each side acquiring weapons out of the fear that the other was about to do so, thus

---

[5] "It is significant that there are not many cases where statesmen, correctly or not, perceive that others are afraid of them." Robert Jervis, *Perception and Misperception in International Politics* (Princeton, N.J.: Princeton University Press, 1976), p. 88; see also pp. 64–5.

driving the other to provide itself with armaments it would otherwise not have built. The nuclear arms race, in this view, has been an action–reaction cycle in which the mistaken policies of each side have produced unintended and unwanted policies by the other.

Provocation, as described here, cannot be proved. It is a matter of retrospective judgment. It cannot be definitively known whether Germany would have been in a better position – that is, whether Britain would have stayed out of the war in 1914 – had the Germans not mounted their naval challenge.[6] China might have been more secure had it never entered the Korean War, but Chinese restraint might also have left the United States equally hostile to the Communist regime and equally or more inclined to try to remove it. Perhaps had either the United States or the Soviet Union, or both, refrained from adding to their respective nuclear stockpiles the other would have showed similar restraint. Both would have acquired fewer than they came to have, and each would have been more secure. But there is no way of knowing this. The proposition, as with Germany and China, is hypothetical.

The historical precedents for provocation are uncertain because the historical evidence is necessarily speculative. This is one reason that states seldom pursue policies to avoid provocation, preferring instead to be as strong as possible. There is another reason: Even if the policy of increasing strength turns out to be mistaken, it at least provides the means to overcome the mistake.

Although Fredonia's policy of becoming stronger may make Sylvania more hostile, it also makes Fredonia better able to cope with Sylvania's hostility. If the policy of strength makes war between the two more likely, it also increases Fredonia's chances of winning. It may do both. If it does, Fredonia will never know whether more

---

[6] In fact, Wilhelmine Germany, although frequently cited (see, e.g., ibid., p. 92), is a dubious case of provocation. The German goal was to overturn, not maintain, the status quo in Europe, at least in the east. Had the Germans not annexed Alsace-Lorraine in 1871, it is true, they might have avoided war with France in 1914. But Germany wanted much more than merely to hold these two western provinces. Berlin sought to expand to the east, which would have made even the British, not to mention the French and the Russians, considerably less secure. In this sense World War I was the product not of misunderstanding, not of policies that were misconceived, but rather of policies that were well conceived to advance interests that were fundamentally in conflict. See Chapter 1, pp. 40–3.

circumspect policies would have averted war; it will, however, have solid grounds for believing that such policies would have damaged its security if war had come all the same.[7] It is possible that World War I occurred because Germany was too strong. It is certain that the Germans lost the war because they were not strong enough. Between the two approaches toward a potential adversary, there is a powerful bias in favor of increasing rather than decreasing strength. Most states attempt to practice policies of deterrence. They are usually willing to risk unintentionally pursuing a policy of provocation instead – on those occasions in which they are aware that such a risk exists at all.[8]

Sometimes, however, a state not only is aware of the possibility of provoking another, but acts to avoid this. Occasionally states give up military assets, thereby making themselves less powerful, or at least pass up the opportunity to acquire more power, with the aim of affecting the intentions of a potential adversary in a favorable way. Such a policy may succeed. Britain reached accommodation in the years before World War I with all the other great powers except Germany in this manner. By abandoning disputed claims or compromising issues that divided them from each of the

---

[7] If Fredonia increases its armaments and then has to fight, it will be just as plausible for Fredonians to believe that their policy was the proper one but was not pursued vigorously enough – that is, that more armaments would have deterred Sylvania from attacking – as to conclude that the policy itself was wrong. Wars may break out because of failed deterrence as well as through provocation.

[8] The bias in favor of increased strength is one reason that the security dilemma does not correspond precisely to the game of Prisoner's Dilemma (for further discussion of this issue see Chapter 6, p. 384). The alternatives that the security dilemma involves are very roughly comparable to the outcomes in Prisoner's Dilemma. Deterrence is the equivalent of DC; provocation of DD; conciliation of CC; and temptation of CD. But the "payoffs" of the alternatives in the security dilemma differ from those of the outcomes of the Prisoner's Dilemma. Although it is difficult to assign numerical values to these payoffs, as some versions of Prisoner's Dilemma do, provocation is not, as in the game, a clearly and significantly worse outcome than conciliation. That is, DD is not necessarily significantly worse than CC. It does not necessarily produce war. If war comes, the first party may win. And if there is war, the first party may conclude not that the policy was misconceived but that mutual interests simply did not exist. It may decide in retrospect that the "game" the two sides were playing was not Prisoner's Dilemma but "Deadlock." See Kenneth A. Oye, "Explaining Cooperation Under Anarchy: Hypothesis and Strategies," in Kenneth A. Oye, ed., *Cooperation Under Anarchy* (Princeton, N.J.: Princeton University Press, 1986), p. 6.

others, the British conciliated the United States, Japan, France, and Russia. In each case the British gave up something of at least potential military value to make the intentions of the other power more benign.[9]

Even when they realize that following the normal impulse to maximize strength may lead to an undesired outcome – even, that is, when they understand that the choice of security policy involves a genuine dilemma – states ordinarily do not give up strength in order to conciliate a would-be adversary. If it miscarries, such a policy can lead to disaster. If Fredonia's policy of being less capable than it might be does not achieve its aim, if Sylvania remains hostile, then Sylvania may be more likely to act on its hostility. It may be tempted to press its claims against Fredonia. It will certainly be in a better position to do so. If war then breaks out, Fredonia will be more likely to lose.

The history of the twentieth century offers a vivid cautionary example of such a mistake: Britain and France's unsuccessful appeasement of Hitler in the 1930s. The western powers gave concessions to Germany in the hope of satisfying German demands, thereby rendering German intentions peaceful and so avoiding war. Instead, their acquiescence in the remilitarization of the Rhineland and their surrender of Czechoslovakia put the Allies in a weaker position to fight when, because Hitler's appetite for conquest had not been satisfied, war did come.[10]

Even if it is misconceived, a policy of becoming stronger can still make a state secure. A mistaken policy of becoming less strong does not have the same built-in basis for safety. And although the costs of excessive strength can never be firmly established since provocation cannot be proved, the costs of insufficient strength – defeat – are all too clear. It will therefore almost always seem better to err on the side of being too powerful than not being powerful enough. Appeasement will seem a greater threat than provocation. Sovereign states, even when they are aware of the possibility of

---

[9] See Chapter 1, pp. 48–9.

[10] See Chapter 2, pp. 108–14. In the terms of the security dilemma, it might be argued that the French mistimed their policies. In 1919 they practiced deterrence when conciliation would have made them more secure. In the 1930s they adopted conciliatory policies, when a greater emphasis on deterrence would have been more appropriate.

both, are more likely to risk the dangers of the second than the perils of the first.[11]

Although it is universal, states rarely recognize the security dilemma or seriously weigh the choice between greater and lesser strength. For those few that do, what is at stake in the choice varies widely. After 1967, Israel's version of the security dilemma was distinctive both because the Israelis did realize that they faced this choice and because the stakes were very high indeed.

From 1948 to 1967, however, the Israeli choice between greater and lesser strength was unusually straightforward. Israel practiced a policy of deterrence. It tried to make itself as powerful as possible.

---

[11] The term "security dilemma" seems to have been first used by the English historian Herbert Butterfield. See his *History and Human Relations* (London: Collins, 1951), pp. 19–20. The most extensive discussion of the concept can be found in the work of Robert Jervis: *Perception and Misperception*, pp. 62–76, and *Cooperation Under the Security Dilemma* (Los Angeles: University of California, Center for Arms Control and International Security, 1977). Jervis's definition of the term is narrower than the one used here. For him it means that "many of the means by which a state tries to increase its security decrease the security of others" (*Cooperation*, p. 4; see also p. 25). A consequence of international anarchy and therefore a fact of international life is that power is relative, so that when one state becomes stronger others become weaker. (This is not the case in the rare but not unprecedented event that a state's newly acquired strength is useful for purely defensive purposes but not for attack and conquest. See *Cooperation*, pp. 25–6.) But if Fredonia's policies make Sylvania less secure, this is not, in itself, a problem for Fredonia. The possibility that this will occur does not pose a dilemma. The dilemma stems from the fact that these policies may prompt Sylvania to take steps that ultimately make Fredonia itself less secure than it would have been had it not strengthened itself in the first place. This unintended consequence of acquiring strength is here called "provocation." It has also been called the "insecurity spiral" (Glenn Snyder, "The Security Dilemma in Alliance Politics," *World Politics*, 36, no. 4 [1984]: 477) and the "spiral model" (Jervis, *Perception and Misperception*, p. 82). The possibility of an insecurity spiral is part, but only part, of the security dilemma. A policy of increasing strength, although by far the most common, is not the only one available to sovereign states. As noted, they can and occasionally do choose to be *less* strong than they might be. That policy also carries the possibility of an unintended and unwanted outcome, which is here termed "temptation." The security dilemma encompasses both. (As it is defined here, the security dilemma is more or less what Glenn Snyder calls the "secondary adversary dilemma." See Snyder, "Security Dilemma," pp. 469–70, esp. the last paragraph of no. 6 and p. 477, n. 13). For the application of the security dilemma, defined somewhat differently than in this chapter, to the Israeli war in Lebanon, see Avner Yaniv, *Dilemmas of Security: Politics, Strategy, and the Israeli Experience in Lebanon* (New York: Oxford University Press, 1987).

Strength portended no unwanted consequences. Arab hostility seemed not only intense but immutable. There was no danger of making the Arab world more hostile, because it was already as hostile as it could conceivably be. A popular Hebrew phrase expressed the basis of the country's security policy: *ein breira* – "no choice." The Israelis believed that they ran no risk of provocation, because there was absolutely no prospect of conciliation with their neighbors.

But after 1967, and especially after 1973, Israel's security problem changed. The Israelis captured territory that both sides agreed belonged to the Arabs. To the south, Egyptian troops were driven off the Sinai Peninsula to the western side of the Suez Canal, which became the new frontier between the two countries. To the east, Israel captured the West Bank of the Jordan River, the territory between the river and the 1949 cease-fire lines – including all of Jerusalem, which had been a divided city since 1949 – from the kingdom of Jordan. The Jordan River became Israel's new eastern border. To the north, the Israeli army assaulted and captured the Golan Heights, the southwestern end of the plateau on which Damascus stands, which overlooks the Hula Valley and northern Galilee in Israel. Israel's conquests established diplomatic possibilities that had not been available before. The choice of security policy, previously easy, became an exceptionally difficult one after 1973. The Israelis were aware that they faced a dilemma. They realized that they might be more secure if they were not as strong. They recognized that conciliation was a possible goal. They pondered whether to trade "land for peace" – that is, whether to surrender territories occupied in 1967 in exchange for Arab promises to launch no further attacks. They had to calculate the effect of their own capabilities on the Arabs' intentions.

The captured territories added to Israel's capabilities. They were military assets. In case of war, Israel would be in a stronger position if it retained control of them.[12] They provided Israel with natural frontiers. The Suez Canal to the south, the Jordan River to the

---

[12] See Edward Luttwak and Dan Horowitz, *The Israeli Army* (New York: Harper & Row, 1975), pp. 299–300, and Nadav Safran, *Israel: The Embattled Ally* (Cambridge, Mass: Harvard University Press, 1978), pp. 258–61, for the basis of the following discussion.

east, and the Golan Heights to the north could be more readily defended than the cease-fire lines of 1949, which had been the country's borders until June 1967. The territories also served as buffer zones between the Arab states and the Israeli population, and so were particularly important for a country as small as Israel. They provided a measure of strategic depth. They made it possible, in case of attack, for Israel to trade space for time in which its army could mobilize.

Israel did trade space for time in the war of October 1973, a war that at first seemed to demonstrate the military value of the occupied territories. Egypt and Syria enjoyed the benefit of surprise, gained an initial advantage, and pushed the Israeli forces back from the lines they had established in 1967. If the war had begun where the border stood before the 1967 war, the heart of Israel would have been in jeopardy, a fact that argued in favor of retaining control of the territories.

But Israel would also gain by giving up the territories, if this would prevent future wars. If returning the territories resulted in a change in the attitudes of the Arab states, if these states agreed to accept Israel as a legitimate sovereign state in the Middle East, if, that is, yielding land produced successful conciliation, then Israel would be *more* secure than it would be simply by retaining what it had captured in 1967. Maximizing national strength was not necessarily the high road to security.

The Israeli version of the security dilemma after 1967 was unusual in another way. Israel was hardly the first state to wish to change the mind of its potential adversary. Pure cases of conciliation, however, in which one side unilaterally reduces its strength to affect the attitudes of the other, are rare. Negotiated agreements are frequent enough; but when agreements involving the reduction of military potential are voluntary, they are almost always mutual. Both sides, not only one, give up elements of military strength. Arms control agreements between the United States and the Soviet Union have imposed restraints on both great powers. The exchange of land for peace would not be comparably mutual. Israel, and Israel alone, would have to give up military assets. The Arab side would be required simply to change its mind. Israel would have to trade capabilities for intentions. The Israeli concessions would be concrete. The Arab concessions would be no less important, but they would be intangible. This made the choice difficult for Israel.[13]

It was a difficult choice for yet another reason. Unilateral concessions, of the sort that Israel would have to make, are unusual but not entirely without precedent. At the beginning of the twentieth century, Britain made accommodation with the United States possible by relinquishing any claim to a political and military role in the New World and did so without demanding a reciprocal concession by the United States. The Anglo-American rapprochement was one-sided. Before World War II Britain and France also exchanged capabilities for intentions. In return for agreeing to the partition of Czechoslovakia, they received only Hitler's promise to make no further demands. There is, however, a significant difference between these two cases and Israel's choice after 1967.

What the British relinquished before World War I, and the British and French gave up before World War II, was not crucial for their security. That is why they could afford to make the concessions. They could reckon that, even if the calculations on which the concessions were based proved to be incorrect, even if their potential adversaries were not better disposed to them but rather tempted to make further demands on them, even if what was intended to be conciliation turned out instead to be unsuccessful appeasement, they would still be able to defend themselves. What they gave up was not without value, but for the safety of the home territories it was marginal.

By contrast, what the Israelis were faced with relinquishing was central to their security. North America was far from the British

---

[13] Henry Kissinger made the point clearly in his memoirs: "All the tangible concessions – above all, territory – had to be made by Israel; once made, they were irrevocable. The Arab quid pro quo was something intangible, such as diplomatic recognition or a legal state of peace, which could always be modified or even withdrawn" (*Years of Upheaval* [Boston: Little, Brown, 1982], p. 169). The Israelis recognized their predicament. Kissinger quotes Prime Minister Golda Meir as saying, when negotiations with Egypt were just beginning, "If we are realistic and honest with ourselves, we Israelis, it [disengagement] really means we have come out of this war, which was as it was, by pulling back. That's what it really is, if you call it by its right name. Just pulling back, that's what it is" (ibid., p. 790). On the asymmetrical character of the exchange see also Yehoshafat Harkabi, *Arab Strategies and Israel's Response* (New York: Free Press, 1977), p. 123.

Isles. Czechoslovakia lay well to the east of Britain and France. But the territories that the Israelis captured in 1967 were located directly on their borders. The immediate risks of surrendering them were far higher than the risks had been to Britain at the turn of the century and to Britain and France in 1938.

Ordinarily, a state will not relinquish such an important military asset. The risks are too great. But for the Israelis the risks of not doing so were also considerable. The return of the territories offered to Israel the prospect of removing the political basis of the Arab–Israeli conflict. It promised real peace, the peace that Israel had sought since its establishment. It offered the hope of an end to the grinding, dangerous round of wars and the chance to build the Jewish state without the constant threat of attack. Muting the hostility of its Arab neighbors, which had burdened, indeed dominated, Israeli national life since the founding of the state, would mean achieving Israel's supreme national goal.[14]

Unlike most sovereign states, Israel after 1967, and especially after 1973, found the choices that comprise the security dilemma both clear and consequential. Because both the risks and the benefits of attempting a policy of conciliation were so great, Israel was the sovereign state in the twentieth century for which the security dilemma was perhaps the most acute. The Israeli case vividly illustrates the security dilemma, because Israel's version of this universal feature of international affairs was an extreme rather than a normal one.

The Israelis preferred to choose conciliation. Conciliation was a powerfully attractive but also a highly risky option. Israeli policies after 1973 were designed to choose conciliation while reducing the risks that the concessions it required would result in unsuccessful appeasement. The Arab–Israeli peace process can be seen as a response to the special problems inherent in Israel's version of the security dilemma.

The character of the international system imposes the security dilemma on all sovereign states. The dilemma is imposed, so to

[14] For an Israeli assessment of the risks and benefits of conceding territory see Foreign Minister Moshe Dayan's account of his speech to the Knesset, the Israeli parliament, in support of the Camp David accords. Moshe Dayan, *Breakthrough: A Personal Account of the Egypt–Israel Peace Negotiations* (London: Weidenfeld & Nicolson, 1981), pp. 194–7.

speak, from the world beyond the state's boundaries. There is no necessary, predetermined way for states to respond to it. Whether a state will make itself more or less strong cannot be inferred from its position in the international system. An "outside-in" explanation cannot account for the choice, which is a product of the state's history, its national temperament, and its domestic politics. Any response to the security dilemma requires an "inside-out" explanation.

Israel was eager for conciliation but also wary of its dangers. The wariness came partly from its size and shape, but also from its history, which consisted both of the experience of the Jewish people in Europe in the twentieth century and of the experience of Israeli Jews with their neighbors since 1948. The attitudes of Israel's neighbors were crucial in shaping that second experience; and those attitudes, in turn, were rooted in the domestic features of the Arab states.

II

Israel's security policy from 1948 to 1967 was shaped by political conflict. The distinctive features of that conflict made the initial Israeli policy for remaining secure a strictly military one.

The Arab–Israeli conflict has, it is true, a number of features in common with many other national enmities in the postwar world. The end of imperial rule gave birth to it. Britain retreated from the Middle East, as from South and Southeast Asia and Africa. The peoples of those regions were left to create new political orders for themselves. This was almost nowhere accomplished without turmoil. The boundaries that Britain devised were frequently contested. Sometimes the British left no boundaries at all.

In both South Asia and the Middle East, minority groups that had managed to coexist with the majority in the days of British rule decided that they needed their own sovereign state. Jewish nationalism in Palestine had a somewhat longer history than Muslim separatism on the subcontinent, but Muslims had ruled in India more recently than an independent Jewish community had existed in the Middle East. Both communities achieved their aim, but not without violence. There was violence on a much larger scale in South Asia, but in the Middle East it was more explicitly organized, more plainly the work of governments. The partition of the British raj in India led to bloody communal riots in which Hindus, Sikhs, and Muslims butchered one another. The partition of Palestine provoked the first, but not the last, Arab–Israeli war.

For all the similarities, however, the conflict between Israel and the Arabs was deeper, more durable, more bitter, and of greater significance for the history of the peoples involved than the conflict between Indians and Pakistanis, or between Ibos and Hausas in West Africa, or Greeks and Turks over Cyprus, or even, perhaps, the oldest of these conflicts, the one between Protestants and Catholics in Ulster. The distinctive bitterness of the conflict made Israel's security singularly precarious during the first quarter-century of its existence and the Israeli version of the security dilemma particularly acute thereafter.

The depth of Arab hostility had several causes. Many of the Jews of Palestine came from Europe. They appeared to some Arabs to be merely the latest in a long line of Western interlopers. Their community seemed another foreign outpost in the region, a descendant of the Crusaders' Latin Kingdom of Jerusalem.[15] The Arab-Israeli conflict can also be seen as a clash between two groups over the same piece of territory. But it was longer lasting, wider in scope, and more bitter in tone than other such conflicts. Perhaps the principal reason for its unusual features was to be found in the character of Arabs' Islamic religion and culture.

The Islamic faith pervades the everyday life of the believer. It is a "complete program for ordering society."[16] It provides rules

---

[15] If Zionism had been a movement only of oriental Jews – that is, of those whose ancestors had lived in the Middle East for generations – the history of the region in the twentieth century might have been different. (For speculation on this subject see David S. Landes, "Palestine Before the Zionists," *Commentary*, February 1976, p. 55.) Muslims in the Middle East did tolerate the partly Christian state of Lebanon, although in the 1970s the tolerance evaporated and Lebanon ceased to be, for all practical purposes, a unified country. The Christians of the region differed from the Jews in a number of important ways, one of which was that they spoke Arabic, the language of the Muslims. This is the basis of Daniel Pipes's speculation that Arab attitudes toward Israel might have been more benign if the Zionists had decided on that language, rather than Hebrew, as their official tongue. Daniel Pipes, *In the Path of God: Islam and Political Power* (New York: Basic Books, 1983), p. 342, n. 14. The following discussion is heavily indebted to this book.

[16] Pipes, *In the Path*, p. 11.

for every aspect of human conduct. Islam does not, therefore, make the distinction between the secular and sacred realms that is central to Christianity. Religious ordinances have a political character. There is no separation between political power and religious authority. They are one and the same.[17] Muslims are enjoined to govern territories where they live so that the all-pervasive Islamic law can be enforced. Non-Muslims who live among them may be tolerated, but they cannot rule. Muslims must hold power.

This is true in theory. The imperative of Muslim rule wherever Muslims live follows logically from the character of the faith. As with other religions, the theory has not always and everywhere been put into practice. It has often been honored in the breach. No Muslim community anywhere has ever conformed perfectly to the entire Sharia, the religious code. Nor have Muslims always dominated the non-Muslims with whom they have lived side by side. Many Muslim communities have lived peacefully under the dominion of unbelievers. Since the founding of the religion, the world of Islam has become a large and diverse one. Customs, and the fidelity with which they have been observed, have varied widely within the Islamic world. The spirit of orthodoxy has been strongest, however, at the center of that world, the place of its birth, the Arab Middle East. The injunction to obey the law and to control the organs of government so as to enforce obedience on the whole becomes stronger the closer to the Arabian peninsula a Muslim community is situated. Even there Muslims have not always held power. For three decades after World War I Britain and France governed the region. But Islamic rule remained an important goal, and with the end of European predominance after World War II came the opportunity to reassert it.

The idea of a sovereign Jewish state in their midst was alien, unwelcome, and unacceptable to the Arab Muslims. It contravened the fundamental tenets of their faith. When the leaders of the surrounding Arab states attacked the new state of Israel in May 1948, however, their motives were not primarily religious. Al-

---

[17] "Islam, from the lifetime of its founder, *was* the state, and moreover one favored with success and victory. The linkage of religion and power, community and polity was thus established for its people by revelation and confirmed by history." Bernard Lewis, "Right and Left in Lebanon," *The New Republic*, September 10, 1977, p. 21.

though they sometimes invoked the idea, they were not waging a *jihad* – a religious war to put Muslims in command of all of Palestine so as to enforce the Sharia there. They were not enforcing it in their own countries. The reasons that they attacked and prolonged the Arab–Israeli conflict by refusing a peace settlement once the war had ended, however, were related to the Islamic character of their societies.

Because Islam was so powerful in the Arab Middle East, it eclipsed all other sources of collective identity and objects of political allegiance. The new states that came into being in the wake of the European retreat were artificial creations. They had no real historical roots. They were formed out of what had been simply Ottoman administrative districts before the Europeans acquired them. Nationalist sentiment, powerful in the West, was weak in the Arab world. The people of the states that emerged in the region thought of themselves not as Syrians, Iraqis, Saudi Arabians, or Jordanians (not to mention Palestinians) but as members of their tribes, clans, and families, citizens of their villages, Arabs, and above all Muslims.

The rulers of the new states needed some way to make themselves legitimate in the eyes of the people whom they aspired to govern. They required policies capable of arousing popular enthusiasm. Religion was the most important source of political legitimacy; the cause of freeing Palestine from Zionism was one in which all the Arab states enlisted in 1948 because it had an Islamic basis and thus served precisely that purpose.[18]

Nationalist sentiment was not entirely absent from the Arab world in the first half of the twentieth century, but it took a particular form. In the days of the Prophet, Islam had been a single political community. The unity of all Muslims ended soon after Muhammed's death. The aspiration to restore it, to gather all believers together under a single jurisdiction, persisted. This traditional aim of Islam fused with the modern concept of linguistic nationalism to form pan-Arabism, the idea that all Arabs should

[18] Daniel Pipes, "How Important Is the PLO?" *Commentary*, April 1983, p. 19. The Arab leaders both helped to create and responded to pressure within their societies to oppose Israel. Harkabi, *Arab Strategies*, p. 409; Barry Rubin, *The Arab States and the Palestinian Conflict* (Syracuse, N.Y.: Syracuse University Press, 1981), p. 199.

belong to a single political unit.[19] It gathered momentum after World War II and helped to deepen and prolong the Arab animosity toward Israel.[20]

The project of destroying Jewish sovereignty in part of what had been the British mandate of Palestine appealed to pan-Arab feeling. It became the focus of pan-Arab sentiment.[21] Israel stood as an obstacle to the unity of all the Arabs. It was a piece of Arab land that outsiders had occupied. The Arab states agreed that uprooting it was the first step toward bringing together all of the Arab people into a single political entity. It was not easy for them to agree on the next step. No ruler was anxious to surrender his sovereign prerogatives to some larger unit, no matter how fervently he supported that goal in his public rhetoric, as various efforts to merge different Arab states after 1948 were to demonstrate.

[19] Pipes, "How Important," p. 18; Pipes, *In the Path*, p. 153. Not all Arabs were Muslims. Some were Christians, among whom were some of the most fervent advocates of pan-Arabism. An important early book on the subject, *The Arab Awakening*, was written by a Christian, George Antonius. Because of their ties with the West the Christian Arabs were the natural transmitters of Western ideas to the world of Arab Islam. Christians tended to be marginal to Arab culture and politics, which was the reason that many were attracted to pan-Arabism. It was not an Islamic creed. It proposed a basis for political community in the region in which, as Arabic speakers, they could share. In a unified Arab state they could hope to escape their marginal, minority-group status. Other radical, secular ideologies held out the same promise. It was not coincidental that the most radical factions of the Palestinian Liberation Organization were led by Christians – George Habash and Nayef Hawatmeh. (The main component of the PLO, Al Fatah, was predominantly Muslim.) Minorities outside the Middle East have also gravitated to revolutionary secular ideologies in the twentieth century. The Jews of Eastern Europe and Russia were powerfully drawn to Marxism, and for the same reason. Like Christian Arabs, they yearned for social and political transformations in which the distinctions that stigmatized them would no longer matter. In fact, the axes of politics in the Middle East remained largely religious and communal despite the nominal allegiance to "Arab socialism" of the rulers of Syria and Iraq. In Lebanon, the one part of the region in which Christians were numerous enough to act cohesively, they too organized themselves on a communal basis.

[20] See, e.g., Bernard Lewis, *The Middle East and the West* (New York: Harper & Row, 1964), p. 94.

[21] Pipes, "How Important," pp. 19–20; Nadav Safran, *From War to War: The Arab–Israeli Confrontation, 1948–1967* (New York: Pegasus, 1969), p. 87. On the variety of political programs that were sheltered under the umbrella of pan-Arabism, especially after 1967, see Fouad Ajami, *The Arab Predicament: Arab Political Thought and Practice Since 1967* (Cambridge University Press, 1981), pp. 38–9.

Pan-Arabism affected the Arab–Israeli conflict in another way. It gave every Arab state license to interest itself in the affairs of all the others. If the Arab people were one, if divisions among them were artificial and temporary, then each ruler had a claim on the people and the policies of the other states.[22] Each of the Arab rulers went to war in 1948 partly out of fear that if he held back while others conquered the rest of Palestine for Islam he would be discredited in the eyes of his own people. After 1948 none was willing to adopt a conciliatory policy toward Israel lest he be charged with insufficient devotion to the Arab cause. A common policy of utter rejection of Israel was in effect enforced on each of the Arab states by all of the others.[23]

Each Arab regime had an incentive to continue the confrontation with Israel because this made it seem more authentically Islamic, and hence more legitimate, to its own citizens. Indeed, none had any real countervailing incentive to settle the conflict. A settlement would have been an admission that the enterprise undertaken in 1948 had failed. It would have opened each government taking part in it to the charge of betrayal, a charge that the general commitment to pan-Arabism guaranteed would find an audience within its own borders.[24]

The Arab policy of rejecting the legitimacy of the Jewish state made Israel's neighbors seem particularly menacing. Its Islamic roots gave Arab animosity a particular intensity. In theory, no compromise was possible: The Arab goal, at least theoretically, was nothing less than the total destruction of the Jewish state. Pan-Arabism also meant that any single Arab state could publicly abandon this goal only at great risk to itself. So the Arab–Israeli conflict

[22] Pipes, "How Important," p. 18; Rubin, *Arab States*, p. xiii; Pipes, *In the Path*, p. 154.

[23] Safran, *From War to War*, p. 66; Safran, *Israel*, p. 336. Kissinger makes reference to "the compulsion for the flamboyant rhetoric of Arab unity, which tilted this, like all other Arab summit meetings, in the direction of militance" (*Years of Upheaval*, p. 757). The process was at work within the Arab world even before 1948. See Rubin, *Arab States*, p. 13.

[24] Safran, *From War to War*, pp. 39–40, 43; Rubin, *Arab States*, pp. xv–xvi; Kissinger, *Years of Upheaval*, p. 945. Jimmy Carter discovered that the dynamics of pan-Arabism produced adamant public expressions of hostility toward Israel from Arab leaders who in private were much more moderate. Jimmy Carter, *Keeping Faith: Memoirs of a President* (New York: Bantam Books, 1982), pp. 286, 302.

assumed a bitterness and persistence that was missing in other postcolonial enmities, even those where, as in South Asia, the death toll was higher.[25]

The Israelis' response to the unremitting hostility of their Arab neighbors was to concentrate on a policy of deterrence. They went to great lengths to make themselves as strong as possible. Settlement patterns were designed to help safeguard the borders.[26] The economy was organized to promote as much independence as possible in the manufacture of defense equipment.

Since its security depended entirely on its military strength, it was incumbent on Israel to muster as massive an armed force as possible. It could not possibly maintain as large a standing army

---

[25] This account of the basis of Arab hostility toward Israel is not the one that Arab spokesmen themselves have usually given. They have generally stressed two points. The first is that the Jews unjustly seized land properly belonging to Arabs, usurping the Palestinian homeland and driving the Palestinians out of it. In the prevailing Arab view, the Arab aim, consequently, has been to restore the rights of the Palestinian people. These rights are not, in the Arab account, compatible with the national rights of the Jewish people. The Jews, however, and this is the second grievance, are members of a religion, not a nation, and so do not have national rights. The charter of the PLO, for instance, makes this last assertion. A statement of the Arab case that emphasizes the first point is George M. Haddad, "Arab Peace Efforts and the Solution of the Arab–Israeli Problem," in Malcolm H. Kerr, ed., *The Elusive Peace in the Middle East* (Albany: State University of New York Press, 1975). This and other such statements invoke the harmony in which Jews and Muslims are supposed to have lived in the Middle East before Zionism infected the region. (For a much less idyllic portrait of Jewish life in Palestine in the nineteenth century see Landes, "Palestine.")

The justice of the Arab case is a matter of opinion. The first point turns on historical episodes that were exceedingly complicated and are subject to widely differing interpretations. The second is a normative, not an empirical, matter. Historically, the resolution of such questions has not depended on the coherence and plausibility of the arguments that the contending parties make. After 1948, the question of the control of Palestine – like other, similar issues – was decided, in Bismarck's indelicate but apposite phase, by blood and iron. The analysis here is not intended to bear on the question of whether the Arab case is right or wrong (although the author is not sympathetic to it). Nor is it meant to imply that the Arabs have never believed what they have said about Israel – another matter that is not easily resolved. Rather, it is intended to explain why the Arab views were deeply felt, insofar as this was so, and why the Arab states acted on them in particular ways.

[26] Safran, *Israel*, p. 229. David Ben-Gurion, Israel's first prime minister, is supposed to have said, "We must go to the borders or the borders will come to us."

as its Arab adversaries. Instead, Israel developed a reserve army, the core of which consisted of a small number of full-time professionals and cadres of conscripts serving three-year tours of duty beginning at the age of eighteen. The army's ranks were filled out during wartime by every able-bodied male from the ages of twenty-one to fifty. All had had military training. All could, in theory, be mobilized and ready for combat in forty-eight hours.

The European neutrals – Sweden, Finland, and Yugoslavia – also maintained standing armies to which civilian reservists were to be added in time of war. Israel's operational strategy, however, was different from theirs.[27] The Israelis made no provision for guerrilla warfare. Their country was too small and too vulnerable for them to count on weathering an Arab occupation while inflicting enough punishment on the occupiers to compel them to withdraw, as the Finns, the Yugoslavs, and the Swedes planned to do in case of Soviet occupation. Nor did Israel need to rely on such a strategy. Although outnumbered by its Arab neighbors, it was not weaker than they: It had the means to defend itself.

Nor, however, was the Israeli strategy one of perimeter defense, which the European neutrals also practiced. Israel did not plan to guard its frontiers and repel Arab attacks wherever they came, which is the common practice of a country whose principal aim is self-protection. Israel's borders were too long to be manned everywhere. An attack on a lightly defended section or a successful assault on a fortified position might lead to an Arab breakthrough. A strategy of perimeter defense must allow for breakthroughs and provide for reserve forces to meet them. But Israel was not populous enough to assemble a sufficiently large reserve force, and the country was too small to risk allowing Arab armies to pierce its frontiers anywhere. Since the 1949 boundaries left the state only nine miles wide at its narrowest point, it could quickly be cut in two by a breach of its border defenses.

Perimeter defense was unattractive for yet another reason. It held out the prospect of a long war of attrition, of the sort that had been fought on the western front in World War I. The Arab armies could attack when and where they chose; even if they failed to break through Israel's line of defense, they could hope to wear

---

[27] See Chapter 4, pp. 238–40.

down the Israeli forces over time. This Israel could not afford. With a larger pool of manpower on which to draw, the Arabs could bear much heavier losses. Israel's factory workers, farmers, and civil servants were also its soldiers. The country's economy could not sustain their extended absence from their regular jobs.[28]

Since Israel would not be able to fight long, inconclusive wars, its army planned instead for short, decisive ones. Its operations were geared for the offensive. It was trained to strike first, to pierce the Arab lines with combined assaults by armor and air forces, to cause disruption and confusion in Arab ranks and gain swift, conclusive victories.[29]

The military strategy led to Israel's post-1967 security dilemma. Israel had won three consecutive wars, each time extending the territory under its control. In 1956 the Israelis conquered the Sinai Peninsula. This they returned, under American pressure, in exchange for measures taken by the United Nations that were intended to prevent further Arab threats. In 1967 the measures of 1956 were revoked, precipitating the third Arab–Israeli war. This time the Israeli territorial gains were even more extensive.

---

[28] The Israelis came to find the prospect of a swift victory attractive as well because the great powers regularly intervened in the Arab–Israeli wars at some point, which usually worked to the disadvantage of the Israelis since they were almost always winning. John Mearsheimer, *Conventional Deterrence* (Ithaca, N.Y.: Cornell University Press, 1983), p. 135; Safran, *Israel*, p. 237.

[29] Mearsheimer, *Conventional Deterrence*, pp. 135–40; Luttwak and Horowitz, *Israeli Army*, p. 172. This is ordinarily the strategy of the would-be conqueror. It was the German strategy in World War II. Ironically, Israeli tactics resembled those of the German blitzkrieg operations of 1940 and 1941 (see Chapter 2, pp. 120–1). There was another similarity between the strategic predicaments of the two countries: Both faced the prospect of war on more than one front. Neither could afford a lengthy conflict, in which each could be worn down by the superior numbers of the adversary. Part of Hitler's response to this predicament was to make peace with one adversary in an effort to isolate the other, in his case through the Nazi–Soviet Pact of 1939. Such an option was not available to Israel.

Israel's purposes were also different from, indeed they were the opposite of, those of Germany in the two world wars. The Israelis wanted simply to protect themselves. Their particular circumstances, however, above all their size, compelled the adoption of an unusual strategy for self-protection. It was a "defensive strategy, executed offensively" (quoted in Mearsheimer, *Conventional Deterrence*, p. 135.) For a detailed account of the evolution of Israeli strategy, see Avner Yaniv, *Deterrence Without the Bomb: The Politics of Israeli Strategy* (Lexington, Mass.: Heath, 1987).

The outcome of the 1967 war created the basis for a trade: the return of captured territory in exchange for guarantees, promises, and signed agreements amounting to the Arabs' acceptance of Israel's right to exist. The foundation was now in place for an exchange of land for peace. The idea of this exchange was expressed in Resolution 242 of the United Nations Security Council, which was adopted on November 22, 1967, and became widely accepted as the framework for settling the conflict.[30]

The 1967 war created the possibility that the special Israeli version of the security dilemma might occur but did not quite bring it about: Israel did not have to confront squarely the question of whether it should trade land for peace. The Arab states were not yet prepared to consider such an exchange. The forces that had kept them from coming to terms with Israel in 1948 were still at work. Defeat once again brought Arab humiliation. As in the aftermath of the first war, the Arabs' inclination was to reverse the result by fighting rather than accept the outcome of the 1948 war – an independent Jewish state in the Middle East – and try to reverse the result of the 1967 war – the occupation of Arab territory by that state – by negotiation.

Each Arab country had to be wary of appearing less resolutely opposed to Zionism than the others. Nor were they under any compulsion to come to terms with Israel. Egypt, Jordan, and Syria survived their losses of territory. Their capital cities were not in danger. The Israeli army was not about to advance beyond the new cease-fire lines. Israel had no ambitions for further conquest. If it had attempted to go farther, the great powers would have intervened to prevent this. Not all of the Arab states accepted Resolution 242. Even those that did also subscribed to the resolution of the Arab summit meeting in Khartoum in August 1967 that committed the Arab world to an uncompromising stance toward Israel of no peace, no negotiations, and no recognition. This was the public position. In private some Arab leaders were less adamant. But

[30] The resolution endorsed two principles: "i) Withdrawal of Israeli armed forces from territories occupied in the recent conflict; ii) Termination of all claims or states of belligerency and respect for and acknowledgement of the sovereignty, territorial integrity, and political independence of every state in the area and their right to live in peace within secure and recognized boundaries free from threats or acts of force." Quoted in Safran, *Israel*, p. 430.

none was willing to negotiate without prior assurances of recovering territory.[31]

For their part the Israelis had, as they saw it, made a one-sided trade after the 1956 war. They had returned the Sinai without direct Arab assurances of an end to the conflict. They had received, in fact, no direct Arab assurances on any subject. Such promises as they did receive had come from the United States and the United Nations, and these had proved worthless in 1967. There *had* been another war. Israel thus required firmer assurances and more explicit promises – and from the Arabs themselves, not third parties – in order to relinquish territory again, as after the 1956 war. Moreover, the Israelis were not of one mind about which territories they would eventually be willing to give up and what they would require in return. They themselves had no incentive to go through the politically difficult process of answering these questions unless and until it became necessary to do so. They could agree that they would make no concessions at all before negotiations. Like the Arabs they would not move first. After June 1967, in the words of Moshe Dayan, they were waiting for a phone call from Cairo or Amman.[32]

No call ever came. Instead, there was another war. In October 1973, on the Jewish holiday of Yom Kippur, Egypt and Syria attacked Israel along the 1967 cease-fire lines. Both broke through lightly defended positions. The Egyptian forces crossed the Suez Canal and established their own defensive line a few miles to the east. The Syrians moved west across the Golan Heights. Caught by surprise, Israel mobilized its army and launched counterattacks on both fronts. To the north, the Israeli army stopped the Syrian advance and drove the Syrian forces back toward Damascus. To the south, the Egyptians held their ground and Israel suffered heavy losses of tanks and planes. A week after the war had begun, however, Egypt tried to advance from its initial defensive positions in the Sinai in order to relieve pressure on Syria. This gave Israel the opportunity to break through the Egyptian line, cross the canal in force, disrupt the Egyptian army's rear, and ultimately, to surround its main units, which were at the mercy of Israel's forces.

[31] See, e.g., Kissinger, *Years of Upheaval*, p. 221.
[32] Ibid., p. 257.

At that point the United States and the Soviet Union finally imposed a cease-fire.

The war was a shock that broke the stalemate in Arab–Israeli relations. In its wake, serious negotiations began, revolving around the possible exchange of land for peace. The 1973 war changed both sides' attitudes toward the conflict; their changes of attitude produced changes of policy.

The most important changes took place in the largest and most important Arab country, Egypt. After 1973, Egypt was willing to negotiate the exchange that Resolution 242 envisioned: giving Israel peace in return for land – the Sinai Peninsula – that the Israeli army had captured in the 1967 war. Egypt was able to offer peace because it was different from the other Arab states. It had greater freedom to maneuver. It was not as deeply affected by the forces that made hostility to Israel so important in the Arab world.[33] Egypt had in fact been the last of the Arab states to enter the 1948 war and the first to sign an armistice.

Its rulers had less need of the legitimacy that the crusade against Zionism conferred. They were more self-confident because they were more firmly established in power; and they were more firmly established in power because the state that they governed was itself more firmly established than the others. It had a longer history as a political unit. Indeed, if its beginnings are traced to pharaonic times, Egypt can be said to have had a longer history than *any* other state. It was relatively homogeneous, without the sharp internal divisions of Syria, for example, with its Sunni and Shii Muslims and its Alawi and Druze; or Jordan, with its Bedouin rulers and Palestinian subjects. It had a sizable middle class, and the country enjoyed a sense of national self-consciousness. An Egyptian nationalist movement had appeared as early as the nineteenth century. Egypt was, in short, a modern nation-state in ways that the other Arab states were not. Its people thought of themselves as Egyptian and felt a sense of allegiance to their national government that was missing among the people of Syria, Jordan, Iraq, and Saudi Arabia.

---

[33] See Ajami, *Arab Predicament*, Chap. 2, on which much of the following discussion of Egypt is based. On Egypt's freedom of maneuver see esp. pp. 101–2.

Egypt was therefore not as greatly affected, and was affected in different ways, by pan-Arab sentiment. Because the state was better established, with deeper historical roots and a stronger political identity, Egypt could be less concerned than other countries with what the other Arab leaders said and did. Other Arabs could not easily interfere with Egyptian affairs; they were more clearly outsiders in Egypt than anywhere else in the Arab world.

Egypt did become one of the most enthusiastic proponents of the pan-Arab cause after 1948. Gamel Abdel Nasser, Egypt's leader after 1952, saw it as the vehicle for Egyptian leadership in the Arab world. He espoused the gathering together of all the Arabs under a single political roof because the great Arab commonwealth was to be dominated by Egypt.[34] Pan-Arabism was for Nasser a matter of choice rather than necessary. It was not so much a policy for consolidating the power of the regime as an instrument for extending Cairo's influence beyond Egypt's borders. It was not imposed because of internal weakness; it was, rather, embraced on the basis of Egypt's strength, which in turn was grounded in the country's political, demographic, and cultural weight in the Arab world. As the strongest of the Arab states, Egypt could aspire to leadership among them. That same strength made it easier for Cairo to disregard the pull of pan-Arabism when this suited its national purposes. It was therefore able to make peace with Israel.

Egypt was never entirely free of the influence of pan-Arabism. It could not, even in the midst of the negotiations that culminated in a peace treaty, ignore the wishes of the Arab world.[35] The disengagement agreement of 1974 between Israel and Syria was negotiated for the sake of Egypt's relations with the other Arabs. Anwar Sadat, Nasser's successor, said that he could proceed with the peace process only if his partners in the war coalition received some benefit from negotiations.[36] Similarly, the final peace treaty

[34] Safran, *From War to War*, pp. 22, 69, 70–1, 77ff.

[35] During at least part of the time that he was negotiating with Israel, Nasser's successor, Anwar Sadat, seems to have believed that, whatever their immediate reactions, the other Arab states would ultimately have to follow his lead in carrying out a policy of conciliation. Martin Indyk, "To the Ends of the Earth: Sadat's Jerusalem Initiative," Harvard Middle East Papers, Modern Series, No. 1 (Cambridge, Mass.: Harvard University, Center for Middle East Studies, 1984), p. 49.

[36] Kissinger, *Years of Upheaval*, pp. 963, 967, 1032.

was accompanied by a negotiated framework for resolving the status of the territory to the east that Israel had captured in 1967, the West Bank of the Jordan River.[37] Egypt could not make peace without receiving some gesture on the Palestinian question; but it did not insist on the actual resolution of that question as a condition for coming to terms with Israel.[38]

Egypt's weight and place in the Arab world gave it the means to terminate its own conflict with Israel if it chose to do so. Anwar Sadat decided to make that choice. His predecessor had given Egypt a series of interrelated policies in the 1950s and 1960s that included the confrontation with Israel. Nasser adopted the pan-Arab cause as a way of extending Egyptian influence. This necessitated adopting a hostile stance toward Israel, which in turn put Egypt at odds with the United States and in alignment with the Soviet Union. Moscow became its principal supplier of weapons and economic assistance. In conjunction with these foreign policies, Nasser put the Egyptian economy on the path of what he called Arab socialism, which meant a degree of central planning and public ownership of a number of industries. Sadat was determined to change these policies. He was doubtless motivated by the desire to escape the shadow of his predecessor; he wanted to distinguish himself from Nasser. There was, however, a less personal reason. The Nasser policies had brought Egypt to a crippling, dangerous impasse.

Nasser's pan-Arab aspirations had led, unintentionally, to two disastrous wars. In the 1950s Egypt had sponsored raids by Palestinian groups from Egyptian territory into Israel. Partly to discourage these incursions, Israel launched the Sinai campaign of

---

[37] Sadat devoted much of his address at the Israeli Knesset during his dramatic visit to Jerusalem in 1977 to this question, and his associates stressed it in private discussions. Melvin A. Friedlander, *Sadat and Begin: The Domestic Politics of Peacemaking* (Boulder, Colo.: Westview Press, 1983), p. 94. See also Carter, *Keeping Faith*, pp. 339, 345.

[38] See Kissinger, *Years of Upheaval*, pp. 618, 770, for indications of this position before the Camp David agreement. Some groups within Egypt were particularly sensitive to the views of the other Arab states and therefore unhappy about the negotiations with Israel. The Egyptian foreign ministry, for example, was generally cool to Sadat's initiatives. It had to deal with the other Arab countries, which the rapprochement with Israel made more difficult. Two foreign ministers resigned during the course of the negotiations. Friedlander, *Sadat and Begin*, p. 47.

1956.[39] Eleven years later, in 1967, Nasser's fortunes stood at a low ebb in the Arab world. Egypt had become bogged down in an unsuccessful effort to unseat the royalist regime in the backward, remote monarchy of Yemen in the southern part of the Arabian peninsula. The Egyptian president's prestige had suffered. Syria was challenging Egypt for Arab leadership. To recoup his standing, Nasser ordered U Thant, the secretary-general of the United Nations, to remove the United Nations observers that had been placed in the Sinai and at Sharm El-Sheikh on the Red Sea as part of the terms of the Israeli withdrawal in 1956. Perhaps to his surprise, they did leave. Their departure was celebrated throughout the Arab world as a great victory. Nasser's prestige soared. Carried along by the wave of enthusiasm that swept through the region, he took further steps – the closing of the Straits of Tiran at the mouth of the Red Sea, the forging of an alliance with Syria and Jordan – which led, in June 1967, to Israel's attack and decisive victory.[40]

The wars with Israel brought defeat and humiliation to the Arab world. Although all of the Arab states had a political stake in the conflict, Egypt did most of the fighting and suffered most of the casualties. In peacetime, Egypt bore the burden of maintaining a large army that had to be ready to fight. It was a burden the country could ill afford. Egypt's strength was also a source of weakness. Its population gave it political weight that the other Arab states lacked, but because it was so populous Egypt was singularly poor. Bereft of natural resources, with its population packed into the narrow strip of land straddling the Nile and more and more of its people crowded against one another in the teeming metropolis of Cairo, Egypt had to struggle to feed itself. The Soviet Union could provide little help in this task and had proved, moreover, to be an unreliable military ally, at least in Sadat's eyes. To make matters worse, the Egyptian economy, weighed down by its large official bureaucracy, was stagnant and unproductive.

---

[39] Safran, *From War to War*, pp. 45, 51; *Israel*, pp. 355–6.
[40] For a detailed account of the events leading up to the 1967 war see Safran, *Israel*, Chap. 21. Of the events that touched off the war Kissinger writes, "It is doubtful that Nasser sought a military showdown; it is even possible that he was astonished by the alacrity with which [UN Secretary General] U Thant acceded to his request. Nasser may have intended to do no more than strike a heroic pose." *White House Years* (Boston: Little, Brown, 1979), p. 343.

Sadat sought to break out of the cycle of defeat, poverty, and dependence on the Soviet Union into which Nasser's policies had led Egypt. He wanted to concentrate on Egyptian rather than pan-Arab issues.[41] He sought to realign Egypt with the United States: A country that suffers from a constant shortage of food will, after all, be better off in the camp of a great power that exports grain than in that of one that must import it. And he had decided to cast off the official controls that Nasser had placed on the Egyptian economy and open it to the West.[42] Peace with Israel was part of this new course.

Sadat launched the 1973 war not to conquer Israel – Egypt's military aims were strictly limited – but to redress the humiliation of 1967 with a modest success on the battlefield, to break the diplomatic stalemate in the Middle East with this success, and to begin the negotiations that would make possible political and economic initiatives toward the West.[43] Indeed, rather than seeking cordial ties with the United States the better to make peace with Israel, there is every indication that Sadat's motives were the reverse: Negotiations with Israel were a means to a more important end, Egypt's political and economic alignment with the West in general, and the United States in particular.[44] For the Israelis the important point was that Sadat was willing to negotiate, which brought them face to face with the question of whether giving him what he wanted – the Sinai Peninsula – would produce conciliation and peace or temptation and another war.

In weighing that question Israel, like its adversary, was influenced by the 1973 war. Israeli attitudes also changed. The change was not quite as dramatic as in Egypt. Israel had been prepared

---

[41] Indyk, "Ends of the Earth," p. 18.

[42] On Egypt's economic dependence on others see John Waterbury, *The Egypt of Nasser and Sadat: The Political Economy of Two Regimes* (Princeton, N.J.: Princeton University Press, 1983), pp. 404–5. On the various international orientations in Egyptian history see Ajami, *Arab Predicament*, p. 109.

[43] This is Kissinger's interpretation. *Years of Upheaval*, pp. 459–60. See also Shlomo Aronson, *Conflict and Bargaining in The Middle East: An Israeli Perspective* (Baltimore, Md.: Johns Hopkins University Press, 1978), p. 181; Ajami, *Arab Predicament*, pp. 98–100.

[44] On the importance of economic motives see Indyk, "Ends of the Earth," pp. 5, 10; Waterbury, *Egypt*, pp. 394, 401, 429–30. On the centrality of friendship with the United States see Kissinger, *Years of Upheaval*, p. 640.

in principle to negotiate with the Arabs since 1967, indeed since 1948. A negotiated peace had been the ultimate aim of Israeli security policy for twenty-five years. After 1967, however, Israel was not prepared to do more than wait for an Arab initiative. In the wake of the 1967 war, as for the two preceding decades, Israel carried out a security policy of almost pure deterrence, of maximizing its military strength without making serious efforts at conciliation with its neighbors. Between 1967 and 1973, although not before or afterward, this policy seemed to the Israelis, if not altogether desirable, at least a comfortable strategy. The military superiority they enjoyed in the wake of their victory was such, they believed, that they could sustain the postwar lines without undue exertion. Israel counted not simply on being able to defend the new borders but on not having to do so. The Arabs' certainty that they would suffer another crushing defeat if they fought to recover what they had lost, the Israelis assumed, would deter them from trying. There was no need, the Israelis further assumed, to mobilize a large army to stand guard along the new frontiers.[45] They believed that time was on their side. They could afford to wait for the Arabs to offer peace proposals and could be cautious in responding to these proposals once they came.

The October 1973 war demonstrated that this view was mistaken. It made clear that, whatever their attitude toward Israel's existence, the Arab states would not accept as permanent Israel's 1967 conquests. They would fight to recover their territories even if they were overmatched in military terms. Israel won the 1973 war, but the fact that it had had to fight at all was a defeat for its policy. The price of keeping the status quo proved higher than the Israelis had calculated; it was a higher price, in the end, than they were willing to pay.[46] The war made Israel, if not more disposed to make peace (since it had always been so disposed), then more willing to compromise in peace negotiations. In weighing the hard choice of the security dilemma after 1973, conciliation looked more attractive to Israel as a result of the war, and provocation – perpetuating

---

[45] Aronson, *Conflict and Bargaining*, p. 164; Luttwak and Horowitz, *Israeli Army*, pp. 359–60.

[46] Israel was in a position at the war's end to crush the Egyptian and Syrian armies. It was plain, however, that the great powers, the United States as well as the Soviet Union, would not permit this.

Arab hostility by retaining control of the captured territories – appeared more costly.

The 1973 war was a turning point in the Arab–Israeli conflict as well because it demonstrated how heavily Israel depended on the United States. The United States was Israel's only reliable political ally and its only source of armaments. Shipments of American military equipment had been hastily dispatched in the middle of the war. The war actually increased Israel's dependence. The costs of fighting and being prepared to fight soared as supplies of expensive weaponry were rapidly depleted. In the postwar period, Israel's adversaries could hope to draw on the ever increasing revenues that the Arab oil producers were receiving to pay for rebuilding their arsenals. The Israelis could not pay for comparable arms by themselves and had to count on the United States not only to supply what they needed but to finance the supply as well.[47] Israel's government necessarily became extremely sensitive to American preferences and susceptible to American pressure.[48] After the war, the United States became far more actively committed than before to a settlement of the Arab–Israeli conflict.

Since 1948, American policy in the Middle East had had two goals: the survival and security of Israel and influence in the Arab world to prevent the Soviet Union from becoming the dominant power in the region. It was not easy to reconcile the two aims. The imperatives of the Arab–Israeli conflict were at odds with the requirements of the East–West competition. In the 1950s the United States placed the second goal before the first. The American

[47] "Israel is dependent on the United States," in Kissinger's words, "as no other country is on a friendly power." *Years of Upheaval*, p. 483; Safran, *Israel*, p. 316; Aronson, *Conflict and Bargaining*, p. 308.

[48] This dependence was particularly unwelcome to the Israelis, who resisted it as much as they could. It was at odds with one of the purposes of Zionism, which was to make Jews independent of the goodwill of others for their survival. But although Israeli dependence on others became more pronounced after 1973, it did not begin then. David Ben-Gurion, the country's first prime minister, was very much aware of the importance of the great powers for Israel. It was his rule not to risk war without the certain support of one of them. (In 1956 Britain and France counted for him as great powers.) (Aronson, *Conflict and Bargaining*, pp. 64, 389, n. 93.) In fact, long before 1948, the Jewish community in Palestine sought assistance from the outside, initially by Zionism's founding father Theodore Herzl and then, with considerable success, by Chaim Weizmann, who became the country's first president. Safran, *Israel*, p. 24.

government tried to organize an anti-Soviet coalition in the region. It was known as the Central Treaty Organization, or the Baghdad Pact; it included Iraq but excluded Israel. In 1956, for the sake of good relations with the Arabs, the Americans compelled the Israelis, along with the British and French, to withdraw from the Suez Canal and the Sinai Peninsula.[49]

With the growth of Egypt's pan-Arab aspirations, however, the United States began to see advantages in Israel's military strength. Nasser maneuvered to displace American-supported monarchies in Jordan and Saudi Arabia. To the extent that he had to concern himself with Israel, he was not free to oppose America's Arab friends. A strong Israel served as a kind of check on Egypt. After 1967, the United States accepted the Israeli view that the postwar state of affairs could be preserved at low cost. Israel's policy of holding the captured territories and waiting for an Arab initiative seemed to serve American purposes as well. But the 1973 war made the status quo intolerable for the United States as it did for Israel.

Just as the war upset Israel's calculations, so it demonstrated that the conflict threatened American interests. When the Arab–Israeli conflict was quiescent, the United States could maintain decent relations with both sides. When the conflict became acute, erupting into open warfare, this was not possible. The war aggravated the tension inherent in American Middle East policy. It pushed the Arab world closer to the Soviet Union, their principal supplier of weapons. All of the Arab states came under pressure to join the fight against Israel, which meant, at the least, distancing themselves from Israel's patron, the United States. When Arabs and Israelis simply glowered at each other across cease-fire lines, the United States could, with difficulty, pass as the friend of each without fatally alienating the other. When the two sides went to war, by contrast, the American government was forced to choose between them; and by choosing Israel, it damaged its relations with the Arabs.

[49] On the history of relations between the United States and Israel see Safran, *Israel*, and Steven L. Speigel, *The Other Arab–Israeli Conflict: Making America's Middle East Policy from Truman to Reagan* (University of Chicago Press, 1985), which examines how Middle East policy was made within the American government.

The October war threatened another American interest – the steady supply of Middle Eastern oil to the West. In the midst of the fighting, the Arab oil producers declared an embargo against the Americans and the Dutch, who had also sided with Israel. The oil weapon was a blunt instrument, incapable of being wielded with accuracy. It was not possible to deny oil to two countries while providing it to all other customers. The world market for oil was an integrated one. But the embargo did reduce the world's overall supply, causing shortages and panic buying that helped to trigger an enormous increase in price.

The Arab oil-producing states imposed embargoes in the wake of previous Arab–Israeli wars. They had little effect; supplies from other parts of the world had easily made up for the reduction. But by 1973, the other sources of oil had become less bountiful. The world needed petroleum from the Middle East.[50] The embargo dealt the severest blow since 1945 to the economies of the industrial democracies. The rise in the price of oil injured many nations, and not only the industrial ones.[51] In retrospect, the 1973 war seems to have been more the occasion than the cause of this increase; but one lesson that impressed itself upon the American government was the need to avoid another embargo.

The war posed an even greater threat than the loss of oil. It led to a confrontation with the Soviet Union that seemed, at the time, the most dangerous episode in Soviet–American relations since the Cuban missile crisis of 1962. With the Israeli army surrounding the main Egyptian forces on the western side of the Suez Canal, the American secretary of state, Henry Kissinger, flew to Moscow to work out the terms of a cease-fire. The belligerents accepted them – the Arabs to prevent further losses, the Israelis because they could not refuse the United States. The cease-fire broke down, however, and the Israeli forces began to tighten their grip on the Egyptian army. The Soviet leader, Leonid Brezhnev, sent a message to the American president, Richard Nixon, threatening that unless the Israelis halted their advance the Soviets would dispatch their own troops to the region to enforce the cease-fire. American

[50] There is a large literature on this subject. A useful early collection of essays is Raymond Vernon, ed., *The Oil Crisis* (New York: Norton, 1974).

[51] For further discussion of the "oil shock," see Chapter 6, pp. 373–5.

intelligence detected troop movements within the Soviet Union that suggested that preparations were indeed underway to carry out the warning. The American government responded quickly: While telling the Israelis, in no uncertain terms, that they had to observe the cease-fire, Washington also warned the Soviets that their presence along the Suez Canal would not be tolerated. To underscore the message American forces worldwide were placed on an unusually high state of alert.[52]

The crisis abated. No Soviet troops appeared in Egypt. But American leaders concluded that the Arab–Israeli conflict threatened to drag them into dangerous confrontations with their nuclear-armed adversary, giving them yet another reason to try to defuse it. Following the war the United States took a more active part than ever before in making peace between the two sides. The American role turned out to be indispensable. The particular features of Israel's security dilemma created problems that could not have been resolved without it.[53]

III

The choice that Israel faced after 1967 was difficult because it was uneven in a way that carried grave risks for the Jewish state. It involved a trade of the tangible for the intangible. The Israelis were called upon to give up real military assets in exchange for a pledge from the Arabs to maintain peaceful relations. The exchange was

[52] The crisis is recounted in Safran, *Israel*, Chap. 24, esp. pp. 490–5, and Kissinger, *Years of Upheaval*, Chap. 12, esp. pp. 575–91.

[53] In his memoirs Kissinger asserts that what was crucial in engaging the United States in the postwar negotiations was Egypt's change of mind. Before the war, he says, he had believed that the Arab states needed to understand that the Soviet Union could not help them get what they wanted. Having learned this, they would turn to the United States, which would then participate in efforts to find a settlement acceptable to both sides (*White House Years*, p. 559). This is, of course, what happened. The United States certainly desired a settlement before the 1973 war, which would have served American interests then as well as afterward. The set of proposals known as the Rogers Plan represented an effort to get one (see Kissinger, *White House Years*, pp. 374–5). In that sense there was continuity in American Middle East policy before and after 1973. But the Rogers Plan was a halfhearted effort. The stakes were higher, the interests to be protected through a settlement were larger, and thus the urgency with which the American government approached the issue as a result of the war was greater.

attractive but also dangerous because it involved reliance on Arab promises. The Arab states could renege on them more easily than Israel could recapture the territory that it would have to yield. The Israelis had reason to be suspicious: The Egyptians had sometimes said one thing about the Middle East conflict to one audience and something quite different to another.[54]

When one sovereign state voluntarily relinquishes military assets, when it makes itself weaker, it usually does so, as noted, in exchange for comparable measures by another. In the Israeli case the exchange was necessarily one-sided. The asymmetry was built into the circumstances. What the Arabs wanted was concrete, something that could be seen, felt, used, and defended. What Israel wanted was, by its nature, intangible. In this sense Israel's position was less like that of an ordinary sovereign state than like that of a bank, which gives money to borrowers in exchange for their promise to repay it. Banks make judgments about the reliability of the promisors. When they loan money they are said to be extending credit, from the Latin word *credere* – "to believe," "to have faith." They make judgments about the "credibility" of the promisor. When one state seeks to deter another from attacking, it strives to make credible its threat to respond. Since deterrence rests on the threat to do something, its credibility can be enhanced by visibly preparing to do it, by amassing military force or, as in the Chinese case, by using it. The Egyptian promise was to forbear from doing something, a promise even more difficult to make credible.

In exchanging land for peace, Israel was making a wager on its capacity to affect Egypt's intentions by adjusting its own capabilities. If its calculations turned out to be wrong, the costs might be high. If another war broke out after the Israelis had surrendered territory, Israel would be in a less advantageous position to fight. The Israelis wanted to trade land for peace. They therefore sought ways to minimize the attendant risks, to gain assurances that the Egyptians meant what they said.

Israel did not make a single, all-encompassing wager but rather several separate bets. It returned the Sinai to Egypt, not all at once but in installments. What came to be called the peace *process*

---

[54] Kissinger, *White House Years*, p. 366; Aronson, *Conflict and Bargaining*, pp. 89, 395, n. 11.

began almost immediately after the guns fell silent at the end of October 1973; it continued for almost a decade. The return of the Sinai Peninsula to Egypt, the condition for peace between Egypt and Israel, took place through a series of carefully calibrated, painstakingly negotiated steps, each building on the previous ones.

Israel negotiated five separate agreements with Egypt and one with Syria.[55] The first of these, known as the Six-Point Agreement of November 8, 1973, confirmed the cease-fire between Egypt and Israel, established a limited United Nations presence between them, and provided for Israel to permit the passage of food to Egypt's Third Army and for the exchange of prisoners of war. On January 18, 1974, came a second agreement between the two. It adjusted the Israeli and Egyptian lines in the Sinai east of the Suez Canal, which in turn required Israeli withdrawals from positions occupied during the fighting, established a buffer zone between them patrolled by the United Nations, and set limits to the forces that both could deploy in specified adjacent areas. This was the first Sinai disengagement agreement. On May 30, Israel and Syria made a similar arrangement to the north, on the Golan Heights: Israeli withdrawal from the points of farthest advance the previous October, including the town of Quneitra, and a United Nations buffer area flanked by limited force zones on both sides. In September 1975, Israel and Egypt concluded a second Sinai disengagement agreement. Israel abandoned approximately one-third of the Sinai, including the strategically important Gidi and Mitla passes and the fields at Abu Rudeis that had been supplying almost all of Israel's oil. Three years later, in September 1978, under the auspices of the American president, Jimmy Carter, a two-week meeting at Camp David, the presidential retreat outside Washington, D.C., produced one framework for negotiating the future of the West Bank and another for peace between Israel and Egypt.[56] Six months after Camp David, in March 1979, after further ne-

---

[55] Those undertaken from 1973 to 1975 are usefully summarized in Safran, *Israel*, pp. 590–4.
[56] On Camp David see William B. Quandt, *Camp David: Peacemaking and Politics* (Washington, D.C.: Brookings Institution, 1984), esp. Chaps. 7–11; Dayan, *Breakthrough*, Chaps. 12–15; Carter, *Keeping Faith*, pp. 319–403.

gotiations, a final peace treaty between the two countries was signed in Washington.[57]

Some of the agreements were more consequential than others; some were more difficult to negotiate than others. They involved three successive Israeli cabinets, headed by Golda Meir, her Labor party successor Yitzhak Rabin, and Menachem Begin, the leader of the Likud coalition that replaced Labor in 1977; two Arab countries – Egypt and Syria; and three American presidents – Richard Nixon, Gerald Ford, and Jimmy Carter.

For all their many differences, however, there were some fundamental similarities among the five agreements. By the terms of each, Israel withdrew from territory conquered in 1967 (and some additional land captured in 1973) in return for a variety of measures and promises. Ultimately Israel vacated the entire Sinai Peninsula. The agreements with Egypt can be seen as successive stages of a grand negotiation, a single transaction broken down into smaller parts. The parts themselves were subdivided. Israel withdrew in stages from the territory it agreed to give up in the second Sinai disengagement accord. The terms of the final Israeli–Egyptian peace treaty were also implemented in stages. The Camp David plan for resolving the status of the West Bank was also to be carried out in stages, although the plan was not implemented. Arrangements were to be negotiated for a transitional period of five years during which the final arrangements were to be worked out.

The separation into discrete segments of the overall exchange of land for peace was deliberate.[58] The "step-by-step" method, as it came to be known, seemed to Israel, Egypt, and the United States superior to the alternative "comprehensive" approach. A settlement of all the outstanding issues in the Arab–Israeli conflict at once would have required a single peace conference that would inevitably have had to include the Soviet Union.[59] This, in turn,

---

[57] Dayan, *Breakthrough*, Chaps. 16–22; Carter, *Keeping Faith*, pp. 404–29.

[58] The idea had been broached more than once before 1974. A partial or interim settlement seemed to some people preferable to no settlement at all. Aronson, *Conflict and Bargaining*, p. 141; Kissinger, *White House Years*, pp. 1280–1, 1289–90.

[59] Immediately after the war, a conference on the Middle East under United Nations auspices did convene, with the United States and the Soviet Union as

would have enhanced the Soviet role in the region, a development that none of the three was eager to promote. Such a conference would also necessarily have brought representatives of all the Arab states together, which would have magnified the influence of pan-Arab sentiment, with its tendency to pull all parties toward the position of the most recalcitrant member.[60]

The comprehensive approach was likely to fail as well because the issues involved in the conflict were so contentious. Some were in fact intractable. The step-by-step procedure was a method for deferring matters on which agreement was not possible. The Camp David accords represented a way of making peace between Israel and Egypt, a goal that it was possible to reach, without waiting for a resolution of the future of the West Bank, over which there remained deep disagreement between Arabs and Israelis.

The step-by-step method also had advantages pertinent to the difficulties inherent in the Israel version of the security dilemma. In the early stages, since the first steps were to be modest, Israel was not giving up significant military assets. The initial unilateral concessions, as is common with most states that make them, were of marginal significance for the nation's safety. The later steps were much more significant, and the risks to Israel were higher. The step-by-step approach addressed the problem of the credibility of Egyptian promises. It helped Israel to decide to accept those risks by providing a test of the sincerity of those promises: the test of time.

One basis for believing that a country will keep a promise is its record of having kept similar promises in the past. Each step, when successfully taken, provided a reason to believe that the Egyptians would observe the terms of another. Israel was willing to give up more and more of the Sinai because Egypt had continued to keep the promises it had made to acquire the parts that Israel had already surrendered. The step-by-step process built Israeli confidence in

co-chairs. This was in keeping with the understanding that Secretary of State Kissinger had reached with the Soviet leaders when negotiating a cease-fire. But it adjourned after its first meeting and never met again. Kissinger, *Years of Upheaval*, pp. 558–9; 645–6.

[60] Ibid., p. 615.

Egypt's good faith, which was, from the Israeli perspective, one of its central purposes.[61]

Although time provided a test of the sincerity of Egypt's commitments, those commitments remained both intangible and revocable. Israel still had to accept what Egypt said on faith. The Israelis wanted a broader, firmer basis for this faith than mere Egyptian observance of the accords already negotiated. Peace for Israel depended on Egyptian intentions, and intentions are states of mind. The Israelis sought some concrete embodiment of these intentions. They wanted an outward expression, beyond mere words, of Egypt's attitudes.[62] They wanted specific measures that would attest to the depth of Egypt's commitment to cordial or at least peaceful relations after twenty-five years of belligerence.

There is a particularly illuminating parallel here with a concept of literary criticism. In his essay "Hamlet and His Problems," T. S. Eliot writes that "the only way of expressing emotion in the form of art is by finding an 'objective correlative'; in other words, a set of objects, a situation, a chain of events which shall be the formula of that particular emotion; such that when the external facts, which must terminate in sensory experience, are given, the emotion is immediately evoked."[63] In the negotiations, Israel sought the objective correlative of benign Egyptian intentions.

One act that Israel counted as evidence of the Egyptians' good intentions was direct negotiations between the two countries. This had been a basic Israeli demand since 1967. From 1948 to 1973 the Arabs refused it. Beginning immediately after the war, however, representatives of the two sides did meet. During the peace process the meetings became more and more direct and increas-

---

[61] Abba Eban, "Camp David: the Unfinished Business," *Foreign Affairs*, 57 (Winter 1978–9): 348; Dayan, *Breakthrough*, pp. 11, 224, 282–4. Jimmy Carter quotes Israeli Defense Minister Ezer Weizmann as saying of the proposal for arrangements for "autonomy" on the West Bank, "We want to have a time factor, to give the idea a test" (Carter, *Keeping Faith*, p. 377). In the terminology of game theory, the step-by-step process increased the "iterative" character of the situation and so lengthened the "shadow of the future" under which the two sides operated, increasing the likelihood of cooperation. Oye, "Explaining Cooperation," p. 117.

[62] On this point see Harkabi, *Arab Strategies*, pp. 107, 112.

[63] T. S. Eliot, *The Sacred Wood* (London: Methuen, 1920), p. 100.

ingly public, and they took place at progressively higher political levels.

The signing of the Six-Point Agreement at kilometer 101 on the Cairo–Suez road marked the first face-to-face encounter between official Arab and Israeli representatives and the first formal accord between them. The Geneva Conference on the Middle East, which met for a single session in December 1973, was the first occasion on which high officials of two Arab states, Egypt and Jordan, were willing to sit at the same table with representatives of the Israeli government. Secret contacts at even higher levels began in 1977. The Israeli and Egyptian chiefs of intelligence met at Casablanca. Messages were exchanged through the Moroccan and Rumanian governments. Foreign Minister Moshe Dayan journeyed to Rabat, in Morocco, again secretly, to meet with Egyptian Deputy Prime Minister Hassan Tuhamy. Their discussions paved the way for the most dramatic episode in the peace process – President's Sadat's visit to Jerusalem.

That visit opened a variety of channels. Sadat and Prime Minister Begin conferred in Jerusalem, met subsequently at Ismailia, in Egypt, and spent two weeks together at Camp David the next year. There were contacts at the ministerial level as well. After their first encounter, Sadat and Begin established political and military committees on which they were represented by their foreign and defense ministers. The foreign ministers spent several days together in the summer of 1978 at Leeds Castle in England, in what proved to be a dress rehearsal for the Camp David meetings. After Camp David, they conducted follow-up discussions. There were informal contacts as well. Sadat and Defense Minister Ezer Weizmann struck up a cordial relationship and had several private meetings. Sadat met, as well, with the leader of the Labor opposition in the Israeli parliament, Shimon Peres.

In addition to direct negotiations, the Israelis sought explicit statements of what the fact of the negotiations implied: Egyptian acceptance of their status as a legitimate state in the Middle East. They wanted formal recognition, of the sort that sovereign states routinely accord each other whatever their differences, and the trappings of recognition, above all an exchange of ambassadors. The first article of the 1979 peace treaty gave them both. Its opening clause stated, "The state of war between the Parties will be terminated and peace will be established between them upon the exchange of instruments of ratification of this treaty." The third clause included the promise that "the Parties will establish normal and friendly relations." The treaty's third article explicitly pledged the signatories to peaceful conduct, stating, "They will refrain from the threat or use of force, directly or indirectly against each other and will settle all disputes between them by peaceful means."[64]

The Israelis sought, as well, connections with Egypt beyond formal diplomatic relations. They were interested in commercial ties, cultural exchanges, and personal contacts. Dayan considered these to be as important as the peace treaty itself.[65] For twenty-five years there had been virtually no contacts of any kind, since the Arab governments had prohibited them. In recognition of their significance, an entire annex to the peace treaty was devoted to commitments to foster Israeli–Egyptian contacts. "The Protocol Concerning Relations of the Parties" committed the two sides to promoting trade, cultural exchanges, freedom of movement, transportation, and telecommunications between them.[66]

Direct talks, formal state-to-state relations, unofficial contacts in the areas of commerce and culture, even exchanges at the level of simple tourism were, for Israel, the objective correlative of peaceful Arab intentions, which the surrender of the Sinai Peninsula was intended to purchase. The Israelis were moved by the intuitively plausible view that promises – which were what they were receiving from Egypt – are more credible when delivered personally by the party making them. Thus Sadat's visit to Jerusalem had extraordinary significance. The Egyptian president went to Israel's capital, he told the Knesset, to remove "all suspicion of fear, betrayal, and

[64] The treaty as well as the Camp David documents are reprinted in Paul A. Jureidini and R. D. McLaurin, *Beyond Camp David: Emerging Alignments and Leaders in the Middle East* (Syracuse, N.Y.: Syracuse University Press, 1981), p. 123; Quandt, *Camp David*, also reprints these and other pertinent documents.

[65] Dayan, *Breakthrough*, p. 200.

[66] Israel also wanted Egypt to reopen the Suez Canal and resettle the cities along its banks, to create an economic stake in peace apart from any commercial ties between the two countries. If war broke out again, the canal and the port cities would be vulnerable, the investments that had been made in them at risk. They would be hostages to Egypt's good behavior. In March 1975 Sadat did agree to reopen the canal – and without any reciprocal concession by Israel. Aronson, *Conflict and Bargaining*, 293.

bad intentions."[67] To a remarkable extent he succeeded. When he met with Golda Meir after the address, she was moved to say, "When you sit here and I look at you and I heard you last night it's not the same. I believe in your sincere desire for peace."[68]

His visit served yet another purpose. It demonstrated to a worldwide audience the Egyptian president's commitment to conciliation with Israel. Its public character made it stronger than a commitment undertaken privately. "Today I tell you, and I declare it to the whole world," Sadat announced, "that we accept to live with you in permanent peace."[69] The "whole world" that formed his audience included the Arab world. His visit in particular, and the peace process in general, had, or were supposed to have, the effect of changing the attitudes toward Israel among the Arab peoples, attitudes that had had a great deal to do with creating and perpetuating the conflict.[70]

The elements of a normal relationship between the two countries served particularly well as the objective correlative of peaceful Egyptian intentions toward Israel because they addressed the basis of the Arab–Israeli conflict. That conflict had arisen from the Arab conviction that Israel itself was *not* normal. It was not, in Arab eyes, like other states. It was illegitimate and transcient. For this reason, contacts of all kinds with Israel, save hostile military ones, were prohibited.[71] In his memoirs Henry Kissinger remarks that "recognition of their existence is where the security problem of all other nations begins, not ends."[72] But it was precisely the question of recognition, of acceptance, of normality that was in dispute in the Middle East. For Egypt to treat Israel like the other one hundred and fifty or so sovereign members of the international

[67] "Transcript of address by President Anwar el-Sadat to the Israeli Parliament, November 20, 1977 (simultaneous interpretation from the Arabic). *New York Times*, November 21, 1977, p. 14.

[68] William E. Farrell, "A Cairo Ex-Legislator Lobbies Members of the Knesset for Peace," *New York Times*, November 22, 1977, p. 17.

[69] "Transcript of the address by President Anwar el-Sadat," p. 14.

[70] Sadat "surprised the Arab world . . . with a psychohistorical shock in November, 1977, with his journey to Jerusalem." Ajami, *Arab Predicament*, p. 83.

[71] Safran, *From War to War*, p. 43; Bernard Lewis, "The Palestinians and the PLO: An Historical Approach." *Commentary*, January 1975, p. 43. The Arab practice of nonrecognition in fact predated Israel's independence. Safran, *From War to War*, p. 26.

[72] Kissinger, *Years of Upheaval*, p. 220.

system was, in symbolic terms, to abandon the basis of twenty-five years of bitter hostility.

The test of time and the establishment of normal relations provided Israel with a measure of assurance that Egypt would keep its promise to remain at peace, but not with absolute certainty. Israel received no ironclad guarantee that Egypt would never change its mind and resume the conflict. No such guarantee was possible.[73] The step-by-step process and the various measures included in the negotiated agreements that counted as the objective correlatives of Egyptian goodwill did not and could not eliminate the stark asymmetry of the exchange that Israel had to make. That asymmetry was built into the country's international position. It was inherent in the Israeli version of the security dilemma.

If Israel was in the position of a creditor, Egypt was no ordinary debtor. An individual borrower has to put up collateral, which the lender may confiscate in the event of default. The lender may also avail himself of the force of the law to compel the debtor to pay or to punish him for nonpayment. Israel had access to neither. In the anarchic international system, self-help is the rule. If Egypt undertook the equivalent of default, if it resumed hostilities, Israel could certainly resist and might hope to punish Egypt for breaking its word. In fact, Israel could seize the Sinai again. That possibility undoubtedly affected Egyptian calculations. Deterrence continued to operate even after the territory was returned. But by returning it, Israel ensured that recapturing the Sinai would cost Israel something as well as forfeit the benefits that conciliation had bought. It would, in all probability, cost Israeli lives.

Trading land for peace necessarily meant giving up capabilities in order to make Egyptian intentions more benign. Beyond asking for concrete expressions of benign Egyptian intentions, Israel also sought capabilities in forms other than territory, in order to compensate for what it was giving up. These other forms of strength were to be insurance in case the trade did not work and Egypt failed to keep its promises. In the terms of the security dilemma, the land-for-peace trade involved giving up military assets in the

[73] "Israel insisted on a 'binding peace.' Only a country that had never known peace could have attached so much importance to that phrase. For what is a binding peace among sovereign nations when one of the attributes of sovereignty is the right to change one's mind?" Kissinger, *White House Years*, p. 346.

hope of promoting conciliation but without tempting Egypt to take advantage of diminished Israeli strength to launch an attack. But as the Israelis relinquished territory, they acquired military strength in other forms, which were less objectionable to Egypt. They tried to bolster deterrence while avoiding provocation of Egypt, as retaining the Sinai was bound to do. Here the United States played a major role.

IV

A critical feature of the series of agreements between Egypt and Israel was that after relinquishing the Sinai the Israelis would no longer be permitted to use it for military purposes. Although they acknowledged that it was sovereign Egyptian territory, they insisted that Egypt not be allowed to make military use of it either. There was a precedent for their demand. Before 1967, the Sinai had in effect been a buffer zone between the two countries. Cairo had stationed troops along the border, but not in heavy concentrations. Each of the Sinai agreements also included restrictions on the forces that Egypt could put in the territory it was reclaiming.[74] The final peace treaty divided the Sinai and a narrow strip of Israel adjacent to it into four different zones and specified the forces that would be permitted in each.[75]

---

[74] On the first Sinai agreement see Safran, *Israel*, pp. 525–7; on the Syrian disengagement agreement see ibid., pp. 530–4; on the second Sinai disengagement agreement, ibid., pp. 554–7.

[75] Jureidini and McLaurin, *Beyond Camp David*, pp. 129–30, 142. An intramural debate took place in Israel over the strategic value of holding the Sinai. Some argued that the country was actually better off, even in strictly military terms, with the peninsula free of any significant military forces belonging to either side than with Israel in complete possession of it. Holding it, the argument went, would involve stationing forces at its edge, along the Suez Canal. But Israel could hardly afford deployments in strength there; its army was not large enough. The canal positions would inevitably be lightly defended, as they had been when war broke out in October 1973. For political reasons, Israel would not, however, be able to pull back from this forward line, especially when it was under attack; any Israeli retreat would send a dangerous signal to the Arabs and the rest of the world. Israel would therefore be forced into a perimeter defense, for which its army was not trained. The perimeter would be thinly manned, with fixed positions and long supply lines. In defending it, Israel's military advantages – speed, mobility, improvisation – would be worth little. By contrast, in a war begun behind the 1949 lines, the argument concluded,

Depriving Egypt of a potential source of military strength was not, for the Israelis, sufficient to compensate them for what they had to give up to make peace. They wanted to increase their own capacity for defending themselves. Since they were giving up one kind of military asset, they sought other kinds to replace it. Here the role of the United States was crucial. Washington did compensate Israel for relinquished territory, which made the land-for-peace trade possible. The American role as the source of military strength that, unlike Israeli control of the Sinai, did not provoke Egypt grew out of its other roles in the peace process.

The American government was initially drawn into the process to mediate between the two sides. This served Egypt's purposes. In the negotiations Egypt's position was the reverse of Israel's. It was giving up peace, so to speak, in order to get land. Just as Israel did not wish to hand back the entire Sinai without receiving everything that constituted peace in return, so Egypt did not want to take all the steps that Israel was demanding so long as Israel still held part of its sovereign territory. Direct contact was an important objective correlative of peace in the eyes of both sides, which was why for twenty-five years Israel had insisted on it and the Arab states had refused. It was a point the Egyptians did not want to concede at the early stages of the negotiations.[76] They, too, wanted to disaggregate the concessions they made. Israel offered a piece of land for a piece of peace. Similarly, Egypt broke recognition of Israel into separate pieces. Although a direct meeting took place at kilometer 101 to sign the Six-Point Agreement, the representatives of the two sides were of relatively low rank. The ensuing

Israel would have time to mobilize before engaging the adversary and could fight a mobile campaign in which its flexibility and speed of response could be used to good effect, as in 1956 and 1967. See Dan Horowitz, *Israel's Concept of Defensible Borders*, Jerusalem Papers on Peace Problems 15 (The Leonard Davis Institute for International Relations, The Hebrew University of Jerusalem, 1975), pp. 20–2, and Yaniv, *Deterrence Without the Bomb*, pp. 184–6. Those who made the contrary argument held that the strategic value of the Gidi and Mitla passes was great enough to justify holding the entire Sinai. Aronson, *Conflict and Bargaining*, p. 270.

[76] At the outset of negotiations Kissinger reckoned that it would be "too dangerous" for Sadat to "treat directly with Israel" (*Years of Upheaval*, p. 804). Syria did not deal directly with Israel at all, although in the aftermath of the war the Syrian government did accept UN Resolutions 242 and 338, of which the second explicitly called for direct negotiations.

negotiations were conducted not face to face but through the United States.[77]

Precisely because recognition was at the heart of the conflict from the beginning, with the Arabs avoiding direct talks with Israel, would-be mediators were a constant feature of Middle Eastern affairs from 1948 onward.[78] For most of the next twenty-five years it was the United Nations that attempted to play this role. But its prompt acquiescence in Nasser's demand for the withdrawal of its forces from the Sinai and Sharm El-Sheikh in 1967, and the automatic majority the Arabs were able to command in its General Assembly for any resolution, discredited the United Nations in Israel's eyes. Into the breach stepped the United States.

The first episodes of American mediation after the 1973 war, Henry Kissinger's "shuttle diplomacy" among the capitals of the region in 1974 and 1975 that produced the two Sinai disengagement agreements and the single accord between Israel and Syria, began more or less by accident. In January 1974 Kissinger went to the region to sound out Israel and Egypt on their negotiating positions in advance of the expected reconvening of the Geneva Conference on Peace in the region. Although he had helped to work out the Six-Point Agreement, he thought of Geneva as the natural forum for further talks. Sadat suggested that the two sides try to reach agreement in the Middle East itself rather than in Switzerland, with Kissinger acting as a mediator. The result was the first Sinai disengagement agreement, and the American role as mediator became institutionalized.

There was more to the development of this American role, however, than mere chance. There was a logic to it. The United States had the confidence of both sides, as the United Nations did not. American mediation was compatible with the step-by-step approach to peacemaking, which both sides favored. For its own reasons, finally, both Egypt and Israel wished to involve the United States as deeply as possible in the peace process.

---

[77] Kissinger reports that Sadat gave him a message for Golda Meir in January 1974 that said: "We never have had contact before. We now have the services of Dr. Kissinger. Let us use him and talk to each other through him." *Years of Upheaval*, p. 836.

[78] This is the subject of Saadia Touval, *The Peace Brokers* (Princeton, N.J.: Princeton University Press, 1982).

The United States had tried to mediate before. The Rogers Plan of 1969 had proposed terms on which the conflict could be settled. The plan appealed to neither Israel nor Egypt, and the United States did not press it. But after the war the American interest in resolving the conflict was all the greater. The American government was prepared to devote time, effort, money, and political capital to the pursuit of a settlement. Washington took an active part in ending the fighting, with Kissinger traveling to Moscow to arrange a cease-fire. Even while the war was in progress, he hinted that the United States would take a prominent postwar role in seeking a political settlement after it had ended.[79] For the next five years, the peace process was a central concern of American foreign policy.

Kissinger was not the only secretary of state to serve as an intermediary between Arabs and Israelis. His successor, Cyrus Vance, did so as well. Officials at lower levels also played this role, as did the highest elected American official of all. At Camp David, President Carter was the principal intermediary. He himself shuttled between the Egyptian and Israeli delegations at the Maryland retreat just as Kissinger had flown back and forth between Jerusalem and Cairo. Carter followed the intensive round of diplomacy at Camp David with a trip to the Middle East the next year to work out the final details of the peace treaty.

The American mediators undertook several distinct, although related, tasks. The simplest was serving as a messenger, relaying proposals back and forth between the two governments. As the negotiations proceeded, Kissinger broadened his duties. He interpreted each party's position for the other, sometimes giving advice on how to respond.[80] This remained important even after 1977, when the two sides had direct and openly acknowledged channels of communication with each other. The third task also remained important after 1977: Kissinger and his successors actually drafted compromise positions, based on their sense of what was acceptable to both sides. They took it upon themselves to define the middle ground.[81] During the Camp David meetings,

---

[79] Kissinger, *Years of Upheaval*, pp. 506, 508.

[80] This was a particularly prominent feature of the negotiations between Israel and Syria. See ibid., pp. 965, 1043, 1093.

[81] On this point on the Syrian disengagement agreement see ibid., p. 1081; on the second Sinai disengagement accord see Safran, *Israel*, p. 524.

the Americans were at work almost nonstop drafting and redrafting the texts.

American mediation appealed to Egypt beyond the fact that it made possible the recognition of Israel in stages rather than all at once. Although the American government attempted, like a mediator in a labor dispute, to be impartial, it could hardly pretend to be disinterested. It very much wanted a settlement. American interests required that another war be avoided, and during the first weeks of the peace process there was additional pressure to show results in order to get the oil embargo lifted.[82] A settlement required that Israel retreat from its lines of advance. This the Israelis were reluctant to do; but they were not in a position to ignore American wishes. When the United States presented an idea for their consideration, it was not purely a matter of academic interest: The implicit and sometimes explicit American endorsement of a proposal inevitably counted heavily in Israel's decision about whether to accept or reject it. In general, the more closely involved in the negotiations the United States became, the greater the pressure Israel felt to make concessions. This was something that Sadat well understood.[83]

The United States applied pressure to Israel both directly and indirectly during the negotiations with Egypt and Syria. Kissinger and his successors reminded the Israeli leaders of the possible consequences of not making concessions: the risk of provocation. The Americans emphasized the need to keep Egypt committed to the peace process and to its decision to realign itself with the West and United States. They compared the dynamics of the process to riding a bicycle: It had to keep moving forward or it would fall. If it collapsed, the Americans warned, Israel would be less secure.[84]

The Israelis could imagine the consequences of a failure to reach agreement without having the Americans spell them out. The case for conciliation, however, took on additional force from the fact that it was Washington that was making it. It was especially forceful

---

[82] Aronson, *Conflict and Bargaining*, p. 207.
[83] Kissinger suggests that Sadat had this in mind even before the war. *Years of Upheaval*, p. 482; see also Indyk, "Ends of the Earth," p. 31.
[84] Kissinger, *Years of Upheaval*, p. 1056; Aronson, *Conflict and Bargaining*, pp. 289–90; Safran, *Israel*, pp. 530, 546; Dayan, *Breakthrough*, p. 67; Carter, *Keeping Faith*, pp. 347–8.

when the Americans hinted, as they did more than once, that Israel would be blamed for any failure to reach a settlement.[85] This the Israelis wished to avoid. Their security depended on support from the United States, which rested on their standing with the American government and ultimately with the American people. Both wanted a settlement. If they came to see Israel as obstructing one, they would have less sympathy for the Israeli cause.

The American advice to the Israelis not to risk provocation was usually tendered in the spirit of friendship. The Americans assumed the role of counselors, warning the Israelis of what third parties would think of their policies. Sometimes, however, American officials were more blunt. A vivid instance of the direct application of American pressure came in the last days of the war. The United States asked the Israelis to stop their operations. Although the Israelis had unfinished business on the battlefield – they were on the brink of surrounding the Egyptian Third Army on the western side of the Suez Canal – they decided that they could not refuse the American request. When the cease-fire broke down and Israeli forces advanced, the United States told the Israeli government in no uncertain terms to go no farther.[86] The fighting stopped, but the Egyptian troops were surrounded. They began to run short of food and water. Israel proposed to extract concessions from Egypt in exchange for giving the Third Army access to supplies. The United States insisted that nonmilitary supplies be allowed to reach the Egyptians without preconditions. Because of the American pressure Israel complied. Dayan later said of this episode: "Israel gave up the surrender of the Third Army because the United States told [it] that if Israel would not allow food and water to reach the Egyptians and made them prisoners, 'we shall disassociate ourselves from you.' The Israeli government had to decide which it was ready to give up – the Third Army or the United States!"[87] In

---

[85] Aronson, *Conflict and Bargaining*, p. 268; Kissinger, *Years of Upheaval*, p. 790; Touval, *Peace Brokers*, pp. 302–3, 314–5; Friedlander, *Sadat and Begin*, p. 218.

[86] Aronson, *Conflict and Bargaining*, p. 187. "As the fighting continued, Kissinger applied intense pressure on Israel to comply immediately with the cease-fire. He summoned the Israeli ambassador and told him that if the fighting continued as a result of Israeli actions, Israel should not count on military aid from the United States." Safran, *Israel*, p. 493.

[87] Quoted in Aronson, *Conflict and Bargaining*, p. 414, n. 54. The United States

the early stages of the step-by-step negotiations, President Nixon demanded concessions from Israel to make progress possible.[88] Kissinger and Gerald Ford, who succeeded Nixon as president in the summer of 1974, launched a well-publicized reappraisal of American Middle East policy, which included restricting the shipment of armaments to Israel and suspending consideration of proposals for economic assistance, after failing to secure Israeli agreement on a second disengagement agreement with Egypt in the spring of 1975. Their aim was to exert public pressure on the Israeli government in the United States.[89]

Israel's leaders were not altogether unhappy with American me-

wanted a supply corridor opened in order to bolster its own blossoming friendship with Egypt. Ibid., pp. 193, 198; Safran, *Israel*, pp. 508, 589.

[88] Kissinger, *Years of Upheaval*, p. 550, 759, 1071. In Kissinger's account these demands were neither inspired nor encouraged by the secretary of state. But it can be surmised that they were not entirely unwelcome to someone trying to persuade the Israelis to make concessions for the sake of conciliation.

[89] Safran, *Israel*, p. 548; Aronson, *Conflict and Bargaining*, p. 294. In the aftermath of the war Kissinger was accused of pressuring Israel in a different and costlier way. It was charged that he had maneuvered to make the Israelis more amenable to concessions in the postwar bargaining that he anticipated by withholding shipments of ammunition and spare parts for several days after Israel had requested them. His aim was to prevent a repetition of the sweeping victory of 1967, which would have made negotiations seem unnecessary (see Walter Laqueur and Edward Luttwak, "Kissinger and the Middle East War," *Commentary*, September 1974; Safran, *Israel*, pp. 478–81). In his memoirs, Kissinger emphatically denies the charge, contending that the Israeli request was not immediately fulfilled because all American officials believed that the war would be over before the equipment could reach the Middle East. As soon as it became obvious that the war would continue longer than had been expected and that Israel was in urgent need of resupply, he says, the American government hastened to provide it (*Years of Upheaval*, pp. 478, 501; see also Aronson, *Conflict and Bargaining*, p. 184). The United States did exert perhaps unintentional influence on Israeli conduct at the outset of the war. When it became clear that Egypt and Syria were about to attack, Israel had to consider preemption. Jerusalem decided against it so as to make certain that the Arab side was seen as the aggressor by the Americans, on whom Israeli claims for support would then be strong (Safran, *Israel*, p. 488). According to Kissinger, the United States did not explicitly tell Israel not to attack, at least not in October 1973: "The morning the war started Golda had volunteered to [American Ambassador Kenneth] Keating that Israel would not preempt. The decision had been her own, without benefit of recent American advice" (*Years of Upheaval*, p. 477; see also p. 455). In fact, Israel had delayed launching a strike for several weeks in the spring of 1967, out of deference to American opinion. On that occasion, however, Israel did ultimately strike first (Aronson, *Conflict and Bargaining*, p. 65).

diation, despite their insistence before 1973 on direct talks. It was the only way to get the peace process underway. In any event, given their reliance on the United States, they could hardly refuse it. Nor were they entirely unhappy that with American mediation came American pressure for concessions to move the process forward. They wanted agreement with their neighbors. A policy of conciliation rather than (or at least in addition to) one of deterrence was the ultimate Israeli aspiration. To achieve better relations with the Arabs they had to make concessions. But the Israeli public, to which the government was accountable, was wary of surrendering territory. At each stage of the peace process some segment of the Israeli public and its parliamentary representatives charged the government with not getting enough in exchange for what it had given up. The government found it convenient to justify concessions on the grounds of American pressure. Washington's insistence, they could say to themselves as well as to their critics, left them with no choice. Their position was comparable to the one in which labor union leaders sometimes find themselves during contract negotiations when their expectations are more modest – and realistic – than those of the rank and file, to whom, however, they must ultimately answer.[90]

The Israelis were not gluttons for pressure. There were limits to the concessions they considered prudent, regardless of what the Americans wanted. If the leadership and the public were not always as one on the issue of what Israel should give up, neither were Israeli officials and their American counterparts always in accord on this subject. Even when they did agree, moreover, both recognized the dangers of Israel appearing to bow to American pres-

---

[90] Safran, *Israel*, p. 540; Kissinger, *Years of Upheaval*, pp. 539, 608, 610. Kissinger dealt with the leaders of the Labor coalition, who had to be wary of parliamentary opposition that was generally inclined to be less conciliatory than they. During the Carter administration, when the Camp David accords and the final peace treaty were negotiated, Labor's opponents were in power in Jerusalem and did not run quite the same risk of being outflanked – although ultimately many members of Begin's coalition voted against the Camp David accords in the Knesset. But American pressure played the same role as before. Some members of the Likud government, such as Foreign Minister Dayan and Defense Minister Weizmann, were more willing to make compromises with Egypt than others, most notably Prime Minister Menachem Begin. Dayan and Weizmann were therefore not entirely unhappy about American pressure on Begin.

sure. This risked inviting the Arabs to press the United States to extract concessions from Israel without giving the Israelis anything. Washington had the delicate task of persuading the Arab world, and Egypt in particular, that the United States could induce Israel to make concessions, but without giving them the impression that this was possible without Arab concessions in return, or that American pressure could force Israel to do anything that Washington desired.[91]

In truth, the United States could *not* compel Israel to comply with any and every American wish. The Israelis resisted American pressure. A favored Israeli tactic was to circumvent the American administration and appeal, instead, to the Congress, where support for Israel was invariably strong, and to the American public.[92] In May 1975, in the midst of the Ford administration's reassessment, seventy-six senators – fully three-fourths of the Senate – signed a letter to the president urging him to "be responsive to Israel's urgent military and economic needs" and to make clear America's general support for Israel.[93] Another tactic, and an effective one, was sheer stubbornness. What was at stake for Israel, ultimately, was survival. The Israelis were determined to do whatever was necessary to survive. On matters they deemed vital, no amount of American pressure could budge them. Kissinger records Golda Meir saying to him during the negotiations with Syria: "We have no oil, we have no nuisance value. We can't say to the United States, 'You won't do this for us, so we will invite [Soviet Foreign Minister Andrei] Gromyko to come.' He won't come, and we have no oil to stop pumping. We have nothing, except one thing: a determination to live and not to have our people killed."[94] The American government was well aware of Israel's determination, which set limits on what it would ask the Israelis to do.

The use or threat of pressure was not the only way the United

---

[91] Kissinger, *Years of Upheaval*, pp. 211, 483, 624, 1055, and esp. 1057. "Perhaps the most important ingredient [in the success of the peace process] was the success of the United States in conveying to the Arab side at one and the same time the sense that it was able to move Israel and that such a feat was by no means easy." Safran, *Israel*, p. 534.
[92] Kissinger, *Years of Upheaval*, p. 485.
[93] Spiegel, *The Other Arab–Israeli Conflict*, p. 296.
[94] Kissinger, *Years of Upheaval*, p. 485.

States attempted to persuade Israel to make concessions. The Americans offered positive inducements as well. They offered measures to make the concessions they favored safe and even, on balance, advantageous to Israel. The peace process involved two parallel sets of negotiations. One set, between Israel and Egypt, concerned the trade of land for peace. The other, between Israel and the United States, centered on what the United States would give Israel as compensation for the land being given up. Israel's negotiating tactics were designed to extract concessions not just from Egypt but from the United States as well. The second set was as important for the peace process as the first.

Israel received assistance from the United States in three forms. One was economic assistance. At the beginning of Kissinger's shuttle diplomacy, for example, the American government converted a 1 billion dollar loan to an outright grant. Even when there was no explicit connection between American economic assistance to Israel and the peace process, an implicit link between the two was present. On occasion, economic aid was tied to a specific concession that Israel had made in the negotiations. The Americans promised a reliable supply of oil to make up for the loss to Israel of the oil wells in the Sinai. They financed the relocation of air bases from the Sinai to sites within the 1949 borders.

The United States also gave promises of continuing political support. This was of particular importance because in the wake of the war and the oil embargo no other country of any consequence was willing to side with Israel in political disputes with its Arab neighbors. In conjunction with the second Sinai disengagement agreement, for example, Israel received a number of political assurances and commitments, including the promise that the United States would "view with particular gravity threats to Israel's security or sovereignty by a world power." The reference was to the Soviet Union. An American "memorandum of agreement" went on to say, "In support of this objective, the United States government will in the event of such a threat consult promptly with the government of Israel with respect to what support, diplomatic or otherwise, or assistance it can lend to Israel in accordance with its constitutional practices."[95]

---

[95] Quoted in Safran, *Israel*, p. 559. A full discussion of the various American

Most important of all, and most pertinent to the security dilemma, Israel received military assistance from the United States
in return for relinquishing territory to Egypt. The pattern predated
the 1973 war. The United States had asked Israel to observe the
cease-fire that was being proposed in the "war of attrition" with
Egypt in 1970. The Israelis agreed to do so in exchange for supplies
of American military equipment and assurances that these shipments would continue. Even before that episode, Nixon had said
that the United States would trade "hardware for software" with
Israel – that it would provide weapons in exchange for Israeli flexibility in negotiations.[96] After the 1973 war, this formula was incorporated into the peace process. In connection with each major
agreement the United States gave Israel either specific weapons,
a promise of a continuing supply of weapons, or both.[97]

There was a logic to this third form of assistance, which stemmed
from the character of the security dilemma. The territory that Israel
was giving up had military value. The United States therefore
provided Israel with the basis of military strength in another form.
Since in returning the Sinai Israel was giving up strategic depth,
the United States undertook to make depth less important for
Israel's security. Just as important for the peace process as returning
the territory was strengthening Israel in such a way as to help it
cope with the failure of conciliation but without making Egypt more
inclined toward hostility.

Egypt did not, on the whole, object to the American assistance
to Israel, even the military assistance, that went hand in hand with
the peace process. There is a fundamental political difference between a country's building up its armaments within its own borders
and its occupying territory claimed by another. The one is almost
always less objectionable than the other. A neighbor's increase in
military strength is not, however, always received with equanimity.
In this case Egypt may have calculated that Israel would receive
American aid under any circumstances and that within the context

undertakings to Israel that accompanied the second disengagement agreement
appears in ibid., pp. 554–60.

[96] Kissinger, *White House Years*, p. 371; Aronson, *Conflict and Bargaining*,
p. 125.

[97] Aronson, *Conflict and Bargaining*, pp. 230, 303; Safran, *Israel*, p. 594; Friedlander, *Sadat and Begin*, p. 289.

of the peace process the weapons went to purchase the recovery of Egyptian territory. Egypt itself also received military and economic assistance from Washington. Indeed, the United States became its principal source of aid. Alignment with the West had been one of the principal purposes of Sadat's policy. Tolerating American ties with Israel was the price Egypt had to pay for it. The American government made an effort to maintain parity of economic aid between Egypt and Israel, which became by far the two largest recipients after the 1973 war. In this sense the United States underwrote peace between the two countries.

The relationship between Israel and the United States as it developed after 1948, and especially after 1973, resembled a military alliance.[98] The United States was more than Israel's principal supplier of weapons, and not only its chief political supporter. The American government suggested privately, although it never said so publicly, that it was prepared to send American troops to fight on Israel's behalf should developments in the Middle East place the Jewish state in mortal jeopardy.[99]

For all the cooperation between them, however, Israel and the United States were not bound by a formal treaty. The United States was not obliged to defend Israel as it was to come to the defense

[98] One of the main arguments of Safran, *Israel*, is that the relationship is to be understood as an alliance. See esp. pp. viii, 557.

[99] Aronson, *Conflict and Bargaining*, p. 186; Shlomo Aronson, "The Nuclear Dimension of the Arab–Israeli Conflict: The Case of the Yom Kippur War," *Jerusalem Journal of International Relations* 7, no. 2 (1984): p. 126. There were no conceivable circumstances in which Israeli forces would be needed to defend the United States; but on at least one occasion Israel was prepared to fight in the Middle East in the service of an American purpose – which was also, to be sure, an Israeli purpose. In 1970, war erupted in Jordan between King Hussein's army and the PLO, which had set up its main headquarters in the Jordanian capital, Amman. Syria began moving troops south to support the PLO. Urgent consultations between the United States and Israel followed. Partly at the behest of the Americans, the Israelis prepared to send forces into Jordan to oppose the Syrians. The Israelis prepared, that is, to defend a regime with which they were technically at war but that was friendly to the United States. After American warnings were issued and American air and naval forces and Israeli ground troops were mobilized, and after meeting Jordanian resistance, the Syrians withdrew from Jordan (Kissinger, *White House Years*, pp. 617–31; Safran, *Israel*, pp. 452–4). The Israelis were not indifferent to the fighting across the Jordan River and were not preparing simply to do a favor for the United States. They much preferred that Hussein rule Jordan rather than the Syrians or the PLO.

of the Western European members of NATO and of Japan.[100] No American troops were stationed in Israel. The Israelis emphasized their self-reliance; they frequently reminded the Americans that they asked no one else to fight and die for them.

Still, the idea of an alliance between the two countries held some attraction and was periodically raised on both sides. In the 1950s Ben Gurion had sought without success a formal affiliation with the United States.[101] During the final stages of the peace process the idea surfaced again. The Israelis expressed interest. But the Americans seemed to be willing to offer an alliance only in exchange for concessions – notably Israeli withdrawal from the West Bank – that the Israeli government of the moment, at least, was not willing to make.[102]

An alliance threatened to inhibit Israel's freedom to retaliate for small-scale attacks across its border, which had been a settled policy since the 1950s. Nor was it altogether compatible with another important American role in the peace process. In addition to mediating between the two sides and compensating Israel for giving up territory, the United States served as the guarantor of parts of the settlement.

The American role as guarantor grew naturally out of its services as mediator. Just as the Arabs were at first unwilling to talk directly with Israel, so they were not prepared to make concessions directly. They thus made them to the United States, which vouched for them to Israel. When the initial Six-Point Agreement was reached, the Egyptian president said to the American secretary of state: "Never forget, Dr. Kissinger, I am making this agreement with the United States, not with Israel."[103] Israel insisted on certain interpretations of the agreement's major points. Sadat was willing to assent to them but would not embrace them publicly. They were therefore put in a separate "memorandum of understanding" between the United States and Israel.[104] In the first Sinai disengage-

---

[100] Robert W. Tucker, "Israel and the United States: From Dependence to Nuclear Weapons?" *Commentary*, November 1975, p. 35.
[101] Aronson, *Conflict and Bargaining*, pp. 29, 43; Safran, *Israel*, p. 167.
[102] Dayan, *Breakthrough*, pp. 12, 25, 56, 145.
[103] Kissinger, *Years of Upheaval*, p. 643.
[104] "What we could not do was what the [Israeli] cabinet seemed to want: turn the Israeli–American Memorandum of Understanding into the basic Egyptian–

ment agreement several months later, the Egyptians refused to extend a formal promise to Israel to limit their forces in certain zones of the peninsula but were willing to declare to the United States that they intended to respect the desired limits and have the Americans convey these assurances to Jerusalem.[105] The last item remaining for settlement in the 1974 negotiations with Syria was the Israeli insistence that Damascus pledge not to permit raids against Israel from Syrian territory. The Syrians would not give such a pledge, although they had always kept tight control of their borders. So the Israeli prime minister, Golda Meir, announced that the United States interpreted the agreement to prohibit such raids and added, "I assume that the United States would not have made such a declaration had it not had a solid foundation for doing so, and I make this statement public with the knowledge of the United States."[106] In each case the United States was far more than a messenger. Washington was implicated in the terms of each agreement and had some responsibility for seeing that they were observed.

This responsibility took concrete form in the second Sinai disengagement agreement. Israel wanted to retain control of the electronic detection and monitoring stations it had built in the Gidi and Mitla passes. Egypt opposed this and suggested, as a compromise, that the United States operate the stations. Israel agreed.[107] In the final 1979 accord between Egypt and Israel, the United States, in a letter from President Carter to both President Sadat and Prime Minister Begin, promised to monitor observance of the

Israeli agreement. This would have required going back to Sadat and asking him to confirm formally what he could only accept de facto. . . . [Kissinger aide Harold] Saunders wisely suggested that Golda [Meir] declare Israel's interpretation to the Parliament and we would not contradict it. However we could not ask Sadat to agree to it formally even while he acquiesced in practice." Kissinger, *Years of Upheaval*, pp. 652–3.

[105] The Egyptians also promised in this roundabout fashion to reopen the Suez Canal.

[106] Quoted in Kissinger, *Years of Upheaval*, p. 1106. See also Safran, *Israel*, p. 531. As with the Sinai disengagement agreement, the force limitations in the Israeli-Syrian accord officially were not formal undertakings given by each side to the other but rather responses to a United States proposal. *Years of Upheaval*, p. 1099.

[107] The United States also promised that it would support Israel's right of passage and overflight in several international waterways.

terms of the peace treaty by aerial surveillance and to consult with each side in the event of a violation, as well as to "take such other action as it may deem appropriate and helpful to achieve compliance."[108] An accompanying memorandum of agreement between the United States and Israel was even more direct and explicit. It said that "the United States will take appropriate measures to promote full observance of the Treaty of Peace" and listed some specific actions that the American government was prepared to undertake, including providing military aid and opposing hostile resolutions at the United Nations, in support of Israeli responses to Egyptian violations.[109]

On these occasions the United States was compensating Israel by giving assurances of American support in exchange for the surrender of territory. But it was assuming responsibility in the first instance not for Israel's security but for the peace settlement itself, to which both sides had agreed and in which each had a stake. Here the American role was similar, in a very modest way, to the one that government plays within sovereign states. There, government enforces contracts: The power of the state stands behind lawfully concluded agreements. Since there is no government in the international system, for international agreements each state is its own judge and its own police force. In the Egyptian–Israeli agreements, the United States acted as a third party with some claim to impartiality, as a government would. Although a violation by either side would probably not precipitate sanctions of the sort that a genuine government would impose, it would at least carry risk of alienating the United States. The prospect of forfeiting American goodwill was bound to have a deterrent effect, rather like the force of law in the domestic setting.

Still, the United States was more the protector of Israel than the guarantor of the settlement, more a traditional ally than that mythical creature, a world government. In this regard there is a parallel between the Israeli–Egyptian peace process of the 1970s and French and British relations with Germany in the 1930s.[110] Just as France took each round of concessions to Germany as an oppor-

---

[108] Reprinted in Jureidini and McLaurin, *Beyond Camp David*, p. 154.
[109] Reprinted in Dayan, *Breakthrough*, p. 154.
[110] See Chapter 2, Section IV.

tunity to strengthen its ties with Britain, so Israel agreed to make concessions to Syria and Egypt in return for increasing support from the United States. There is an important difference between the two historical episodes: The French wanted to make certain that when they fought Germany British troops would be fighting at their side. The Israelis, by contrast, always fought the Arabs alone and sought American assistance so that they could continue to do so. But there was also a similarity, which was troubling from the Israeli point of view. Allies, no matter how close, always have different interests and therefore occasionally prefer different policies. Britain was less alarmed about Germany and more optimistic about chances for conciliation than France. The British were generally more reluctant to fight. It was their empire that concerned them. Moreover, they had a margin of safety – the English Channel and France itself. The French did not. Germany was next door.

Similarly, the Israelis lived next door to the Arabs; the Americans did not. It was Israel, not the United States, that was threatened. Like British policies in Europe, American policy in the Middle East was subject to a variety of influences, including the influence of commitments in other parts of the world; Israel, like France, did not have the luxury of concerning itself with commitments beyond its own region. American interests would be served by almost any settlement at almost any price. But for Israel, it was the price above all that mattered. The United States was more willing to run risks to reach agreement; but Israel would have to bear the burden of those risks.

Their security dilemma required the Israelis to accept Arab assurances in order to make peace. The long history of Arab hostility made them less than sanguine about the credibility of those assurances. So they sought and received *American* assurances of support, to complement the Arab promises and to compensate for the territory they had to yield. They sought to reinforce deterrence even as they practiced conciliation. But even American assurances were not guaranteed. The United States had not always made good on them in the past. The American government had tried to organize a multinational effort to break the Egyptian blockade of the Straits of Tiran in 1967 but had failed.[111] At the outset of the June

---

[111] When Israel withdrew from the Sinai in 1957, the United States made clear

war, the Israelis had felt isolated. Three years later, in 1970, there was disagreement between the United States and Israel about whether Egypt had violated the terms of the cease-fire in the war of attrition. The Israelis worried both about an American policy in the Middle East that was too strong for their liking, involving pressure on them to make concessions they thought unwise, and a policy that was too weak, with the American government unwilling to make good on the commitments it had given to Israel. Like Egyptian pledges of good conduct, American promises of assistance were, in the end, intangible. Israel could not enforce them. And not only the Israeli experience of thirty years, but also the Jewish experience of five thousand years lent itself to the conviction that in the end a people can rely only on itself. This was one of the animating principles of Zionism.

There was one way of compensating for what Israel had to give up, one form of military might for which the Israelis did not have to depend on the United States. This form of national strength, an important if shadowy presence in Israeli security policy, was nuclear weaponry.

In 1960 an experimental nuclear reactor was built at Dimona, in the southern part of the country, with help from France. It had the capacity to produce enough fissionable material to make several bombs each year. During the 1960s the United States insisted that the facility be open to international inspection so that it could be determined whether material was being diverted for use in making bombs. After 1969 the inspections stopped. There were periodic reports that Israel had made a bomb, or was on the brink of making one. Speculation was particularly intense about Israeli preparations for nuclear use during the 1973 war.[112] Israel certainly possessed the materials and expertise necessary for fabricating nuclear weapons. The Israeli government never confirmed these reports. It

that it supported the right of free passage in the international waterways of the region. Although not a formal commitment, this gave the Israelis some basis for feeling that they could expect the United States to act to enforce that right when the issue arose in 1967. Safran, *Israel*, p. 357.

[112] Ibid., p. 489; "How Israel Got the Bomb," *Time*, April 12, 1976, pp. 39–40. For a summary of these reports, most of which appeared in the American press, see Shai Feldman, *Israeli Nuclear Deterrence: A Strategy for the 1980s* (New York: Columbia University Press, 1982), p. 215.

consistently took the position that it would never be the first to introduce these weapons into the Middle East.

Beginning in the early 1960s, fragmentary and half-public debate took place in Israel about whether the country ought to have the bomb. Two different positions could be discerned. One downplayed the importance of nuclear weapons, maintaining that Israel's security should rest on its nonnuclear forces and on close ties with the United States. From this it followed that the strategic depth provided by the occupied territories was of some value.[113] The other looked more favorably on an Israeli nuclear arsenal because it made possible the deterrence of the Arab states without reliance on the United States or possession of territory. Strategic depth is less important for a strategy of deterrence through the threat of retaliation – that is, punishment – than for deterrence through preparations for defense – that is, denial.[114]

Although Israel consistently said that it did not have nuclear weapons, the belief that it did, or easily could, have them influenced Middle East politics and the peace process. There is some evidence that even before the 1973 war the Egyptian government was convinced that Israel had come into possession of the bomb. Sadat alluded to this belief in his address to the Knesset when he said, "Missiles and warheads and nuclear weapons cannot establish security. Instead they destroy what peace and security build."[115] The belief that Israel had nuclear weapons helps to account for the limited aims the Egyptians and the Syrians set for themselves in the war. They may have feared that, if the Arab armies attacked the core of the country, Israel would retaliate with its nuclear

---

[113] The debate has been reconstructed by Shlomo Aronson. See "The Nuclear Dimension" and *Conflict and Bargaining*, pp. 50–3, 310. He imputes this first view to the Mapai and Achdut Ha'Avoda political parties.

[114] Aronson says that Ben Gurion was attracted to this second view, as were his disciples who broke with the Labor party to found an independent group, Rafi, but subsequently returned to hold high office in Labor cabinets: Moshe Dayan and Shimon Peres. "The Nuclear Dimension," p. 123; *Conflict and Bargaining*, pp. 54, 97, 434–5, n. 66. Shai Feldman calls for an overt Israeli nuclear force because, among other reasons, this would make possible relinquishing control of the West Bank. *Israeli Nuclear Deterrence*, pp. ix, 103. On the distinction between punishment and denial see Chapter 4, pp. 235–8.

[115] "Transcript of address by President Anwar el-Sadat," p. 14; see also Friedlander, *Sadat and Begin*, pp. 92, 122.

arsenal.[116] The Egyptian conviction that Israel had become a nuclear power may also have reinforced Cairo's desire to reach accommodation, in order to avoid future wars in which nuclear weapons might be used.[117]

The prospect of a nuclear-armed Israel influenced American policy as well. The American attitude on this subject changed over time. Washington was more troubled by it in the 1960s than in the 1970s but was never happy at the prospect. The United States consistently preferred to keep nuclear weapons out of the Middle East entirely. This preference created an incentive to supply Israel with nonnuclear armaments so as to make a nuclear stockpile unnecessary.[118]

Nuclear weapons presented Israel with another of the difficult choices to which the security dilemma gives rise. Acquiring the bomb was a way of deterring without also unintentionally provoking the Arab world. The bomb was, on the whole, a less provocative form of military strength than the occupation of land claimed by others. Egypt would go to war to recover the Sinai but not, in all likelihood, to destroy Israel's nuclear arsenal. Still, nuclear weapons were more provocative than the nonnuclear armaments the United States was supplying. The bomb belongs to a special political category; it has a powerful political resonance. Had Israel announced or demonstrated that it possessed nuclear armaments, it might have prompted the Arabs to obtain the bomb themselves or to accelerate ongoing efforts to obtain it.[119] The United States

---

[116] Aronson, "The Nuclear Dimension," pp. 116, 117–8, 127–8; *Conflict and Bargaining*, p. 178. This is not the only possible explanation for the limited Arab aims. For purely military reasons, the Egyptians in particular may have planned to remain behind fortified lines beneath the cover of their surface-to-air missiles where they could ward off Israeli attacks, rather than wage mobile battles in which they would be at a disadvantage. They did fight and lose such battles during the second week of the war.

[117] On this general point see Tucker, "Israel and the United States," p. 42.

[118] Safran, *Israel*, pp. 489–90; Feldman, pp. 210–11.

[119] China did not face this problem. Its two adversaries already had nuclear weapons. Nor was another danger that Israel faced pertinent to the Chinese case. Israel was superior to its adversaries in nonnuclear terms. A competition in nuclear armaments might leave it comparatively worse off. China, by contrast, was so much weaker than the United States and the Soviet Union that nuclear weapons on both sides would reduce its margin of inferiority. See Chapter 4, Section V.

might have distanced itself from Israel in deference to the general American policy of opposing the spread of nuclear weapons.

The status of its nuclear weaponry – rumored but not confirmed to exist – gave Israel the best of both worlds: a measure of deterrence of its Arab neighbors and some leverage on and independence of the United States without forcing either the Arabs or the Americans to take steps that would make Israel less secure.[120]

V

In the end, Israel agreed to exchange land for peace with Egypt. All the territory to the south that it had captured in 1967 was returned to Egyptian control through a series of negotiations that stretched over six years, ending in 1979. The Israelis' security dilemma encompassed territories they captured from their neighbors to the north and east as well. Israel did not make the same exchange with them. Syria and Jordan differed from Egypt in crucial ways, and the territories in question – the Golan Heights to the north and the West Bank of the Jordan River to the east – were more difficult to exchange than the Sinai Peninsula. The elements of their relationship with Egypt that disposed the Israelis to the policy of conciliation were missing.

Israel did reach one agreement with Syria, in May 1974. The Israeli army withdrew from its lines of farthest advance toward Damascus of the previous October. As part of the withdrawal, Israeli forces evacuated the town of Quneitra. The negotiations with Syria were undertaken to permit Egypt to continue its dealings

---

[120] Although calling for an explicit Israeli policy of nuclear deterrence, Shai Feldman is careful to advise that the nuclear option be adopted in a way that does not alienate the United States. The American government is likely to be least unhappy about an Israeli announcement that it has the bomb if this comes in response to the news that an Arab state has acquired it. Hence the policy of ambiguity described above is appropriate even in Feldman's terms as long as no other country in the region has nuclear weapons (Feldman, *Israeli Nuclear Deterrence*, p. 192). He also argues that American objections would be blunted if the announcement were made as part of an Israeli proposal for an overall peace settlement (ibid., p. 229). For a different view, which proposes a series of measures to avoid the need for an explicit nuclear capacity, see Yaniv, *Dilemmas of Security*, Chap. 6.

with Israel. Neither side felt a pressing need to settle the larger conflict between them.[121]

Giving back the Sinai to Egypt was easier for Israel than returning the strip of land captured from Syria. The Golan Heights formed an elevated plateau overlooking Israel's Hula Valley, an important agricultural area, and the Sea of Galilee. It was a much smaller piece of territory than the Sinai; troops could be moved through the Golan up to the 1949 Israeli border much more quickly. If Israel retreated from the Golan Heights in return for the promise that the territory would be demilitarized and if Syria then violated its promise, the Israelis would have much less time to mobilize and resist than a comparable violation by Egypt in the Sinai would allow.[122] Once having reoccupied the Golan, Syria would be in a position to launch an offensive against northern Israel or, short of that, to harrass farmers in the Hula Valley and fishermen in the Sea of Galilee. Before June 1967, Syrian forces had periodically fired on Israeli towns and workers from elevated positions overlooking northern Israel. The Israeli army had attacked and captured those positions at the end of the Six Day War partly in response to demands by residents of the northern part of the country that the government take advantage of the opportunity to push Syrian guns beyond the range of Israeli homes. It could be argued that Israel would be stronger in military terms without the Sinai as long as it was demilitarized. The same argument was far less persuasive when applied to the Golan.

Just as the Golan Heights differed from the Sinai Peninsula, so Syria itself was different from Egypt in a way that made the exchange of land for peace difficult. As suspicious as they were of Egyptian declarations of peaceful intent, the Israelis were even less disposed to trust Syrian goodwill. The Syrian regime was unwilling and probably unable to address these suspicions by offering

---

[121] Kissinger, *Years of Upheaval*, pp. 1045, 1061. As part of the May agreement, Syria promised to repopulate Quneitra, a gesture that, like the Egyptian resettlement of the towns along the Suez Canal, was to serve as evidence of peaceful Syrian intentions by creating a hostage to Syrian good behavior. The Israelis would then be encouraged to pull back further. Unlike the Suez Canal cities, however, Quneitra remained deserted.

[122] Horowitz, *Israel's Concept*, p. 28; Kissinger, *Years of Upheaval*, p. 1077.

the kinds of assurances that Egypt had provided. Damascus did not have the flexibility, because it lacked the legitimacy, of the Egyptian government.

Syria, unlike Egypt, was a recent creation. Damascus had once been an important city as the seat of the caliphate. Its significance, however, had been religious rather than national. It was an important part of Islamic, not Syrian history. Before the twentieth century there was, strictly speaking, no such thing as Syrian history. Syria was smaller than Egypt and carried less weight in the Arab world. It was also a less homogeneous society. Its largest group was Sunni Muslim, but there were Shia Muslim and Druze communities as well. The rulers in 1973 and afterward were Alawis, a sect that had split off from the Shias. Traditionally poor and backward, the Alawis had managed to seize control of the government in the 1960s. They were triply disadvantaged and vulnerable: The Sunnis looked askance at them because they were Shias; the Shias scorned them because they were Alawis; and both disliked them because the regime they controlled professed a secular ideology, the Ba'ath version of Arab socialism.[123]

The Syrian Alawi leader, Hafez Asad, did not and could not have the authority that Anwar Sadat enjoyed. "Whoever rules in Cairo," the scholar of Middle East politics, Fouad Ajami, quotes a Lebanese politician as saying, "is a pharaoh; whoever rules in Damascus is a 'wali' [a provincial governor]."[124] Asad could not break with the pan-Arab consensus on Israel, as his Egyptian counterpart did. His rule was insecure. He stayed in power through repression and terror. What legitimacy he possessed came from zealous pan-Arabism, which was expressed in uncompromising hostility to Zionism. The Israeli threat also provided an excuse for the suppression of opposition at home.[125] Because the conflict with Israel was so important to Asad, he lacked Sadat's incentive to turn to the West. The United States did not establish the same kind of relationship with Syria, which remained a Soviet client. Nor did Washington,

---

[123] Alasdair Drysdale, "The Asad Regime and Its Troubles," *Merip Reports*, 112 (November–December 1982): 4, 7–8.

[124] Ajami, *Arab Predicament*, p. 101. See also Kissinger, *Years of Upheaval*, pp. 780, 936.

[125] Kissinger, *Years of Upheaval*, p. 1066.

the 1974 disengagement agreement notwithstanding, serve as the mediator and guarantor of a settlement between Syria and Israel.[126]

The same obstacles, geography and politics, that prevented the Israelis from exchanging the Golan Heights for peace with Syria, stood in the way of the return of the West Bank to Arab control. The military problems that relinquishing the territory presented, and the lack of a firmly established legitimate authority to negotiate for it and offer Israel public promises of good conduct in return, kept the Israelis from following the course of conciliation on their eastern border. Like the Golan Heights, the West Bank was linked to the negotiations on the Sinai Peninsula. Just as Egypt would not move forward without parallel negotiations between Syria and Israel in the early months of the peace process, so in its latter stages Sadat insisted on some declaration concerning the status of the West Bank. At Camp David the two sides agreed to a "framework" for settling its political future. This called for two sets of negotiations, the first to establish a transitional regime to preside for five years, during which time the second would determine the ultimate disposition of the territory. The initial negotiations soon bogged down and were not completed; but Egypt did not permit the unresolved questions of the West Bank to interfere with its own bilateral settlement with Israel.

The geographic features that made the Golan Heights difficult for Israel to return were even more pronounced in the case of the West Bank. It was smaller and closer to Israel's population centers than the Sinai. The 1949 lines made Israel less than nine miles wide at its narrowest point. Shorn of the West Bank, Israel assumed an awkward and not easily defended shape, which was one of the

---

[126] The requirements for remaining in power in Cairo and Damascus differed. Sadat enjoyed political legitimacy. He was judged on his regime's economic performance. Its most dangerous moment was the eruption of riots in the capital after the government decreed a rise in the price of bread. Although he could feed the Syrians, Asad did not enjoy comparable legitimacy. Much of whatever popular support he enjoyed outside the Alawi community came from his role as the resolute adversary of Zionism. His most dangerous moment was the uprising against his rule by the Muslim Brothers in the city of Hama and elsewhere in 1981, which he brutally suppressed. (On this episode see Ze'ev Chafets, *Double Vision* [New York: Morrow], Chap. 2.) The difference between the two, it might be said, was that Sadat needed bread and Asad needed circuses to stay in power. The United States could supply the first; hostility toward Israel was necessary for the second.

reasons that Israeli military strategy had had an offensive cast through 1967.

Moreover, although Anwar Sadat could and did negotiate the return of the Sinai and Hafez Asad was the person with whom Israel would have to deal over the Golan Heights, it was not at all clear who would be the interlocutor for the West Bank. There were two principal candidates. One was the king of Jordan. In the course of the 1948 war, his grandfather, Abdullah, had seized the territory where, according to the terms of the United Nations partition resolution, a third independent state (in addition to Israel and Jordan) was supposed to be established in Mandatory Palestine. Hussein had ruled it until 1967, when his forces had attacked Israel, suffered defeat, and been driven out. Those Israelis who sought a settlement comparable to the one that had returned the Sinai to Egypt wanted to negotiate with Hussein, who was the Americans' preferred interlocutor as well. A number of secret meetings between him or his representatives and Israeli officials took place over the years. The two sides were never able to reach any agreement, however, and Hussein was not willing to meet publicly with the Israelis. His reluctance stemmed from his uncertain position at home.

Like his neighbor and rival to the north, Hafez Asad, Hussein had an unsteady grip on power. Like Asad he did not have the negotiating latitude, because he did not possess the political legitimacy, of Sadat of Egypt. Like Syria, but unlike Egypt, the state over which he presided wàs a recent, artificial creation. Asad, at least, had seized power in Syria himself. Hussein's throne was originally a gift from Great Britain, although he himself had defended it over the years.

Hussein's great-grandfather had been the sherif of Mecca, a tribal chief in the Arabian peninsula who had joined the British in fighting the Turks during World War I. (Britain's liaison with the sherif was Colonel T. E. Lawrence, known to history as Lawrence of Arabia.) One of the sherif's sons believed that the British had promised his family the throne in Damascus in payment for their services. In 1920 he went there to claim it, only to find the French installed in power. Another son, Abdullah, raised an army in Arabia and set out for Damascus to help his brother evict the French. Alarmed at this development the British colonial secretary, Winston Churchill, intercepted him and suggested that he settle, with a regular subvention from London, in western Palestine, which the British had received as part of the postwar division of Ottoman possessions that gave Damascus to France. It was to be a temporary arrangement; but sixty years later Abdullah's grandson, Hussein, was still there.[127]

To many of the Sunni Muslims who were the majority of his subjects, Hussein, although a fellow Arab, was an interloper imposed by foreigners, with no mandate to govern. The king was therefore wary of departing from the pan-Arab consensus on the subject of Israel. He was especially wary of agreeing to a settlement that consigned any territory that he had once controlled, including Jerusalem, to Israel.[128] These were terms that almost nobody in Israel was prepared to contemplate seriously.

Hussein was particularly cautious about violating the taboo against dealing directly with Israel, moreover, because he was not the only claimant to Arab Palestine, however it was defined.[129] His rival was the Palestine Liberation Organization, or PLO, an association of several distinct groups of various sizes. In 1974 an Arab

---

[127] Briton Cooper Busch, "Great Britain and Jordan, 1918–1956," in Anne Sinai and Allen Pollack, eds., *The Hashemite Kingdom of Jordan and the West Bank* (New York: American Academic Association for Peace in the Middle East), 1977, p. 37.

[128] When he met Moshe Dayan secretly in London in 1977, Hussein said that the only kind of settlement he could contemplate was one in which Israel returned completely to its borders before June 1967 (Dayan, *Breakthrough*, pp. 35–7). Kissinger portrays Jordan as being more flexible before 1973 (*Years of Upheaval*, p. 220; also Aronson, *Conflict and Bargaining*, p. 108). In early 1974, Kissinger suggested that Israel yield a small piece of the West Bank, perhaps the city of Jericho, as a way of engaging Hussein in the peace process. The Israeli cabinet refused, in part because this would have created considerable political turmoil within Israel. Aronson, *Conflict and Bargaining*, p. 251; Kissinger, *Years of Upheaval*, pp. 787, 847–8.

[129] The Arabs who considered themselves Palestinians could be divided into four distinct groups: those who lived on the West Bank and Gaza; those living in Jordan proper (who formed a majority of the kingdom's population); those in Lebanon, many of them in refugee camps; and those scattered throughout the rest of the Arab world, especially the oil-exporting states along the Persian Gulf. The 400,000 or so Arab Christians and Muslims living within Israel's 1949 borders qualified as Palestinians on ethnic grounds, but almost all had accepted Israeli citizenship. Of course, if the term "Palestinian" is taken to refer to anyone born within the boundaries of Mandatory Palestine then about 2.5 million of the Palestinians are Jews.

summit meeting at Rabat, Morocco, revoked Hussein's mandate to speak for the Palestinians – at least those under Israeli control – and conferred it, instead, on the PLO. In the competition for primacy, this was a severe setback for Hussein.[130]

The PLO was founded under Egyptian auspices in the early 1960s. It reached the apogee of its influence when the Arab states anointed it the rightful spokesman for the Palestinians.[131] The rise of the PLO marked a change in the way the Arabs conducted their conflict with Israel, at least in public. In 1948 they had objected to the existence of a sovereign Jewish state. With the growing role of the PLO, the emphasis shifted to the national rights of the Palestinian people. The declared Arab goal changed from liquidating Israel to creating Palestine.

But it was not at all clear where it was to be created. Sometimes the West Bank seemed to be the focus of Palestinian national aspirations. But the PLO's official position was that this ambition extended to what had since 1948 been Israel. According to the organization's charter, Jews had no national rights in the Middle East (or anywhere) and so the Jewish state was illegitimate, which was the position the Arab states had taken in 1948.[132] Moreover,

---

[130] In the aftermath of the 1973 war and especially the 1974 Rabat summit, thwarting the PLO became a more immediate objective for Hussein than recovering the territory he had lost in 1967. Since he needed to present himself as the likely interlocutor in any negotiation with Israel, he strove to appear interested in negotiating. Because he needed American support he had, in fact, to seem positively willing to negotiate. But since he could not make the kinds of compromises that Israel would accept, he generally attempted to set terms for negotiations that could not be fulfilled but that would allow him to place the blame elsewhere, usually on Israel, for their failure to begin. See, e.g., the Jordanian response to the Camp David agreements. Dayan, *Breakthrough*, pp. 201–3.

[131] The rivalry between Hussein and the PLO, although at its most intense in the decade of the 1970s, had a historical precedent. When Abdullah had reigned on one side of the Jordan River, there were local notables who were active politically on the other side. The most prominent of them in the interwar period was Haj Amin al-Husseini, who had the title of grand mufti of Jerusalem. During World War II he sided with Germany. Abdullah remained loyal to Britain. Three decades later a relative of the mufti, Yasir Arafat, the chairman of the PLO, aligned himself with the illiberal great power of the postwar period, the Soviet Union, while Abdullah's grandson was in the camp of Britain's successor as the principal liberal world power, the United States.

[132] See, e.g., Bernard Lewis, "Settling the Arab–Israeli Conflict," *Commentary*, June 1977, p. 51.

the PLO made clear in private that it considered Jordan, which was as much a part of Palestine as Israel, part of its domain.[133] Although it had never directly challenged Israel militarily, confining itself to random attacks on civilians, it had actually fought part of the Jordanian army in 1970.

The similarity between the PLO's official attitude toward Israel and that of the sovereign Arab states thirty years earlier was not accidental. The organization itself resembled the Arab world. It was fragmented, made up of various groups some of which, for reasons of ideology or because they wanted to reclaim land that had been Israeli since 1948, had no interest in conciliation. The largest of the constituent groups, Al Fatah, was itself divided into contentious factions. None of the elements of the PLO was particularly strong. Each claimed to speak for all Palestinians. Each was afraid of being outflanked by the others, as all of the Arab states had been during the first two decades of the Arab–Israeli conflict. None was prepared to take a conciliatory position toward Israel in public, for fear of the wrath of the others.[134] The same dynamic that had enforced hostility to Israel throughout the Arab world was present, on a smaller scale, within the ranks of the PLO.

There was more than a parallel between the Arab world's attitude toward Israel and that of the PLO; there was a connection. The PLO was not an independent body. Some factions were wholly controlled by individual Arab states. The others depended on the rest of the Arab world for money and political support. They could not disregard their patrons' wishes. The PLO's positions reflected those of the sovereign Arab states.[135] For them, in turn, the dynamic of pan-Arabism still held sway over the Palestinian question.[136] Even three decades after 1948, the regimes in Syria, Jordan,

---

[133] Kissinger, *Years of Upheaval*, p. 626.

[134] A regular feature of Middle Eastern politics after the rise of the PLO was the recurrent expectation that Yasir Arafat, the PLO chairman, would announce that he was willing to recognize and negotiate with Israel. Like Hussein, Arafat was adept at seeming to wish to negotiate without ever actually doing so – or indeed actually saying so.

[135] Rubin, *Arab States*, p. 20; Pipes, "How Important," p. 20. Similarly, local figures in the West Bank could not disregard the PLO's position. They were subject to reprisals if they did. Dayan, *Breakthrough*, p. 306.

[136] The Palestinian question remained at the heart of the pan-Arab enterprise. Indeed, by the end of the 1970s it was all that remained of the once-grand

Saudi Arabia, and Iraq still felt themselves vulnerable. Their credentials to rule were still less than solid. Championing the Palestinian cause continued to be a way for them to seek legitimacy at home. None except Egypt was strong enough to break with the Arab consensus. When Egypt did break with it dramatically, by signing the Camp David accords, the others reacted by trying to drum the Egyptians out of the Arab world.

Thus, even if the PLO had wanted to reach a settlement with Israel, its Arab sponsors would have blocked it. So Israel found itself, on the issue of the West Bank, in the same position in which it had been placed in its relations to the entire Arab world after 1948. There was no chance to trade land for peace as in the Sinai because there was no entity with which to make the trade. There were no negotiations on the West Bank because the politics of the Palestinian question within the Arab world had reproduced the conditions that had created the Arab–Israeli conflict in the first place.

For Israel, as well as for the Arab states, the Palestinian question had become, by the end of the 1970s, a smaller version of the Arab–Israeli conflict as a whole. But the West Bank was different from the Golan and the Sinai for Israel, in ways that not only made it difficult to choose conciliation but also transformed the problem that the territory represented.

It did not, in the first place, pose the same kind of problem for Israeli security as the Sinai and the Golan Heights. The land itself was strategically situated, but the Arab claimants to it were far less dangerous than Egypt, which had ten times Israel's population, or Syria, whose army was generously supplied by the Soviet Union. Jordan was smaller than either of the other bordering countries, with more modest armed forces and close ties to Israel's great patron the United States. Israel and Jordan worked out tacit terms of coexistence after 1967. Considerable traffic passed back and forth across the Jordan River in both directions. The relationship between the two countries lacked the formal trappings of peace: There were no treaties, ambassadors, or formal meetings between officials of the two governments, and Israeli passports were not honored

schemes of pan-Arabism. The PLO became "the conscience, symbol, and pivotal institution of pan-Arabism." Pipes, "How Important," p. 22.

on the other side of the river. Despite this, the relationship was a peaceful one.

As for the PLO, it had never amounted to a significant military threat to Israel. It had taken over southern Lebanon and established a state in miniature there, amassing a large stockpile of weapons that it used to harass Israel's northern border areas. A PLO rocket occasionally struck a town in northern Israel. But insofar as the PLO had a military strategy at all, it called for provoking another general Arab–Israeli war in which the other Arab states, with unspecified assistance from PLO forces, would finally triumph. Southern Lebanon was ostensibly a base for the final assault on Israel. In fact, it was a small fiefdom for Yasir Arafat and his colleagues and rivals in the PLO. They received large stipends from the rulers of the other Arab states, who were happy to keep them out of their own countries. The arrangement was satisfactory to all except the Shia Muslims, who were the original inhabitants of southern Lebanon but who were too weak to do anything about it until 1982.

In that year the Israeli army crossed the border, pushed all the way to the outskirts of Beirut, and drove the PLO out of Lebanon. Arafat was forced to set up camp in Tunis, far from the territory that he claimed. Shortly thereafter a Syrian-sponsored faction broke with him. A minor military threat to Israel before 1982, the PLO was not even that thereafter.

If it was not the source of a military threat, however, the West Bank was important to Israel in other ways. Unlike the Sinai or the Golan, it was populated.[137] It was thus a potential haven for terrorists.[138] There was another, more important consequence. Is-

---

[137] The territory Israel captured from Syria in 1967 included the town of Quneitra. But its inhabitants fled. The Israelis governed no Syrians. The town was returned, but not resettled, in 1974. Israel established a few settlements on the Golan Heights, as it had in the Sinai. The Sinai settlements were abandoned as part of the peace treaty with Egypt.

[138] The danger of terrorism, although not a threat to Israel's existence, complicated the problem of returning the West Bank to Arab sovereignty. The Israelis were uneasy at the idea of relying on an indigenous government to prevent it. Such a government would have to have effective police power, which would contradict the powerful Israeli desire to keep it from having armed forces of any consequence. The Israelis could have decided to police the West Bank themselves, sending their own forces across the border to hunt down and punish raiders. The policy of reprisals for border raids was well established. But such a policy would violate the sovereign prerogatives of whatever successor regime

rael had to put a government there, rather than simply station troops, as in the captured territory to the north and south. Israeli authorities had to keep order and provide for some public services.[139] Nor did this put the Israelis in the same position as the Europeans, who had governed other peoples until the middle of the twentieth century. They did not live thousands of miles from their subjects, as the British did from India. The West Bank was next door. Its inhabitants quickly became integrated into the Israeli economy. The West Bank was part of the daily life of Israel as the Sinai and the Golan were not.

For some Israelis this was natural and proper. They considered the territory, which they called by its biblical names, Judea and Samaria, to be part of Israel. Menachem Begin and his associates, who formed the core of what became the governing Likud coalition in 1977, had opposed the United Nations decision in 1948 to partition the section of the British Mandate of Palestine between the Jordan River and the Mediterranean. (Mandatory Palestine east of the river became the kingdom of Jordan.) Its biblical and historical associations made Hebron and Jericho as much parts of the land of Israel for them as Tel Aviv or Jerusalem. They never accepted the legitimacy of Arab rule west of the Jordan River. The 1967 war

to the Israeli occupation came into being. It would poison Israel's relations with the newly installed Arab authorities, thereby subverting the purpose of relinquishing the territory in the first place. On the policy of reprisal for terrorist raids see Mark Heller, *A Palestinian State: The Implications for Israel* (Cambridge, Mass.: Harvard University Press, 1983), p. 140; Safran, *Israel*, p. 237; Luttwak and Horowitz, *Israeli Army*, pp. 106, 110.

   Israel could not protect the entire length of its borders and did not wish to launch an all-out war in response to low-level raids. Hence it adopted a policy of "collective punishment," which held governments responsible for terrorist acts launched from within their borders. The idea was to force these governments to police the borders themselves. By and large the policy succeeded. The 1956 war was a large-scale reprisal raid against Egypt. After 1967 the Israelis forced King Hussein to control the PLO, leading to the 1970 showdown between the two and the expulsion of the PLO. The "war of attrition" of 1970, in which Israel made air strikes on Egyptian cities, can also be seen in this light. The border with Syria was generally quiet because the various Syrian regimes took care to keep it quiet. The great failure of the policy occurred in Lebanon. Israel could not compel the Lebanese government to control its southern border because the regime in Beirut was, after 1970, not strong enough to do so. Partly as a result, Israel launched its own assault against the PLO there in 1982.

[139] Many of the civil servants on the West Bank continued to be paid by Jordan.

had, in their eyes, set right a historic wrong. For them, the West Bank did not present the same choice that Israel faced in negotiations with Egypt. The Sinai could be surrendered in return for the appropriate concessions. But the West Bank could not be vacated under any circumstances. It was part of their country.

If the West Bank was part of their country, the Israelis had to decide what to do with the Arabs who lived there. A handful of people called for their expulsion. The Likud position, which Begin offered after the Camp David agreements, was to partition the functions of government in the region. Its Arab inhabitants would take responsibility for governing themselves – up to a point. "Autonomy" was what Begin called the cluster of responsibilities that he proposed for the residents of the West Bank. But Israel would retain sovereign title to the territory along with control over police and defense. The implicit pattern was in fact a familiar one in the Middle East,[140] but no Arab representatives were prepared to accept it and the Israeli government was reluctant to enact it unilaterally.

Not all Israelis were resolved that none of the West Bank would ever leave their control. Geography and demography, however, made even those willing in principle to return part of it to Arab governance insistent on terms more stringent than those the return of the Sinai had involved. There was a general consensus in Israel in favor of retaining the settled areas around Jerusalem and Tel Aviv beyond the 1949 border that had become virtually suburbs of those cities since 1967. There was an essentially unanimous determination to keep Jerusalem a united city under Israeli control. The consensus also included the retention of Jewish settlements along the length of the Jordan River[141] and military control of the crest of the Judean mountains, which bisected the West Bank and commanded the Plain of Sharon along the Mediterranean where most Israelis lived.

These requirements were roughly embodied in the Allon Plan,

[140] See James R. Kurth, "U.S. Policy and the West Bank," *Middle East Review*, 17, no. 2 (1984–5): 6–10.

[141] Dayan considered these settlements necessary from a military standpoint. Israel had to control the West Bank, he believed, for reasons of security; and the army could be counted on to defend territories only in which there were Jewish inhabitants. Dayan, *Breakthrough*, pp. 61, 184–5.

a scheme for the West Bank devised by the one-time deputy prime minister Yigal Allon. It was never officially adopted by any government; but it expressed the general views of his Labor party, which in turn represented most of those for whom trading land for peace to the east was at least conceivable.[142] Although it was conceivable for Israel, however, neither the kingdom of Jordan nor the PLO nor any other group was willing or able to negotiate such a trade from the Arab side. Well after 1979, in fact twenty years after the 1967 war, the Israeli government was still waiting for the phone call that would initiate serious negotiations on the West Bank.

Israel therefore confronted the uncertain prospect of governing more than a million Arabs indefinitely. These people were not citizens of the Jewish state. Although they enjoyed more political rights than the citizens of any of the Arab states, they were not fully self-governing. Whatever their freedoms in comparison with those of their neighbors, moreover, and despite the rise in their standard of living during the period of occupation, the Muslim and Christian inhabitants of the West Bank did not want to live under Israel's rule. Israel found itself governing others without their consent.

This raised the question of what rights these people ought to have under Israeli rule, indeed who should be a citizen of Israel and therefore what kind of political community the Zionist state itself should be. Israel's rule in the West Bank called into question the aspirations of its founders. Governing a million people without their consent was not compatible with the democratic purposes for which the state had been established.

[142] Heller, *Palestinian State*, pp. 35–6; Aronson, *Conflict and Bargaining*, pp. 87, 392, n. 115; Horowitz, *Israel's Concept*, p. 26. The positions of Israel's two main political groupings on the question of the West Bank were not, in the end, as far apart as each side often claimed. The Likud favored a "functional" partition of the territory, with Israel retaining sovereignty over all of it while an Arab authority supervised some governmental functions; Labor wanted a "territorial" partition, in which the land itself would be divided between Arab and Jewish sovereignty. (The terms are from Mark Heller, "Begin's False Autonomy," *Foreign Policy*, 37 [Winter 1979–80]: 111–32.) But Labor insisted on some Israeli sovereign prerogatives, such as the right to pursue terrorists, even in land ceded to an Arab authority; and the Likud version of partition would likely have led to effective Arab control over the sections of the West Bank not deemed to be of strategic importance.

The Palestinian problem had become the latest version of the question that had stood at the heart of the Arab–Israeli conflict since before 1948: whether the Arabs would accept Zionism. But it had also come to pose a different question: how the Israelis would define Zionism. The West Bank presented the Israelis with the profoundest kinds of problems. They were problems that all states face. Important as they were, however, they were not problems that arose, ultimately, from membership in the anarchic international system. The basic problem the West Bank raised was determining the kind of state the Israelis wanted, not how to defend the state they had. It was a problem of national purpose, of national authority, and of national identity. It was not, strictly speaking, a problem of national security.

6

Collective Approaches

The International Economic Order and Japan, 1945–1985

I

The ordinary meaning of security is physical protection. This the state provides. It offers protection both from other individuals and from other states. In addition to law, it provides national defense. In the twentieth century the state has assumed responsibility for something else: the economic well-being of its citizens. Governments have undertaken to provide not only for the common safety but also, in some manner, for the general welfare.

This more recent responsibility is a legacy of the industrial revolution. New techniques of production have made wealth available on a scale previously unimagined. The belief has spread that governments can encourage, foster, and even supervise these techniques. This belief is most firmly a part of the socialist tradition. In Communist countries, whose governments are offshoots of that tradition, the state has full control of virtually all legal economic activity. In the non-Communist world, management, although not ownership or complete control, of the national economy is generally taken to be one of the duties of the state.

The new responsibility for securing the national well-being is a legacy, as well, of the French Revolution and the political developments that it set in motion. Once it became an article of public faith that the state had the capacity to encourage the creation and take a hand in the distribution of wealth, the conviction took root that it had the obligation to do so.

329

Eighteenth-century public rhetoric celebrated political rights. To these were added, by the second half of the twentieth century, the right to a minimum standard of well-being. Prosperity joined liberty, equality, and fraternity as something to which all people were deemed entitled. The aim has been enshrined in various international declarations in the second half of the century. Indeed, along with the establishment of public safety – that is, the protection of citizens from internal disorder and foreign attack – and representativeness, a third feature – the provision of some level of well-being – has come to be a principal test of a state's legitimacy. Not every regime has met each test, of course; but all have been expected, and most have in some manner attempted, to meet them.

Security by definition involves international considerations. One state's security depends on its relations with others. This is not necessarily the case for prosperity. In theory, the government can help to foster the economic well-being of its citizens simply by attending to economic activity within its own borders. In practice, the determinants of well-being are seldom purely internal. The circle of economic activity has widened since the beginning of the Industrial Revolution. Modern states have grown rich by practicing the economies of scale, selling things to and buying them from people far away, making more and better products available to everyone. If they were confined to trading, investing, and producing only within their own borders, most states would be considerably poorer than they are. For most of them well-being depends on transactions that cross national borders.

Borders are at the heart of the problem of security. According to one body of doctrine, however, they are far from central to economics. They are, or at least ought to be, irrelevant. This is the reigning economic orthodoxy in the West. It is based on the economic theories of Adam Smith, David Ricardo, and their successors, who include most of the professional economists in the West today. The body of "neoclassical" economic doctrine that they have created conceives of markets, the nexus of economic activity, as standing apart from politics and the exercise of state power. Trade, in neoclassical economic thought, proceeds according to the principle of comparative advantage. Each country devotes its resources to making what it can produce most cheaply and efficiently and buys the rest of what it needs from others, who, on the same principle, specialize in other things. In Ricardo's well-known example, Britain, the industrial nation, emphasizes machine-made cloth, while Portugal, a nation of farmers, produces wine. Each will sell as much cloth and wine as is profitable. No other considerations govern their economic decisions. Similarly, capital gravitates to the places where it can earn the highest rate of return.

In Adam Smith's and Ricardo's conception of it, economic activity is spontaneous in that no official body plans or directs it. The economy operates according to impersonal rules based on profitability. This is a "constitutional" view of the economy; all are bound by its rules.[1] Getting and spending, investing and producing are the business of individuals and firms, not of organized political collectives. The state has no role to play.

These principles, especially as applied to economic activity within organized political communities, are known as the doctrine of "laissez faire:" the government leaves merchants and industrialists alone to do as they will. What they do follows the laws of the market. The principles are also known as the doctrine of classical economic liberalism. When these principles are observed by members of the international system in their relations with each other, an "open" international economic order exists. Each sovereign state is open to economic transactions originating beyond its borders.[2]

Sovereign states have seldom behaved entirely in accordance with the precepts of international economic liberalism. Governments have intruded where the doctrine of laissez faire holds they do not belong. They have intervened to make the volume and direction of international economic activity as it affects their own countries different from what the unimpeded play of market forces would have produced. An open international economic order may be desirable but it is not, judging from the historical record, natural.

---

[1] The phrase is from Fred Hirsch and Michael W. Doyle, "Politicization in the World Economy: Necessary Conditions for an International Economic Order," in Fred Hirsch, Michael W. Doyle, and Edward L. Morse, *Alternatives to Monetary Disorder* (New York: McGraw-Hill; 1980s Project/Council on Foreign Relations, 1977). p. 14.

[2] The liberal approach to economics and alternative approaches are summarized in Robert Gilpin, *U.S. Power and the Multinational Corporation* (New York: Basic Books, 1975), pp. 25–31.

A tax on incoming products, a tariff, which reduces the volume of imports, is a familiar source of state revenue. In the twentieth century governments have come to have at their disposal many other devices for influencing the movement of goods across their borders.[3] They have often regulated the international passage of money and capital as well. Their purposes go well beyond raising revenues for themselves.

These purposes conflict with what international economic liberalism takes to be the aim of economic activity. The result of the observance of liberal rules by individuals whose aim is their own economic advantage is the maximum possible *total* wealth. Liberal doctrine does not concern itself with the *distribution* of wealth that results when its rules are followed. The free play of market forces yields an uneven distribution among states. Some always do better than others. Generally speaking, for example, clothmakers do better than winemakers. Neoclassical doctrine is concerned only with the highest possible output of cloth and wine, regardless of who produces and who consumes the products.

Governments, by contrast, tend to be less concerned with the total worth of the world's output than with the value of their own country's share of it. They consider the single state, not the community of states, to be the salient economic unit even as it is the basic unit of international politics. Governments are thus often willing to violate the rules of the market, to interfere with economic transactions, to lower the world's net welfare, if these actions will provide more wealth for their own citizens. Not only are they willing to control economic activity to make themselves richer at the expense of making the world as a whole poorer, but they also often redirect commerce and production to reward some of their own citizens at the expense of others. They often favor a particular distribution of wealth within their own countries.

Governments also interfere in production and investment to promote goals other than economic well-being. They have often sought to foster military strength, which in the twentieth century has depended largely on industrial development. Governments have encouraged industrial development beyond the point of profita-

---

[3] These are discussed in John Hicks, *A Theory of Economic History* (Oxford: Clarendon Press, 1969), p. 163.

bility in order to produce the weapons of modern warfare. A state wholeheartedly committed to liberal principles would purchase weapons from other countries with a comparative advantage in manufacturing them. Historically, few states have displayed such unswerving allegiance to economic laissez faire.

Liberalism assumes that individuals, and therefore states (which, for purely economic purposes, are simply the sum of all individuals who live within their borders), will seek to maximize their wealth. Since the world is the sum of all individuals living in it, the world's total wealth will similarly be maximized. In the real world, however, states act to maximize their own but not necessarily others' wealth, and sometimes they sacrifice wealth to accumulate power. Government interference with the workings of the market is neither unknown nor even uncommon. In the words of Friederich List, a German economist of the nineteenth century who was unsympathetic to liberal principles, the world is emphatically *not* "one indivisible republic of merchants."[4]

Thus the international economic order has not always and everywhere been open. At some times, in some places, it has been closed. This is not to say that there has been no international trade and investment. It is to say that there has been less than the unfettered free market would have produced; that national borders have served as gates guarding national economies, with governments as gatekeepers that do not always permit trade and investment to pass in and out unimpeded and that decide, on grounds other than profitability, what does enter and leave. The opposite of an open international economic order is not, strictly speaking, a "closed" one. It is rather one based on the "authoritative allocation" of resources, with the established authority, the government, deciding what will enter and exit according to political criteria rather than by impersonal market rules.[5]

---

[4] Quoted in David P. Calleo and Benjamin M. Rowland, *America and the World Political Economy: Atlantic Dreams and National Realities* (Bloomington: Indiana University Press, 1973), p. 27.

[5] Hirsch and Doyle, "Polititicization," pp. 11–12; Stephen D. Krasner, *Structural Conflict: The Third World Against Global Liberalism* (Berkeley and Los Angeles: University of California Press, 1985). pp. 5, 66–7; Robert O. Keohane, *After Hegemony: Cooperation and Discord in the World Political Economy* (Princeton, N.J.: Princeton University Press, 1984), p. 21.

The temptation for governments to intervene in economic affairs has grown as they have come to be held responsible for the well-being of those they govern. But no matter how widely it has been practiced in the second half of the twentieth century outside the Communist countries, government interference in international economic activity has been considered exceptional. It has almost invariably been acknowledged as a departure from the desirable and economically proper norm of openness. Before the industrial revolution, however, before Adam Smith and Ricardo, government regulation of international commerce was the norm. It was what established doctrine prescribed. That doctrine was mercantilism. It held that wealth, like power, is relative: When some states become richer, others necessarily become poorer. The government's task, according to mercantilist doctrine, is to enhance its nation's wealth at the expense of others by ensuring a net inflow of precious metals.[6]

In this form the seventeenth-century doctrine of mercantilism no longer commands any credence. Metals are not the source of wealth, and no one doubts the possibility of joint benefit through international economic transactions, which is, after all, the founding assumption of international economic liberalism. But mercantilist behavior, defined here as state interference in international economic activity, remains a feature of modern life, whether to promote national well-being at the expense of global welfare, or to help some sectors or groups within a national economy at the expense of the overall wealth of the nation, or to achieve non-economic aims.

Together the international dimension of national well-being and the mercantilist approach to international economic activity create a parallel between the goal of prosperity and that of security. They are, to be sure, distinct goals, but to the extent that a sovereign state must have access to the economies of others to ensure a desired level of welfare for its citizens, and to the extent that others are disposed to mercantilist policies that inhibit access, the task of fostering public welfare has certain similarities to the problem of

[6] On mercantilism see Albert O. Hirschman, *National Power and the Structure of Foreign Trade*, expanded ed. (Berkeley and Los Angeles: University of California Press, 1980; first published, 1945), p. 4, and Hicks, *Economic History*, p. 161.

remaining secure. In both cases the point of departure, the core of the problem, is the division of the world into separate sovereign states. The parallel can be taken even farther. The problem of creating and preserving an open international economic order, in which the free flow of goods and capital and therefore the prosperity of states that depend on this is guaranteed, is a collective task. It can be compared to the task of achieving collective arrangements for security.[7] They have three cardinal features in common.

First, each is a property of the international system as a whole. No single state can achieve either by itself. To put it differently, both an open international economic order and collective security arrangements involve a relationship among sovereign political units rather than characteristics of these units themselves. Second, each requires national policies of self-restraint that are in some sense unnatural. Each, that is, requires national conduct that runs counter to a state's normal impulses, the mercantilist approach to economic policy being here defined as normal in the same way that the search for national advantage can be considered the norm in the realm of security. Third, each is difficult to achieve because no overarching authority, no global sovereign, exists to enforce the required conduct, which must therefore be voluntary.

The extent to which particular states face such a problem in promoting the welfare of their citizens varies widely. The more a state depends on an open international order for its well-being – and dependence is not always simple to calculate – the more the goal of prosperity will resemble the problem of achieving security in collective fashion.[8]

Japan has depended heavily on an open international economic order. Japan's prosperity since 1945 has, arguably, owed more to international trade than has the well-being of any other member of the international system. Closing national gates to international commerce would do greater damage to Japan than to any other

[7] On collective security arrangements see Chapter 1, Section II, and Chapter 2, Section II.
[8] In this respect the problem of national well-being is like the security dilemma. Since it is a consequence of anarchy, the basic feature of the international system to which all sovereign states belong, it is potentially relevant for each of them. But it is not equally important for all. Like the security dilemma, it matters more to some than to others.

nation. Mercantilist policies practiced by others are potentially more costly to the Japanese than to any other people.[9] After 1945, Japan confronted a security problem in the ordinary sense of the term. It faced a military threat from the Soviet Union and adopted a familiar policy to cope with it: an alliance with the United States. Since the United States was crucial for Japan's prosperity, the conditions for Japan's economic well-being and physical protection were related. In relying on another power for protection Japan was not unusual, nor did it employ a collective approach to security as the term has been defined here. The extent of its reliance on access to other economies was atypical, however, and Japan's prosperity did depend on collective arrangements.

The simplest relevant statistic does not, at first glance, bear out Japan's unusual economic dependence on others: Japan devotes a smaller percentage of its gross national product to trade than do many other industrial countries. Almost every country of Western Europe has a higher proportion of its total national economic activity in international commerce.[10] It is the *composition* of Japan's trade that has, in the first instance, made it so dependent on the rest of the world. It is one of the great industrial nations of the twentieth century. Industrial production requires raw materials. Japan has none within its borders; virtually all must be imported. The industrial countries for which imports have constituted a higher percentage of total economic activity have bought consumer products abroad, which they could either forgo or produce at home (albeit less efficiently) if foreign supplies were withheld. Japan could neither substitute for imported raw materials nor do without them. To lose access to them would mean losing the capacity to function as an industrial country and so to suffer a radical decline in economic well-being.[11]

---

[9] "Of all the industrial countries, Japan has the greatest stake in a smoothly functioning international economic system subject to agreed norms and rules. Its dependence on foreigners for the necessities of life is greater than that of any other major industrial country." Isaiah Frank, "Introduction," in Isaiah Frank, ed., *The Japanese Economy in International Perspective* (Baltimore, Md.: Johns Hopkins University Press, 1975), p. 13.

[10] Clark A. Murdock, "Economic Factors as Objects of Security: Economics, Security, and Vulnerability," in Klaus Knorr and Frank N. Trager, eds., *Economic Issues and National Security* (Lawrence: Regents Press of Kansas), pp. 82–3.

[11] The characterization of Japan's international economic position is drawn from

In order to import raw materials, Japan had to export finished goods to pay for them. The Japanese were unable to sell much of what they made to the primary producers themselves, who were too poor to buy a great deal. They found their main foreign markets in the industrial world, especially the United States.

Other industrial countries had to import raw materials as well. None of the Western European nations was wholly self-sufficient. But Japan's requirements were larger because the Japanese economy was bigger – it was the largest importer of raw materials in the world – and so more vulnerable to mercantilist policies. The Europeans, too, had to export their manufactures, but they could trade with their neighbors – that is, with each other. Both Japan's sources of supplies *and* its markets were located thousands of miles from the Japanese archipelago. Rather than short railway journeys, as in Europe, long ocean voyages, susceptible to disruption, kept the Japanese economic machine working.

Japan was more vulnerable than the European countries that, from a purely statistical point of view, had more economic interaction with others, because the Europeans were closer not only geographically but also politically and culturally to their trading partners. There was a long history of close relations among the European states. Not all of it was peaceful, to be sure, but history did lend an organic character to economic ties among them, which was fortified by the establishment of the European Economic Community. This was something that Japan's international economic relations lacked.[12] The Japanese did not have a long history of

Masataka Kosaka, "The International Economic Policy of Japan," in Robert Scalapino, ed., *The Foreign Policy of Modern Japan* (Berkeley and Los Angeles: University of California Press, 1977); T. J. Pempel, "Japanese Foreign Economic Policy: The Domestic Bases for International Behavior," in Peter J. Katzenstein, ed.: *Between Power and Plenty: Foreign Economic Policies of Advanced Industrial States* (Madison: University of Wisconsin Press, 1978), pp. 143–4; Edwin O. Reischauer, *The Japanese* (Cambridge, Mass., Harvard University Press, 1978), pp. 369–71; Leon Hollerman, "Foreign Trade in Japan's Economic Transition," in Frank, ed., *Japanese Economy*, pp. 177–8; J. J. Kaplan, "Raw-Materials Policy: Japan and the United States," in Frank, ed., *Japanese Economy*, p. 233.

[12] Japan's security policies were also both similar to and different from those of the Western Europeans. Both protected themselves against the Soviet Union through an alliance with the United States. Both the Atlantic and Pacific alliances suffered the stresses to which all alliances are subject, the complementary

dealing with the countries either from which they bought raw materials or to which they sold what they made. Nor were they like these other countries culturally. Japan was unlike *any* other country. All peoples feel themselves to be unique, and to some extent all are. Some, however, are more distinctive than others, and the Japanese sense of their own singularity and the feelings of isolation and vulnerability to which this gave rise seemed more pronounced than those of other nations.[13]

Japan's reliance on an open international economic order, in sum, was greater than that of any other country, because it could not do without foreign raw materials and overseas markets, because the economic network on which Japan depended was unusually broad, stretching to the Persian Gulf, the source of its oil, and to

dangers of abandonment and entrapment (see Chapter 2, p. 101). During the postwar period, the Europeans and the Japanese were concerned with both dangers, but the sequence was different in the two cases. From 1950 to 1970 the Europeans feared that the United States would not defend them if the Soviet Union attacked. The American government constantly reaffirmed its commitment to protect them. In the 1970s, the fear of entrapment supplanted the anticipation of abandonment. The Europeans did not expect to be entrapped in a war they did not want but did fear that the United States would push them into a worse relationship with the Soviet Union than they desired. Détente between the United States and the Soviet Union ended at the close of the 1970s. The Europeans wished to preserve their own détente with the East and so dragged their feet at joining the United States in political reprisals for the invasion of Afghanistan. The deployment of intermediate-range nuclear forces in the early 1980s was controversial for the same reason. The Western Europeans did not wish to be drawn into worse relations with the Soviet Union and the Eastern Europeans, who strongly objected to the weapons.

Japan experienced the inbuilt stresses of alliance in the reverse order. Throughout the postwar period the threat of a Soviet attack generally seemed less pressing in the Pacific than in the center of Europe. But insofar as they were concerned about their alliance with the United States, the Japanese were at first leery of being drawn into the American wars in Korea and Indochina. In the 1970s the sources of Japanese unhappiness with the United States more closely resembled the fear of abandonment. President Nixon's trip to China affected Japanese interests, but Tokyo was not consulted. At the beginning of the 1980s, President Carter proposed to withdraw the American ground troops that had been stationed in Korea since the end of the war there in 1954, which was a sensitive matter for the Japanese because the Korean peninsula served as a kind of first line of defense for their islands.

[13] See Reischauer, *The Japanese*, p. 379; Robert Shaplen, *A Turning Wheel: Three Decades of the Asian Revolution as Witnessed by a Correspondent for "The New Yorker"* (New York: Random House, 1979), p. 298; Kosaka, "International Economic Policy," p. 221.

North America as well as to countries closer to the Japanese archipelago, and because the cultural and political distance between the Japanese and those with whom they had to do business to sustain their standard of living was unusually pronounced. For Japan, more than for any other country, therefore, the problem of ensuring economic well-being was like the problem of providing collective arrangements for security.[14]

II

An open international economy, with economic relations among sovereign states based on impersonal, constitutional, market principles, is a recent development. For most of recorded history the norm was localized barter or production according to political direction, along with subsistence agriculture and a trickle of trade in very expensive commodities such as spices and precious stones. The industrial revolution, with its new products and swifter, surer means of transportation, made economies of scale more productive and the division of labor more extensive than ever before. Adam Smith, Ricardo, and their followers propagated the idea that free exchange was the best way to create wealth.

Since the coming of the machine age there have been two periods in which the international economic order has been relatively open. The first began in the 1840s and lasted, although in considerably modified form, until the outbreak of World War I in 1914. The second began after World War II and endured, although not, again, in precisely the form in which it was established, for more than forty years. In neither period was international economic activity wholly uninhibited. In the first, the major countries on the European continent erected tariff barriers in the late 1870s. The United States also practiced protection for much of the time.[15] In

---

[14] One conspicuous difference between them is that, while collective security arrangements must include all the major powers of the international system to be effective, an open international economic order need not do so. Even Japan, for which the extent of international economic openness had to be greatest, did perfectly well without access to China and the Soviet Union for most of the postwar period.

[15] Calleo and Rowland, *World Political Economy*, p. 26. On both periods see also Arthur A. Stein, "The Hegemon's Dilemma: Great Britain, the United States

the second the rules of economic interaction were not entirely liberal from the start,[16] and the policies of the principal economic powers became more mercantilist in the decades following the end of the war.

Still, national economies in these two periods were considerably more open to transactions with other countries than before the middle of the nineteenth century, when mercantilist policies were the rule. For much of both, the volume of international economic activity steadily expanded. There was, during most of each era in most countries, a presumption, even if it was not always honored, in favor of liberal economic precepts and against government interference with trade and investment across national borders.

The economic liberalism of these two periods, imperfect though it was, stands, finally, in contrast to the predominant practices of the years that separate them, the period between the two world wars. Especially during the 1930s the international economic order was not at all open. Mercantilist policies reigned. Tariffs, competitive devaluations, and the general philosophy of trying to use them to gain economic advantage known as "beggar-thy-neighbor" were widespread. Far from being an integrated market, the world was divided into several more or less self-contained economic blocs having little to do with one another.

The degree of openness of the international economic order affected Japan's economic policies, and its security policies as well. Isolated from the rest of the world until 1854, when the American Commodore Matthew Perry's fleet arrived in Tokyo Bay, the Japanese thereupon set about making themselves a modern industrial nation. Within fifty years, by the outset of the twentieth century, they had succeeded. One condition of their success was access to the raw materials and markets of other countries. The characteristic Japanese pattern of the postwar period was in evidence well before 1945. The open international economic order of the nineteenth and early twentieth centuries contributed to Japan's early industrial

and the International Economic Order," *International Organization*, 38, no. 2 (1984): 355–86.

[16] This is one of the principal themes of John Gerard Ruggie, "International Regimes, Transactions and Change: Embedded Liberalism in the Postwar Economic Order," in Stephen D. Krasner, ed., *International Regimes* (Ithaca, N.Y.: Cornell University Press, 1983).

development. The breakdown of international economic liberalism in the interwar period, and especially in the 1930s, in turn had a substantial effect on Japan.

In the 1920s Japan's relations with its neighbors and with other industrial countries were relatively good. The decade was a peaceful one in Europe as well. The major powers tried to work out satisfactory arrangements for security and to restore the level of economic cooperation they had achieved before 1914.[17] In the 1930s both economic and political relations worsened, and in 1939 World War II began. Japan's foreign policies underwent a similar shift, from an emphasis on international cooperation to unilateral military measures.[18] The Japanese took a series of steps in Asia that brought them into conflict with the Western powers. Japan, like other great powers, had obtained economic concessions in China. The Japanese thought of themselves as having a special proprietary interest there and in 1931 moved to assert it by forcibly establishing a puppet regime in the province of Manchuria. For this they were eventually expelled from the League of Nations. In 1937 the Marco Polo Bridge incident marked the beginning of a full-scale, albeit undeclared, war with China. In 1940, with Europe already at war, Japan issued a declaration of common cause with Fascist Italy and Nazi Germany. Finally, at the end of 1941, the war in the Pacific began with a Japanese attack on the American naval base at Pearl Harbor, Hawaii, and on British and Dutch colonial possessions in Southeast Asia.

The Western historical reconstruction of the origins of World War II has placed the blame on Japan's internal politics, which are generally considered to have produced an aggressive foreign policy that culminated in the December 1941 attack. An "inside-out" explanation of Japanese behavior gained broad acceptance in the aftermath of the war.[19]

---

[17] See Chapter 2, Section II.

[18] Akira Iriye, "Japan's Policies Toward the United States," in James William Morley, ed., *Japan's Foreign Policy, 1868–1941: A Research Guide* (New York: Columbia University Press, 1974), p. 444. See also Michael A. Barnhart, *Japan Prepares for Total War: The Search for Economic Security, 1919–1941* (Ithaca, N.Y.: Cornell University Press, 1987), which stresses the quest for economic self-sufficiency as one of Japan's chief aims in the interwar period.

[19] James B. Crowley, *Japan's Quest for Autonomy: National Security and Foreign Policy, 1930–1938* (Princeton, N.J.: Princeton University Press, 1966), p. xiv;

There is certainly some truth to this general explanation. The growing militance of Japanese foreign policy in the 1930s coincided with the rising influence of the armed forces within Japan. The Mukden incident of 1931, which led to the establishment of the puppet regime of Manchukuo, was initiated by officers of the Kwantung Army in Manchuria without their having consulted, or received permission from, the civilian authorities in Tokyo. In the Marco Polo Bridge episode six years later, the cabinet was again subject to pressure from the military.[20] Over the course of the decade, the role of the military in shaping foreign policy increased.

Japan's imperial policy was not, however, purely the initiative of the armed forces. Japan's leaders and the society as a whole broadly supported the drive to secure a sphere of control in East Asia, especially in China.[21] Virtually all Japanese believed that, to survive, their country had to dominate its neighbors. The ideology of expansion, which was born at home, explains many of the actions Japan took abroad between 1931 and 1945. But Japanese policies were neither wholly the result of strictly political considerations nor entirely the product of internal forces. They responded as well to international events, and in particular to developments in the international economic order.[22]

Japan's imperial design for Asia had an economic component. The Greater East Asia Co-Prosperity Sphere that the Japanese aspired to establish in China and Southeast Asia was to be an integrated economic bloc as well as a zone of Japanese political dominance. They had to obtain raw materials and to sell what they produced somewhere. The rise of mercantilist policies among the industrial countries in the 1930s denied them access to countries

---

Dorothy Borg, "Introduction," in Dorothy Borg and Shumpei Okamoto, eds., *Pearl Harbor as History: Japanese–American Relations, 1931–1941* (New York: Columbia University Press), 1973, pp. xii–xiii; Richard W. Leopold, "Historiographical Reflections," in ibid., p. 19. The Borg and Okamoto volume, a collection of essays by Japanese and American scholars, itself reflects a bias toward an explanation based on domestic factors. Almost all the essays concern specific institutions in each country such as the armed forces and the foreign ministry.

[20] Akira Iriye, *Across the Pacific: An Inner History of American–East Asian Relations* (New York: Harcourt, Brace & World, 1967), pp. 172–3; Crowley, *Japan's Quest*, p. 380.

[21] Ibid., p. xvii, 32.

[22] Iriye, "Japan's Policies," p. 444.

with which they had previously traded. The British Empire, for example, was not as open to them as it had once been.[23]

In the 1920s Japan had attempted to follow a program of cooperation with the Western powers, a program known as "Shidehara diplomacy" after the foreign minister with whom it was closely identified. But with the onset of the world depression and the adoption of beggar-thy-neighbor policies by the major countries, the others would not cooperate. The growing illiberalism of the international economic order reinforced the imperial trends within Japan by closing off an alternative approach to foreign policy.[24]

The mercantilist blocs that formed during the decade served not only as obstacles to Japan's well-being but also as political models for the Japanese. Exclusive economic zones protected from the outside world by tariffs and other mercantile barriers with powerful countries at their centers seemed to be the wave of the future. The division of the world into separate blocs was already well underway by the mid-1930s. Britain had abandoned the gold standard and the venerable British commitment to international liberalism in 1931; the Ottawa Preference System of 1932 appeared to be a step toward the conversion of the empire from the free-trade area that it had been since the nineteenth century to a closed economic unit.[25] The French had their empire. German economic policies were designed to create a dependent economic sphere in Central Europe. The Bolsheviks had closed Russia's borders after their victory in the civil war that followed the 1917 revolution. International commerce resumed on a modest scale with Lenin's

---

[23] Crowley, *Japan's Quest*, p. 391; Crowley, "Japan's Military Foreign Policies," in Morley, ed., *Japan's Foreign Policy*, p. 85; Iriye, "Japan's Policies," pp. 443, 447, 454; Iriye, *Across the Pacific*, p. 207; Kosaka, "International Economic Policy of Japan," p. 213; see in particular the story cited in Chalmers Johnson "MITI and Japanese International Economic Policy," in Scalapino, ed., *Foreign Policy of Modern Japan*, pp. 260–1; Ian H. Nish, "Japan's Policies Toward Britain," in Morley, ed., *Japan's Foreign Policy*, p. 235.

[24] Iriye, "Japan's Policies," p. 437; Iriye, *Across the Pacific*, p. 175. On the different tendencies within the Japanese foreign ministry see Leopold, "Reflections," p. 5.

[25] Robert Skidelsky, "Retreat from Leadership: The Evolution of British Economic Foreign Policy, 1870–1939," in Benjamin M. Rowland, ed., *Balance of Power or Hegemony: The Interwar Monetary System* (New York: New York University Press, 1976), p. 180. Skidelsky argues that in fact an integrated mercantile bloc was *not* created.

New Economic Policy of the mid-1920s but ceased again when Stalin came to power and set the country on the path of economic autarky. And with the Montevideo Agreement of 1933, the United States appeared to be consolidating its own mercantile bloc in the Western Hemisphere.[26]

In seeking to establish Greater East Asia the Japanese were, in their own view, only doing what other great powers had already done. They were doing what they believed they *had* to do to remain a great power. They compared their aspirations for dominance in East Asia to the American Monroe Doctrine, which warned the European great powers not to trespass in Latin America. They were simply asserting a right in their own part of the world that the United States had long enjoyed in its own region.[27]

---

[26] Calleo and Rowland, *World Political Economy*, p. 36.

[27] Iriye, *Across the Pacific*, p. 210; Leopold, "Reflections," p. 17; Mashakoji Kinide, "The Structure of Japanese–American Relations in the 1930s," in Borg and Okamoto, eds., *Pearl Harbor*, p. 597. There are striking similarities between Japan during the period leading up to World War II and Wilhelmine Germany before World War I. Both came late to the status of great power. Japan remained in virtual isolation from the rest of the world until 1854; Germany was unified only in 1871. Each undertook a program of rapid economic modernization and became an industrial giant. In each case economic development served as the foundation for military power. Each won a sudden, unexpected military victory that heralded its arrival as a great power: Germany over France in 1871, Japan over Russia in 1905. In fact, Germany served as a kind of model for Japan until 1914. Isaac Shapiro, "The Risen Sun," *Foreign Policy*, 41 (Winter 1980–1): 66.

There are, as Alexander Gerschenkron noted, certain advantages to being a "late industrializer" and replicating the stages of economic development that others have already passed. ("Economic Backwardness in Historical Perspective," in Alexander Gerschenkron, ed., *Economic Backwardness in Historical Perspective: A Book of Essays* [Cambridge, Mass.: Harvard University Press, 1966]). Coming late offers the possibility of accelerating the process and even overtaking those that have gone before. As "late developers" in international *political* terms, however, both Germany and Japan suffered from a common handicap: The international stage was already crowded when they stepped onto it. Both felt entitled to the same privileges, influence, and spheres of predominance that their predecessors as great powers already had. But these great-power prerogatives were in short supply. Most of the world had already been parceled out. Those who had acquired empires in an earlier day were not eager to share what they had with newcomers. The Germans felt a sense of grievance against the British. The Japanese felt the same way toward the United States and Great Britain, powers that had acquired their own imperial domains but wished to deny the Japanese an empire in East Asia. To the established great powers, the newcomers seemed dangerously aggressive. To Germany in the

Although the roots of the Japanese–American conflict lie ultimately in radically different visions of Japan's proper role in East Asia, it was economic issues that triggered the outbreak of war. The United States never recognized Japan's conquests in China. In the 1930s the Americans came to see Japan as a threat to world peace, an image reinforced by its tripartite pact with Hitler and Mussolini in 1940. The United States protested widening Japanese control in China and the brutal methods Japan employed to consolidate it, ultimately putting in place economic sanctions against Japan. These posed serious problems for the Japanese, who depended, after all, on foreign sources of supply for raw materials. In 1941 the Japanese government was simultaneously pinched by the American trade embargo, especially as it affected the delivery of oil, and tempted to seize the European colonial possessions in Asia by the collapse of metropolitan France, the occupation of the Netherlands, and the defeat of Britain in Europe. Oil and other

first decade of the twentieth century and to Japan in the 1930s, Britain and the United States appeared selfish and hypocritical.

Both Germany and Japan felt themselves to be victims of the mercantilist policies of others. The Germans launched a war to win a middle European empire in 1914 for some of the same reasons that the Japanese tried to establish Greater East Asia several decades later. Both countries felt themselves being surrounded by hostile powers: The Triple Entente that confronted Germany corresponds to Japanese fears of an "ABCD" (American, British, Chinese, and Dutch) encirclement (Seizaburo Sato, "The Foundations of Modern Japanese Foreign Policy," in Scalapino, ed., *Foreign Policy of Modern Japan*, p. 380). Both Germany and Japan started wars because they feared that time was working against them. In 1914, the Germans worried that the Russians would soon surpass them in military strength. In the 1930s, the Japanese were concerned that the rising tide of nationalism in China would ultimately force them out. In 1941 they foresaw economic ruin if the stalemate with the United States continued.

The parallels extend to the domestic politics of the two countries. Both governments in the years leading up to war were odd, unstable hybrids of authoritarian and democratic forms, a mixture that, arguably, contributed to their erratic and ultimately counterproductive foreign policies. When war came in each case, the military dominated the government.

There is a final, ironic point that the two countries have in common. The German historian Fritz Fischer has argued that the 1914 conflict was a "war of illusions" for the Germans because they wrongly believed that they needed formal political control to dominate Central Europe, when in fact their economic strength was already giving them a position of informal dominance without war. Similarly, Japan achieved a position of economic if not political primacy in much of Asia after 1945 without firing a shot.

raw materials were available in the Dutch East Indies and the British Malay Peninsula.[28]

The Japanese leaders calculated that to strike southward would bring war with the United States. They faced a choice, therefore, between an accord with the Americans and an empire in Southeast Asia. Negotiations to resolve the dispute between the two countries failed. Once again the sticking point was China. In return for lifting its embargo, the United States demanded the restoration of the status quo before 1931 in East Asia. Washington demanded, that is, that Japan quit China.[29] The Japanese refused to abandon their imperial possession. The country's leaders decided to solve their economic problems by bringing Southeast Asia into their empire. Rather than wait for the United States to respond, they took the initiative themselves and, as a prelude to a sweep to the south, attacked the American Pacific Fleet at Pearl Harbor.

In the aftermath of the war that began with that attack and ended with Japan's crushing defeat, international economic conditions continued to play an important role in defining Japan's foreign policies. In the open international economic order of the postwar period Japan flourished. Its economic requirements had not changed; they were the same as they had been since early in the century. Japan still needed to import raw materials and export finished products. After 1945, the Japanese obtained access to the markets they required not only without constructing an imperial bloc but without even mustering large military forces. It is neither fanciful nor altogether exaggerated to say that the liberal international economic order created after World War II served the same purpose as, or at least one of the central purposes of, the Greater East Asia Co-Prosperity Sphere that Japan had tried, brutally, with considerable bloodshed, and finally without success, to assemble between the two world wars.

Although Japan drew considerable benefit from the open international economic order before World War I and after World War

---

[28] Ibid., pp. 201–2; Robert A. Scalapino, "Perspectives on Modern Japanese Foreign Policy," in Scalapino, ed., *Foreign Policy of Modern Japan*, p. 396.

[29] This was the substance of the "Hull note" from American Secretary of State Cordell Hull on November 26, 1941, which sealed Japan's decision to strike south, and therefore east. Iriye, *Across the Pacific*, pp. 218–9; Iriye, "Japan's Policies," p. 456.

II, the Japanese did little to make it possible. Others assumed responsibility for supporting and enforcing liberal international practices. Both periods were associated with the economic predominance of a single power. On each occasion the policies of an economic hegemon, which far surpassed other countries in economic strength and was also powerful in military terms, underwrote the arrangements by which goods and capital passed more or less freely across the borders of sovereign states. In the nineteenth century the predominant power was Great Britain. After 1945, it was the United States.

On neither occasion did the open order arise spontaneously, out of a happy coincidence of uncoordinated national policies. Like other social institutions, it had to be created and sustained.[30] A free market both within and among sovereign jurisdictions is like an old-fashioned watch. Most of the time it ticks away automatically. But from time to time the equivalent of a watchmaker is required to fix and wind it. It is the state that first helps to establish and then tends the market within its borders. There is no international sovereign, but in the nineteenth and twentieth centuries Britain and the United States performed the functions for the international economic order that the state undertakes where its writ runs.

Economic transactions in an open international order are voluntary. That is the essence of liberalism. Neither the British nor the Americans compelled others to trade. But they did encourage trade and supported a setting in which trade flourished. Liberal international economic rules require both internal acceptance and external support. The term "hegemon" perhaps has a more ominous connotation than is warranted, implying as it often does the exercise of coercion. There was some in each case, but both Britain and the United States provided services to other members of the international system as well. Both served as the international economic leader.

Like national governments, the two hegemons induced others to follow the rules of international liberalism in economic transactions. Once they did, once the open order was in place, Great Britain and the United States, like national governments, per-

---

[30] Gilpin, *War and Change*, p. 130; Skidelsky, "Retreat from Leadership," pp. 152–3.

formed two types of service. They helped to maintain the liberal procedures in good repair, and they intervened when cyclical disturbances threatened to damage or destroy them and send the members of the international economic system back to national mercantilist policies.[31]

An open international economic order requires a secure political basis. No one is forced to buy, sell, or invest, but everyone who does so must know that the business he undertakes will proceed as agreed. There must be enforceable law or, among sovereign states, something analogous to it to ensure that contracts are honored and property rights respected and that transactions can proceed without interruption.

To sustain a large volume of exchanges, the international economy needs the kind of foundation that the state provides for markets within national borders.[32] In the nineteenth century, Britain, with its empire and navy, performed this service. The "Pax Britannica" underpinned the first global expansion of the free market. Within its far-flung imperial boundaries Britain *was* the government. The Royal Navy ensured uninterrupted seaborne commerce and on occasion enforced proper commercial behavior far from the British Isles (especially where Britain had commercial treaties) through shows of force, bombardment, and occasionally even invasion. The British government intervened abroad to enforce commercial agreements but not, on the whole, to press for advantages for British merchants or investors.[33]

---

[31] The role of the international economic hegemon in supporting an open system is found in Charles P. Kindleberger, *The World in Depression, 1929–1939* (Berkeley and Los Angeles: University of California Press, 1973), Chaps. 1 and 14; Robert Gilpin, *The Political Economy of International Relations* (Princeton, N.J.: Princeton University Press, 1987), pp. 72–80, 85–92; Skidelsky, "Retreat from Leadership," pp. 151–62; and Keohane, *After Hegemony*, pp. 136–41. The account that follows is based on these sources. David Calleo argues that Britain was not a hegemon before 1914 in the same way that the United States was after 1945 but bases his distinction on a single difference between the two: the greater degree of freedom from international monetary rules that the United States enjoyed. Even accepting this difference, in other ways Britain and the United States acted similarly as leaders in the international economic arena. David Calleo, "The Historiography of the Interwar Period: Reconsiderations," in Rowland, ed., *Balance of Power*, pp. 245–50.

[32] Skidelsky, "Retreat from Leadership," p. 155; Gilpin, *War and Change*, p. 155; Hicks, *Economic History*, p. 71.

[33] D. C. M. Platt, *Finance, Trade and Politics in British Foreign Policy, 1815–1914* (New York: Oxford University Press, 1968), esp. pp. xvi, 33, 41, 92.

After 1945, the United States played the same role as had the British. As with Britain, American military commitments had mainly political rather than economic purposes.[34] They were not undertaken primarily to guarantee unimpeded international commerce, but they had that effect. After 1945, American military deployments were more extensive and on the whole more costly than were Britain's in the nineteenth century.[35] But the United States rarely felt impelled to punish violations of international liberal economic practices by military reprisals. There was little in the way of American military intervention to compel wayward countries to pay their bills. Most of the important members of the open international economic order belonged to the American security coalition. They depended on American arms for protection against attack, which gave liberal policies among them a firm foundation.

Both Great Britain and the United States coaxed and occasionally coerced others to join the open international economic order, to discard mercantilist policies and abide by liberal norms. Liberal policies almost always brought benefits over the long term, but often had short-term costs for some sectors of national economies, and so were not always automatically adopted. Britain's imperial might and the lure of access to what was in the mid-nineteenth century the most powerful economy on earth helped to overcome the obstacles that short-term costs presented and to draw other countries into the open order.

Similarly, after 1945, the United States offered inducements and threatened sanctions to persuade others to abide by liberal principles. Immediately after World War II, for example, the British themselves, once the champions of liberalism, were reluctant to adopt free-trade policies and to make the pound convertible into other currencies. Their economy had been damaged by the war, and they feared that it could not stand up to the exposure of international competition. At the same time, the British desperately needed loans from the United States. The Americans made it clear that to receive them Britain would have to adopt the liberal policies the United States favored. In exchange for British agreement to comply with liberal norms the United States not only extended loans but also agreed, among other concessions, to postpone con-

[34] See Chapter 3, p. 136.
[35] Gilpin, *U.S. Power*, p. 83.

vertibility of the pound sterling in order to allow the British economy a grace period in which to strengthen itself. The American
government adopted a similar approach to other countries: carrots
and sticks, threats and bribes – sometimes known to economists
as "side payments" – to draw them into a network of liberal economic exchanges.[36]

In addition to a political environment in which market exchanges
across national borders could be made with confidence, and a combination of pressure and enforcement that drew others into a system
of free market relations, Great Britain and the United States provided a third service without which an open international economic
order could not have functioned. While the first of these services
had its roots in their military might and the second depended on
both military and economic power, the third was made possible
almost entirely by the strength of their domestic economies. An
integrated market requires an accepted medium of exchange in
order to operate smoothly. It needs a currency that all are willing
to hold and to use. In the modern era the state has monopolized
the supply of money to national economies. In the absence of
international government, Britain in the nineteenth century and
the United States in the twentieth provided a unit of exchange for
international economic activity.

The pound sterling (which was linked to gold) in the earlier
period and the dollar (with a similar but weaker link) were almost
universally accepted as a means of settlement for international
transactions or in exchange for other national currencies. The two
served as reserve currencies as well. Other governments held them
to back their own money, which they promised, in effect, to exchange upon request for sterling or dollars. The pound sterling and
the dollar were attractive, in turn, because the national economies
of Britain and the United States stood behind them. Others had
confidence in these economies, believing that they themselves
would always wish to purchase goods that Britain and the United
States produced and so would always have a use for sterling and
dollars and that third countries would have similar confidence and
so would accept their own currencies.[37]

---

[36] Keohane, *After Hegemony*, pp. 72–3, 149–50; Krasner, *Structural Conflict*,
   pp. 64–5; Hirsch and Doyle, "Politicization," pp. 30–2.
[37] Hicks, *Economic History*, pp. 64–8; Gilpin, *War and Change*, pp. 130–1;
   Joanne Gowa, *Closing the Gold Window: Domestic Politics and the End of*

In neoclassical economic theory in its pristine form, the buying and selling, investing and producing that take place in a free market, once begun, gain a momentum of their own and continue indefinitely. The market, in this conception, is a kind of perpetual motion machine. The locus of commerce and industry may change. Particular goods go in and out of production. Firms are born and die. Prices rise and fall. But through it all, economic activity proceeds steadily.

In fact, it has turned out to be cyclical. Economic activity in market systems has peaks and valleys. Within national economies these valleys can bring bankruptcy, unemployment, and widespread hardship. When the international economic order suffers a decline, states have tended to attempt to protect themselves either by withdrawing or by taking unilateral measures. Cyclical declines in the international economy foster mercantilist behavior. The hegemonic powers played important roles in combating this behavior. Both Great Britain and the United States, during their periods of predominance, acted at moments of economic stagnation to help revive economic activity, discourage mercantilist policies, and sustain the openness of the international economic order.

Each sustained international trade by providing a market for exports when other countries were closed to them. In the nineteenth century Britain resolutely practiced free trade even when the other major economic powers favored and practiced protection.[38] In periods of economic contraction, countries are tempted to close their borders to protect their own producers. When one does so, others reciprocate. Protection, itself economically disadvantageous, can have other adverse consequences. Without the foreign exchange that trade brings, countries may be forced to default on foreign loans, for example. By keeping its market open, Britain helped limit such mercantilist cycles.

The United States did the same after 1945. Access to the Amer-

---

Bretton Woods (Ithaca, N.Y.: Cornell University Press, 1983), pp. 17, 37, 41. Since both the pound sterling and the dollar were initially linked to gold, others accepted them in the belief that they could be redeemed for bullion. Once the two currencies were used widely, others had an interest in continuing to use them that was independent of the performance of the British and American economies. Nonetheless, each initially attained its status as a key currency because of the power of the economy that issued it.

[38] Kindleberger, *The World in Depression*, pp. 293–4; Skidelsky, "Retreat from Leadership," pp. 157–8; Platt, *Finance, Trade and Politics*, pp. xv, xxi, 152.

ican market was especially important for reviving the European economies that had been shattered by war. Recovery was partly driven by demand. The demand for European products among the impoverished, dislocated peoples of Europe was initially modest and was supplemented by demand from the United States.

Economic recovery was driven by supply as well, which requires capital, the seeds of economic activity. Britain in the nineteenth century and the United States in the twentieth provided capital when it was unavailable from other sources. The City of London served as a kind of capital market for the world in the earlier period, channeling investment funds to the European continent, to Latin America, to the empire, and to the United States.[39] The United States performed the same role after 1945, especially, again, in the immediate aftermath of the war, when capital was in particularly short supply.[40] The European Recovery Program, better known as the Marshall Plan after the American secretary of state George C. Marshall, who first proposed it, provided capital to reignite the engines of European industry. After 1945, the United States also supplied capital through private banks and American-based multinational corporations.

Finally, Britain in the nineteenth century and the United States after 1945 (for much of the period in conjunction with others) served as the lender of last resort for national currencies under pressure.[41]

The services that Britain and the United States performed for the international economy as a whole – as guarantors of its political foundations, entrepreneurs of a liberal order, markets for goods that could not be sold anywhere else, sources of an internationally accepted currency, purveyors of countercyclical capital flows, and lenders of last resort – can be seen as the costs of maintaining a liberal order. The two hegemonic states paid these costs. Of all members of the international system they could most easily afford to pay them. They were the wealthiest. It is easier, moreover, for

---

[39] Gilpin, *U.S. Power*, p. 97; Skidelsky, "Retreat from Leadership," p. 160; Platt, *Finance, Trade and Politics*, p. 3.

[40] Capital is the surplus of resources over and above what is consumed. The Europeans had no surpluses of anything. They did not, in 1945, have enough to satisfy the minimal requirements for consumption.

[41] Skidelsky, "Retreat from Leadership," pp. 160–1; Kindleberger, *The World in Depression*, p. 307.

one country, with a single locus of decision making, to pay such costs than to take up a collection among several countries.[42]

Although Britain and the United States paid the costs of sustaining the open international economic order, it does not follow that any country so placed will necessarily act as they did. There have always been dominant economic powers; only recently have liberal economic practices been common. Historically, most hegemons have not supported systems of market rules but instead have engaged in the mercantilist exploitation of their weaker neighbors. Britain and the United States differed from other states in similar positions in the international system in that their leaders, and to a lesser extent their publics, strongly believed in the principles of international economic liberalism.[43] For each, the importance of free markets was an article of faith and of conviction. For the British free trade was "itself a good, like virtue, holiness and righteousness, to be loved, admired, honoured and steadfastly adopted for its own sake."[44] The United States was equally dedicated to international liberalism after World War II. It was widely believed in the United States that the mercantilist policies of the major European powers in the 1930s had been important causes of that war. Free markets, as a saying popular in both the United States and Britain has it, make free men. After 1945, Americans also believed that free markets made for world peace.

The British and American policy of defraying the costs of an open international economic order was neither purely ideological nor idealistic, although it was partly both. Each country also had an economic interest in carrying out these policies; in each case, self-interest reinforced conviction.

[42] The point is strongly asserted by Kindleberger: "With a duumvirate, a troika, or slightly wider forms of collective responsibility, the buck has no place to stop." *The World in Depression*, pp. 299–300. The issue is addressed below, pp. 382–3.

[43] Ruggie argues that an open order requires both a concentration of power and a "social purpose" – that is, a commitment to liberal economic precepts. "International Regimes," pp. 198–201. Gilpin argues that the conflict between Britain and France at the end of the eighteenth century was a clash between a proponent of a liberal order and a champion of mercantilism. If France had won, the international order would have been far less open (Gilpin, *U.S. Power*, pp. 80–1). The conflict between the United States and the Soviet Union after 1945 can be characterized in the same way.

[44] Quoted in Calleo and Rowland, *World Political Economy*, p. 23.

A free market is a setting for open competition for customers and investors. It is a level playing field, where all compete on equal terms. In such circumstances, those who are strongest and most adept at the game will invariably win. Since Britain and the United States in their periods of predominance had the strongest and most productive economies in the world, each enjoyed an enormous advantage in the competitive environment of an open international economic order.[45] Given a free choice, consumers everywhere would be apt to buy British and American goods, which were often of higher quality and less expensive than those that other countries produced.

In addition, the hegemonic powers controlled the largest pools of capital and thus benefited the most from unlimited opportunities to invest it. Liberal practices are attractive because they help everybody; but they help the strong so much that they are willing to pay to get others to follow them. Economic strength not only gave each hegemon the wherewithal to pay the costs of liberal rules; it also gave each an incentive to do so. The resources devoted to supporting an open order amounted to a profitable investment for each dominant power.

The open order in the postwar period was immensely profitable for Japan as well. Insofar as it rested on services rendered by the United States, which were in turn made possible by the enormous concentration of economic power in North America, Japan's well-being depended on American hegemony.

III

An open international economic order can be compared with the nineteenth century managed balance of power system as well as with a cartel among firms in a particular industry[46] in that all three

---

[45] The historical literature has termed British overseas policy for much of the nineteenth century an example of "the imperialism of free trade," since the British received economic benefits that imperial powers have often sought, not by direct control but rather through the enforcement of liberal rules. John Gallagher and Ronald Robinson, "The Imperialism of Free Trade," *Economic History Review*, 2nd ser., 6, no. 1 (1953): 1–15; Tony Smith, *The Pattern of Imperialism: The United States, Great Britain, and the Late-industrializing World since 1815* (Cambridge University Press, 1981), pp. 20–35.

[46] See Chapter 1, pp. 31–40.

can be thought of as examples (although economic openness is not a perfect example) of what economists call public goods. These are goods or services that are relevant to groups of people rather than to individuals alone. They are "inclusive" in that they are consumed, in some manner, by all members of the group in question. A public good is defined as something that, if provided to one member of a group, cannot be denied to any of them.[47]

Clean air is a familiar example of a public good, as is national defense. They are enjoyed by entire populations rather than purchased and consumed individually. Antipollution devices in factories or on automobiles purify the air that everyone in the vicinity must breathe; an army generally defends an entire country. Since they are properties of collectives, not individuals, public goods are sometimes also called collective goods.

Cities acquire clean air and nations raise armies through the mechanism of government, which imposes regulations to secure the first and collects taxes to pay for the second. In general, public goods are most easily and therefore most often supplied by groups through the good offices of government. Without the coercive power of organized authority, these goods are difficult to obtain. The reason is what is sometimes called "the fallacy of composition" or the "collective goods problem." Simply stated, what is in the interest of a group as a whole is not necessarily in the interest of each of its individual members. The group interest may thus differ from the sum of the interests of the individual members of the

---

[47] Mancur Olson, *The Logic of Collective Action: Public Goods and the Theory of Groups* (Cambridge, Mass.: Harvard University Press, 1971; first published, 1965), pp. 5–22; Russell Hardin, *Collective Action* (Baltimore, Md.: Johns Hopkins University Press, 1982), pp. 17–20. Another common feature of public goods, which is not, however, universal and therefore cannot be said to be a defining characteristic, is jointness of supply, whereby the consumption of the good by one member of the group does not diminish the consumption of any other member. Ibid., p. 19. International economic openness does not qualify unambiguously as a public good because not all of its elements have the feature of "inclusiveness." Its monetary component does have this characteristic; no single country can readily be denied the use of the dollar as a reserve and vehicle currency. In contrast, the open trading system *is* something from which individual states can be excluded. In this sense Japan was not truly a "free rider," as it is defined below, for trade. See Duncan Snidal, "The Limits of Hegemonic Stability Theory," *International Organization*, 39, no. 4 (1985): 590–3; see also Stein, "The Hegemon's Dilemma," p. 367.

group.[48] Everyone has an interest in breathing clean air, but no one has an interest in bearing the cost of installing an antipollution device in his or her automobile. If no one else installed one, the cost of a single device would not purchase materially cleaner air for the person who bought it. But the same calculation of self-interest applies if everyone else were to equip his or her automobile with an antipollution device. Then, too, the effect on the overall quality of the air of one more device would be too small to notice. Individuals ordinarily will not, on their own, contribute to the cost of collective goods. They must usually be compelled to do so. It is the state that compels them.[49]

The nineteenth-century managed balance of power system in Europe and the open international economic orders of the nineteenth and twentieth centuries can be understood as public goods in the sense that the benefits that each set of arrangements provided went to all or most of the members of the international system. The peace established by the rules and customs that the major European powers followed in the nineteenth century and the prosperity fostered by the liberal practices of the international economy before 1914 and after 1945 were "consumed" by all those who took part. The "goods" in each case were not confined to particular states. Europe was peaceful for all Europeans; the benefits of the open economic order were available to all who were part of it.

The behavior that each set of arrangements required from all states was not in the interest of individual states acting alone. Self-restraint is a foolish and counterproductive method of becoming secure unless others practice it as well; mercantilist policies are also, arguably, both natural and rational for sovereign states in the international economic system. Military and political restraint and liberal economic policies can thus be seen as the price that states had to pay to acquire the public goods of equilibrium in the first instance and international openness in the second. No single state alone has an interest in paying that price. Similarly, the oligopoly

---

[48] The point is clearly stated in Hardin, *Collective Action*, pp. 8–9.

[49] Democratic governments are not coercive in the usual sense of the word. They are duly elected, and in this sense the majority votes in favor of whatever public goods they cause to be provided. But to supply these goods requires a mechanism to ensure unanimity of contribution, which is the role that government plays.

price that all members of an economic cartel enjoy is purchased by the willingness of the cartel's members to forgo production and thus an increment of income, a policy that violates each firm's natural impulse for maximal profit.

If all members of each group behaved according to its individual interest – if the European powers in the nineteenth century had attempted to expand their power and influence as far as possible, if nations had practiced mercantilist policies, and if firms sought the largest possible market shares – all would be in less favorable situations than they could achieve by behaving, in concert, unnaturally, by restraining themselves, by cooperating. But none could gain from cooperating if the others did not follow suit.

Thus far the European equilibrium of the nineteenth century and the international economic liberalism of the nineteenth and twentieth centuries are comparable to clean air and national defense. There is, however, an important difference. The common condition for the provision of a public good was missing in these historical episodes. In none was there an all-powerful world government to compel the required behavior. There was no state to force members of the group to pay the costs of the public good, whether in forgone political power and territorial acquisition or potential economic gain given up. The contributions had to be voluntary.

Great Britain in the nineteenth century and Japan in the twentieth had a similar relationship to the European political equilibrium and the open international economic order, respectively, a relationship expressed by another concept familiar to economists: the free rider. A free rider is a member of a group that does not itself contribute to the cost of the collective good that the group enjoys, like someone who travels on a train, a bus, or a boat without paying the fare. There is a natural inclination to ride free. It involves, after all, getting something for nothing, a universally held, if seldom realized, aspiration. It is to overcome this inclination that government is usually necessary, which is the reason that the "collective goods problem" is sometimes also called the "free-rider problem."[50]

[50] As noted, Japan was not, strictly speaking, a free rider, because it could have been denied access to some parts of the open international economic order;

Great Britain received the benefits of Continental equilibrium without making any contribution to it, that is, without sacrificing anything to achieve it. Peace in Europe was a boon to the British. Although they themselves did not live on the Continent, they were inevitably affected by developments there. They found themselves drawn into its conflicts because a concentration of power in Europe would threaten them. To keep a single power from dominating the Continent, the British periodically provided financial assistance to others, as in the eighteenth century, and sometimes even dispatched troops across the Channel, as in the Wars of the French Revolution and World Wars I and II. After 1815, the Continental states created a balance of power by restraining their ambitions to expand in Europe. The British had no such ambitions and so gave up nothing by observing the basic precept of the managed balance of power system. They in fact expanded elsewhere during the nineteenth century, beyond Europe, where balance of power rules did not apply.

Similarly, in an industry where a cartel holds sway a free rider is a firm that produces the maximum possible output. It thereby gains the benefits of a higher price for its products without paying for it with voluntary limits on its own production. Such limits constitute the cartel members' contributions to the collective good that the oligopoly price represents.

Japan was a kind of free rider on the liberal international economic order after 1945 in the sense that it did not pay any of the costs of establishing or maintaining it while nonetheless enjoying its advantages. In this, of course, Japan was not alone. Since the United States bore the burden of sustaining liberal practices, all others qualify as free riders. The Japanese enjoyed a free ride in an additional way. Not only did they not pay the costs of supporting the system for much of the period after 1945; they did not even obey its rules. The Japanese drew enormous benefit from an open economic order while themselves conducting largely mercantilist policies.[51]

individuals, by contrast, cannot be denied access to clean air (see note 47). But even where it could have been excluded, Japan did ride free in the sense that it enjoyed a benefit – through choice rather than automatically – for which it did not have to pay.

[51] "Japan's highly restrictive foreign economic policies differed sharply with the

Japan carefully regulated its own trade. Although its volume of imports was substantial, the Japanese government tightly controlled what could be brought into the country. Almost all imports were raw materials necessary for industry that had to be purchased abroad. Industrial products of the kind the Japanese themselves made were kept out. Other countries that accepted Japan's products did not themselves have access to the Japanese market.

The Japanese government had a decisive influence as well on the country's exports. Its aim was to promote rather than restrict them. It provided subsidies so that firms could sell products at low prices abroad. The Japanese tax code also encouraged exports. The government sponsored cartel arrangements in some industries so that, with assured market shares at home, its member firms could compete more effectively with foreign producers abroad. The government went even farther. It helped to shape the country's overall industrial structure, nurturing particular industries at the expense of others. It had considerable say over the distribution of credit, which it steered to industries that it favored. The chief agent of this policy of organizing industry to create advantage in international markets was MITI, the Ministry of International Trade and Industry. MITI was active in forming cartels. It controlled foreign exchange and so could help some industries to grow and force others to stagnate or shrivel.[52]

The Japanese government also closely monitored the influx of capital from abroad. Japan welcomed foreign technology and sometimes admitted foreign capital. But foreigners were required to be passive investors, without effective control over any significant part of Japanese industry.[53]

gradually liberalizing outlook of much of the rest of the non-Communist developed world. Japan's position in the postwar world may be realistically assessed as historically unique." Gary R. Saxonhouse, "The World Economy and Japanese Foreign Economic Policy," in Scalapino, ed., *Foreign Policy of Modern Japan*, p. 292.

[52] There is a large and growing body of literature on the Japanese economy that emphasizes the role of the government. See, inter alia, Johnson, "MITI and Japanese International Economic Policy," and Johnson, *MITI and the Japanese Miracle* (Stanford, Calif.: Stanford University Press), 1982; Pempel, "Japanese Foreign Economic Policy," Frank, "Introduction," Yoichi Ohita, "Japan's Fiscal Incentives for Exports," in Frank, ed., Japanese Economy.

[53] Gilpin, *U.S. Power*, p. 239; Saxonhouse, "World Economy," p. 288.

In each case, the government intruded into the economy, producing results that were different from what the free play of market forces would have yielded. It practiced mercantilist rather than liberal policies. Japan's policies violated the letter of neoclassical economic teachings and the spirit of the economic order that Britain sustained in the nineteenth century and the United States led and managed in the twentieth.

The Western Europeans conducted mercantilist policies also, but not as extensively or as successfully as the Japanese. They formed the European Economic Community, or Common Market, a customs union with significant external tariffs. But the members of the Common Market could not discriminate against one another and did not discriminate against the rest of the world as completely as Japan did. Nor did the Europeans restrict the influx of foreign capital in the Japanese manner. American multinational corporations made substantial investments in Common Market countries, as they did not in Japan. Although the European governments tried their hands at creating internationally competitive industries, they did not have anything like Japan's success. None of them played the role in coordinating their countries' industrial evolution that their Japanese counterpart did.[54]

Japan's mercantilist policies were designed to overcome obstacles to the development of advanced industries. They were sophisticated twentieth-century versions of the nineteenth-century practice of protecting infant industries against foreign competition until they had grown strong enough to hold their own in international commerce. Without protection, without guaranteed markets, such industries would be stifled at birth by older and more efficient foreign competitors.

These policies offered a way not only of overcoming the head start of other countries, notably the United States, that enjoyed postwar industrial development – Japanese industry had been se-

---

[54] Japan had a freer ride than the Western Europeans in national defense as well. Neither paid the full cost of their own security. Both enjoyed the protection of the United States. Like Japan, the Europeans supplemented American forces with a military establishment of their own. But the Europeans, on the whole, devoted a greater proportion of their national wealth to the task than the Japanese, for whom defense spending never rose above 1 percent of the gross national product in the four decades after 1945.

verely damaged in 1945 – but also of coping with natural conditions unfavorable to the desired pattern of economic development. By the standards of neoclassical economics, Japan should not have been a great industrial power at all. With sparse natural resources and a large population, its specialty should have been labor-intensive manufacturing. The American occupation authorities in fact encouraged the development of light industry. The law of comparative advantage did not prescribe an emphasis on the steel, ships, and automobiles that Japan produced after 1945. The Japanese, however, did not wish to be relegated, as they saw it, to the niche that geography, geology, and demography had intended for them. Since the terms of trade in the postwar world favored heavy industry, this would have given them a lower standard of living than the one to which they aspired. The path that the United States had followed was the path to wealth. The Japanese chose to flout the rules of international economic liberalism in order to embark upon it. Following that path required guiding the development of industries and ensuring that foreign exchange was used first and foremost for purchasing the necessary raw materials abroad.

Other members of the international economic order had an incentive to follow Japan's example. But the Japanese, almost alone, had the capacity to organize themselves to this end. Their mercantilist policies followed from the way they understood economics. They were not as wedded to the liberal view as the British in the nineteenth century and the Americans after 1945. Of greater influence was the alternative school of economic analysis that grew up in Germany in the nineteenth century and whose best known spokesman was Friederich List; this school stressed the need for protection as the prelude to free competition in an open international economic order.[55] Liberal principles come naturally to those with economic advantages; mercantilist ideas are attractive to late developers who are trying to catch up.

Japanese society is marked by a high degree of social cohesion, which grows out of the Japanese sense of their singularity as a people and also out of the feeling of vulnerability that comes from being crowded together on a few islands off the coast of Asia. For

[55] Saxonhouse, "World Economy," p. 292; Pempel, "Japanese Foreign Economic Policy," p. 149.

the sake of investment on a scale necessary for rapid industrial growth, Japanese wage earners were willing to forgo consumption. Government and business were naturally drawn to cooperative relations with each other. The strict separation between the two that the laissez faire approach to economic activity assumes was unnatural for the Japanese. This cooperation, without the smothering grip of government control that is the rule in Communist countries, made it possible for Japan to conduct mercantilist policies that, taking advantage of the open international economic order, led to rapid industrial progress and a high rate of economic growth fueled by ever expanding exports.

The free ride that both Britain and Japan received was more than a pleasant bonus, a welcome addition to the national treasury. It was in both cases a subsidy underwriting a central feature of national policy. In the British case the European equilibrium made possible far-reaching imperial expansion in Asia and Africa in the nineteenth century. If Britain had had to take as active a role on the Continent as it did in the eighteenth and the twentieth centuries, London would have had much greater difficulty acquiring and governing territory overseas.

Similarly, Japan's international free ride subsidized its extraordinarily rapid economic growth after 1945, so rapid – the economy increased about six and one-half times between 1952 and 1974 – that it is often called the Japanese economic miracle. The combination of access to the open international order and freedom from the discipline of its rules made the miracle possible. The Japanese would probably have prospered, and perhaps even built the same industries, without the particular relationship to the international economy that they had; but they could not have done so on the scale or at the pace that they achieved.[56]

As with Japan's foreign policies before World War II, the large and growing body of literature on the causes of the Japanese economic miracle after the war generally adopts "inside-out" explanations that single out features of Japanese society, such as its educational system, its strong sense of social solidarity, the dedi-

[56] Pempel, "Japanese Foreign Economic Policy," p. 168.

cation of Japanese workers, and the delicate psychology of the country's industrial relations.[57]

These were unquestionably important. The Japanese made things the world wanted to buy. The skills that went into the creation of these products came, obviously, from within Japan. But "outside-in" explanations also bear on Japan's success. The configuration of the international economy provided the indispensable setting in which Japanese products were made and sold. Certainly without an open order and perhaps without national mercantilist policies – the first the relationship of sovereign states to one another, the second, in effect, Japan's relationship to that relationship, and both, therefore, features of the international system instead of Japanese society – the Japanese miracle would not have occurred as it did.[58]

Although similar to Britain's relationship to the nineteenth-century European balance of power system, Japan's status in the open international economic order after 1945 also differed from Britain's and from free riders in general. That status was not wholly the result of the inclusiveness of the public good in question. Free riders cannot be denied the benefits of the public good that they consume without paying. The benefits of the European equilibrium were automatically available to the British, who could not be prevented from enjoying them. This was not entirely so for Japan and the practices of international liberalism. The Japanese *could* have been denied some of their benefits. They could have been refused access to some parts of the international economic order. Other countries could have erected barriers to Japanese exports; the Western Europeans in fact did so.

Japan received access to the international economic order despite violating its fundamental precepts through the good offices of the United States. The American government sponsored Japan's admission to the international trade organization, the General Agree-

[57] See, among many others, Ezra F. Vogel, *Japan as Number One: Lessons for America* (Cambridge, Mass.: Harvard University Press, 1979); William Ouchi, *Theory Z: How American Business Can Meet the Japanese Challenge* (Reading, Mass.: Addison-Wesley, 1981).
[58] Johnson, "MITI and Japanese International Economic Policy," p. 277; Saxonhouse, "World Economy," p. 289.

ment of Tariffs and Trade (GATT), for example, despite the objections of the Europeans. More important, the United States opened its home market to Japanese products even though its own goods were barred from Japan. This was partly the result of American confidence, indeed overconfidence, in its own industrial prowess. Americans did not suspect, in the early postwar years, that Japan could become a serious competitor in the production of finished goods. The United States was also playing its role as the entrepreneur of the economic order, providing inducements – side payments – in the form of partial exemptions from certain international liberal norms in the short term in order to achieve compliance with other liberal rules over the long term. But the United States could have played this role for others while excluding Japan.

The Americans had political reasons, as well, for giving Japan a free ride. With the Cold War with the Soviet Union underway and Communist forces triumphant in China at the end of the 1940s, and with the outbreak of the Korean War in 1950, the American government wanted to encourage strong, friendly, prosperous allies. Permitting Japan to conduct mercantilist policies seemed an effective way of fostering a bulwark against further Communist expansion in East Asia. America's security requirements took precedence over its economic principles.

There is another important difference between Japan and Britain. Both can be understood as having benefited from a collective good; but the goods in question were supplied in different ways. All the major European powers except Britain contributed to the managed balance of power system of the nineteenth century. Each, that is, made a sacrifice – each agreed to forgo political gains it would otherwise have tried to secure – for the sake of equilibrium. Although most followed its rules to some extent, none of the major economic powers after 1945 except the United States contributed to the cost of sustaining the liberal international economic order. Political equilibrium was supplied jointly, pluralistically; economic openness was provided individually, hegemonically.

The chief threats to the continued provision of the two collective goods therefore differed. For political equilibrium, the danger was greater inequality in the international system; in the case of economic openness, it was the opposite – less international economic inequality. The nineteenth-century managed balance of power system was finally destroyed because Germany became too strong to be willing to pay the costs of equilibrium. The post-1945 economic order has seen a challenge comparable to the one that Germany posed to the nineteenth-century security arrangements. It, too, stemmed from changes in the distribution of power, in this case economic rather than military power. It was a shift that made the United States relatively weaker in economic terms and thus less willing to pay the costs of supporting international economic liberalism.

IV

In the decade of the 1970s, mercantilist policies were more widely practiced than they had been in the first quarter-century after 1945. The international economic constitution of liberal rules was increasingly disregarded. There was an erosion of the open character of the economic order that the United States had helped to establish and sustain. One important reason for this was the rising significance of public welfare as a national goal. Since governments were increasingly held responsible for the public well-being, they were more and more disposed to use state power to promote it, whatever the effect on other countries.[59]

The erosion of the liberal order coincided with the decline of American dominance in the world economy. Throughout the 1970s, as in 1945, the United States had the largest economy in the world. It was in fact much larger in absolute terms in 1980 than it had been in 1945. But because others also grew, the American margin of superiority was steadily reduced over this period.[60] Since he-

---

[59] Hirsch and Doyle, "Politicization," p. 51; Ruggie, "International Regimes," pp. 202–4. The international economic policies of the industrial states depended in large part on internal political competition among different groups, sectors, and interests. On this subject see Peter Gourevitch, *Politics in Hard Times: Comparative Responses to International Economic Crises* (Ithaca, N.Y.: Cornell University Press, 1986), Chap. 5.

[60] Statistical measures of the relative decline of the United States are listed in Krasner, *Structural Conflict*, p. 70, Keohane, *After Hegemony*, pp. 196, 199, and Gilpin, *The Political Economy*, p. 344. For an emphasis on misconceived American domestic economic policies as a cause of international economic disorder, see Henry Nau, "Where Reaganomics Works," *Foreign Policy* 57 (Winter 1984–5).

gemony is the product of *relative* economic strength, the United States was considerably less "hegemonic" in the 1970s than before.

The relative American decline was as natural and predictable as any political or economic development can be. American predominance in 1945 was artificial, the consequence of an unusual set of circumstances. The other industrial nations had been devastated by war. The continental United States was untouched. American economic production actually expanded as a result of the conflict. As the others recovered, the gap between them and the United States was bound to close.

There is in fact a familiar historical tendency for economic inequalities such as that which marked relations in 1945 between the United States, on the one hand, and Western Europe and Japan, on the other, to lessen over time, as techniques that have made one or more states rich diffuse to others. The tendency is pronounced in an open international economic order, where capital and know-how circulate freely. Liberal rules of economic procedure forbid any effort by the hegemonic (or any other) state to block the creation of economic strength elsewhere.[61] The United States did not, in any case, seek to prevent the development of economic power overseas. To the contrary, it was the purpose of American international economic policies – the Marshall Plan in Europe, for example, and the special dispensations permitted Japan – actively to help the newly allied countries regain their economic health. Hence the same Japanese economic miracle that it helped to sustain contributed to the erosion of the hegemony of the United States. In general, to the extent that an open order depends on the services of a hegemon but also tends to nullify extreme inequalities in economic power, that order can be said to contain within itself the seeds of its own subversion.

In the first period of international economic liberalism, the decline of the founding and sustaining hegemonic power coincided with the collapse of the open economic order. Indeed, the decline was arguably the cause of the collapse. By the end of World War

---

[61] The general historical tendency for economic power to diffuse is the subject of Gilpin, *War and Change*. The form it took after 1945, and especially the role of one feature of the postwar order, the transfer of capital by American multinational corporations, is the theme of Gilpin, *U.S. Power*. See also Chapter 3, pp. 165–6.

I, Britain's economic advantage over the rest of the world had disappeared. At the end of the 1920s, the world economy experienced the severe disruption known as the Great Depression, in which most countries turned to mercantilist policies. Liberal practices disappeared. The Depression occurred, according to one interpretation, because Britain was no longer able, and the United States not yet willing, to counteract the fluctuations in the world market. The absence of a hegemon turned a cyclical slump into a deep depression, which in turn destroyed the practices of international economic liberalism.[62]

The history of the international economic system in the 1970s did not precisely reproduce the experience of the 1930s. The open order eroded but did not collapse. But as in the earlier period, the diminution of the margin of the hegemon's economic superiority over other countries was directly connected to the rise of illiberal policies. The United States was no longer as able or as willing to bribe and coerce others to resist mercantilist impulses and conform to the rules of the open order. Indeed, the United States itself succumbed to the temptation to violate liberal rules, a temptation that had not been present in the immediate postwar period.[63]

International trade practices were not uniformly liberal after 1945. There were exceptions to the rule of free trade. But the exceptions were understood, at the outset, as temporary measures.

---

[62] This is the argument of Kindleberger, *The World in Depression*. See, e.g., p. 292.

[63] Krasner, *Structural Conflict*, pp. 70–1. Robert Keohane gives an "inside-out" explanation for American mercantilist impulses, arguing that they had domestic origins (*After Hegemony*, pp. 150, 215). But these impulses arose because of a change in the American international position – because of the decline in American predominance. With a predominant position, the United States could satisfy the requirements of international leadership and the needs of domestic interests. With the decline of its dominance, the two came into conflict. When the margin of superiority was enormous, as in 1945, for example, the United States could permit protectionist policies by others and still provide large enough markets for American industries at home. By the 1970s it was difficult to do both; pressure for protection for American industries mounted. Similarly, in international monetary affairs the United States found itself, in the 1970s, caught between the international obligation to restrain the creation of dollars and the domestic imperative to increase it. The American government abrogated the Bretton Woods system in 1971 as a way of choosing the second over the first. When its economic predominance was at its zenith (which is when the system was established), there was no need to make such a choice.

It was assumed that tariff barriers would be progressively dismantled. By the 1970s it had become clear that this would not happen.
The momentum of tariff reduction waned. The restrictions that had
once been thought temporary took on the appearance of permanence. At the same time, new forms of protection appeared. To
shelter their home industries countries increasingly enacted various
types of nontariff barriers such as quotas and orderly marketing
agreements. These violated the spirit, if not always the letter, of
liberal international commercial regulations.

In the 1940s, the United States had coaxed others to join the
free trading system and had permitted mercantilist exceptions on
some issues in order to encourage fidelity to liberal rules on others.
By the 1970s, the Americans were no longer willing to make such
concessions, insisting on the principle of reciprocity in tariff reductions. Besides abdicating the hegemonic responsibility of in-
ducing others to observe liberal rules, the United States ceased
observing some of them itself. It adopted mercantilist trade policies
in some areas, extending protection to textiles, steel, and
automobiles.

The liberal rules for money were also abandoned. The Bretton
Woods agreements of 1944 had provided for fixed exchange rates
among national currencies, with the dollar at the center of the
system. These arrangements were liberal, or perhaps more accu-
rately constitutional, because they meant that the value of a nation's
money was determined by impersonal rules, and ultimately by
market forces, rather than by government manipulation. Fixed
exchange rates were discarded largely as a result of the American
decision not to redeem dollars for gold, a step that eliminated the
fixed standard to which other currencies were linked. The floating
exchange rates that succeeded the Bretton Woods system were
compatible with mercantilist policies in that they gave governments
a greater opportunity to manipulate the value of their money, just
as tariffs manipulate the volume of trade. Again, the relative decline
of American economic power lay behind the scrapping of liberal
rules. The dollar was the linchpin of the system. As the one currency theoretically convertible to gold, it provided a fixed standard
for all others. Thus its value could not be changed, nor, in theory,
could the United States refuse to redeem gold at the fixed price.
This role, which encouraged the use of the dollar as a reserve and

an internationally acceptable currency, obliged the American government to pursue cautious domestic economic policies to maintain confidence in the system. With America's enormous economic superiority in the early postwar period, these international obligations were compatible with policies that the American government considered necessary for domestic well-being. Washington was able to provide enough dollars to keep employment high at home without encountering resistance from the rest of the world. Starved for capital and liquidity, others wanted all the dollars they could get.

As the margin of American superiority evaporated with economic recovery in Europe, Japan, and elsewhere, a tension arose between the international and domestic requirements for the dollar. The world wanted fewer dollars than successive American administrations deemed necessary to keep economic activity within the United States at their preferred level. To carry out their domestic policies they sacrificed the norm of international good behavior, and with it the liberal procedures on which that norm rested.[64]

As trade barriers multiplied in the 1970s and the liberal monetary arrangements of the 1940s fell apart, new restraints appeared on the international circulation of capital. International investment had never proceeded entirely unhampered. Japan itself had imposed strict controls. In the 1970s others followed the Japanese example. Prominent among them were states that had achieved independence from foreign rule after 1945, the less developed countries (LDCs), or, as they were sometimes called, the members of the Third World. Their governments imposed limits on direct foreign investment and moved to take control of investment in the form of fixed assets that had already been made, a practice known as nationalization.

Restrictions on foreign capital formed part of a larger program for a "New International Economic Order" (NIEO) that the LDCs

---

[64] This is the thesis of Gowa, *Closing the Gold Window*; see esp. pp. 23, 31, 171, 174. Another vulnerability of the Bretton Woods systems stemmed from the "Triffin Paradox," formulated by the economist Robert Triffin, which holds that a national currency cannot simultaneously provide liquidity and serve as a reserve asset in the international economic system. The first requirement invariably calls for a greater supply of the currency than the second function will permit. But with the extraordinary economic strength of the United States in the aftermath of the war, the Triffin Paradox temporarily did not apply. Ibid., p. 42.

proposed, which posed a fundamental challenge to the open international economic order of the postwar period. Its expressed aim was to restructure international economic relations between the LDCs and the industrial countries in a manner more favorable to the LDCs. The change was to take place through extensive government control of economic activity. The program was an overtly mercantilist one, calling explicitly for the "politicization" of international economic transactions. In addition to investment codes, it included elaborate trade regulations designed to increase the earnings of Third World nations through price supports for their products, chiefly raw materials, and guaranteeing access to the markets of the industrial countries for their exports. It also called for direct transfers of resources to the LDCs in the form of aid, subsidized credits, and the provision of modern technology.[65]

The proposals for a new international economic order, Japan's international and domestic mercantilist practices, and the trade restrictions that the United States and Western Europe erected were all mercantilist policies in the sense that they involved government interference with the workings of the market. In each case, economic decisions were made by political authorities rather than by recourse to impersonal rules. The ultimate purposes of the three, however, were different.

Japan's goal was national wealth and also national power, prestige, and prominence insofar as these follow from wealth and are available without military might in the second half of the twentieth century. Other industrial nations, notably the United States, practiced mercantilist policies less systematically, usually in response to domestic pressures rather than as part of an overall design. Their policies sought to protect particular domestic economic sectors or industries from pressure from foreign competition. Japanese mercantilism placed the goal of national well-being ahead of that of global welfare. The tariffs, quotas, and orderly marketing agreements of the Americans and Western Europeans promoted the welfare of particular sectors at the expense of the overall welfare of their national economies.[66]

---

[65] Krasner, *Structural Conflict*, pp. 69, 190–5; Hirsch and Doyle, "Politicization," pp. 18–19.

[66] Japan's government was strong enough to design and implement coherent economic plans. The governments of the other industrial states did not have the

Proponents of the NIEO ostensibly sought what Japan had achieved: the enhancement of their own national welfare, if necessary at the expense of the welfare of others. Other, more explicitly political purposes were also evident in the LDCs' proposals and policies. They wanted a dramatic change in the distribution of power in the international system. They were occasionally even willing to forgo economic advantage to enhance their own power.[67] The special arrangements and privileges they sought had another political purpose: to shelter their governments from the buffeting to which they were subject from the normal workings of the world economy. Poor, often dependent on a single crop, and with a precarious hold on foreign markets, these countries were subject to severe dislocations through the normal fluctuations of the international market. The shocks of an open order interfered with the capacity of many of such regimes in these countries to govern, and even to stay in power. A downturn in the international economy that could easily be absorbed by the industrial countries could bring disaster to them. The NIEO therefore represented a search for an insurance policy, for a more stable, predictable environment for weak regimes with shallow roots in the societies they governed.[68]

The LDCs' proposals for a new international economic order differed from the Japanese, American, and European varieties of mercantilism in another way. They posed a direct, explicit challenge to liberal principles. The Japanese honored these principles in the breach; they had a strong interest in the observance of these norms by others, if not by themselves. The Americans and Europeans similarly pledged fidelity to an open order. Tariffs, quotas, and even floating exchange rates were considered exceptional; the norm remained liberal. The proponents of the NIEO took issue not only with particular liberal practices but also with the idea of a liberal order. A body of economic doctrine called dependency

same authority within their own societies. Therefore, on the one hand, they did not have the same competence to direct the economy, and on the other, they were more vulnerable than the Japanese government to pressures for protection from different sectors. On the variations among Western governments see Katzenstein, ed., *Between Power and Plenty*.

[67] Krasner, *Structural Conflict*, pp. 114, 236. See also Robert W. Tucker, *The Inequality of Nations* (New York: Basic Books, 1977), esp. pp. 57–65.

[68] This is an important theme of Krasner, *Structural Conflict*. See, e.g., pp. 28, 33, 38–9, 40, 41.

theory was assembled to support their position. The open international economic order was, they asserted, the engine of inequality, and so had to be overturned.[69]

The erosion of the open order threatened the prosperity the Japanese enjoyed. They recognized that the conditions in which they had thrived were in jeopardy. What particularly convinced them of the danger was not so much the gradual accretion of barriers to trade during the 1970s or the growing frequency with which foreign investments were nationalized in the Third World. It was, rather, two sudden and dramatic events in the early part of the decade that shook the foundations of the liberal economic order. The new American economic policies of August 15, 1971, and the crisis brought on by the Arab oil embargo of October 1973 were the political equivalents of earthquakes, shaking the ground on which the open system stood. Each made a deep and disturbing impression on the Japanese, for whom they were landmark events in postwar history and who came to refer to them as "shocks."[70]

The first of them, known as the "Nixon shock" after the president who was largely responsible for it, had two parts, each potentially harmful to Japanese interests. Both were in fact aimed at Japan. The United States announced on August 15, 1971, that it would no longer redeem dollars for gold, thereby severing the last remaining connection between the American currency and the universal store of value and dismantling the Bretton Woods system of fixed exchange rates. Fixed exchange rates were important to Japan because they were considered essential for the trade on which the Japanese depended. Long-term international exchanges were easier to undertake when those involved could be confident of the future value of the currencies they were using. Fluctuating exchange rates brought with them an element of uncertainty that would, it was thought, depress the volume of international commerce below what fixed exchange rates would sustain.

The new American monetary policy affected Japan in a more direct way. One of its purposes was to force the Japanese to increase the value of their own currency. Under the Bretton Woods system, the yen had come to be substantially undervalued in relation to

[69] Ibid., pp. 82, 85–7, 88.
[70] Reischauer, *The Japanese*, p. 372.

the dollar. The rate of exchange between the two could not readily be changed, at least not through an American initiative, since the system depended on the value of the dollar remaining fixed. The undervalued yen served, in turn, as a kind of subsidy for Japanese exports, permitting Japan to sell products abroad at lower cost than they could have if the yen had been more properly priced. An export surplus was crucial to Japan's overall economic policy. By 1971 the surplus came in large part at the expense of the United States. The Nixon shock was designed to redress the balance.[71]

Redressing the American trade deficit with Japan was also the aim of the second part of the Nixon shock. In addition to closing the gold window, the American government imposed a 10 percent surcharge on all imports to the United States. (At the same time the president also announced a freeze on wages and prices.) This was a direct blow to the Japanese because they relied so heavily on the American market.[72] Since they also relied on American military protection, an abrupt change in any policy of the United States toward them was doubly distressing. It was an indirect blow as well, because it rocked the trading system as a whole. It was a flagrant defection from the principles of international liberalism by the country that had been their most powerful and effective champion since 1945.[73]

The Arab–Israeli war of October 1973 triggered the first oil shock, which was the second political earthquake that Japan experienced in the 1970s. To support Egypt and Syria, Arab oil producers declared an embargo on shipments to two countries they deemed too friendly to Israel: the United States and the Netherlands. They did not succeed in denying oil to either country, but they did reduce the world's total supply of oil, sparking panic buying that raised the price of crude oil fourfold – from three to twelve dollars per barrel – in a matter of weeks. The first oil crisis (and the second,

---

[71] Frank, "Introduction," p. 9; Saxonhouse, "World Economy," p. 287.

[72] From the early 1950s to the early 1970s, 30% of Japan's exports and 30% of its imports involved trade with the United States. Pempel, "Japanese Foreign Economic Policy," p. 144.

[73] It was especially ominous because it came on the heels of a wrangle over Japan's exports of textiles to the United States and at a time when protectionist legislation was gathering support in the United States Congress for the first time in more than two decades.

in 1979, sparked by the Iranian revolution) was a crisis of price, not one of supply – although this was not immediately apparent.

Like the collapse of the postwar international monetary rules, the oil shock was due in part to the erosion of American power – in particular, in this case, the diminished share of the world's total oil being produced in the United States. During the 1956 Arab–Israeli war, Arab oil producers also imposed an embargo. It had no effect on the world market because American stocks easily compensated for the loss of Arab petroleum. But by 1973, world demand was sufficiently high and American capacity beyond what was being produced was sufficiently low that this was not possible. Since there was no increase in the supply of oil, there was an increase in its price.[74]

Japan had to pay that price. Since virtually all of its oil was imported, Japan's energy costs skyrocketed. In effect, the oil shock imposed a huge tax on the Japanese economy.[75] Given their dependence on oil, the Japanese had no choice, in the short term, but to pay. Oil was indispensable. As one government official reportedly put it, "With or without a nuclear deterrent there is no national security without oil."[76]

Given the extent of Japanese dependence on oil, moreover, what seemed to be a clear implication of the embargo – that the supply of oil could be manipulated for political purposes – was particularly disturbing. Japan had tried to avoid political positions that might harm its economic activities. It had studiously played no political role in the Middle East. The Japanese government quickly issued a statement of sympathy for the Arab side in the 1973 war, thereby

---

[74] Robert J. Lieber, *The Oil Decade: Conflict and Cooperation in the West* (New York: Praeger, 1983), pp. 15, 20.

[75] It imposed such a tax on the economies of all the consuming countries, which triggered the kind of cyclical disruption – that is, a recession – to which market economies are prone. The recession was a deep one, in part because, with its margin of economic superiority diminished, the United States was less well placed than before to offer the countercyclical services that hegemonic states provide.

[76] Quoted in Makato Momoi, "Are There Any Alternative Strategies for the Defense of Japan?" in Franklin B. Weinstein, ed., *U.S.–Japan Relations and the Security of East Asia: The Next Decade* (Boulder, Colo.: Westview Press, 1978), p. 76.

risking the displeasure of the United States. Yet even so, Japan did not escape the effects of the embargo.

The oil shock was an ominous portent for the Japanese in another way. It seemed to herald the fulfillment of the LDCs' plan for a new international economic order. Oil producers from Asia, Africa, and Latin America had formed OPEC – the Organization of Petroleum Exporting Countries. By 1974, with agreed production targets and the price of their product soaring, they seemed to have established an effective cartel, changing the procedures of the oil trade to favor the producers at the expense of the industrial consumers. This was not, precisely, a shift from liberal to mercantilist norms. Oil had previously been controlled by a cartel. That cartel, however, had been made up of Western oil companies, which were subject to the influence of Western governments and had therefore kept the price relatively low. OPEC seemed to have succeeded not only in redistributing the world's wealth but also in transferring power from the industrial nations to the Third World, which were precisely the aims of the NIEO. It was widely thought, in the mid-1970s, that other commodities and other areas of international economic activity would follow the same course.

Such developments would have been deeply disadvantageous to Japan, the country with the largest stake in the international order being challenged by the LDCs. One of the principal tenets of the NIEO posed a particular threat. Many of the LDCs exported raw materials, whose prices they naturally wished to raise. As the world's largest importer of raw materials, Japan had a powerful interest in keeping these prices low.

V

As with Great Britain in the late nineteenth century, Japan recognized in the 1970s that the international circumstances that had proved so favorable to its fortunes were coming under pressure. The collective international economic measures and the restraints they embodied began to fray, as had the security arrangements that had survived from the Congress of Vienna down to the end of the nineteenth century. Like the British, the Japanese responded to the new conditions. They did what they could to bolster the collective international framework in which they had flourished after 1945. As with the British, the Japanese could not sustain the framework alone. But they did not have to act alone to sustain it. In the middle of the 1980s, international economic openness seemed more durable than the remnants of the nineteenth-century managed balance of power system had finally proved to be in 1914; and this was so in large part because of the basic differences between economic relations and security issues.

An alternative to either a wholly liberal or an entirely mercantilist economic order was theoretically available and potentially attractive to Japan. This was a world of mercantilist blocs, encompassing more than one country but not the international system as a whole, with each bloc integrated internally but closed to the rest of the world. Although it offers a market broader than that of a single sovereign state, a mercantilist bloc is not as large and therefore not as difficult to sustain as a liberal order embracing most of the international system. A world of such blocs would be composed of several separate, self-contained or loosely connected systems, each with a hegemonic power at its center.[77]

This was very roughly the world of the 1930s. The United States, Britain, France, Germany, Russia, and Japan organized – or tried to organize – integrated economic blocs.[78] It was the aim of Japan's Greater East Asia Co-Prosperity Sphere. That was not, however, a happy political precedent. Those countries that the Japanese compelled to join resented and resisted it. The resentment lingered after the war. Japan became the leading economic power in East Asia, establishing a pattern of economic relations that in a sense recreated Greater East Asia; but this took place in the shelter of an American security guarantee to Japan and many of its neighbors. The Japanese had no political or military role. Even their economic presence aroused some resentment. During a tour of Southeast Asia in 1974, Prime Minister Tanaka encountered anti-Japanese protests and rioting. To form a separate, coherent, economic bloc,

---

[77] Gilpin, *U.S. Power*, pp. 234–7; Gilpin, *The Political Economy*, pp. 397–408.
[78] See above, p. 344; Skidelsky, "Retreat from Leadership," p. 178; David P. Calleo, "The Decline and Rebuilding of an International Economic System: Some General Considerations," in David P. Calleo, ed., *Money and the Coming World Order*, A Lehrman Institute Book (New York: New York University Press, 1976), p. 59.

Japan would have to undertake the political and military responsibilities of the hegemonic power.

Nor would it be simple for Japan to obtain free access to all economically important parts of the region. North China, for example, had been part of Greater East Asia. Although trade between Japan and the People's Republic increased in the 1970s, it is doubtful that China would choose to integrate its economy fully with the others of the region. Nor would the Soviet Union do so. There is a natural economic complementarity between Japan and the eastern part of the Soviet Union, especially Siberia, which is rich in the minerals, timber, and other raw materials that Japan needs. But political relations between the two countries have been strained. Soviet forces occupied several islands at the northern tip of the Japanese archipelago claimed by Japan. Even in a more cordial political climate, the leadership of the Soviet Union was hardly likely to permit unimpeded commerce with Japan.

Even if a bloc excluding the Communist countries could be organized, it would be neither large nor rich enough to support the standard of well-being that Japan had attained by the 1970s within a global order. It could not supply all the necessary raw materials. It could not provide markets to replace the West, particularly the United States. Asian countries, even prosperous ones like South Korea, Taiwan, and Singapore, were simply not large enough or rich enough. A partial version of the postwar liberal order, therefore, was not, for Japanese purposes, a substitute for an open order of global dimensions.[79]

Rather than attempt to form an economic bloc in East Asia, Japan responded to the two great shocks of the early 1970s by adjusting its own economic policies. Beyond addressing their most pressing problems, the Japanese moved to bring their international economic practices more into line with liberal norms. The same features of Japanese society that had made successful mercantilist policies possible – indeed, the same characteristics that had transformed an isolated, backward, semifeudal agricultural country into an industrial power in the three decades between 1870 and 1900

---

[79] Scalapino, "Modern Japanese Foreign Policy," p. 400; Kosaka, "International Economic Policy of Japan," p. 221; Kindleberger, "Systems of International Economic Organization," p. 31.

– gave Japan the capacity to respond to sudden shifts in international conditions.

By the 1980s, the Japanese had altered their economic relations with the rest of the world in a number of important ways. In the wake of the first oil shock they reshaped their energy policies. They reduced their consumption of oil through conservation and sought alternative sources of energy. They also looked for new sources of oil.[80] Still, the Japanese could not do entirely without imported oil. So they increased their exports of industrial products to bring in the currency they needed to pay for the suddenly more expensive energy. The Japanese government also began seeking long-term contracts with suppliers and tried to develop supplementary political and economic relations with producers of raw materials, particularly oil. Resource diplomacy, as this policy came to be called, was a way of fostering political goodwill to help ensure that resources would be continuously available.[81]

In addition to reliable supplies of raw materials, Japan's access to the markets in which it had sold its manufactured products, in particular the American market, was also in jeopardy in the 1970s. So the Japanese negotiated bilateral restraints on their exports, known as quotas or "orderly marketing agreements." They agreed to limit the number of televisions, automobiles, and other finished products sold in the United States and elsewhere.[82]

---

[80] Kosaka, "International Economic Policy of Japan," pp. 207–10; Joseph S. Nye, "Japan," in Joseph S. Nye and David Deese, eds., *Energy and Security* (Cambridge, Mass.: Ballinger, 1981), p. 216.

[81] Shapiro, "The Risen Sun," p. 74; Momoi, "Alternative Strategies," p. 86; *Asian Security, 1981* (Tokyo: Research Institute for Peace and Security, 1981), p. 195; Terutomo Ozawi, *Multinationalism: Japanese Style: The Political Economy of External Dependency* (Princeton, N.J.: Princeton University Press, 1979), pp. 140–53.

[82] As well as "structural" problems created by the threat of the closure of the international economic order, Japan faced "cyclical" difficulties stemming from the changing international costs of production. As technology spreads and labor markets change, some countries gain and others lose advantage in producing particular goods. Comparative costs shift and the economic profiles of different countries shift with them. Where Britain once made cloth and Portugal wine, by following the rule of comparative advantage Britain might subsequently specialize in steel, Portugal in cloth, and some third country in wine. Just as Japan had taken markets away from countries that had industrialized earlier by making products less expensively, so newer entrants into the industrial world began to press Japan. Korea, Taiwan, Singapore, and others started to produce

As a way of coping with the threat to their supplies of raw materials as well as to their access to foreign markets, the Japanese began to invest abroad. The practice was a familiar one for countries with large trade surpluses. Both Britain in the nineteenth century and the United States in the twentieth had exported capital in large quantities. The Japanese invested in extractive industries overseas to ensure that they would receive a share of the minerals that were extracted.[83] They invested in manufacturing industries in the United States to circumvent barriers to products made in Japan and to avoid the political stigma of taking jobs from American workers. The Japanese began to make automobiles, refrigerators, and even computer components in North American plants that they financed, owned, and, in some cases, managed.[84]

The measures Japan adopted did not entirely solve the problems they addressed. Some were even self-defeating. The efforts to strike long-term bargains with producers of raw materials and the quotas on imports simply added to the mercantilist trends in the international economy. The increased volume of Japanese exports that paid for oil at its higher price aggravated protectionist sentiments in the countries in which Japan's goods were sold. Still, the negotiated restraints on imports did help to keep protectionist feeling in the United States from shutting out Japanese products altogether. And with the drop in oil prices and the easing of the pressure on other minerals, the international market for raw materials began, in the 1980s, to favor buyers like Japan once again.

The new Japanese international economic policies, moreover,

---

textiles, steel, and even automobiles for export, which they could sell for less than Japan because their costs of production were lower. In the postwar world, Japan was adept at shifting out of products in which its comparative advantage was waning and into products in which it could compete effectively (see Peter J. Katzenstein, *Small States in World Markets: Industrial Policy in Europe* [Ithaca, N.Y.: Cornell University Press, 1985], p. 26). This presupposed the existence of a world market – that is of an open international economic order. In this way, therefore, the structural and cyclical problems were related.

[83] Saxonhouse, "World Economy," p. 309.
[84] In the mid-1980s, as the value of the yen climbed sharply, Japan's foreign investment accelerated. The change in exchange rates made production abroad cheaper than in Japan. Most of Japan's capital exports did not go into building factories, however. In 1985, $60 billion went to purchase securities issued in the United States and only $6.5 billion into fixed assets. *New York Times*, August 9, 1986, p. 35.

went beyond the specific problems that the wave of mercantilist measures of the 1970s raised. Sensitive to the charge that they flaunted the very rules that had sustained their own prosperity, the Japanese took major steps to conform to those rules in the 1970s and 1980s. They abandoned many of their most egregiously illiberal practices. They removed the formal tariff barriers that they had erected after the war. They began to open their financial system to the rest of the world. Foreigners were permitted, for example, to purchase seats on the Tokyo stock exchange. To demonstrate their good intentions and perhaps to encourage others, Japan became one of the world's largest producers of internationalist rhetoric. The slogan "comprehensive security," denoting economic access as well as military protection, gained currency. There was a great deal of talk about the need to be a good "global citizen."[85]

The new policies, substantial though they were, had limited results. The rhetoric carried little weight. Although formal restraints on some foreign goods were abolished, Japan still excluded many new kinds of imports, such as services, which were not covered by GATT rules. There were, moreover, a host of nontariff barriers that kept foreign products from finding Japanese buyers. A daunting array of informal obstacles to imports remained, some deeply embedded in Japanese society itself. Japanese retail networks, for example, were intricate, long-established, and based on personal ties sometimes going back generations. It was, accordingly, difficult for foreign products to gain access to these networks and to be distributed.[86] Often the Japanese came by their success in a most straightforward way: Japanese products were simply superior to others. The fact that Japan succeeded even while following liberal rules did not, however, eliminate resentment and threats of protective retaliation on the part of others. And in the end, no matter how liberal its policies, Japan could not sustain the open international economic order alone. The continuation of that order depended on liberal economic policies by others. Like Britain before World War I, Japan did not have the power to do everything

---

[85] *Asian Security, 1981*, p. 200; Johnson, "MITI and Japanese Economic Policy," p. 278; Pempel, "Japanese Foreign Economic Policy," p. 145.

[86] Hollerman, "Trade," p. 169; Kosaka, "International Economic Policy of Japan," p. 217; Pempel, "Japanese Foreign Economic Policy," p. 180; Frank, "Introduction," p. 8.

that its interests required. Like Britain and the European equilibrium of the nineteenth century, the Japanese alone could not sustain the conditions in which they had flourished. Fortunately for them, they did not have to act alone.

American hegemony did not have to be fully replaced. The United States remained the most powerful and important member of the international economic system in the 1970s. The American market was still the largest of any country's, and it was far from entirely closed to foreign products. The dollar retained its central role in international commerce and banking. American military power continued to undergird international economic activity. By the 1970s the Soviet Union had become the equal of the United States in many important categories of military might. But to provide a foundation for an integrated international economic order (although one that did not include the Soviet Union and its empire), military equality turned out to be adequate. The superiority that Britain had deemed essential, at least in naval terms, during the nineteenth century was not necessary for the United States in the twentieth.[87]

Still, the American economy was not as powerful in the 1970s as it had been during the previous three decades. The American capacity to provide the services of the hegemonic state to the international economic order had declined. Nor was another, successor hegemonic power on the horizon. Thus the members of the international economic system, including Japan, found themselves, in the 1970s, in the same position as the European powers in the aftermath of the Wars of the French Revolution. They faced a kind of collective goods problem, the collective good being an open international economic order in the later period as it had been European equilibrium in the earlier one. The United States would no longer pay the costs of sustaining liberal procedures by itself. With the decline of American superiority, international openness had to be supplied pluralistically, as in the nineteenth-century

---

[87] American nuclear weapons were in some ways the equivalent of the British navy. But nuclear parity sufficed in the twentieth century, whereas naval superiority had been required in the nineteenth. See Michael Mandelbaum, *The Nuclear Revolution: International Politics Before and After Hiroshima* (Cambridge University Press, 1981), Chap. 4.

managed balance of power system, rather than hegemonically, as in the international economic order before 1914 and after 1945.[88]

As the precedent of the nineteenth-century European equilibrium shows, the pluralistic provision of a collective good in the anarchic international system is not a hopeless task. It can, however, be a difficult one. The literature on collective goods explains why this is so.

Whether or not a public good is provided has been found to depend on the distribution of power within the group.[89] When power is highly concentrated in one of its members, the group is "privileged." The powerful member will have an interest in supplying the public good by itself. This is the condition of the international economic order when there is a hegemonic power, such as Britain in the nineteenth century and the United States in the twentieth. If, however, power is dispersed among many members of the group, if the group is large and those belonging to it relatively equal, in the absence of a sovereign power the public good will not be provided. In such a "latent group," the collective goods problem will prove insurmountable. If there were no government, cars would not have pollution control equipment. No individual driver would have a sufficient interest in buying it.

When there is no hegemon but a few members of a group are considerably more powerful than the others, an "intermediate" group exists. Here the public good may or may not be provided; the outcome is undetermined. The group is small enough and its members powerful enough that each can have a perceptible impact on the supply of the public good, which is not the case with a latent group. Each can monitor what the others do and can respond to what they do "strategically," by attempting to punish those that fail to contribute.[90] Again, this is not true of automobile owners

---

[88] This is an important theme of Keohane, *After Hegemony.* See, e.g., pp. 9–10.
[89] This is a central theme of Olson, *Logic of Collective Action,* esp. Chaps. 1 and 2. See also Hardin, *Collective Action,* pp. 40–2.
[90] A parallel can be drawn between group size and market size for a particular industry. A privileged group corresponds to a monopoly, a latent group is the equivalent of perfect economic competition, and an intermediate group is the analogue of an oligopoly. In the first case cooperation is unnecessary. In the second it is impossible. In the third it is possible but not inevitable. Olson, *Logic of Collective Action,* pp. 48–50.

and pollution. If all members of an intermediate group recognize their common interest and if there is some mechanism for serving that interest, the group may succeed in supplying itself with a public good.

The great powers of Europe in the nineteenth century constituted such a group. There were five of them in 1815: Britain, France, Prussia, Russia, and Austria. Each had a noticeable impact on the European balance. They were able to coordinate their policies to achieve equilibrium. The international economic order of the 1970s and 1980s also qualifies as an intermediate group. The United States, Japan, and the major nations of Western Europe – Britain, France, the Federal Republic of Germany, and Italy – were much more important than any other countries. Together they controlled a very substantial proportion of the world's wealth.

The Third World's challenge to their power could be seen, by the end of the decade, to have failed. The New International Economic Order was not enacted. Its proponents' rhetoric in international forums was not translated into commercial policy.[91] Oil proved to be an exceptional commodity. The producers of other raw materials did not succeed in raising their prices or controlling their supply. By the early 1980s, moreover, even oil was no longer exceptional. OPEC, if it had ever functioned as an effective cartel, had ceased to do so. Conservation, the substitution of other forms of energy, economic recession in the industrial countries, and increased production outside OPEC countries combined to draw the price of oil steadily downward. So the principal industrial powers could largely ignore the wishes of the LDCs in organizing the international economy. By themselves they formed an intermediate group.

The literature on public goods and the related literature on game theory[92] offer reasons to expect the provision of the collective good of international economic liberalism to be *less* difficult than the

---

[91] Most LDCs pursued a two-track policy. While advocating the principles of the NIEO in public forums, they continued to deal with one another and with the industrial countries on the basis of the liberal rules that they denounced. Krasner, *Structural Conflict*, pp. 16, 18, 56.

[92] Hardin shows that "the problem of collective action and the Prisoner's Dilemma are essentially the same" (*Collective Action*, pp. 25–30).

establishment of collective security arrangements, reasons that
have to do with the differences between security, on the one hand,
and economics, on the other.

In one game that is often cited in this literature, the Prisoner's
Dilemma, two prisoners are held separately. Each is asked to implicate the other in a crime. If one does and the other does not,
the first one will go free while the other receives a long sentence.
If both remain silent, each will get a brief sentence. If each implicates the other, each will receive a much longer sentence than
if both remain silent but a somewhat shorter sentence than one
will receive if the other implicates him but he does not implicate
the other. Each can, to use the language of game theory, either
"cooperate" by remaining silent or "defect" by implicating the
other. But if both cooperate by remaining silent, each will be
considerably better off than either will be if both defect. Cooperation in this setting is the equivalent of paying the cost of a collective
good, either financially or by behavior that entails sacrifice of some
kind. It is the equivalent of political and military restraint by the
European powers in the nineteenth century and of liberal economic
policies. Defecting in the Prisoner's Dilemma is the equivalent of
avoiding these costs, of attempting to "ride free." It is the optimal
strategy only if the other, in the case of Prisoner's Dilemma, or all
of the others, in the case of security and an open international
economy, cooperate. It is therefore the rational course for each
individual but counterproductive for all if every member of the
group adopts it.

If the players in a game of Prisoner's Dilemma interact with each
other repeatedly over time, it has been shown, cooperation is likelier than it would be if there were only a single encounter between
them.[93] Familiarity and the understanding that the present round
will not be the last one foster cooperation. Security arrangements
are single-play games. If one player defects – if one country asserts
its own interests without restraint, if it attacks another – it does so
anticipating no further repetitions of the same situation. Economic
relations bear a closer resemblance to multiple-play games. Trade,
investment, and monetary dealings are recurrent. Countries do not

---

[93] Robert Axelrod, *The Evolution of Cooperation* (New York: Basic Books, 1983);
Hardin, *Collective Action*, pp. 3, 13.

buy single shipments of cloth or wine or oil from one another. Long-term collaboration is assumed. Cooperation is therefore likelier.[94]

Another difference between security and economic affairs that the vocabulary of public goods and game theory helps to express is pertinent to the prospects for cooperation in each. Cooperation is likely to the extent that the enterprise in question can be seen as a positive-sum game, in which both sides (or all parties) stand to gain from it. Prisoner's Dilemma is a positive-sum game. Public goods are also, indeed by definition, like positive-sum games. This is the sense in which the two can be equated.

Such enterprises are distinct from zero-sum games, in which a gain for one party is necessarily a loss for the other. Security can be seen as both a positive *and* a zero-sum game. The nineteenth-century managed balance of power system provided both: peace (or at least the absence of general war) and a particular distribution of power, territory, and influence in Europe. The first can be seen as a positive-sum game. Each power restrained itself and all enjoyed – in the parlance of public goods, they "consumed" – the resulting peace. The second bears a closer resemblance to a zero-sum game. What one state had, others could *not* have.

A country that defected from the European equilibrium would likely find itself in a worse position where peace was concerned. If others defected as well, as they surely would, the initial defector could no longer benefit from peace. But it might be in a *better* situation in terms of the distribution of power. It might get more territory as a result of defecting – that is, of fighting and winning a war.

If considerations of power, influence, and territory dominate a state's calculations, it is less likely to "cooperate" than if peace is uppermost in its policies. Peace, in turn, is likely to be important to *all* states to the extent that war is anticipated to be so destructive as to be unacceptable *whatever* its outcome. It was out of this broadly shared anticipation that the European equilibrium of the nineteenth century emerged. A similar assumption has been cen-

---

[94] See Robert Axelrod and Robert O. Keohane, "Achieving Cooperation Under Anarchy," in Kenneth A. Oye, ed., *Cooperation Under Anarchy* (Princeton, N.J.: Princeton University Press, 1986), p. 232.

tral to relations between the United States and the Soviet Union at least since the 1960s, because of the advent of nuclear weapons. Neither side could expect to win a nuclear war by any reasonable definition of victory.

The final blow to the balance of power system, the outbreak of World War I, occurred because the Germans concluded that the distribution of power was more important than peace. They came to believe that what they could hope to gain by upsetting the European status quo was more valuable to them then the public good of peace that they would have to forfeit to achieve it. Indeed, this is, in general, the calculation that causes wars. Historically, the distribution of power, a zero-sum game, has from time to time weighed more heavily on national policies than has the desire for peace – a positive-sum game. At some point, sovereign states have become less concerned with avoiding wars than with winning them.

Economic activity, by contrast, especially in the neoclassical view, is a positive-sum game. It more clearly and unambiguously involves a public good. It is therefore more likely than security to involve cooperation. If all cooperate to obey liberal rules, all will be better off absolutely. Some will gain more than others, but none will suffer an absolute loss, as occurs when power is redistributed. This fact provides an incentive to cooperate rather than to defect. It is all the more powerful because if all states fail to cooperate each one not only fails to gain but actually suffers an absolute loss. Not only is each not richer; all are poorer. International economic activity, and in particular an open international economic order, offer the prospect of joint gain with cooperation *and* joint loss without it.[95]

To supply a public good on a pluralistic basis in the absence of a sovereign authority, two conditions must exist. The members of the intermediate group, in the case of the international economy sovereign states, must recognize the situation in which they find themselves. They must understand their collective goods problem and the need for cooperation to address it. And they must have a mechanism for cooperating, some means of ensuring that oth-

---

[95] Hardin, *Collective Action*, p. 62.

ers also recognize the common predicament and will behave co-operatively.[96]

The shock that produced the recognition of a common predicament and the need for cooperation among the European powers of the nineteenth century came from the Wars of the French Revolution. The distinctiveness of the conflict, the threat that the new forms of warfare posed to the regimes in power on the Continent, created a common interest in the public good of peace. Cartels often require similar traumatic experiences to jolt its members into cooperation.[97]

No precisely equivalent event demonstrating the value of liberal procedures for the international economic order occurred in the 1970s. But the major economic powers did appear to recognize their common interest in an open order. They announced that they recognized it. There was broad support, at least rhetorically, for free trade, the free flow of capital, and monetary rules that did not lend themselves to mercantilist manipulation. Although no longer a recent memory, the Great Depression of the 1930s, when mercantilist policies led to severe economic dislocation, when the absence of cooperation led to joint losses, still served as a cautionary example. The lesson of that period – that mercantilist policies, when all pursue them, lead to disaster – had entered the common stock of Western political ideas. The postwar economic history of the West offered a happy counterexample. The unprecedented prosperity of the quarter-century following 1945 was widely imputed to the existence of an open international economic order. The major industrial powers recognized their common stake in preserving it.

The best evidence of this common recognition was a series of annual economic summit meetings that began in 1975. They were born out of the shared concern of three Western ministers of economics – George Shultz of the United States, Valéry Giscard d'Estaing of France, and Helmut Schmidt of Germany – with the mercantilist trends that developed in the wake of the first oil shock.

---

[96] Ibid., p. 172.
[97] "...narrowly defined, spontaneous groups commonly require some coordinating event to stimulate group-oriented behavior." Ibid., p. 31.

The three were convinced of the need for the great industrial powers to cooperate to resist these trends.[98] The heads of government of the United States, Britain, France, Germany, Japan, and Canada, as well as a representative of the European Common Market, accordingly began to convene annually in one of their capitals (the site rotated) to consider economic issues. The participants reflected the uneven distribution of economic power in the world. Their number was appropriate for an intermediate group among whose members cooperation to supply a public good is possible.

On two occasions in the 1970s these summits· produced actual plans for cooperative economic policies, although they were modest and not fully implemented. In 1978 the leaders agreed on a series of macroeconomic measures to stimulate economic growth worldwide. Each of the major powers agreed to adopt a policy that others wanted. The Germans and Japanese pledged to stimulate their economies; the United States promised to reduce its oil imports; the French gave assurances that they would permit a successful conclusion to the Tokyo Round of trade negotiations. In 1979, in the midst of the second oil shock, the leaders agreed to set targets for imported oil in order to relieve pressure on the market and stabilize the international price.[99]

For the most part, however, the meetings were taken up with general discussions and ended by issuing very general communiqués rather than announcing specific economic plans. The series of summits was significant not as a forum for the joint management of the global economy but as a symbol of the common recognition of the need for cooperation to sustain a liberal economic order.

By attending the meetings the leaders showed, in effect, that they recognized the existence of a collective goods problem. They demonstrated their understanding that their own prosperity depended upon the economic policies of the others. By meeting regularly they acknowledged that the general problem the gatherings had been initiated to address was a continuing one. The

---

[98] Robert Putnam and Nicholas Bayne, *Hanging Together: The Seven-Power Summits* (London: Heinemann, 1984), Chap. 2.
[99] Ibid., pp. 92–6, 123–7.

meetings also signaled the leaders' common realization that to secure the public good of international economic openness they would all have to contribute. They would have to limit mercantilist policies, for which there were often powerful political constituencies at home, for the sake of the general well-being, which was ordinarily less well represented in the political systems of the industrial democracies. The summits served to educate national leaders about the international dimensions of economic policy, with which they were seldom familiar upon entering office. The leaders were occasionally even able to resist domestic pressures for mercantilist policies at home on the grounds that these would create difficulties at the summit.[100]

The summits symbolized fidelity to the norm of international liberalism. To function, however, an open system requires more than allegiance to the norm of openness; it needs specific rules for different areas of economic activity.[101] These, too, were available in the 1970s and 1980s. They were embedded in international organizations, to which the major economic powers (and sometimes all the members of the international economic system) belonged and whose work the economic summits often endorsed. If the liberal international economic order was constitutional in that economic activity proceeded according to impersonal predetermined rules rather than ad hoc government decisions, these organizations could be said to be the various articles of the world's economic constitution.

The GATT and the International Monetary Fund (IMF), the principal organizations concerned with trade and monetary issues, were born at the beginning of the postwar period. The regulations they codified were generally, but not entirely, liberal.[102] Although the United States had been instrumental in establishing them, it

---

[100] Ibid., pp. 137, 199, 205.
[101] On the distinction between broad norms and narrower, more specific rules, see Krasner, *Structural Conflict*, p. 4.
[102] John Ruggie terms the postwar order one of "embedded liberalism," in which liberal rules were embedded in political systems with some provision for mercantilist policies. Governments were permitted to intervene in international economic transactions to cushion their societies against the shocks of the normal workings of the market. Ruggie, "International Regimes," pp. 209–14.

did not follow that the organizations or their rules would lapse with
the erosion of American economic superiority. Indeed, they appeared not only to survive but to remain at least partly effective.[103]

They were voluntary organizations, without sovereign powers of
coercion. The GATT and the IMF, like the pope, had no divisions
and so could not enforce whatever decisions they made. They did,
however, contribute in two ways to efforts to cope with the collective goods problem that the maintenance of an open international economic order presented in the absence of American
hegemony. First, they addressed the need for a common recognition of the problem, a precondition for a cooperative effort by
an intermediate group such as the major economic powers. Membership in these organizations, like attendance at the economic
summits, served as a sign of good faith, a gesture of the commitment
to continue to observe liberal rules. The organizations gave each
member a way of monitoring the others, to be sure that they were
complying with these rules.[104] Second, international organizations
provided forums for apportioning the costs of sustaining the open
order, just as a cartel's formal mechanism distributes market shares
among its members. The task requires coordination. This is a service that organizations, even without enforcement powers, are able
to render.[105]

The GATT rules, with their emphasis on free trade, remained
in place throughout the 1970s and into the 1980s. The major economic powers found ways to get around them, engaging in the
protection of their own industries without recourse to the formal
tariffs that GATT forbade. The allegiance to the rules and the
underlying norm of free trade that membership in GATT demonstrated might be taken as a form of hypocrisy – the tribute that

[103] Keohane, *After Hegemony*, pp. 101–1.
[104] Ibid., pp. 92, 97.
[105] In the 1970s the term "international regime" came into use to refer to the
rules that states follow in particular areas of economic activity. The term denotes
the fact that cooperation often extends beyond the borders of formal organizations. Regimes play the same role as organizations, helping to overcome the
collective goods problem. Stephen D. Krasner, "Structural Causes and Regime
Consequences: Regimes as Intervening Variables," and Arthur A. Stein, "Coordination and Collaboration: Regimes in an Anarchic World," in Krasner, ed.,
International Regimes.

vice, in this case mercantilism, paid to virtue, in the form of international liberalism. But the world trading system did not collapse. Liberal procedures coexisted with mercantilist ones. The Tokyo Round of tariff reductions, which concluded in 1979, did remove some barriers to commerce, although many remained in place. Other countries in addition to the United States made concessions at Tokyo. The volume of international trade continued, on the whole, to grow, although not as rapidly as in the immediate postwar years and although the growth was concentrated in a few sectors and in trade within the industrialized world.[106] In general there was little sign of a collapse like the one that took place in the 1930s.

Liberal practices, although not precisely those with which the postwar period began, survived as well for international monetary transactions. The rules that emerged from Bretton Woods were not purely liberal. They did not reestablish the classical gold standard, under the terms of which payments imbalances were set right by automatic adjustments in national economic activity. Under a gold standard, at least as described by Hume, Mill, and others if not as practiced in every detail in the nineteenth century,[107] all national currencies must be backed by gold. When there is a balance-of-payments deficit, gold is shipped to surplus countries. The deficit country's supply of money and credit shrink, economic activity contracts, prices fall, and the demand for imports declines until payments are once again in balance. In surplus countries the opposite economic processes occur. The adjustment of domestic economic activity is the liberal, impersonal, constitutional way of coping with a payments deficit. The mercantilist methods of doing so are to borrow – to "finance" the deficit – or to lower the exchange rate – to devalue. Both are illiberal in that they involve government interference with economic processes. Both tend to be attractive

---

[106] Charles Lipson, "The Transformation of Trade: The Sources and Effects of Regime Collapse," in Krasner, ed., *International Regimes*, p. 236, 268–9; Ruggie, "International Regimes," pp. 216–17; Gilpin, *The Political Economy*, pp. 199–228.

[107] Skidelsky, "Retreat from Leadership," pp. 158, 170; Calleo, "Historiography," p. 233. For a brief account of how the gold standard operated in practice, see Gilpin, *The Political Economy*, pp. 123–7.

to governments because they can protect domestic constituencies from having to make sacrifices in the form of lower employment and consumption, at least in the short term.

The Bretton Woods system, however, established the IMF, which was authorized to make loans to countries in imbalance.[108] There was also a provision, although it was not often invoked in the early years of the postwar period, for changing exchange rates – that is, for devaluation. The system was imperfectly liberal, finally, in that the United States, because of the central role of its currency, was more or less immune to market discipline.[109] The American economy was able to run deficits that were not permitted to other countries.

After 1971, the monetary procedures changed. But there remained a more or less open order; the world did not fragment into currency blocs as it had in the 1930s. The costs of sustaining it were borne multilaterally, not by the United States alone. The dollar remained the central currency while others absorbed the costs that this entailed. Although it was formally detached from gold in August 1971, well before then many more dollars were in foreign hands than the United States could possibly have redeemed for gold. The American government therefore took a number of steps to avoid having to convert them. The Japanese and the Germans, in particular, gave assurances that they would not trade in the dollars they held.[110]

Several motives lay behind the Japanese and German assurances. They depended on the United States for military protection; they could not afford to risk it by refusing a major American request. Since they themselves held the dollar as a reserve currency, a run on it would have severely damaged them. As Keynes is said to have put it, if you owe a bank a thousand pounds you are in its power; it you owe the bank a million pounds *it* is in *your* power.

---

[108] The loans were subject to "conditionalities" that ordinarily involved adjustment. Thus the IMF functioned in a liberal way. Benjamin J. Cohen, "Balance of Payments Financing: Evolution of a Regime," in Krasner, ed., *International Regimes*, pp. 319–22.

[109] Ibid., p. 327. The dollar's central role was also an element of openness, since it made possible a larger volume of international transactions than could have been sustained by a pure gold standard.

[110] Gowa, *Closing the Gold Window*, p. 54, 172; Hirsch and Doyle, "Politicization," pp. 39, 41.

By the end of the 1960s, the United States in effect owed the other great trading nations billions of dollars. Japan and Germany were also willing to absorb dollars because this helped to keep the value of their own currencies low, which subsidized the exports on which they depended. But they and other countries also cooperated in propping up the Bretton Woods system, with the dollar's special place in it, because they were committed to an open system, they recognized that this required a central role for the dollar, and they were therefore willing to pay a price – in accepting excess dollars and with it imported inflation – to maintain the dollar's role.

With the demise of the Bretton Woods system, national currencies floated against each other. Opportunities for nations to engage in the mercantilist manipulation of their own currency values were far greater than under the rules of fixed exchange rates. Most of the major economic powers did intervene in currency markets to affect the value of their own money. Floating was generally managed, or, as it was called, "dirty." But monetary transactions did not degenerate into the free-for-all "beggar-thy-neighbor" competitive devaluations that had been feared. The major economic powers managed their money with some sense of responsibility for the economic order as a whole. In September 1985 the finance ministers of the United States, Japan, West Germany, Britain, and France met at the Plaza Hotel in New York to plan ways to bring their currencies into more suitable alignment and in particular to reduce the relative value of the dollar. The next May, at the economic summit in Tokyo, the seven national leaders gathered there (the five who had met in New York plus two from Italy and Canada) agreed to a formal mechanism to monitor exchange rates. Balance-of-payments deficits were addressed by domestic adjustments as well as through financing and rate changes. In one way, the new monetary procedures were more liberal than the old. The United States was subject to greater discipline. In the late 1970s the American government responded, among other things, to payments deficits by adjustments in the domestic economy, in the form of a deep recession, as it had not done before.

Liberal rules remained partly in force, with the United States neither bribing nor coercing others to obey them on the same scale as in the 1940s or thereafter. The industrial nations as a group compensated for the decline of American leadership. The task of the economic hegemon in the nineteenth century and after 1945 involved countercyclical "emergency" services as well. Here, too, there were signs in the late 1970s and 1980s that the public good would be supplied by the major economic powers acting jointly. They responded to changes in the oil market by forming a consumers' organization, the International Energy Agency (IEA). This signified the recognition that oil presented a collective goods problem.[111] The purpose of the IEA was to foster cooperation among the consuming countries, especially in times of crisis. Its members agreed that in the event of shortages they would reduce their consumption and pool their supplies so as to avoid the panic bidding that had driven prices up so rapidly in 1973. The United States proposed creating the organization and used its influence to convince others to join.[112] But the sacrifices were to be borne by all members.

The IEA did not succeed in preventing the second oil shock of 1979, when, once again, prices soared. But in 1980 informal cooperation under its auspices contributed to the avoidance of a third oil shock. The war between Iraq and Iran reduced oil exports from both countries. The world price, however, remained stable. Conditions were favorable for the consumers. Their oil stocks were high. Demand was low because of the recent increases of the second oil shock and the consequent recession in Western economies. But the exchanges of information and informal consultations that took place in the IEA also contributed to the prevention of another price spiral.[113]

Another cooperative effort was mounted in response to the crisis of LDC debt in the early 1980s. The crisis had its origins in the two oil shocks. The poorer countries could not earn enough foreign exchange to defray the rising cost of fuel, nor were they willing to sacrifice economic activity by restricting imports of oil. So they borrowed from Western commercial banks. They chose to finance their oil deficits rather than adjust to them. In the early 1980s interest rates rose sharply and export markets, with the industrial countries in recession, contracted. The heavy borrowers encoun-

---

[111] See Keohane, *After Hegemony*, p. 223, on oil purchases on the world market as a collective goods problem.
[112] Lieber, *The Oil Decade*, pp. 19, 21; Keohane, *After Hegemony*, pp. 217–18.
[113] Lieber, *The Oil Decade*, pp. 7, 9, 36–8.

tered difficulty in servicing their debts and renewing their loans. This raised the danger of large-scale defaults, with the potential for damaging the world's banking system.

Cooperation among the banks, the governments of the major industrial countries, the IMF, and the debtor countries produced a series of national programs combining fresh loans with plans for internal adjustment to prevent default. The American government and American banks took leading parts in the operations, but they did not act alone. The role of the IMF was important. It served as a shield to protect Western governments from the LDCs' unhappiness with the economic retrenchment they were required to undertake. It also served as a mechanism for sharing the burden of avoiding default. The IMF made loans itself, drawing on reserves contributed by all the economic powers.[114]

In all this, the Japanese were faithful, even eager, participants. They were willing to bear a share of the costs of sustaining an open international economic order. They took an active part in the annual economic summit meetings and played host to two of them, in 1979 and 1986. The holding of the GATT negotiations in the late 1970s in Tokyo symbolized Japan's eagerness to preserve an open trading system and perhaps also the conviction of the other industrial countries that in the matter of abolishing barriers to trade the Japanese had a great deal to do. Japan also joined in the effort to cope with the problem of Third World debt in the 1980s.

In these collective efforts, however, Japan's role was modest. Although theirs was the world's second largest economy, and in the second half of the 1980s arguably the most powerful one in financial terms because of its huge trade surplus, the Japanese did not assume major responsibility for any international economic issue. In supplying the collective good of international openness, Japan contributed no more, and sometimes even less, than the other principal industrial powers. In the debt crisis, for example, the country's efforts centered on places where its own banks were exposed. In monetary affairs, while the 1980s saw the beginnings of a "Euroyen" market similar to the one for dollars that existed

[114] See Miles Kahler, "Politics and International Debt: Explaining the Crisis," and Charles Lipson, "International Debt and International Institutions," in Miles Kahler, ed., *The Politics of International Debt* (Ithaca, N.Y.: Cornell University Press, 1985).

outside the United States, Japan's currency was not used to supplement the dollar as a medium for international transactions or as a reserve. The Japanese government spoke of the need to redirect the country's economic activity toward social welfare and consumption so as to increase the demand for foreign products. Its proclaimed goal was similar to one of the services that economic hegemons have performed: counteracting cyclical downturns by serving as a market to which others can export. In practice, however, Japan resisted acting as the engine of the international economy. It resisted reflating its economy. The Japanese authorities did not wish to risk the inflation and trade imbalances that might follow.

Nor, finally, did Japan do much to assist the United States in providing the framework of military security in which the open economic order had operated since 1945. Tokyo stated its intention to assume responsibility for protecting the sea lanes up to one thousand miles from the Japanese archipelago, a task performed in the postwar period by the United States Navy. This remained an intention; it did not become Japanese policy. Japan held steadfastly to its postwar rule of spending no more than 1 percent of its gross national product on defense.

The Japanese were, in short, followers, not leaders. They would agree to cooperate to support liberal international economic rules and procedures but would not assume a major part of the costs or even attempt to rally others to contribute. By the latter years of the 1980s, at least, they had not suffered major damage from their reluctance to do either. The conditions of Japanese economic wellbeing were being sustained, although not without strain and surely not indefinitely, both by American leadership and by joint action among the industrial countries, even as they had once been supported principally by American hegemony. The fruits of the Japanese miracle could continue to flourish because the international conditions that had made that miracle possible were more or less intact. The international economic order was still open enough to keep Japan prosperous.

Index

World War II (*cont.*)
  origins of, 345–6
  and the postwar settlement, 70,
    100
  and problem of alliance formation,
    94–5
  and relations between the great
    powers, 30
  and relations between the USSR
    and China, 214
  use of guerrilla tactics in, 240

Xinjiang, 210, 221–2

Yalta, summit conference at, 130
Yalu River, 206
Yellow Sea, 214
Yenan, 241
Yom Kippur, 276
Young Plan, 87
Young, Robert J., 78 n.14
Yugoslovia, 73, 98–9, 104, 202, 239–
  40

zero-sum game, 50 n.42, 385–6
Zhou Enlai, 218
Zionism, 267 n.15, 269, 275, 277,
  312, 317